Major Tooley receives the Regiments's first Guidon from King Edward VII at Worsley on 6 July 1909. The Guidon was donated by Colonel J. Rutherford TD MP and was presented by the King along with colours to four battalions of the Lancashire Fusiliers, two battalions of the East Lancashire Regiment and six battalions of the Manchester Regiment at a mass review of the East Lancashire Division. Kneeling is Lieutenant Shaw and standing at the rear in service dress is Captain Ridley ASC. The Guidon was marched past as part of a mass review of the division and carried SSM France.

Chain Mail
THE HISTORY
OF
THE DUKE OF LANCASTER'S OWN YEOMANRY

By the same author

The 7th Queen's Own Hussars
The Horse in War
A History of the 4th/7th Royal Dragoon Guards
A Guide to the Regiments and Corps of the British Army
The British Soldier – A Social History
A History of the Royal Regiment of Wales

With Major A C S Savory:
A History of the Duke of Wellington's Regiment (West Riding) 1702–1992

Chain Mail

THE HISTORY
OF
THE DUKE OF LANCASTER'S OWN YEOMANRY

by
John Brereton

Picton Publishing (Chippenham) Limited

© Copyright DLOY Regimental Trustees
Published in Great Britain by
Picton Publishing (Chippenham) Limited
Queensbridge Cottages, Patterdown,
Chippenham, Wiltshire SN15 2NS
ISBN 0 948251 67 0

All rights reserved
No part of this publication may be reproduced,
stored in a retrieval system or transmitted, in any form
or by any means, electronic, mechanical, photocopying,
recording or otherwise without the express written
permission of the copyright owners.

Typeset in Linotype Melior
by Mike Kelly Typesetting 'Avalon' Hartham Lane Biddestone Chippenham
Printed and Bound in the United Kingdom by
Picton Publishing (Chippenham) Limited

Contents

Regimental Battle Honours vi
Acknowledgements vii
Trustees Acknowledgements vii
Forword by The Most Hon. The Marquess of Anglesey, DL, FSA, FRHistS, D.Litt ix
Preface by Major-General Sir Michael Palmer, KCVO, Honorary Colonel xi
Prologue xiii

Chapters

I	'Gentlemen and Yeomanry'	1
II	The Duke of Lancaster's Own Yeomanry	13
III	Victorian Peace	29
IV	Imperial Yeomanry	41
V	Last Days of Summer	59
VI	The Great War	73
VII	'Peace in Our Time'	99
VIII	The Second World War	109
IX	Resurgence	137
X	Epilogue	149

Appendices

I	Roll of Honour	163
II	Honours and Awards	171
III	Regimental Music	193
IV	The Lancashire Hussars	215
V	Honorary Colonels and Commanding Officers	218

Illustrations

Pictures between pages . . . . 78–79, 142–143 and 158–159

Index 223

Battle Honours

Boer War
South Africa 1900–1902

The Great War
Somme 1916, 1918; Albert 1916, 1918; Ypres 1917; Passchendaele;
St Quentin; Bapaume 1918; Amiens; Hindenburg Line; Epehy;
Cambrai 1918; Selle; Sambre; France and Flanders 1915–1918.

The Second World War
Honorary Distinction:
A badge of the Royal Regiment of Artillery with the year dates '1944–1945'
and two scrolls 'North West Europe' and 'Italy'

Acknowledgements

It goes without saying that a regimental historian must rely not only on the archives of the regiment itself, but on the co-operation of its members, past and present, and it is my pleasant duty to record my indebtedness to the following.

First, I express sincere thanks to Lieutenant Colonel J. D. V. Woolley (17th/21st Lancers) who as Commanding Officer entrusted me with the authorship of this history, and to his successor, Lieutenant Colonel M. T. Steiger, TD (a true Yeoman of 'the family'). Both have afforded every facility for research and have been generous with hospitality on my several visits to Regimental Headquarters and Museum. The bulk of the work was carried out during Colonel Martin Steiger's tenure, and despite his dual commitments as Commanding Officer and busy barrister in Manchester, he has found time to devote personal attention to my labours, to check drafts and to proffer valuable suggestions. Without his continued support my task would have been onerous indeed.

From the Second World War to the present day I owe much to the past and present officers and other ranks who have so freely responded to my pestiferous queries and offered reminiscences. To the following retired officers and Old Comrades I tender thanks: Brigadier J. F. Lindner, OBE, MC; Lieut-Col N. H. Phillips; Major N. Haddock, TD; Major J. R. G. Harrop; Major R. E. Heaton, MC; Mr L. Hargreaves (ex-Gnr, 77th Medium Regiment); Mr A. Harris (ex-Sgt, 77th); Mr A. Hartill (ex-Gnr, 77th); Mr R. D. Nuttall (ex-Bdr, 77th); Mr B. Richardson (ex-Bdr, 78th – RQMS, DLOY); Mr N J. Sharp (ex-Sgt, 77th); Mr E. White (ex-Gnr, 78th); Mr J. Wilson (ex-BSM, 77th).

My gratitude is no less due to members of the Permanent Staff at Regimental Headquarters, especially to Major E. Sheen, MBE and Captain B. G. Stocker.

I must also express thanks to those officials of the Lancashire County Museums Service at Preston who did much to ease my researches in the Regimental Museum: Mr John D. Blundell, County Museums Officer, and the successive Curators, Mr Fergus Read and Dr Stephen Bull.

While most of the illustrations in this book emanate from Regimental sources, others have been generously provided by individuals, among whom I thank Major Philip Bates, RMVR, VRD (son of Colonel D. E. Bates, MC, TD, former Honorary Colonel); Mr Arthur Harris (ex-Artificer Sgt, 77th); Mr B. Richardson (see above); Mr R. J. Smith (co-author of *The Uniforms of the British Yeomanry Force 1794–1914*); Mr J. Wilson (see above).

Acknowledgement is due to my London research agent, Mrs Elizabeth Murray, for tenacious delving among the file of the Public Record Officeand elsewhere .

Finally I pay tribute to the present Marquess of Anglesey, to whose monumental *History of the British Cavalry* I owe so much.

Trustees' Acknowledgements

The Regimental Trustees commissioned this regimental history from Mr John Brereton, an established and respected military historian, in 1987. The main manuscript was completed in 1989, but, pending publication, two further short sections were added to deal with the Guidon Parade in October 1990 and the impact of Options for Change in 1992. Appendix I was compiled by Fergus Read Esq., Curator of the Regimental Museum 1984–89 in collaboration with Mark Abbott, formerly of A Squadron, and with help from Major J M A Tamplin, Mr Alan Case, the Commonwealth War Graves Commission and the staff of Liverpool City Library. Mr Abbott compiled the sections of Appendix II dealing with long service and good conduct medals, assisted by Major Tamplin who furnished details of Territorial Decorations awarded. The Trustees would also like to acknowledge the generous support made available by past and present members of the Duke of Lancaster's Own Yeomanry without which this history would not have been possible.

Foreword

A sense of historical perspective and an understanding of social customs and usages at different periods are just as important for the regimental historian as is a knowledge of the military mind.

This is especially so when it comes to chronicling the doings of a yeomanry regiment. By definition, everyone in a voluntary unit is as much a civilian as a soldier.

It has interested me to observe how John Brereton, the distinguished historian of regular cavalry regiments, has subtly and dexterously changed his tune when writing of the yeomanry. He has used his experience and skill to fulfil all three of the qualifications listed above, dwelling more on the first two than on the last.

Further, he has avoided the pitfalls inherent in writing about a living organization. He has steered adroitly between the charybdis of 'warts and all' (not many, I think, in this case!) and the scylla of hagiography. Then again his biographical portraits of members of the regiment are very telling indeed.

I love, too, the amount of humourous anecdotes he has unearthed. I laughed aloud when I read about the horse called 'Blouse', whose owner when asked why he was thus called, said "Well, Sir, he ain't no bloody jumper like".

To say that the regiment has had a chequered career is not to exaggerate one jot. All yeomanry have always been used at times as dogs-bodies — jacks of all trades — but the DLOY does seem to have had to serve in that capacity more than most: that is until it became artillery in the Second World War. The detailed account of its actions, triumphs and frustrations in that role are brilliantly yet soberly recounted.

As one who has read the histories of every one of the mounted regiments, I can assert that there are some excellent ones, too many indifferent ones and, alas, many feeble ones. John Brereton's scholarly and readable record falls without doubt into the first category.

I congratulate him and the regiment most heartily on a splendid achievement.

The Marquess of Anglesey,
FSA, FRHistS, Hon. D.Litt.

The Marquess is the author of *A History of the British Cavalry, 1816–1919*.

The Colonel-in-Chief presenting the Regiment's new Guidon at Stonyhurst on 18 October 1990: The Guidon is being received by the Second-in-Command Major John Eastham TD and the kneeling Guidon Bearer is WO2 (RQMS) John Cavanagh.

[x]

Preface

by
Major-General Sir Michael Palmer KCVO

Throughout nearly two centuries of service to Sovereign and Country, the Yeomen of Britain have been remarkable for their patriotism, dedication, and above all, their readiness to sacrifice what others would regard as leisure in the performance of their duties.

The regular soldier has a full-time job with few other concerns or commitments. When the Territorial is carrying out arduous exercises at week-ends and at Annual Camp, or attending weekly drill nights, he is doing so in his spare time (sometimes with little support from his civilian employer). When he has taken off his combat dress and handed in his arms he must resume the demands of his civilian career, which many would reckon as full-time in itself. Such splendid quixotic spirit has always been the hallmark of the Territorial Army and its predecessors, and nowhere has it been better exhibited than in the Yeomanry.

The Duke of Lancaster's Own Yeomanry, in displaying the true yeoman spirit of dedication in peace and war, has demonstrated the typical adaptability of its arm. Horsed cavalry, infantry mounted and dismounted, medium artillery, armour, reconnaissance; all these multifarious roles have been carried out with characteristic verve and professionalism.

Today, phrases such as "Service to Sovereign and Country" and "Spirit of dedication" are regarded by some as outmoded cliches. Sentiments once considered noble are now often derided, as is sadly the concept of patriotism itself. Horses first, men second, self last is a philosophy inculcated in a fortunate minority, but would be dismissed by the uninitiated today as irrelevant.

The special relationship, respect and friendship between leaders and led within a British Regiment is almost impossible to define to those who have not had the good fortune to experience and benefit from it. John Brereton is well qualified to explain how this relationship was adapted to the peculiar circumstances within a Yeomanry Regiment, and right well has he done it in this book.

The Territorial Army has always embodied this inestimable sense of values, which it has taught to many thousands of citizen soldiers in peace and war. Successive Governments have used and discarded this force for good, as a luxury affordable or not at the whim of political and economic crises. It is difficult to believe that the present Government can have fully appreciated the loss to the country caused by the recent blow dealt to the

Yeomanry. It is some consolation that in the past similar blows have been considered mortal, until wiser counsels prevailed.

The Duke of Lancaster's Own, the last remaining county Yeomanry, is now, at least temporarily, part of history. I hope this book will ensure that The Regiment and its service to Sovereign and Country will not be forgotten.

Prologue

Within the Mess Tent the Squadron Leader accosted his Commanding Officer:

> 'My dear Charles, do let's be reasonable! What *is* the point of ordering a parade for seven a.m. when only you want it at that ungodly hour and three hundred of us prefer it at nine?'

Such a (factual) confrontation could only have taken place at the pre-war annual camp of one of those unique bodies of part-time volunteer horse-soldiers, the Yeomanry Cavalry. Rejoicing in such distinctive titles as The Duke of Cambridge's Own, The Earl of Chester's, The Queen's Own Worcestershire Hussars, The Yorkshire Dragoons – and The Duke of Lancaster's Own, these 'Gentlemen and Yeomanry', as the original term had it, were long remarkable for their spirit of patriotism, their keenness, their independence, and a certain disdain for irksome rules, regulations and military 'bull'.

The senior regiments boasted pedigrees stretching back to 1794 when the French revolutionaries forced the Government to raise volunteer forces for internal security, thereby relieving the regular army of such tasks. Thus committed, the Yeomanry saw no overseas service until the Boer War, but instead were periodically subjected to the distasteful business of dispersing what we should now term 'demonstrators', as at 'Peterloo' and during the Reform Bill and Chartist disturbances.

Police action 'in aid of the Civil Power' could earn no Battle Honours, only brickbats and odium from fellow-citizens and neighbours. Nevertheless, such was the Yeomanry spirit that there was never any shortage of recruits, while on occasions some regiments actually elected to serve without any Government remuneration, to save themselves from extinction. Being horsemen – and providing their own mounts – the Yeomen always regarded themselves as several cuts above the footslogging, enlisted Militiamen and the Volunteer Infantry. As late as 1869 Charles Clode could write: 'As unpaid soldiers they are drawn from a higher social class than the men of the Militia.'[1] The original designation 'Gentlemen and Yeomanry' served to emphasise the status: the Oxford Dictionary defines Yeoman as 'man holding and cultivating small landed estate . . . '

Most, but not all, of the Yeomanry were countrymen bred and born, very often tenants or employees of the landed gentlemen who were their Troop or Squadron Leaders or Commanding Officers. For generations the regiments strove to perfect their mounted drill and evolutions in the oak-studded parklands of stately homes, such as Lowther Castle, or on some broad expanse of seashore, such as Southport sands. Occasionally they would indulge in the 'plumed pomp' of escort duties when, resplendent in the gorgeous

---

1. Clode, Charles M. *The Military Forces of the Crown* (London 1869)

panoply of dragoon, hussar or lancer full dress, they would clatter through the High Street of their county town on escort to some visiting royalty or a circuiting Assize Judge.

Often unconventional if not eccentric, always independent-minded, the Yeomen of the 19th century soldiered much as the spirit moved them in their shires and provinces. Never taking themselves too seriously, they accepted with goodwill, if not rejoicing, the fun-fingered pokes of the regulars and the public, and the not-too-flattering sobriquets that grew up around them. That loyal unit, The Queen's Own Oxfordshire Hussars, or QOOH, inevitably became 'The Queer Objects on Horseback'.[2] Naturally, The Welsh Horse were 'Taffy's Lancers'.

Sir John Fortescue, the British Army's historian, served briefly as a subaltern in the North Devon Yeomanry, and he has left some revealing recollections of that very exclusive Corps.[3] Mounted parades usually began thus: 'The Commanding Officer lifted up his voice and uttered the words Walk March, which were received for a minute or two with complete indifference, and then suddenly and spasmodically obeyed. The regiment shuffled in a leisurely fashion through the desired movement amid a babel of tongues and contradictory orders and advanced for a short distance in the new formation before it was halted again.' When an eminent Inspecting General complimented a Squadron Leader on the quality of his men and asked how he managed to enlist such splendid fellows, the straight-faced reply was, 'I have a pedigree Shorthorn bull, sir, and I let my recruits send their heifers to him.'

In a regular regiment, at any rate during the 19th century, the officers were firmly entrenched behind class barriers as well as those of rank: the gulf between them and their men was virtually unbridgeable. But in the county Yeomanry the officer would very likely know many of his NCOs and troopers as neighbouring farmers or estate workers, while some indeed might even be his equals in civilian society. Kipling's 'gentlemen rankers' were rare in the regular army; not so among those enthusiastic bodies of part-time cavalrymen. It is related that when a Warwickshire corporal was fined by his Squadron Leader for some peccadillo of turnout, the response was 'Dammit, sir, I'll raise your rent for this!' With such a make-up it was inevitable that some degree of democracy should prevail. The trooper receiving a rocket from his Troop Leader for a rust-spotted sword scabbard one Saturday afternoon, could next week be advising the same officer about the stopping of earths prior to the meet of hounds. And both men would be at the meet, on their own horses.

Following the establishment of an effective police force throughout the country in 1855, the Yeomanry regiments were relieved of much of their hitherto primary role of maintaining law and order. The last occasion on which a unit was called out to the summons of the magistrates was in 1867 when the Royal 1st Devon Yeomanry confronted a mob during food riots at Teignmouth. Thenceforth the part-time 'Dragoons', 'Hussars' and 'Lancers' had little to do other than display their volunteer spirit by sacrificing their spare time in striving to emulate their Regular cousins in weekly drills, annual camps and the

---

2. In the early 1900s one of the Queer Objects was a Lieutenant Winston S. Churchill, Troop Leader.
3. Published in *My Native Devon* (1924)

occasional Review Order ceremonial when they were inspected by the Lord Lieutenant or some other dignitary. Unkindly, the 'Saturday afternoon' cavalrymen became the butt of *Punch* and other media cartoonists who saw them as rather comic amateur soldiers, more concerned with flaunting extravagant uniforms and boosting their own prestige rather than contributing to the Defence of the Realm. Thus in June 1850 *Punch* evoked hilarity among its readers with a woodcut depicting an obese yokel on a scraggy nag confronted by a superbly-mounted, beplumed inspecting officer. Noticing the medal on the trooper's chest, the officer remarks, 'Ah, my fine fellow, I see you've been in the wars, eh?' Proudly the stout Yeoman replies, 'Noa, Colonel Sir, I warn't in no war, but me old sow won this medal in last County Show.'

Confined to home service, the Yeomanry had no opportunity to show what they could do against a real enemy, and could only practise their mounted drill, fire off the niggardly allowance of live rounds on the ranges, and perhaps organise 'sham fights' with obliging units of the local volunteer infantry on their annual camps. But in 1899 their chance came when Britain declared war on the Boers of South Africa. Within three weeks a total of 10,900 Yeomen had volunteered for overseas service, and by the end of hostilities in 1902 some 35,000 Imperial Yeomanry had served in the theatre of war. Several thousand did not return.

The conflict in South Africa had witnessed the cavalry discarding their hallowed *arme blanche* for the rifle and becoming relegated to that hybrid creature, the mounted infantryman. But even after the advent of the Maxim machine gun with its astonishing rate of fire of 600 rounds per minute, there were still military pundits, notably Haig, who maintained that 'the magnetism of the charge and the terror of cold steel' could never be ousted by the rifle.

Thus the cavalry and the Yeomanry joyfully resumed their swords and the squadrons once more thundered knee-to-knee over Aldershot Plain or private park, convinced that traditional shock action was still a match for firepower. Before very long some of the Yeomen were to confound the critics of the sword with splendid éclat.

In 1908 came Lord Haldane's creation of the Territorial Force (later the Territorial Army), the Yeomanry forming the cavalry element and the Volunteers the infantry. There were then no fewer than 55 regiments of Yeomanry, organised to provide a second-line force of fourteen cavalry brigades. Although still officially home defence troops, all were now able to volunteer for overseas service in the event of war. And this they did, almost to a man, in August 1914. By September six regiments were fighting alongside the Regulars in France and Belgium, to be followed by more within a few months. By the time the combatants had burrowed into trenches and dugouts, the battlefield was dominated by machine guns, field guns and barbed wire, and the frustrated horse-soldiers, Regular and Territorial, could only picket their mounts in rear bases and slog with rifle and bayonet, awaiting the 'cavalry breakthrough' promised by their generals. The breakthrough was indeed to come; but not on the Western Front.

The last full-scale mounted campaign in history was that of General Sir Edmund Allenby's Desert Mounted Corps which drove the Turks out of Palestine in 1917 and sealed the fate of the Ottoman Empire. With the Anzacs were fifteen Yeomanry regiments, plus batteries of (converted) Yeomanry Horse Artillery. There was no Regular cavalry, and so the swan-song of the British mounted arm was performed by those one-time cartoonists' delights, the part-time horse soldiers. The names Huj and El Mughar became celebrated as scenes of death-or-glory charges which evoked the admiration (and envy) of all those dismounted Regular cavalrymen on the Western Front, besides earning unstinted praise from a High Command that had so recently decried the sword.

At Huj in 1917 three weak squadrons of the Warwickshire and Worcestershire Yeomanry put in a Balaclava-like charge to ride down and capture a battery of field guns together with pack guns and machine guns. They sabred 90-odd enemy, captured 70 and routed two battalions of infantry. Theoretically such a task should have been impossible. The Yeomen enjoyed no fire support of any kind and had to gallop across nearly a mile of completely open desert to come within sabring range. The penalty of 36 all ranks killed and 57 wounded out of the 190 who charged was not, perhaps, too high a price for such a victory. Just a week later a force of some 3,000 Turkish infantry was put to flight by Buckinghamshire, Dorset and Berkshire Yeomanry squadrons at El Mughar. These splendid actions not only raised the Yeomanry image, and morale, to unprecedented heights, but seemed to demonstrate that horsemen still had a part to play in modern warfare.

But the two decades after the Great War saw radical developments in weapons technology and a corresponding reorganisation in the British Army. The tank and the armoured car rapidly ousted the horse. By 1939 only three Regular cavalry regiments were still unmechanised,[4] and all but the fourteen senior regiments of Yeomanry had been converted to Gunners, Tankmen and Signallers. As in 1914, Yeomanry units were among the first to cross the Channel with the British Expeditionary Force in September 1939. Away in Palestine eight regiments served briefly as horsed cavalry before conversion to tanks or signals. The Cheshire Yeomanry proudly boast that they were the last British cavalrymen to see action on horseback when they skirmished with the Vichy French and captured a bridge in June 1941.

As gunners, tank crews, signallers, infantrymen, even paratroops, Yeomen fought in every theatre of the Second World War from Northern Europe to Malaya. Fifteen regiments were in action at El Alamein; six landed on D-Day; three fought against the Japanese in Malaya, their survivors suffering on 'the Railway of Death' as prisoners in Thailand. In all, no fewer than 77 regiments of Yeomanry served during the war – the largest number ever to be mobilised.[5] As many senior commanders averred, the expertise and professionalism of the Yeomen in their varied roles was such that there was nothing except their cap badges to distinguish them from Regular soldiers. Their contribution to the final victory **was** immeasurable.

In the years following that victory the Yeomanry received scant thanks for their devotion.

---

4. The Household Cavalry, The Royal Dragoons and The Royal Scots Greys.
5. These figures include those regiments which split into two, e.g. The Duke of Lancaster's Own Yeomanry became for the duration the 77th and 78th Medium Regiments RA.

Between 1951 and 1961 many regiments were amalgamated, to lose their honoured old titles and be given new roles. Others were ruthlessly disbanded.

Then in 1967 Harold Wilson's Labour Government virtually destroyed the Territorial Army with more drastic reductions and disbandments. Of the 53 distinct Yeomanry regiments that had existed in 1939 only The Duke Lancaster's Own retained its identity. Sixteen others suffered a curiously complex process of amalgamation to produce four new regiments, each composed of squadrons from the original regiments.

Cherishing the title granted by King William IV in 1834 and proud to serve as the only Yeomanry unit representing Lancashire, The Duke of Lancaster's Own Yeomanry retained its identity for another twenty five years. In 1991 the Government's curiously named "Options for Change" smote the Army with yet more amalgamations and disbandments and The Duke of Lancaster's Own Yeomanry were merged with the Queen's Own Mercian Yeomanry to form the Royal Mercian & Lancastrian Yeomanry. In which D(DLOY) Squadron alone represents the former Regiment.

A Simkin original portraying a trooper of the Bolton Troop *circa* 1820.

This original water colour by Richard Simkin in the possesion of the Officers's Mess is erroneously described as the uniform of the Lancashire Corps of Yeomanry Cavalry, 1828. The uniform actually depicted is that of the DLOY *circa* 1840.

[xviii]

CHAPTER I
'Gentlemen and Yeomanry' 1794–1816

In 1794 the Government of England was in a state of some alarm at the course of events across the Channel. In January the previous year the Paris mob had beheaded their rightful King and set up a revolutionary convention; a month later this body formally declared war on England. And thus for the sixth time in just over a century the country found itself embroiled in hostilities with its traditional enemy.

In the House, Prime Minister William Pitt declared that 'This has given a more fatal blow to the liberties of mankind than any they have suffered . . . Unless we wish to stand by, and to suffer State and State to be subverted under the power of France, we must now declare our firm resolution to oppose those principles of ambition and aggrandisement which have for their object the destruction of England, of Europe and the world . . . '

Fine rhetoric, but how was the 'firm resolution' to be put into effect? After the conclusion of the Seven Years' War in 1763, and the humiliating loss of the American colonies in 1782, Parliament, as always, had pared the armed forces of the Kingdom to a minimum. By 1793 the total establishment of regular troops in England had dwindled to some 17,000 all ranks, with another 12,000 in Ireland,[1] In addition there were some 17,500 part-time Militia, not available for overseas service. It was reliably reported that the French could put at least 600,000 troops in the field, while it became common knowledge in London that the French War Minister, Lazau Carnot, was actively planning a 'descent', or invasion.

Pitt, outstanding statesman though he was, evinced certain character traits that evoked dissension among his Cabinet and in the House. Essentially a man of peace and believer in appeasement, he had hitherto shut his eyes to the disturbing events in France. In 1792 he had been confident that 'the present convulsions in France must sooner or later culminate in general harmony and regular order', while that country would enjoy 'just the kind of liberty which I venerate'.[2] Another cause for Government concern was an undercurrent of English sympathy towards the Revolutionaries, sometimes coming to the surface with seditious pamphlets and public meetings, addressed by such arch-radicals as Tom Paine whose inflammatory book *The Rights of Man* led to his arrest.

And so, on the declaration of war Pitt was at last forced to abandon his over-optimism and hastily repair the ravages that previous Parliaments had wrought on the defence forces. Between January 1793 and November 1794 no fewer than fourteen new regiments

---

1. Until the Act of Union in 1801, Ireland had a completely independent military establishment, with its own Commander-in-Chief and staff.
2. Quoted in *The Years of Endurance* (Sir Arthur Bryant, 1942).

of cavalry and 72 battalions of infantry were added to the Regular Army.[3] Also, in February 1793, two Troops of a novel form of mobile artillery were raised, their gun detachments being mounted on horses instead of on limbers. These were the origins of the Royal Horse Artillery which was to add such gallant fire-support to the cavalry.

For home defence and internal security the Militia were embodied and augmented, while in the same period the Fencibles, cavalry and infantry were expanded to give a total of 42,000 auxiliary troops. Then in 1794 came an Act empowering Lords Lieutenant of counties to raise local bodies, mounted or foot, termed Volunteers. This Act (34 Geo III c. 31), promulgated in March 1794, saw the emergence of the corps with which we are primarily concerned; the Yeomanry Cavalry.

As a result, on 14 March 1794 the Home Secretary (William Grenville) despatched to all the Lords Lieutenant of Counties a circular entitled 'Plan of Augmentation of the Forces for Internal Defence . . . '[4] After authorising them 'to form Volunteer Companies in particular Towns' and 'Volunteer Troops of Fencible Cavalry', the circular went on to direct them:

> To form other Bodies of Cavalry within particular Counties or Districts, to consist of the Gentlemen and Yeomanry, or such Persons as they shall bring forward . . . And the Officers to receive temporary Commissions from His Majesty; and the Muster-Rolls also to be approved by His Majesty, or by the Lords Lieutenant, at Periods to be fixed. No Levy Money to be given, and the Horses to be furnished by the Gentry or Yeomanry who compose the Corps, but the Arms and Accoutrements to be supplied at the Expense of the public.[5]

Here we have the first appearance of that rather curious term 'Gentlemen and Yeomanry' which continued until the next century, and which deserves a little notice. 'Gentlemen' is self-explanatory, (it becomes 'Gentry' a few sentences further on), but it implied not only breeding and position but wealth. Until 1871 all Regular cavalry and infantry officers had to pay for their commissions and subsequent steps up the promotion ladder. In the 1790s a young gentleman needed to find £700 for the privilege of serving King and country as a humble Cornet or Ensign. Aspirants to the command of a Light Dragoon regiment would have to put down at least £3,200 – a Croesus-like sum in those days. But the Gentlemen of the Yeomanry (and Light Horse Volunteers) were always exempt from the contentious Purchase System: their commissions were granted without payment and so was their promotion. As for the term 'Yeomanry', this seemed to hark back to mediaeval times when a Yeoman was deemed to be a 'person qualified by possessing free land of annual value 40 shillings to serve on juries, vote for knight of shire, etc.' (*Concise Oxford Dictionary*). Later it was applied to a retainer or man-at-arms of the Lord of the Manor, but by 1794 it had acquired a more familiar meaning – simply a man possessing some modest holding of his own, or a tenant or employee of the local squire. Thus we see the

3. All the cavalry were subsequently disbanded, as were all but fourteen of the infantry battalions.
4. PRO 30/8/245
5. It should be recorded that the very first Yeomanry unit to be formally enrolled was the Earl of Winchelsea's Rutland Light Dragoons, their three Troops mustering in April 1794 – only a month after the Home Office circular.

traditional image of a Yeomanry regiment: officered by gentlemen of wealth with their tenants or 'yeomen' farmers in the ranks.

The 'Gentlemen and Yeomanry' came under the authority of the Lords Lieutenant of Counties, and through them to the Home Department. Thus they were divorced from the Regular Army authorities at Horse Guards (later the War Office) and in fact remained so until 1871. Normally they were required to '... act within the County or in adjacent Counties, for the Suppression of Riots and Tumults'. In other words, they began life as a form of local paramilitary police force – all the more necessary in the absence of any constitutional civilian equivalent. But in the event of an invasion they could be called out to confront the enemy in any part of the country where required (though not beyond its shores). Such Yeomanry roles remained virtually unchanged until Britain went to war in South Africa 100 years later.

The response to the Home Secretary's circular was a remarkable demonstration of loyalty and patriotism. Within nine months, [i.e. by the end of the year], 28 distinct units of Yeomanry had been raised and accepted, some of them comprising a single Troop, others with two or more. Twelve months later the number had risen to 40. It is noteworthy that the great majority of these units originated in the rural districts of England's southern counties and in East Anglia. The northern counties were represented only by Yorkshire.

With the creation of the Yeomanry there were now four distinct forces of auxiliary soldiery behind the regulars, and in 1796 a fifth appeared. It is as well to distinguish them, thus:

> *The Militia*: Exclusively infantry, this body was composed of conscripted men chosen by ballot from those aged between 18 and 45, each county being allotted a statutory quota. The Militiamen had to serve a minimum period of three years and attend 21 days' drills and exercises annually. Officers were commissioned by the King, on recommendation from the Lords Lieutenant. But there was a legal loophole for any man seeking to evade Militia service. This was the Substitute system, by which, if he could afford it, he could pay another man to take his place. In 1793 the regulation 'Subsidy Payment' was £10, but as the war progressed, so illegal trafficking became rife: Fortescue records that by 1803 substitutes could not be 'bought' for less than £21. 10s. All this led to the Militia ranks being filled with undesirable elements and the force as a whole was unpopular with the public.
>
> *The Fencibles*: Both of cavalry and infantry, these were full-time volunteers paid as Regulars, but enlisted only 'for the duration'.
>
> *The Volunteers*: This body had been established in 1778, and as the name implies consisted entirely of volunteer ranks willing to serve for internal security and home defence. Although later associated chiefly with infantry, as for instance, the numerous battalions of Rifle Volunteers in Victorian times, the original force included many mounted units, among them the Bolton Light Horse Volunteers whom we are shortly to meet. The various county units were directly responsible to the Lords Lieutenant, who approved their raising and recommended the officers for commissions.

Yeomanry Cavalry: As seen above, the Yeomanry (or 'Gentlemen and Yeomanry') was officially created in March 1794, and both in role and administration the force was almost identical to the Volunteer Cavalry. In fact, even among contemporary authorities there was some blurring (if not confusion) of nomenclature: we often find the term 'volunteer cavalry' applied to a unit which had been raised as Yeomanry, and vice versa – as was the case with the Bolton Light Horse.

Provisional Cavalry: Like the Fencible Cavalry, this was another hostilities-only body, created in 1796, and arousing much antipathy among those concerned. The Provisional Cavalry Act compelled every owner of riding horses to produce one man and one horse for every ten he owned, so that the measure was as unpopular with the gentry as with the co-opted soldiers. The Act could be circumvented, however, by any who elected to join the Yeomanry or Volunteers, or to raise additional Troops thereof. Thus very few Provisional Cavalry units actually paraded and the scheme had died an unlamented death by 1803.

We must now focus on the year 1798 and on the Lancashire town of Bolton (or 'Bolton-le-Moor' as some contemporaries had it). At that date Bolton was a busy centre for the spinning and manufacture of cotton goods, its citizens including many wealthy mill-owners and merchants. Among these was one John Pilkington, whose name is respected by The Duke of Lancaster's Own Yeomanry as the first Commanding Officer of its progenitors. John Pilkington was well known in and around Bolton as the proprietor of a manufactory turning out dimity fabrics. He also owned one of the town's leading hostelries and is referred to in Clegg's *Chronological History of Bolton* (1888) as a 'builder'. Married, he dwelt in one of the town's superior residences named Silverwell, in the Bradshawgate suburb, which he is said to have had built for himself. That he was a gentleman of some substance and repute is evidenced by the fact that at various dates between 1803 and 1824 he is listed as one of the Deputy Lieutenants for the County of Lancaster. He was also a friend and patron of his fellow-Bolton citizen, Samuel Crompton, whose invention of the mechanical spinning machine or 'mule' became one of the causes of unemployment and unrest among the hand-loom workforce.

The middle class gentry and factory owners of Bolton had already displayed their patriotism by raising, at their own expense, Companies of Volunteer infantry[6] and, unlikely though it might seem, a body of 160 Marines. Since opportunities for 'sea service' were lacking around Bolton, these were promptly posted to Chatham.[7] It was now John Pilkington's turn to come forward with an offer.

In early March 1798 Pilkington, having been promised support from other influential (and moneyed) citizens of Bolton, submitted to the Lord Lieutenant of the County of Lancaster (the Earl of Derby) his proposal to raise two Troops of Volunteer Cavalry. The offer was gladly accepted and on 28 March the Troops were duly enrolled. This of course is a red letter date in the history of The Duke of Lancaster's Own Yeomanry, for it is

---

6. Loyal Bolton Volunteers. Raised 1794, disbanded in 1802.
7. Raised in April 1793, the Marines were commanded by a Captain Hindle. (Corry, J. *A History of Lancashire* (1825))

regarded as the true 'birthday' of the Regiment. All the more regrettable therefore, that the official authorisation, and indeed all correspondence between Pilkington and the Lord Lieutenant and between the latter and the Home Secretary, have eluded every attempt to trace them. Nothing exists in the Lancashire Record Office, not even in the Lieutenancy Office, while the Public Record Office at Kew is likewise barren.

The latter repository maintains a detailed index to its references to Yeomanry regiments from dates of raising, all listed under counties: but for Lancashire the sole entry is 'Lancashire Hussars' (1848).

However, we can catch a few glimpses of the Bolton Troops from other sources. We know that as 'Commandant' John Pilkington was granted a commission as Major, this being gazetted on 19 April 1798. The first muster roll of officers is as under:

BOLTON LIGHT HORSE VOLUNTEERS
(1798)

		Date of Commission
Major Cmdg	John Pilkington	19 April 1798
Captain	James Carlisle	19 April 1798
Captain-Lieutenant	Matthew Fletcher	22 November 1798
Lieutenant	William Slater	22 November 1798
Cornet	William Wright	19 April 1798
Adjutant	Ralph Boardman	22 November 1798
Chaplain	Robert Dean	4 July 1798
Surgeon	Edward Bolling	4 July 1798

The above is compiled from sources in the Lancashire Record Office.[8] Unhappily the roll of other ranks for 1798 seems no longer extant: the earliest to come to light is for 1804. A previous historian quotes this as being the 1798 roll, but although many of the NCOs and men serving at the former date might well have been present on the first muster, we have no means of knowing, since enrolment dates do not appear. The same historian also states that a Captain Ralph Fletcher was Pilkington's Second-in-Command: here one can only assume that the author confused Ralph with Matthew, the Captain-Lieutenant,[9] for the former never served in the Bolton Light Horse. Ralph Fletcher, whom we shall meet again, was a local dignitary and magistrate, who as Lieutenant-Colonel actually commanded ten Companies of the Bolton Volunteer infantry for a brief period. Arrogant, of considerable self-esteem, he does not seem likely to have submitted to anyone as a second-in-command.

The title 'Light Horse' reflected the recent vogue for light cavalry in the Regular Army. Between 1759 and 1783 twelve regiments of Dragoons had been converted to 'Light

---

8. *A List of the Officers of the Gentlemen and Yeomanry Cavalry and Volunteer Infantry of the United Kingdom* (War Office 1 Oct. 1804) *Militia and Yeomanry Lists* (Undated)
9. This oddly-sounding rank was a curious system whereby the Commanding Officer of a regiment also had titular command of the Troop; the *de facto* command was given to a Lieutenant who was distinguished by the prefix 'Captain-'.

Dragoons', whose image thereby acquired a certain aura of dash and panache (they later became Hussars and Lancers).

There is no authoritative record of the actual strength of the two Troops of the Bolton Light Horse Volunteers in 1798, but one unidentified source in the present Regimental Museum says 160 all ranks, and this seems quite possible. Home Office regulations demanded that a single Troop should consist 'of not less than 33 nor more than 63 mounted Men . . . including Captain, Lieutenant and Cornet'. Since we know that there were six officers (excluding the Chaplain and Surgeon, who were not commissioned) this leaves 156 rank-and-file for the two Troops – a creditable total for speedily-raised volunteers.

The 'Gentlemen and Yeomanry' were required to provide not only their own horses, but also their uniforms and saddlery: the Government supplied only arms and ammunition. The former comprised the curved light cavalry type of sabre (essentially a cutting weapon) and a flintlock, muzzle-loading pistol. The sword in its metal scabbard was slung from a waistbelt of buff leather; the pistol was carried, when mounted, in a holster secured to the front arch of the saddle. But there was no provision for carrying it when dismounted – no holster on the man – so one can only assume that the trooper had to keep the cumbersome 12-inch weapon in his hand, or perhaps he stuffed it into his waistbelt. The horse-soldier, whether Regular or Yeoman, always regarded the sword as his true weapon, and there is scant evidence that the pistol was ever used offensively. Since the allowance of ball for practice was a niggardly total of twelve rounds per man *per year*, it is unlikely that much proficiency was achieved. Not until after the introduction of the carbine in the 1840s was greater attention paid to small-arms training.

The matter of uniforms was left entirely to the whims and fancies of the officers, who formed a sort of 'Dress Committee' to decide on design, material and colours. Here once more there is an unhappy hiatus in the archives: there is no record of the original dress of the Bolton Light Horse Volunteers. In fact it is not until the 1820s that we have details, by which time the Bolton Troops had merged with others to become the Lancashire Yeomanry Cavalry. However, it might be conjectured that as the Troops were 'Light Horse', their dress would be modelled on that of the regular Light Dragoon, who wore short jackets, laced in front, buckskin breeches and black leather kneeboots. The *de rigeur* light cavalry headdress was then the imposing 'Tarleton' helmet of black-jacked leather surmounted by a large bearskin crest and often bound with a coloured pagri (or 'puggaree'). But in the absence of firm evidence, all this must remain conjecture. The actual supply of uniforms was the responsibility of the Commanding Officer and his officers, all of whom had to pay in full for whatever finery they chose. For the other ranks there was a sliding scale of clothing allowances from Government: for a sergeant £3. 3s. 9d.; a trumpeter, £2. 3s. 6d.; corporal, £1. 11s. 3d.; 'Private Man', £1. 9s. 3d.[10] These sums were for initial kitting only. There was no allowance for replacements or wear-and-tear, and whether they covered the expense depended on the tastes of the officers, extravagant or otherwise.

10. Sebag-Montefiore, C. *A History of the Volunteer Forces from the Earliest Times to the Year 1860* (1908)

As noted above, all officers received their commissions free of purchase, but unlike those of the Regulars they were signed by the Lord Lieutenant, not the King. As befitting the character of Yeomanry and Volunteers, there was a curiously democratic system of selecting candidates for commissions: this was done by a ballot among the whole corps. The NCOs were appointed by the Commanding Officer.

All self-respecting Volunteer units carried some form of Colours, or Standards or Guidons in the case of mounted corps. Thus, as soon as the two Bolton Troops were mustered, Major Pilkington's wife co-opted the good ladies of the town to embroider 'two handsome silk Guidons' which were presented at a ceremonial parade in Bolton in July 1799. Guidons were the swallow-tailed design of regimental 'flag' borne by all Light Dragoons, and until the 1820s were carried by subaltern officers on ceremonial parades. The Bolton Guidons were later laid up in the Parish Church, but sadly, they seem to have disappeared after the rebuilding of the church in the 1880s.

The terms of service of the Volunteer Light Horsemen were not too demanding. First, as already observed, they were to be employed only within their own county, though they could be summoned to neighbouring counties to suppress riots. Only in the event of enemy invasion were they liable for service elsewhere in the country. Each member was required to attend drill or exercises on two days of each week (totalling a minimum of six hours), while the whole unit had to undertake 'Permanent Duty' for at least eight days each year. This somewhat ambiguous term was applied to the collective training at what would later be known as Annual Camp. Officers received pay of rank for two days per week and for the whole period of Permanent Duty; other ranks were paid two shillings for each day of training. However, when called out for service in aid of the Civil Power or in the event of invasion, all members became entitled to the rates of pay for regular Dragoons. These were as under:[11]

Rank	Pay and allowance per day
Colonel	£1. 12s. 10d
Lt Colonel	1. 3s. 0d
Major	19s. 3d
Lieutenant	9s. 0d
Cornet	8s. 0d
Sergeant	2s. 11d
Corporal	2s. 4d
Trumpeter	2s. 4d

Such was the remarkable spirit of democracy in the 'Gentlemen and Yeomanry' that many units elected to pool their Government remuneration and distribute it evenly among all ranks – but whether Major John Pilkington agreed to such a departure from the rule is unknown.

As volunteers, the Bolton Light Horse [and the rest] were not subject to military discipline unless actually called out for service. At all other times they obeyed their own agreed

---

11. Quoted by Fortescue: *History of the British Army* Vol. IV, pt. II.

rules, regarding it as a matter of honour to attend parades, carry out orders – and submit to punishments if incurred. The harsh disciplinary measures of the Regular Army, based on the barbarous 'cat-o'-nine-tails', never defamed the Volunteer force. The only punishments inflicted were the relatively mild forms of fines or -ultimate disgrace – expulsion from the corps. There was a sliding scale of fines relating to the gravity of the offence. Thus, a man absent from a drill parade without valid reason had to forfeit two shillings; repeated absences up to eight incurred a twenty shillings penalty. Beyond that he was liable to be expelled from the Troop – 'discharged with ignominy' as the later term had it. Should a member – officer or other rank – desire to soldier no more, he was free to resign voluntarily, provided he gave fourteen days' notice in writing, to be forwarded to the Lord Lieutenant.

Each Troop was allowed one regular or ex-regular sergeant as drill instructor, also one Trumpeter who received Regular pay. The former was the prototype of those personnel who later became known as PSIs, or Permanent Staff Instructors. Since these were not always freely forthcoming, a Commanding Officer might bribe suitable NCOs from his own pocket, but there is no evidence that Major John Pilkington did so (although he could well afford it).

The archetypal image of a Yeomanry unit of yeoman farmers with the local landowners as their officers did not apply to the Bolton Light Horse. Its members, commissioned and non-commissioned, were almost exclusively townsmen from Bolton itself. While it might therefore seem odd that all of them should be able to provide their own mounts, we must remember that the horse was then the sole means of transport and mobility, and one did not need to be wealthy to own at least one 'nag' of indeterminate breeding. Gentlemen of course would maintain a stable of more elegant equines, both for riding and for their equipages, while among the rank-and-file there were merchants, innkeepers and tradesmen whose stables could turn out ride-and-drive animals, equally useful between the shafts and under the saddle.

In the 1790s the regular cavalry were supposed to adhere to certain regulations concerning breed, height and age of their remounts: the Light Dragoons' animals were to stand 'between 14 and 15 hands and not above'. But as in all other matters the Yeomanry were a law unto themselves. They could only parade what they could produce; and that must have been a very motley herd indeed, with hairy-legged 14-hand cobs and 16-hand carthorses alongside superior hunter types and hackneys. The latter was not the high-stepping carriage horse of today, but a very useful ride-and-drive animal, while the development of fox-hunting saw the breeding of specific mounts able to keep pace with fast-running hounds and to tackle any fence. There were no foxhounds within hacking distance of Bolton, but the old-established pack of Holcombe Harriers was kennelled not far away and offered sport over the local fells and moors.

The Light Horse Volunteers enjoyed several welcome concessions: not only were they exempted from the Militia ballot, but also from the iniquitous taxes on riding horses – and hair powder. The absurd military coiffure of greased and powdered hair done up in a queue was the regulation style throughout the Army, but no doubt the Volunteers had their own ideas of hair style.

In the summer of 1801 rumours of imminent invasion again alarmed the Government, and in July the Secretary of State for War, Lord Hobart, issued a circular to all Lords Lieutenant urging them to ensure that their 'several Corps of Volunteer Cavalry and Infantry . . . may be kept in a state of the utmost readiness for such immediate service as may be conformable to their respective engagements. At this date there is nothing equivalent to a permanently established Regimental Headquarters or Drill Hall, but in the event of call-out each officer and soldier made his own way, mounted and armed, to a designated place of assembly, which in Bolton was the Market Square. The summons for turn out was by means of the Trumpeter who rode around town repeatedly sounding the 'Assembly', no doubt to the alarm of slumbering citizens. In order that 'utmost readiness' could be achieved, it was enjoined that 'the uniforms, arms and accoutrements of the gentlemen serving in the Volunteer Corps should ever be kept contiguous to their beds so that they may be armed and assembled at the shortest possible notice'.[12] Presumably the horses were also kept contiguous – if not to beds.

However, there was no call on the services of the Bolton Light Horse, nor of the other Volunteers. Events took an unexpected turn when Napoleon Bonaparte, now First Consul, agreed to peace terms, and in March 1802 the Treaty of Amiens was signed. No one (except Napoleon) could foresee that this peace was to last for little more than twelve months. And so, ever blind to the future, the Government decreed that all the volunteer corps raised 'during the late hostilities' should be disbanded. As a sop to their pride, on 6 April 1802 Parliament passed a Vote of Thanks to all those volunteers 'for the seasonable and eminent Services they had rendered to their King and Country'. But it must be admitted that the services of the loyal Horsemen of Bolton had not been noticeably 'eminent'. Hedging bets, Parliament also passed an Act in June, allowing any unit that might wish to do so, to continue on a 'voluntary' basis, that is without Government remuneration. It seems that the Bolton Light Horsemen were among those dedicated corps who elected to continue, for *A View of the Volunteer Army of the United Kingdom* published by James Willson in 1806, has the following entry:

> Bolton Cavalry: Commandant John Pilkington, Establishment: one troop of 116. Strength: one field officer, two subalterns, three Staff Officers, six sergeants, two trumpeters, 100 rank and file. Date of acceptance 3 August 1802.

There are a few anomalies here. 'One troop' should obviously read 'two', while 'Staff Officers' would include the Commandant, Adjutant and Quartermaster, so that with only 'two subalterns' there seems a shortage of other officers.

The Peace of Amiens turned out to be a fragile one. Napoleon's expansionist designs in Europe, Egypt and the Mediterranean were followed by his amassing an army of 160,000 men at Boulogne, the threat being obvious. In the face of this, in May 1803 Britain once more declared war on France, and once more disbanded corps were resuscitated, and new ones raised. There was to be no lasting peace until Wellington's victory at Waterloo.

The feared invasion never materialised and the Bolton Light Horse Volunteers were not summoned beyond the limits of their own district. On 12 June 1805 the unit was

12. Sebag-Montefiore, *op. cit.*

inspected by Colonel Bulwer (North-Western District Staff) and a muster roll of those on parade and absent on leave, compiled by a 'respected friend . . . and worthy son of a long-deceased member', was published in Barton's *Historical Gleanings of Bolton*. Although incomplete, this is the only record of the make-up of the Troops (totalling 168 all ranks) of that date. The Officers listed were as under:

Major, Cmdg	John Pilkington
Captain	Matthew Fletcher
Lieutenant	William Wright
Cornet	Ralph Boardman
Cornet (Adjutant)	John Mawdsley
Quartermaster	James Morris
Surgeon	Edward Bolling
Chaplain	Richard Snape

All but Mawdsley, Morris and Snape were the original members of 1798. Six sergeants, 24 corporals and two trumpeters are named and we find that many of these were citizens of some substance and position in Bolton.

Sergeant Nathaniel Greenhalgh was a co-manager of a cotton mill; Corporal William Balshaw owned a plumbing and glazing business and was also a boroughreeve, or magistrate; Corporal Nathan Butcher was an inspector of weights and measures; Corporal William Hulton was a solicitor; Corporal John Manghall was a manager of Bolton Public Waterworks; Corporals John Moore and John Rainforth both became medical practitioners. These and several other remarkable NCOs added a degree of tone entirely lacking among the ranks of a regular unit, but not uncommon in the Yeomanry.

While the Regular Army was heavily engaged with the Napoleonic menace overseas, the Lancashire Volunteers were frequently called upon to deal with rioting and 'tumultuary business' carried on by gangs of Luddites who claimed that the introduction of machinery in the mills (such as the Crompton 'mule') was the cause of unemployment and consequent poverty. In April 1811 a body of Luddites was reported to be heading for the large mill at Westhoughton with intent to destroy the new steam machinery. The Bolton Light Horse were speedily despatched for its protection, but on arrival they found no sign of rioters, so trotted back whence they had come, unaware that they had been outwitted. The arsonists were lying concealed: as soon as the horsemen disappeared they attacked the mill and left it a gutted shell.

Soaring food prices and unemployment now resulted in widespread rioting and disorder in the northern counties, so much so that there was fear of a general uprising in the country. The Government therefore introduced the 'Spy System' or intelligence network by which local magistrates were empowered to hire informers to give warning of trouble, and so secure the arrest of agitators. Bolton's Chief Magistrate was Ralph Fletcher – 'Colonel' as he liked to be known – and his methods gained him considerable notoriety.[13] Not only

---

13. As previously noted, Ralph Fletcher was not a member of the Bolton Troop, having been confused by previous historians with Matthew Fletcher, who was.

did he evince strong bias in any case brought before him, but he was alleged to bribe informers into giving false evidence in order to secure convictions. Through his efforts, four were convicted of arson at the Westhoughton mill and conveyed to Lancaster Castle for execution. The youngest to suffer was a boy of fourteen. A detachment of the Light Horse had the dubious privilege of escorting the condemned to Chorley, where they were handed over to the Militia.

Whatever the feelings among the impoverished working classes, the attitude of Bolton's 'respectable citizens' was one of gratitude to the magistrates and the soldiery for 'suppressing the riotous proceedings of misled and ignorant people', and as a token of this, gold snuff-boxes were presented to Major Pilkington, Corporal William Balshaw, alias boroughreeve, and others. Colonel Ralph Fletcher was given a silver vase.[14] Since the attempt to preserve the Westhoughton mill was not altogether successful, we can only wonder what other riotous proceedings were suppressed. No details are forthcoming.

But in June 1813 the Light Horse were involved in a curious affair which had no connection with the disaffected working classes. 'One T. Standish of Blackrod, assuming himself to be the heir of the late Sir F. Standish, with numerous followers, assembled at Duxbury Hall and took forcible possession, turning out the servants.'(Clegg), The late Sir Frank had amassed a considerable estate which had been left to his cousin, Frank Hall Standish. Peaceable attempts to evict the usurper having failed, on 4 June a detachment of the Bolton horsemen, accompanied by Colonel Ralph Fletcher as magistrate, surrounded the mansion and, confronted by this show of force, Thomas Standish surrendered without resistance.

Inevitably, with the return of peace after Waterloo came reductions in the armed forces, and the Volunteers suffered with the Regulars. Since Government decreed that the annual allowances to all volunteer units were to be drastically cut by one half, many Volunteers felt it impracticable to continue, particularly as the end of hostilities seemed to remove much of the necessity for their existence. And so in March 1816 Major John Pilkington wrote thus to his Lord Lieutenant, the Earl of Derby:[15]

> Bolton, 4th March, 1816
>
> *My Lord*
>
> I have the Honor to inform your Lordship that at a Meeting of the Corps under my command held on Wednesday 28th ult., it was resolved unanimously that as the causes for which the Bolton Light Horse Volunteers were originally raised have now happily ceased to exist, Major Pilkington be requested to make known to His Majesty's Government their wish to be freed from their Military engagement on 5th April next, at which period the 18th year of their Services will be completed. I have therefore to beg that your Lordship will be pleased to forward this their resignation accordingly.

14. These details are taken mainly from Clegg, *op. cit.* and some anti-Fletcher correspondence published under the title *The Blackfaces of 1812 . . . containing some Notice of the Spy System in 1812, 1817 and 1819* (Bolton, 1839).
15. PRO HO51/137

I have the honor to be My Lord, your Lordship's most obedient and humble Servant

(Sgd) *JOHN PILKINGTON*

Commandg, Bolton Light Horse Volunteers

On 8 March the Home Secretary, Lord Sidmouth, informed Lord Derby that 'His Royal Highness in the name of and on the behalf of His Majesty', was 'pleased to accept' the resignation, and so the Bolton Light Horse Volunteers ended their first period of service as an independent unit. Perhaps it had not been a distinguished one – any more so than the numerous other Volunteer Horsemen and Yeomanry – but they had performed their patriotic duties 'to the satisfaction of Government as well as to the public at large', observed Corry's *History of Lancashire*.

However, this was not the final *Nunc Dimittis* of the Bolton Light Horse Troop: they were to be reborn.

Officer in the Bolton Troop of Yeomanry *circa* 1820 from an original water colour by Simkin.

CHAPTER II

The Duke of Lancaster's Own Yeomanry 1819–1876

The Regiment resulted from an amalgam of three independent units which did not emerge as The Duke of Lancaster's Own Yeomanry until 1834. Having dealt with the prototype, the Bolton Light Horse Volunteers, we must now glance at the others.

Furness Troop of Yeomanry Cavalry

Taking its title from the Furness peninsula on the northern side of Morecambe Bay, this Troop was formally raised in September 1819. In 1937 Alfred Fell, an amateur historian of Ulverston, published *A Furness Military Chronicle* in which he devoted a whole chapter to the Furness Troop, and it is owing to his industry that we have a detailed account of its raising. The founder was Thomas Richmond Gale Braddyll, a magistrate and influential member of the local gentry who resided at Conishead Priory near Ulverston. Unlike John Pilkington of the Bolton Light Horse, Braddyll had seen service in the Regular Army, first in the 17th Foot and then in the Coldstream Guards. He was commissioned Lieutenant in the 17th in 1779 and transferred to the Coldstream in 1808. He retired in 1811 with the regimental rank of Captain, but as a Guards officer he was ranked as Lieutenant-Colonel in the Army. In 1819 Braddyll was 41 years of age.

On 19 August 1819, Braddyll wrote to the Lord Lieutenant of Lancashire (Edward Stanley, Earl of Derby) informing him that consequent on meetings held in Ulverston, 'between fifty and sixty gentlemen and yeomen have declared themselves anxious to form a Troop of Cavalry for the service of the Hundred of Lonsdale North, if His Majesty's Government deem it requisite . . .' There followed a flurry of correspondence between Braddyll, Lord Derby and the Home Secretary (Lord Sidmouth), as a result of which the formation of the Troop was formally approved by the Prince Regent on 7 September 1819. An establishment of 47 rank-and-file was allowed and the first officers to be commissioned were, on 22 September:

Thomas Richmond Gale Braddyll	*Captain Commanding*
Thomas Gale Braddyll	*Captain, Second-in-Command*
William Dodgson	*Lieutenant*
William Fell	*Cornet*

As might be surmised, the Second-in-Command was the Commanding Officer's son, and in 1823 yet another son, Edward, joined as Cornet (later he became Deputy Lieutenant of the County of Lancaster).

As regards the original uniform, there has always been an element of doubt. At this date nearly all the Yeomanry wore some form of Light Cavalry dress (as did the Bolton Troop), but tradition says that in their early days the Furness Troop were popularly known as 'Furness Cuirassiers', implying that they resurrected the obsolete form of breast and back armour or cuirasses that was to survive only in the Household Cavalry. In 1898 Major J. E. Willan of Silverdale, writing in the *Yeomanry Record*, claimed that the Furness Troop were Cuirassiers in fact as well as in name. He related that some local residents could remember seeing the Troop riding across Morecambe Sands 'with their armour flashing in the sun'. Their head-dress was an imposing steel helmet with bearskin crest. At one time such a helmet was displayed in the Barrow-in-Furness Museum: the crest was lacking and the steel shell had been coated with black varnish. The front bore the inscription 'G. R. Furness Yeomanry'. If the above is true (but there is no documentary evidence), the Troop was surely unique in its dress. No other Yeomanry unit ever wore the cuirass, and in fact after the 1690s neither did any Regular cavalry until the Life Guards and Royal Horse Guards permanently reassumed it in 1820. The uniform itself was said to be blue with either buff or scarlet facings.[1] Whereas the other Yeomanry carried the Light Dragoon curved sabre, Captain Braddyll chose the 'heavy cavalry' straight sword as used by Dragoon Guards. This seems appropriate to 'Cuirassiers', which of course had been heavy cavalry.

In June 1821 the Home Secretary approved of the Troop's augmentation to 70 rank-and-file and the addition of one lieutenant. By 1828 the Troop had acquired other officers:

William Town	*Lieutenant* (1823)
John Cranke	" (1825)
Willaim Postlethwaite	" (1826)
Henry Fell	*Cornet* (1828)

The Surgeon was Dr Bernard Gilpin, a noted practitioner of Ulverston. A muster roll of *c.* 1835 laconically shows William Johnson and William Fell as 'Dead'.

In December 1827 the Home Secretary announced that any Yeomanry unit wishing to remain in service should be able to parade at least three Troops, each of no fewer than 50 men. Any not meeting these totals were either to disband or be amalgamated with other units to bring the combined unit up to strength. Since Captain Braddyll had only one Troop, he resolved that rather than face extinction he must submit to amalgamation.

By this date a number of other Yeomanry units had been raised, or re-raised, in the County Palatine, among which were the Bolton Light Horse and the Wigan Light Horse. As we have seen, the Bolton Troop had been disbanded in 1816, but it was resurrected in 1819, the Wigan Troop being formed in that same year. Both were but single Troops with no more than 50-odd rank-and-file and thus in the same situation as the Furness Troop as regards continued existence. At Captain Braddyll's suggestion, therefore, a meeting between the three Troops' officers was held at Preston in March 1828, at which it was

---

1. Barlow, L. *and* Smith, R. J. *The Uniforms of the British Yeomanry Force 1794–1914. The Duke of Lancaster's Own Yeomanry* (1983)

unanimously agreed that the Troops should merge to form a single regiment. The plan was approved by Lord Derby who forwarded his recommendation to the Home Department, and on 18 April 1828 King George IV (former Prince Regent) signified acceptance.

Thus at that date there came into being *The Lancashire Regiment of Yeomanry Cavalry* – a title which, however, had only a brief currency. According to Fell, Braddyll and the other Troop Commanders had petitioned for the distinction of the 'Royal' prefix but this was not approved. Braddyll himself was given command and, since he now had a corps of three Troops, he was promoted Major. His son Edward became Captain and Second-in-Command.

Wigan Volunteer Light Horse

In October 1819 a committee of Wigan factory owners and local gentry proposed to raise a Troop of Volunteer horsemen, to be led by John Hodson Kearsley. At this date the re-raised Bolton Troop was commanded by Captain James Kearsley, Major Pilkington having retired after the 1816 disbandment. The relationship between James of the Bolton Troop and John of the Wigan is not clear. The proposal was forwarded through the usual channels: from Kearsley to Lord Derby, from him to the Home Secretary (Sidmouth), and finally to the Prince Regent. His Royal Highness granted approval on 20 October, and by 15 December the Troop had mustered 48 men with John Kearsley as Captain in Command. The only other contemporary officers recorded were Lieutenants James Alexander Hodson and Richard Perryn, together with Cornet John Marsh. Unlike the Furness Troop, details of this Troop are scant. Barlow and Smith state that it paraded for exercises and drills at Southport in 1820 and carried out 'Permanent Duty' of eight days (i.e. annual camp) at Liverpool in October 1823. On this occasion it was inspected by Major Watts of the North-Western area staff and his report on their excellent turnout and discipline afforded 'the greatest satisfaction' to the Home Secretary (now Sir Robert Peel). As seen above, the uneventful career of the Wigan Light Horse as an independent unit came to an end in April 1828 when it was amalgamated with the Furness and Bolton Troops to form The Lancashire Yeomanry Cavalry.

Complete Muster Rolls for the new Regiment are preserved in the Public Record Office (Ref. WO 13/4009): the following is necessarily an abstract:

LANCASHIRE YEOMANRY CAVALRY
Muster Roll 1st April 1828 – 31st March 1829

Bolton Troop	Furness Troop
Capt. Cmdg James Kearsley	Capt. Cmdg Edward R. G. Braddyll
Lieutenant John Langshaw	Lieutenant John Cranke
Cornets John Woodhouse	Cornet William Postlethwaite
John Fletcher	Quartermaster Thomas Gibson
Quartermaster Robt Brookes	

Bolton Troop cont.
4 Sergeants
4 Corporals
1 Trumpeter
63 Privates

Furness Troop cont.
3 Sergeants
4 Corporals
1 Trumpeter
67 Privates

Wigan Troop
Capt. Cmdg John Hodson Kearsley
Lieutenant James Alexander Hodson
Cornet John Lord
Quartermaster John Mather
2 Sergeants
2 Corporals
1 Trumpeter
41 Privates

Total strength of Regiment:
14 officers (incl. Major Braddyll)
193 other ranks

In January 1820 Captain James Kearsley drew up a set of *Rules and Regulations for the Bolton Yeomanry Cavalry*, a copy of which is preserved in the Museum and forms the earliest extant specimen of 'Standing Orders' for the Regiment.

The Corps was to consist of two Troops commanded by a captain, with one other captain, two lieutenants, two cornets and 90 other ranks, including four sergeants. Officers were to be chosen by ballot at a general meeting of the Corps, and similarly the enrolment or expulsion of members was by general ballot, but NCOs were to be appointed only by the Commandant.

A sliding scale of fines for misdemeanours was laid down. Members appearing incorrectly dressed on parade were to forfeit 5s. if an officer, 2s. 6d. if a private. For repeated absences from parade without satisfactory reason, a fine of 20s. was imposed. 'If any Private shall talk in the Ranks after the Word "Attention!" has been given, or be guilty of any other Irregularity or neglect of Duty, he shall forfeit the Sum of one Shilling for every Offence.' Instances of 'great Misconduct' or refusal to pay fines would be punished by expulsion. All fines were to be collected by the Sergeant-Major and handed to the Captain-Commandant as Treasurer.

Field days and drill parades were to be 'regulated by the Commanding Officer, and altered according to Seasons and Circumstances: but always adapted as much as possible to the general convenience of the Members' (in rural areas the haymaking and harvest seasons were always sacrosanct for Yeomen, but whether this applied in Bolton is debatable).

If at any time the Services of the Corps shall suddenly be required the Sergeant-Major shall immediately assemble the Trumpeters, and order them to sound the 'Turn-Out' in various parts of the Town of Bolton and shall use his utmost diligence to communicate to every Member . . . this Call made upon the Corps and dispatch with the utmost expedition an Orderly to the Commanding Officer, to give him Intelligence.

Every Member was obliged to provide himself, at his own expense, with a pair of Wellington boots 'with Heels at Least one inch high', white leather gloves and a black silk handkerchief.

At this juncture it is fitting to add a valedictory for the founder of the original Troop of 1798. Having resigned his commission on the disbandment of the Bolton Light Horse Volunteers in 1816, John Pilkington saw no more military service, but retired to his new residence of West Farm, near Bolton. He did, nevertheless, continue to serve in a civil capacity, for in 1824 he was acting as a Deputy Lieutenant for the County of Lancaster. Coincidentally, his death occurred in the same year that saw the emergence of The Lancashire Yeomanry Cavalry: he died on 28 November 1828, aged 69 and was buried in Bolton Parish Church.

The formation of the new Regiment naturally involved some discussion among the component Troops about the style of dress to be adopted. By now the Bolton Troop had acquired a splendid if rather curious amalgam of Light Dragoon and Lancer get-up, consisting of the Light Dragoon bell-topped shako with drooping plume, dark blue coatee, grey overalls and wellington boots. But the chest was embellished with a white Lancer-type plastron. Unhappily, there are no details of the Wigan Troop's dress, though as 'light' cavalry they may be assumed to have worn the regulation Light Dragoon kit, similar to the above but without the plastron. On the other hand, the Furness Troop had always considered themselves as 'heavy' cavalry (with or without cuirasses). In March 1828 the Furness and Wigan Troops sent privates in their full dress to a meeting with Captain Kearsley of the Bolton Troop in Preston. After much debate, Major Braddyll's attempt to impose his own Troop's heavy cavalry style on the others failed and the new dress was inspired by the Light Dragoon pattern. As seen in a portrait of Braddyll, painted c. 1830, this consisted of the regulation blue coatee, pouch-belt, sword-belt and overalls, all crowned with the bell-topped shako.

However, it seems that Braddyll must have got his way in the end, for by 1840 the Regiment was sporting the old 'Roman'-type heavy dragoon helmet with glazed black skull, gilt chinscales and fittings, all crowned by an enormous black bearskin crest. The independence of Yeomanry officers with regard to irksome regulations is reflected in the continuing mixture of dress: although the head-dress was unmistakably 'heavy', the rest of the attire was perversely 'light', with light dragoon scarlet coatee and blue overalls, as in the former Bolton Troop.

In September 1834 Major Thomas Braddyll was privileged to attend a private audience with King William IV at St James's Palace. At this meeting His Majesty informed the Major that he had been pleased to approve that the Regiment should henceforth be dignified with the title 'THE DUKE OF LANCASTER'S OWN YEOMANRY CAVALRY'.

This significant honour, unchanged to the present day (except for the dropping of 'Cavalry'), was formally conveyed by Lord Duncannon (Home Secretary) to Lord Derby on

15 October 1834. Apart from the facts that the well-connected Braddyll (ex-Coldstream) was a familiar figure in Court circles, and the component troops were of course loyal Lancastrians, while the Duchy of Lancaster was in the holding of the Sovereign, the reasons for such distinction are not at all clear. Braddyll was ever an ambitious man and it is possible that the proposal was his own. As Commanding Officer, he himself gained two steps in rank, to full Colonel.

The first Muster Roll of The Duke of Lancaster's Own Yeomanry shows the following:[2]

    Commanding Officer   Colonel Thomas Richmond Gale Braddyll

Bolton Troop	*Furness Troop*
Capt. James Kearsley (Cmdg)	Capt. Thomas Richmond Braddyll (Cmdg)
Lieut. John Langshaw	Lieut. William Postlethwaite
Cornet John Fletcher	Cornet William Fell
	Quartermaster Thos Gibson
3 Sergeants	3 Sergeants
3 Corporals	3 Corporals
1 Trumpeter	1 Trumpeter
48 Privates	69 Privates

        Wigan Troop
        Capt. John Hodson Kearsley (Cmdg)
        Lieut. John Lord
        Cornet (*Vacant*)
        Quartermaster (*Vacant*)
        3 Sergeants
        2 Corporals
        1 Trumpeter
        44 Privates

Soon after William IV came to the throne in 1830 he caused new Dress Regulations to be issued, in which his personal preference for red or scarlet uniform was revealed. Thus, much to their resentment, all Light Dragoon regiments were ordered to give up their traditional blue dress and substitute red (the King even demanded red facings for the Navy). Although the Yeomanry were still under control of the Home Department rather than the War Office, they as Light cavalry were required to follow suit, and now we have some firm details of the original dress of The Duke of Lancaster's Own Yeomanry.[3] For reasons unexplained, this conformed to that of the 3rd or King's Own Light Dragoons (later Hussars): scarlet dress jacket with gold lace, blue facings and brass shoulder-scales; gold-laced and blue-striped girdle, broad-topped shako, also gold-laced, with drooping horsehair plume. Dark blue overalls and **Wellington** boots were retained. Officers' pouch-belts were generously embellished with gold lace, as were their sabretaches which displayed a device incorporating crown, monogram and the Red Rose of Lancaster. Other

2. PRO WO13/4009
3. Barlow and Smith, *op. cit.*

ranks' dress was of similar pattern but of cheaper material, with yellow worsted instead of gold lace. For drill order, white overalls were worn – a curious practice, since they must have needed frequent laundering. The full dress attire was completed by white buckskin gauntlets.

Horse furniture consisted of black leather saddlery, with black sheepskin over the saddle and underneath it a highly ornamental shabraque bearing more gold lace and the Regimental device in the rear corners. The Regiment's blue facings reflected their newly-acquired honour of 'royal' status, for the Duke of Lancaster was of course the King himself. It is uncertain which pattern of sword was then in use: it should have been the curved light cavalry sabre, but a few years later the straight Dragoon Guards (or heavy cavalry) pattern had been adopted. Although all the Regular cavalry had been armed with carbines (or muskets) ever since the creation of the Standing Army, most of the 1834 Yeomanry still had to be content with the single (muzzle-loading) flintlock pistol. It was only in 1843 that the carbine became a general issue.[4] In May of that year the Adjutant-General informed Sir George Murray, Master-General of the Ordnance that 'the Yeomanry Cavalry are to have Carbines, not Pistols'.

From a few contemporary manuscripts and newspaper cuttings preserved in the Regimental Museum we can catch glimpses of the now-shadowy original Regiment. Thus in February 1836 the Bolton Troop Order Book: 'The Bolton Troop will muster for eight days Training and Exercise in Field Drill order with Cloaks across the Holsters – old overalls – on Tuesday the 8th March at 9 o'clock in the morning at the usual places of parade. Such as have not received their new Clothing are requested to apply to Sergeant-Major Adams immediately.' On 11 August the Troop was to 'muster for Sword Drill on foot . . . at ¼ before one o'clock in Bradford Square – Stable Dress – white overalls – no Pouch, nor Sabretache'. It seems that the complete new dress and horse furniture had not yet been issued, for a fortnight later it was announced that 'Sheepskins are now ready for delivery at Sergt. Major Adams's, who will give the necessary directions as to fitting them on'.[5]

The *Wigan Gazette* of 23 June 1838 carried a notice of the Regiment's appearance at Lancaster for annual training or 'Permanent Duty'. 'The Regiment assembled at Lancaster for training and exercise under Capt. Kearsley in the absence of Major (sic) Braddyll.' And on the 27th there was some ceremonial when in Full Dress the Regiment underwent an inspection and then marched to the Parish Church ' . . . with their Brass Band, and the crowds assembled were evidently struck with the soldier-like and really fine appearance of the Corps. The regimental Light Cavalry jacket with blue facings and gold lace, Chaco and black horsehair plume is extremely becoming, and the effect as the men marched to and from the parish church was very imposing.' This, incidentally, is the earliest reference to a Regimental band.

Only some two months after the first parade of The Duke of Lancaster's Own, the Bolton Troop suffered the loss of its second Commanding Officer. Captain James Kearsley died

4. Blackmore, Howard L. *British Military Firearms 1650–1850* (1961)
5. Barlow and Smith, *op. cit.*

on 29 December 1834, aged 54, and was buried in his own parish church of Deane. In Bolton Parish Church there is a handsome memorial incorporating bas-reliefs of crossed Guidons, light cavalry sabre and shako, and a lengthy inscription recording that it was erected by all ranks of The Duke of Lancaster's Own Yeomanry 'in testimony of the sense they entertained of his uncompromising loyalty and . . . impartiality, firmness and efficiency with which he commanded the Troop'. Command of the Bolton Troop now passed to Captain John Langshaw.

It so happened that one year after the Regiment's acquisition of the new title, the War Office took the unusual step of issuing a cavalry training manual specially 'Adapted to the Use of Yeomanry Corps.'[6] The manual deals with mounted and dismounted drill, arms drill, and Troop, Squadron and Regimental drill, together with Government regulations concerning establishment, organisation and administration. Since it was the first official manual specifically addressed to the Yeomanry, a few extracts are merited.

Dealing with establishments, the manual laid down that 'No Troop must consist of less than 40 or more than 100 Privates (Farriers included)'. Troops under 70 men were to have one Captain, one Lieutenant, one Cornet, one Quartermaster and one Trumpeter. A 'Corps' of 120 Privates was allowed a Sergeant Major, while one of 300 was entitled to an Adjutant. The former, who was to have been an NCO in the Regulars, or Embodied Militia, was paid 3s. 2d. per day, plus 2s. for forage. The Adjutant received 6s. per day (and 2s. forage) and should have had at least four years' service in the Regulars or Embodied Militia.

The arms issued by Ordnance comprised one pistol and one sword per officer and other rank, plus 'Carbines (12 per Troop)'. The latter seems a little pre-emptive, for as we have seen, it was only between 1842–43 that all Yeomanry were to be armed with carbines 'not pistols'. The ammunition allowed was still only ten rounds of ball per man per year, plus 24 blank cartridges.[7]

While discipline was left very much to the honour of the corps, and to the efforts of the officers and NCOs, for the first time a recommended scale of monetary fines for various offences was published. The maximum fine for a commissioned officer was set at 10s.; for an NCO, 4s. and for a Private 2s. Then followed the sliding scale: failure to attend parade without valid reason, the maximum fine; for every 15 minutes late on parade, one quarter maximum; leaving the ranks without permission, talking in the ranks, improperly dressed, one quarter the maximum. 'Drunkenness on parade is a fault so degrading and disgraceful to the whole Corps that, although the whole of the regulated fine for the *first* offence may be accepted, a repetition of the offence should invariably be punished by expulsion.' Should any officer or man fail to parade when called out in aid of the Civil Power, the fines were more severe: £5 for officers, £2 for NCOs, £1 for Privates. All such fines were to be promptly paid to the Quartermaster and would 'be appropriated for the use and benefit of the Troop'.

6. *An Abridgement of the Regulations for The Formation and Movements of The Cavalry (as last corrected by the Board) Adapted to the Use of Yeomanry Corps* . . . (Wm Clowes & Sons, London, 1835)
7. Blackmore, *op. cit.*

Any member was at liberty to resign from the corps at any time, (except when called out) on giving 14 days' notice in writing. Before leaving he had to return all his clothing, arms and accoutrements and pay for any damage 'beyond reasonable wear and tear'.

Drill parades (or 'Exercise') should not exceed fourteen days annually while a maximum of six consecutive days was permitted for 'Permanent Duty' (or Camp). For such duties each man was entitled to 2s. daily plus 1s. 4d. for his horse.

There were some changes in rates of pay when called out in aid of the Civil Power. While the officers received virtually the same scale as they had in 1798 (Lieutenant-Colonel £1. 12s. 10d., Major 19s., Lieutenant 9s.) all other ranks from Sergeant- Major to Private were given a flat rate of 7s. each – another odd instance of Yeomanry 'democracy'.

There was detailed advice for kit and arms cleaning:

> The Scabbards, Hilts and Blades of Swords are to be cleaned with Bath brick occasionally, but usually kept oiled. The Barrels of the Carbines and Pistols are on no account to be cleaned with any rough substance which would take off the browning; but when perfectly dry and clean must be polished with a little bees' wax. The Brass Mountings of the Carbines and Pistols, the Buckles of the Belts, and the Shoulder and Helmet or Cap scales are to be cleaned with a leather or buff-stick and finely powdered rotten- stone made damp (the rotten-stone may be purchased at any druggist's shop). The Buttons of the Jackets, if tarnished, must be rubbed lightly with a piece of soft wash-leather, or a button-brush and whiting. Every man should provide himself with a button-stick. The Saddlery should be cleaned with soft soap, the bits, buckles and stirrups should always be kept oiled, except when brightened for parade. The men should be cautioned to keep all saddlery in their homes when not required, as the damp of the stable has a much greater effect on leather not in constant use than is usually supposed.

White-haired old cavalrymen of today with memories of such indispensable soldiers' friends as Bluebell, Brasso, Properts' saddle soap and the rest, may spare a thought for those early Yeomen striving for a smart turnout with only primitive materials. At least the button-stick probably remains familiar.

The Manual devotes a complete chapter to advice concerning measures to be taken when in aid of the Civil Power or 'On the March in Disturbed Districts', of which only a few more pertinent hints can be given here.

When likely to be called upon to suppress disturbances 'everything depends on the promptitude with which an armed force can be displayed'. Thus in such circumstances, recognised alarm posts should be fixed at some central billet and a picket should be on duty night and day with horses saddled. Occasional patrols should also be sent out, preferably under an officer. When on the march the advance and rear guards were to have their loaded carbines or pistols ready in their hands: 'without such precautions the best cavalry in the world are in danger of surprise and disgrace from a few opponents well posted in hedges and such places of concealment.'

On riding at a mob, the utmost steadiness and good order would be more effectual than 'any misplaced impetuosity . . . as long as cavalry maintain their ranks with steadiness and order, and do not allow themselves to fall into confusion by attempting too great rapidity of movement, they are irresistible by any except thoroughly disciplined infantry formed in square to receive them'.

Finally, there were some cogent remarks about the often delicate question of whether action could be taken without the authority of a magistrate. The Law Officers made it clear, however, that just as any citizens were entitled to 'arm themselves and use ordinary means of force' to suppress a riot, so were the military. In other words, a Yeomanry officer could act on his own initiative if no magistrate were available.

Despite a temporary setback in public image after the 'Peterloo Massacre' of 1819 when the Manchester and Salford Yeomanry were accused of over-reaction, by the 1830s the Yeomanry had acquired repute as a reliable, disciplined force for the preservation of law and order in support of the civilian constabulary.[8] The very fact that Yeomen themselves were mostly men of some property and substance gave them a personal interest in quelling destructive mobs – a factor which did not apply to Militiamen and Regular soldiers. The Duke of Wellington was a firm advocate for the use of mounted troops rather than infantry in the quelling of public disorder. ' . . . for this reason: cavalry inspires *more terror* at the same time that it *does much less mischief*. A body of 20 or 30 horse will disperse a mob with the utmost facility, whereas 400 or 500 infantry will not effect the same object without the use of firearms, and a great deal of mischief may be done.'[9]

There was, however, some dispute among both Whig and Tory members of the House about the expense of employing the volunteer Yeomanry. Whereas Regular troops were paid whether or not they were employed, the Yeomanry received pay only when called out on such duties, thus adding to Government expenditure.

But, expensive or no, there were many calls upon The Duke of Lancaster's and other loyal Yeomanry units during the troubled times of the 1840s when the Chartist disturbances erupted throughout England. So-called from their 'Peoples' Charter', and led by radical agitators, the Chartists' basic aims were to secure universal suffrage and what they termed 'social equality for all'. Resulting from soaring food prices and trade depression, there was much poverty among the working classes, particularly in the Lancashire manufacturing districts. 'Great distress in Bolton' recorded Clegg; out of 50 mills 30 were idle and some 5,000 workers had neither jobs nor wages. These and many more were very willing to be swayed by the Chartist dissidents in their attacks on factories and mills. In 1842 the so-called 'Plug Riots' of Lancashire became widespread, with mobs gathering to withdraw the plugs of factory boilers and locomotives. According to records in the Museum, the three Troops of The Duke of Lancaster's were called out on numerous occasions between 1842 and 1848, although details of their actions are regrettably lacking. A few references are vouchsafed from contemporary newspapers, some of which

---

8. Sir Robert Peel's blue-coated 'Peelers' appeared on the streets of London in 1830, but many years passed before all counties could deploy their properly organised constabulary forces.
9. Quoted in Clode, *op. cit.*

seemed more concerned with the doings of the mob rather than the forces of law and order. Thus after describing at length some disturbances in Bolton, *The Bolton Free Press* of 27 August 1842 concluded: 'The Cavalry [i.e. the Yeomanry] are still in quarters, but we hope soon to hear of their dismissal to their homes.' This organ was noted for its satirical, if not hostile attitude to the local Troop. In the previous June it reported that 'this body of irregular horse left this town on Thursday for eight days' exercise in Lancaster. It is expected that on their return, they will volunteer for service in India, so, Look out Affghana!' (The first Afghan War was then in full spate.) In August the finger of fun was poked at 'a bold Yeoman' who galloped after an old woman. 'In her haste and agitation her cap fell from her head and her hair streamed in the wind. The sight had such a ludicrous cast, that a universal laugh of derision resounded from every side . . . and the zealous trooper returned to his place.'

The less radical-minded newspaper, *The Bolton Chronicle*, gave unbiased reports. On 13 August 1842 ' . . . the Bolton Cavalry under the command (in the absence from England of Captain Langshaw) of Lieutenant John Fletcher were called out and drawn up in front of the police-office . . . The men of both Troops were kept under arms the whole of the night, ready to be called at a moment's notice.' Next morning, with the help of a company of the 72nd Highlanders, they dispersed a threatening mob in Bolton's Market Square. 'Several skirmishes took place and stones were thrown, but nothing more material than one of the soldiers and one or two of the police being slightly wounded occurred.' There was another incident on 14 August when the busy Lieutenant Fletcher led his men to disperse would-be rioters attempting to enter the town. The mob was approaching along the canal bank, and the outcome had a touch of comedy. Seeing the horsemen bearing down upon them, the mob promptly leaped into the canal, whence some struggled to the other bank while others stood immersed to waists 'staring about them with considerable astonishment'. There were no casualties, but the Yeomen captured 'a wheelbarrow full of bludgeons and cudgels', said the *Chronicle*.

By the end of August the streets of Bolton were peaceful once more. Some 80 rioters (mostly from Heywood and Bury) had been arrested, and, linked together by ropes, the dejected rabble was escorted by the Bolton Troop to the railway station for conveyance to their trial in Manchester. *The Bolton Chronicle* (20 August 1842) reported that on marching through Bradshawgate the escort was assaulted by showers of stones, 'but on [the Troop's] turning round and galloping among the crowd, the people fled and did not resume the attack'.

It is noteworthy that among all accounts of the disturbances there are no reports of casualties other than injuries to troops from brickbats and stones. There was no 'Peterloo' here, and it seems that the military acted with considerable discipline and restraint.

By this date the first Commanding Officer of The Duke of Lancaster's Own Yeomanry, as such, had resigned (1841). Retiring to his Ulverston home, Colonel Thomas Richmond Gale Braddyll lived until 1862, when he died at the age of 84.

Although firm details are lacking, it seems that The Duke of Lancaster's received an issue of the new percussion carbines converted from the old flintlock 'Paget' weapon around

1847.[10] It was now a simple matter for the trooper to slip a cap over the breech nipple instead of the delicate business of pouring priming powder into the pan (often on a restive horse). The weapon was still muzzle-loading and smooth-bored: the rifled version did not appear until the early 1850s. In mounted order the carbine was suspended from a swivel sling, the muzzle resting in a miniature bucket on the horse's offside.

So far The Duke of Lancaster's Own had been the sole Yeomanry regiment representing the County Palatine, but in August 1848 they were joined by a new body of fellow-Lancastrians, styled The Lancashire Hussars. There was long a legend that this Regiment, raised by Sir John Gerard, member of an influential Catholic family of Garswood, near Ashton-in-Makerfield, was formed by 'milking' Catholic officers and men from the mainly Anglican members of the DLOY, but as seen in Appendix III, such a legend is in fact a myth, with no substance in fact.

However, The Lancashire Hussars remained in many respects closely associated with their Lancashire brethren, often doing duty and providing escorts together, while the Army Lists of the 1850s even went so far as to list all the officers under the single joint heading 'Duke of Lancaster's Own and Lancashire Hussars'. But the Hussars were nevertheless a separate body, and do not merit more than the outline of their services given in the Appendix.

The latter half of Victoria's reign may, as Gibbon remarked of a Roman Emperor, be said to have 'furnished very few materials of history', as far as the Yeomanry were concerned. The fact is, with the establishment of a constitutional police force throughout the country, the prime *raison d'être* of the Yeomanry's existence seemed to have been nullified. And although Napoleon III's expansionist designs had aroused some fears of aggression in 1851 and 1859, the threat of invasion never became real. Nevertheless the spirit of selfless service continued to flourish, and when the Government authorised the formation of a new Volunteer Force in 1859, men flocked to enrol, totalling 161,000 within two years. These, however, were mainly infantry, soon to be known as Rifle Volunteers; but a few troops of Mounted Rifles also came into existence, in some cases reverting to the old title of 'Light Horse'.[11]

It must be confessed that the half-century between the 1850s and 1900 was really one of marking time for Volunteers and Yeomen. Mounted or dismounted drills once or twice a week, the annual collective training of all Troops as a regiment in camp (until the 1900s still termed 'Permanent Duty'), the annual inspection by some Colonel or General of the Regular Cavalry; such was the uneventful lot of the part-time cavalryman. Occasionally there might be a flurry of spit-and-polish and ceremonial drill when the Regiment was called upon to provide escorts or guards of honour for visiting royalty. In July 1840 Queen Adelaide, widow of William IV, made a tour of the Lake District, and the Furness Troop under Captain Thomas Michaelson had the honour of receiving her at Newby Bridge and escorting her to Windermere. In June 1857 Queen Victoria and the

10. The name was derived from the cavalry General, Sir Henry Paget, later 1st Marquess of Anglesey, who was responsible for introducing a flintlock carbine around 1808.
11. Examples are: Huntindonshire Mounted Rifles (Duke of Manchester's Light Horse) (1860); Norfolk and Suffolk Light Horse Volunteers (1862).

Prince Consort paid a visit to Manchester when a detachment of the Regiment and the Lancashire Hussars provided a mounted escort through the streets. There was another royal visit to the city in July 1869, this time by the Prince of Wales, who was previously entertained at Worsley Hall by the Earl of Ellesmere (whose father had commanded the Regiment). The Duke of Lancaster's escorted the Prince from Worsley station. In June 1873 the Prince once again honoured Lancashire with a tour of its manufacturing districts, and on this occasion he visited Wigan to open a new infirmary. The escort was once more provided by Troops of The Duke of Lancaster's and The Lancashire Hussars, together with a company of the Wigan Volunteer Rifles. Needless to say, all these prestigious duties were carried out in the resplendent panoply of Review Order, or Full Dress.

When The Duke of Lancaster's Own went to Lancaster for their annual training in June 1871 under Colonel Egerton, they mustered a creditable strength of fourteen officers and 248 other ranks, including five Trumpeters and five Farriers.

By the 1860s the dress had lost all vestiges of Light Horse attire, becoming closely assimilated to that of the Regular Dragoon Guards and Dragoons. A scarlet, skirted tunic replaced the coatee; the old shako gave way to the new heavy cavalry pattern 'Albert' helmet, bearing a detachable plume of white horsehair drooping from a socket on top of the skull. Named after the Prince Consort who had approved its introduction, this was the original pattern of the Full Dress headgear still worn today by the Household Cavalry and Dragoon Guards. Nether limbs were clad in blue overalls with gold stripe, the ankles and inside legs being protected by leather strapping. Horse furniture included the black sheepskin and the gold-embroidered shabraque: all saddlery was still of black leather. It is scarcely necessary to add that the facings remained blue: ever since the Regiment was honoured with the title 'The Duke of Lancaster's Own', this royal distinction of dress has continued to be cherished. The above style remained virtually unchanged until 1871 when blue breeches, or 'pantaloons', were substituted for overalls. For Drill Order a blue stable jacket was worn, and a flat, peaked cap replaced the helmet. But on occasions the helmet was still to be seen on drill parades, though minus the detachable plume.

Since the 1820s the favoured venue for 'Permanent Duty' or annual camp had been Southport, or Birkdale, where the vast expanse of firm sands, seldom reached by the tide, formed an ideal terrain for mounted drill and manoeuvres. It is on record that the early Wigan Troop carried out their training there in 1820 and 1822, while a group photograph of 1897 shows the officers of The Duke of Lancaster's 'at annual training at Southport'.[12] Other centres frequently visited were Lancaster and Liverpool. In July 1855 The Duke of Lancaster's shared a camp with The Lancashire Hussars at Liverpool, the men being billeted around Edge Hill station, the officers enjoying more elegant accommodation in the Adelphi Hotel. May of the following year saw both Regiments again in camp together, this time at Lancaster, where they drilled on land at Scale Hall Farm, two miles outside the town.[13]

12. Reproduced in Barlow and Smith, *op. cit.*
13. Earle, T. A. *The Annals of the Lancashire Hussars* (1880)

For a period of 50 years, that is, from about 1850 until after the Boer War, the Regiment's Headquarters were located at Worsley, on the western fringe of what is now Greater Manchester. Here was located the manor house of Worsley Park, seat of the Egerton family whose Earls of Ellesmere served the Regiment as Colonels and Commanding Officers.

In addition to their blue facings, The Duke of Lancaster's received infusions of blue blood. Among the Captains in the 1860 Army List were Spencer Compton, Lord Cavendish, of Holker Hall, Lancashire (later 8th Duke of Devonshire) and the Viscount Brackley of the Egerton family, which also provided Lieutenant the Hon. Algernon Fulke Egerton. The Cornets were headed by the resounding entry of A. E. H. G. G. Viscount Grey de Wilton, followed by the Hon. Walter Harbord whose father was Lord Suffield. Viscount Grey de Wilton was seconded from the 1st Life Guards.

With such a roll call of aristocracy the Regimental aura had been elevated since those early days of mill owners and factory managers. Always holding themselves superior to the footslogging Militia and Volunteer infantry, the Yeomanry were now undoubtedly the most prestigious of the auxiliary forces, and some Regiments' rolls of officers read like excerpts from Debrett. In 1856 The Royal Wiltshire, for example, outdid The Duke of Lancaster's with four earls, a marquess, two viscounts and an 'Hon.'.

A regretted departure from The Duke of Lancaster's was that of Major John Langshaw who had served continuously since the re- raising of the Bolton Troop in 1819. He retired in 1855 and in July the following year the Regiment presented him with a dress sword, now to be seen in the Museum. On his death (at Lancaster) in 1883 he had reached his 82nd year and was claimed to be the oldest surviving member of the Regiment.

The majority of the rank-and-file of bygone years naturally remain shadowy, if not invisible, figures, but occasionally some noteworthy 'character' emerges out of the mists. Such a one was Sergeant-Major Richard Hall Williams who was appointed Drill Instructor at the Worsley Headquarters in 1867. As a 23 year old, Williams had enlisted in the 17th Lancers in 1842 and served throughout the Crimean War, riding as Troop Sergeant in the charge of the Light Brigade at Balaclava. He emerged unscathed, and later attributed this to his ' . . . visage so fearful that the Russians held their fire . . .' It so happened that he was suffering from a burst abscess on his nose and charged with a gory bandage covering his face. Promoted Troop Sergeant-Major in 1855, Williams continued with the 17th until his discharge from the Regular Army in 1867, aged 58. At the personal submission of the Earl of Ellesmere, commanding The Duke of Lancaster's, he was then posted to the Regiment as Drill Sergeant-Major, at the same time being appointed Postmaster of Worsley village. Regimental archives suggest that he was a colourful character, with a fetish for mounted drill to music provided by the Band. However, his enthusiasm for drill and discipline was not confined to his Yeomen: the children of the Worsley estate, including those of the Commanding Officer, were also subjected to regular 'parades' on the meadow behind his post office. On his final retirement in 1878 the Regiment presented him with a sword which was acquired by the Monks Hall Museum, Eccles, but is now on loan to the DLOY Museum. This worthy old soldier lived for 91 years, dying on 7 July 1910, when his funeral cortege to Worsley church was followed by 'most of the population of Worsley'. His only son, Clement, was reported to be still living in 1969, aged 95.[14]

Another noble veteran of the Regiment was William Adams who was Drill Sergeant-Major of the Bolton Troop in the newly-formed Duke of Lancaster's Own during the 1830s. Clegg's *Chronological History of Bolton* records that he died in 1876 aged 92 years: 'He fought in the battle of Waterloo, and from 1828 to his death was connected with the Lancashire Yeomanry Cavalry. Altogether he served his country 72 years and his remains were interred with military honours in the Bolton cemetery.' On his death *The Bolton Chronicle* of 21 October 1876 published two columns of obituary and an account of the funeral, from which only the following digest must suffice: William Adams enlisted in the 1st or King's Dragoon Guards in 1805, aged 21, and served continuously with that Regiment until retiring as Troop Sergeant-Major in 1827. At the Battle of Waterloo 'Adams was severely wounded and his horse was killed . . . but he instantly seized another horse which had lost its rider, a French Cuirassier, and upon this he rode in the subsequent stages of the strife'. After retirement in 1828, Adams was appointed Sergeant-Instructor to the Bolton Troop, and was transferred to the Worsley Troop in 1849 as Troop Sergeant-Major, soon after being promoted Regimental Sergeant-Major. Of his 72 years' total service, 48 were spent with the Lancashire Yeomanry. He died on 14 October 1876. His funeral at Bolton on 20 October was conducted with full military honours, the cortege including detachments of the Kings Dragoon Guards, the Bolton and Worsley Troops of The Duke of Lancaster's and one of the Lancashire Rifle Volunteers, together with the Band of the Worsley Troop.

14. Details mainly derived from: Fortescue, Hon. J. W. *A History of the 17th Lancers*(1895) and Lummis and Gwynn *Honour the Light Brigade*(1973), together with newspaper cuttings in the DLOY Museum.

Major T. R. G. Braddyll of Conishead Priory painted by T. R. Stewardson *circa* 1830 wearing Review Order of the newly-amalgamated Lancashire Regiment of Yeomanry Cavalry.

Sergeant Major Adams; he was born in 1784, enlisted at the 1st (Kings) Dragoon Guards in 1805, fought at Waterloo and became Sergeant Instructor to the Bolton Troop in 1828. He transferred to the Worsley Troop in 1849 and was later RSM. He died in 1876 and is shown here wearing the Waterloo medal on the left and what is presumed to be a Regimental Medal on the right.

[28]

CHAPTER III

Victorian Peace 1860–1899

Though the period between 1860 and 1899 was anything but peaceful for the Regular Army embroiled in far-flung 'small wars' in China, South Africa, Afghanistan, Egypt, Burma, New Zealand, not to mention almost constant operations on India's North-West Frontier, for the home-based Yeomanry regiments this span saw only the yearly routine as before: weekly drills, periodic inspections, the occasional escort duty, the annual camp (still referred to as 'Permanent Duty').

However, these years brought The Duke of Lancaster's several domestic and wider changes which must be noticed. Among these was the incorporation of several independent Troops to come under command of Regimental Headquarters at Worsley. In 1798 a Troop had been raised by Captain Ralph Kershaw at Oldham. The only extant record of the early years of this Troop is an unpublished typescript by J. H. Fielding, *The Story of the Oldham Horse Association and the Oldham Troop Yeomanry Cavalry 1789–1873*, held in the Regimental Museum. The author obviously had little to go on, for apart from noticing inspections and occasional call-outs, he could find little until 1873 when 'the Oldham Yeomanry became absorbed by The Duke of Lancaster's Own Yeomanry as the Oldham Troop'. However, in June 1819, the Troop was presented with 'a superb silk flag by Mrs Taylor, the mother of Capt. John Taylor, commandant of the Corps . . .' This 'flag' or guidon has survived and at the time of writing is being restored for display in the Regimental Museum.

In February 1844 a Troop was raised at Rochdale; in March 1846 another appeared at Worsley, and in 1877 a third was formed at Broughton, near Manchester. After some 61 years' service the Wigan Troop was struck off in 1880. In November of that year a new Troop came into being at Blackburn, raised by Captain Herbert Shepherd-Cross, whose son Captain (later Major) T. A . S. Shepherd-Cross founded the Blackpool Troop in 1899. The same year saw a Troop raised at Liverpool by Captain R. H. Tilney who as Lieutenant-Colonel commanded the Regiment during the 1914–18 war.

In 1857 Lieutenant-Colonel George Egerton, 2nd Earl of Ellesmere assumed command from his father, Lord Francis, the first Earl. When the second Earl died in 1862 he was succeeded in command by his younger brother, the Hon. Algernon Fulke Egerton who held the post for 23 years, retiring in 1885 to become Honorary Colonel. As shown in Appendix IV, the family of the Earls of Ellesmere maintained an active association with the Regiment for the remarkable span of more than half a century – a record equalled, curiously enough, only by those fellow-Lancastrians, The Lancashire Hussars, with their Gerards.

Among the present Regimental archives is a manuscript Order Book of the Bolton Troop, covering the period 1863–1872, and providing us with a few glimpses of the not very eventful routine and domestic details.

On 10 March 1863 Edward, Prince of Wales was married to Princess Alexandra of Denmark in St George's Chapel, Windsor. This event was celebrated throughout the country with ceremonial parades, civic functions, banquets and 'Loyal Addresses', and the Order Book briefly notes that the Bolton Troop 'paraded on foot in Full Dress with carbines, without swords, or Tuesday 10th March - Marriage of the Prince of Wales'. In the same month it was ordered that foot drills were to be carried out in 'Stable Dress, without spurs, with swords, carbines and gloves'.

In June of that year a new, single-breasted tunic replaced the earlier double-breasted pattern, and Troop Captains were directed to provide all their men with these before the next year's Permanent Duty . . . the pattern to be procured from Sergt. Major Adams, Worsley'. Most of the entries refer to uniform and saddlery details: thus in May 1869 'The Stirrup leathers of Bolton and Rochdale Troops are to be altered to Regt. pattern', while in May 1872 a Regimental patrol coat was approved by the Colonel, and 'Officers desirous of providing themselves with one will find the pattern at Mr. Hawkes, 14 Piccadilly, London'. This 'Mr Hawkes' headed the well-known firm of military tailors whose business flourishes today as Gieves & Hawkes.

There was an establishment change in December 1872 when the Furness Troop at Ulverston was disbanded as such, most of its men being transferred to Oldham.[1]

Between 1870 and 1881 the Regular Army underwent a sweeping reorganisation as a result of the Cardwell reforms.[2] Here it is only necessary to mention his more radical changes: the 'linking' of infantry battalions (later their amalgamation), replacement of time-honoured numerical titles by the new 'territorial' or county names, and most radical of all, the abolition of the age-old Purchase system for officers (in 1871). At last it was no longer necessary for a gentleman to lay out large sums for his commission and subsequent promotion in the service of his Queen and country. This of course meant that the Yeomanry officer, who had never been so burdened, lost his advantage over his Regular counterpart. A minor change in 1871 was the disappearance of the ancient ranks of Cornet and Ensign, replaced by Sub-Lieutenant. But this naval-sounding term lasted only six years: it gave way to Second Lieutenant in 1877.

Cardwell's Regulation of the Forces Act of 1871 was chiefly concerned with the Regular Army, but it also touched on the Yeomanry. The establishment for the whole country was set at 36 regiments totalling 11,850 all ranks. This allowed an average of some 350 officers and men per unit, but of course not all were up to strength. In 1877 The Duke of Lancaster's could parade fifteen officers and 250 other ranks, including the Band.[3] Any regiment with fewer than four Troops or 160 all ranks was to be broken up, or in special circumstances might be allowed to continue as 'mounted volunteers' without Government pay.

1. Fell, Alfred *A Furness Military Chronicle*
2. Edward Cardwell, later Viscount, was Secretary of State for War, 1868–74.
3. Report of Annual Inspection, *The Lancaster Guardian* 30 June 1877.

The whole of the Yeomanry were now organised in two large commands termed 'Cavalry Districts for Auxiliary Forces', The Duke of Lancaster's (and Lancashire Hussars) coming under the 1st District, which embraced all the northern counties of England and the whole of Scotland. The District Headquarters was established at York. A regular Inspecting Officer of Yeomanry was appointed for each District, that of the 1st District being Colonel the Hon. C. W. Thesiger (late 14th Hussars).

Although the Lords Lieutenant retained some authority over their county Yeomanry, being empowered to approve officers for commissions, training periods and other matters, the body as a whole conformed to the Regular Army in being brought under control of the War Office, not the Home Department as previously, while officers' commissions were signed by the Queen like those of all the Regular forces.

The last three decades of the century witnessed no changes in drill or tactics either for Regular or Yeomanry cavalry: troops, squadrons, regiments, and on occasions whole brigades, still performed their complex evolutions on the broad expanse of their training areas – such as Southport Sands – manoeuvring from line to column of sections, column of troops or squadrons, and back again, changing front to left or right, and the other dozen or so 'movements' laid down in the *Cavalry Training* manual. As far as most Commanding Officers were concerned, the prime object of all this effort was really that of impressing the Inspecting Officer on the annual inspection, who was usually content with smart parade-ground drill and turnout, and seldom bothered about such practical tasks as patrolling, picqueting, reconnaissance, skill-at-arms and the like. Provided the regiment was smartly turned out and well drilled in all movements, little else mattered, and it would receive the Inspector's commendation (after fitting hospitality by the officers in the RHQ Mess).

During the period under review both Regular and Yeomanry cavalry were required to train with an almost bewildering succession of firearms. In 1866 the rifled, breech-loading Westley-Richards carbine (.45 in.) was issued. Three years later came the Snider (.57 in.), issued to Yeomanry; then the Martini-Henry (.45 in.) and finally the Martini-Metford of .303 in. calibre which remained in service until the Boer War. The exact dates when all these were received by The Duke of Lancaster's Own Yeomanry cannot be established, but we know that by 1900 the Martini- Metford was in use.[4]

Despite the technological advances in firearms, the sword – that hallowed *arme blanche* – was still regarded as the only weapon for the mounted soldier, and the Yeoman, like the Regular, spent hours practising its offensive use. As a recruit he squatted, knees bent, on an imaginary horse on the drill ground, obeying such injunctions as 'Engage! Infantry right – point! Withdraw!' and so forth. Later he was allowed to mount the live animal and, sword 'in line', to gallop at a straw-stuffed dummy.

However, musketry training was not ignored. Following Cardwell's recommendation, authority decreed in 1872 that all Yeomanry regiments should send their Adjutant and one sergeant for a two-week course at the Army School of Musketry which had been

4   Photographs in Museum.

established at Hythe (Kent) in 1854. By 1880 all ranks of The Duke of Lancaster's from Sergeant to Private had been armed with the breech-loading, rifled Martini-Henry carbine of .45 in. calibre, and there was a Government allowance of 40 rounds of ball per year for live firing on the ranges. If they thought fit, Commanding Officers could supplement this with extra issues – at their own expense. Officers, Sergeant-Majors, Quartermasters and Trumpeters carried pistols only (and swords of course). As issued, the pistols were still the somewhat primitive single-shot, muzzle-loading patterns with 10 in. barrel, but of course most officers preferred to purchase the more sophisticated breech-loading 'revolving pistol' such as the Adams, Colt, and Smith & Wesson, which had been in service with the Regulars since the 1860s.

Successive issues of the Army List had been meticulous in showing all Regular regiments in order of seniority, or precedence, but the Yeomanry were listed simply in alphabetical order of their counties, regardless of their seniority. Thus in 1878 The Duke of Lancaster's appeared seventeenth in the roll, below many that were junior in terms of continuous service. In an attempt to establish a correct order of precedence, on 5 December 1884 the War Office issued 'A Proposed Precedence Table for Yeomanry Regiments', in which The Duke of Lancaster's had moved up one place. This hastily botched list was replete with so many anomalies and inaccuracies that it only served to evoke indignation and objections among the regiments. For instance, pride of place was given to the Derbyshire Yeomanry, alleged to have been raised in 1731 – 63 years before any Yeomanry had come into existence! Later it was revealed that '1731' was a printer's error for '1794'. In the face of criticism, the War Office then asked Commanding Officers to provide firm evidence of their regiments' origins, and as a result a revised, and accurate, Table was published in January 1885.[5] This Precedence allotted The Duke of Lancaster's Own Yeomanry twelfth place in order of seniority, a ranking based of course on the 1798 formation of the Bolton Light Horse, and one which was retained until the drastic 'reorganisation' of the Territorial Army by the Labour government of 1967. However, the official Army List continued to ignore this precedence table and persisted in listing all Yeomanry under alphabetical order of their counties.

In May 1889 a new edition of *Regulations for the Yeomanry Cavalry* appeared from the War Office, and as this remained in force until after the Boer War, it deserves a little attention. The minimum rank-and-file establishment for a regiment was now to be no fewer than 200 NCOs and privates, while a troop should muster at least 42 other ranks. Any regiment falling below 200 other ranks for two successive years would be liable to disbandment 'without further notice'. Candidates for first commissions as subalterns had to be at least 17 years of age and to be approved by the Lord Lieutenant, who would forward their names to the Secretary for War for submission to Her Majesty. Before the commission could be granted, however, the aspirant was now required to pass an examination set by the School of Auxiliary Cavalry, which had been set up at Aldershot in 1876. The syllabus was as under:

    Practical examination in drilling squadron
    Practical sword and carbine exercises
    Equatation and stable management
    Duties of escorts, advanced and rearguards, out posts and reconnaissance.

5. Army Order 648, 10/85.

    Aiming drill and firing point duties
    Command of a troop in field movements
    Duties in billets
    Equipment of the Yeoman and his horse
    Knowledge of regulations applicable to Permanent Duty and duty in aid of the Civil Power

There were further examinations for promotion to Field rank, so that the Yeomanry officer was now on a par with his Regular brother as regards professional qualifications. An Adjutant, of Captain's rank, was appointed from a Regular regiment for a five-year tour of duty, such appointments being made (or approved) by the Commander-in-Chief of the Army. Yeomanry Commanding Officers were cautioned not to solicit for their own choice of Adjutants, though the C-in-C would 'give every consideration to any suggestions or objections' which they might put forward. All Yeomanry officers would normally be retired at the age of 60, but if specially recommended by the GOC the District, continuance for another seven years might be permitted.

Apart from Permanent Staff NCOs, the other ranks ('enrolled members') were to be not younger than 17 and not above 49 years of age. No height limits were specified, but recruits had to be 'of good physique and unexceptionable moral character'. Since most volunteer Yeomen were of a superior class to that of the enlisted recruit of the Regulars, there could have been little difficulty in meeting the latter demand.

The Regulations required a regiment to carry out Permanent Duty (or Annual Camp) for at least six successive days per year 'exclusive of the days of marching to and from the place of assembly'. In addition, each Yeoman had to put in a minimum of six squad drills (mounted or dismounted) and five mounted troops drills annually. Not a very demanding year's duties, perhaps, but Commanding Officers were allowed some discretion about frequency of parades, while it must never be forgotten that the Yeoman also had his civilian employment to attend to.

Government-issue arms were still the rifled Martini-Henry carbines for all ranks below Sergeant-Major, with 'pistols revolving' for officers, WOs, trumpeters and a few others.

The perpetual dispute about the best type of sword for the cavalryman (and Yeoman) was temporarily, and unsatisfactorily, compromised in 1890 with the Ordnance issue of a dual-purpose 'cutting-and-thrusting' pattern. Slightly curved, this was very similar to the pattern now seen in service with the Mounted Squadrons of the Household Cavalry. Other ranks had to be content with what was served out, and judging by photographs in the Museum, between 1870 and 1900 there was little uniformity, some ranks carrying the sabre type, others the straight heavy cavalry pattern. Much the same applied to the officers, most of whom purchased their preferred pattern from Wilkinson's. It was not until 1908 that the final pattern of straight sword became a regulation issue. Still in service with The King's Troop RHA, it is known as the '1908 Pattern'.[6]

By 1889 the Maxim machine gun (forerunner of the Vickers) had been accepted by the Army, and all Regular cavalry regiments deployed a section of two guns (on wheeled

---

6. The evolution of the cavalry sword into its final pattern of 1908 is well described in the present Marquess of Anglesey's work *A History of the British Cavalry* Vols 3 and 4 (1982, 1986).

horse-drawn carriages). None were authorised for the Yeomanry, but, as always, it appears that some regiments (with official approval) made their own arrangements. Thus, the Regulations declared that 'Any machine gun which may become the private property of a regiment of Yeomanry Cavalry should be .45 in. calibre and chambered to take Martini-Henry solid case ammunition'. The cost of such weapons is not revealed, nor that of the 1,000 rounds of ball ammunition per gun per year, obtainable from Ordnance 'on pre-payment'. However, there is no record of The Duke of Lancaster's purchase of any type of automatic weapon: the earliest mention is that of two Colt guns issued before sailing for South Africa in 1900.

More serious attention was now devoted to musketry with the carbine, and the Regulations laid down that all Yeomen should fire an annual musketry course at ranges up to 600 yards, when they would be classified in four categories up to 'Marksman'. All this was of course carried out dismounted: the hazardous practice of firing from the back of a possibly unsteady, 'part-time' Yeomanry horse had been abandoned some 50 years ago.

A complete chapter of the Regulations was devoted to 'Finance', which was a somewhat complex subject, involving different scales of pay for different duties, and only a summary can be given here. First, the officers; they were paid only when attending Permanent Duty (or when called out in aid of the Civil Power), and as seen from the following table, they had suffered some reductions from the rates of 1854.

Daily Rates	
Lieutenant-Colonel	£1. 3s. 0d.
Major	19s. 3d.
Captain	14s. 7d.
Lieutenant (after 3 years' service)	9s. 0d.
Lieutenant (less than 3 years')	8s. 0d.
Second Lieutenant	8s. 0d.
Medical Officer	11s. 4d.
Veterinary Officer	8s. 0d.

The attached Regular Adjutant, however, received from 7s. to 10s. per day, according to the strength of the regiment, during the whole of his attachment. Permanent Staff NCOs were paid as Regulars; all other ranks were entitled to 7s. for each day's service on Permanent Duty, or 3s. 6d. per day on Troop Drills. There were several contingency allowances, such as £2 per NCO and Yeoman per annum for clothing and accoutrements. And here the Regulations seemed to hark back to the nefarious practices of 18th-century colonels who strove to make a profit out of their commands: 'The contingent and clothing allowance . . . is *not* the property of any individual, and will not be applied to increase the income of any of the officers, non- commissioned officers, or men of the regiment.'

A note on uniforms stressed that no deviations from the current regimental patterns would be permitted without the Queen's sanction, while we learn that The Duke of Lancaster's Own and twelve others 'wear gold lace, buttons, braids and plates', all others having silver lace. Exactly when the Ducal Coronet (Duke of Lancaster's) became authorised as a distinctive arm-badge for sergeants and WOs is not recorded, but this was certainly in wear by the 1880s.

Regarding horses, no standards were specified, but 'every non-commissioned officer and private . . . except the orderly room clerk, saddler and tailor, will be required to ride either his own horse or one borrowed from some relative, friend, or employer, who shall engage to the commanding officer that the horse will be provided for the Yeoman's use whenever required'. Compensation up to £30 was admissible for the loss or permanent disablement of a horse in the performance of duty.

It is noteworthy that in the section headed 'Discipline' there is now no reference to the regulation scale of fines for offenders. This is because the War Office scale was abolished in 1880 and such fines were now left to the discretion of the Commanding Officer.

Finally, it was reiterated that when on Permanent Duty or called out for service, either in aid of the Civil Power or in the event of war, the Yeomanry were subject to Military Law in common with the Regular Army.

We now arrive at the year 1893, which is an important date in Yeomanry history. Early the previous year a War Office Committee had been formed to enquire into the general state of the Yeomanry and to make suggestions for greater efficiency. The Committee's report appeared in May, was duly digested by the Army Council (and debated in the House), and as a result in January 1893 Army Order 22/93 was published under the heading YEOMANRY REGULATIONS. The more important changes, to take effect from 1 April, can be summarised thus:

1. All Yeomanry regiments to be organised in Squadrons, as in the Regular cavalry, the maximum strength of each squadron to be 100 enrolled members, the minimum 70. Any squadron that had not reached the minimum by 1 April 1895 was to be broken up.
2. All the Yeomanry to be formed in Brigades, each brigade to consist of not more than three regiments. Regiments forming a brigade would train together in a brigade camp at least once in every three years under the senior commanding officer of the component regiments.
3. If a regiment failed to attend Brigade Camp for three consecutive years it would forfeit the government contingency allowance for the last of those years.
4. As Permanent Staff, one Brigade Adjutant was allowed, and within a regiment, one NCO per squadron and one for general duties.
5. An extra grant of £1 per year to be made for each NCO and private who obtained a 3rd Class classification in the Annual Musketry Course. If any member failed this classification in two consecutive years he was to be struck off the strength.
6. In addition to the normal allowance of ball ammunition, 20 rounds per man per year would be issued free if indented for.

The novel reorganisation into brigades was intended to create a reserve cavalry force which in the event of war could be mobilised to operate as brigades in the same manner as the Regulars. Such was the scheme, but in fact when war came, the brigade organisation was largely ignored.

A total of 18 Yeomanry Brigades were formed, designated by numbers, and each comprising regiments within the same or adjacent counties. It might be thought it would have been practical to brigade The Duke of Lancaster's Own with their fellow-Lancastrians, The Lancashire Hussars. But not so. On 1 April 1893 the Regiment was ordered to form the 14th Yeomanry Brigade with The Westmorland and Cumberland Yeomanry, whose Regimental Headquarters was at Penrith. The Duke of Lancaster's Own RHQ at Worsley now also functioned as Brigade Headquarters, and Captain E. W. N. Pedder, 13th Hussars, was appointed Brigade Adjutant. The two Commanding Officers at this date were Lieutenant Colonel Francis Egerton, Earl of Ellesmere (Duke of Lancaster's) and Lieutenant-Colonel the Earl of Lonsdale (Westmorland and Cumberland). As Lonsdale was the senior, he assumed command of the Brigade.

The late Victorian era saw a remarkable display of interest and enthusiasm by the Press in the doings of the Yeomanry and Volunteers. The arrival of the county regiment at some local centre for annual camp and inspection was an event which warranted the 'attachment' of a reporter for the whole period, who regaled the paper's readers with detailed descriptions of everything that went on.

Thus, in its issues for 15 and 22 June 1872, *The Preston Guardian* devoted three closely-printed columns to the visit of The Duke of Lancaster's Own Yeomanry to Preston. This was an event indeed, for it was claimed that it was the first time the whole Regiment, as The Duke of Lancaster's, had been seen in the town. The 'Corps' comprised five Troops, one each from Worsley, Wigan, Bolton, Rochdale and Ulverston, the men being billeted 'in various public houses in the town centre' – a somewhat questionable arrangement one might think. But there were no reports of disorderly conduct. In command was Lieutenant-Colonel the Hon. Algernon Fulke Egerton, MP, and the other officers were recorded as under:

> Major A. E. H. G. Visct. Grey de Wilton ('late Lieut. 1st Life Guards')
> Captain and Adjutant C. B. Molyneux
> *Worsley Troop*: Capt. The Earl of Ellesmere [Francis Egerton], Lieut. H. Ashton, Cornet B. J. Wilson Patten; *Wigan Troop:* Capt. Walmesley, Lieut. Part, Cornet the Hon. R. G. Molyneux; *Bolton Troop*: Capt. [R. H.] Ainsworth, Lieut. [H.] Cross, Cornet H. Ashton; *Furness Troop*: Capt. the Rt. Hon. Marquess of Hartington, MP, Lieut. J. P. Chamberlain Starkie, MP, Cornet the Rt. Hon. Lord F. C. Cavendish, MP; *Rochdale Troop*: Capt. Patrick, Lieut. C. M. Royds, Cornet E. M. Royds.

With such a parade of aristocracy among the officers, it is not to be wondered at that the local Press took notice. A contemporary Muster Roll, now in the Museum, shows an other-ranks strength of 257, many of the men having more than 20 years' service.

The Annual Inspection was held on a ground termed 'the Marsh' on 22 June. The Inspecting Officer was Lieutenant-Colonel R. T. Godman (late 5th Dragoon Guards), who expressed himself 'well satisfied with the appearance of the regiment and the general conduct of the men'. However, 'he should have been much pleased to have seen a little more expertness and proficiency in the handling of the weapons; but that could scarcely have been expected, taking into consideration that the men were only drilled for one full week in the year and had to attend to their [civilian] labour daily with the exception of that week'.

The *Preston Guardian* reporter, perhaps a horseman, was not greatly impressed with the horses, 'although for the most part they appeared in good condition . . . a few emaciated old nags were here and there to be seen'.

In 1877 the Regiment carried out its annual training in the more familiar environs of Lancaster. In the absence on leave of Lieutenant-Colonel the Hon. A. F. Egerton, command was assumed by Major Viscount Grey de Wilton, who deployed 264 all ranks. As at Preston, the men were billeted in the town's inns, while the officers enjoyed the amenities of the leading hotel, The King's Arms. From the detailed newspaper accounts it is noteworthy that during this late Victorian period the annual inspection was no longer the mere formality of a few drill movements and a glance at turnout, but now embraced quite ambitious schemes and exercises. Reporting the Lancaster visit of 1877 the *Lancaster Guardian* of 30 June described a realistic reconnaissance and attack on a local village, followed by withdrawal, the whole being witnessed by the Inspecting Officer of the Northern Military District, Colonel H. Segar.

As always, a feature of the Yeomanry's presence was their Band which, at Lancaster, 'played nightly a choice selection of instrumental music in front of the Officers' Mess at The King's Arms'.

On 12 June 1896 *The Carlisle Patriot* spread itself over four pages to record the combined camp of The Duke of Lancaster's and the Westmorland and Cumberland Yeomanry, near the town. The former Regiment was commanded by Lieutenant-Colonel C. M. Royds, MP (late of the Rochdale Troop) and paraded 1 major, 5 lieutenants, 5 quartermasters, 18 sergeants, 19 corporals, 6 farriers, 4 trumpeters and 127 privates, plus a medical officer and chaplain. The Westmorland and Cumberland, under Lieutenant-Colonel H. Senhouse, was slightly stronger with 233 all ranks.

Around 1897 The Duke of Lancaster's acquired a mascot in a singular (nearly tragic) fashion, as related in *The Volunteer Service Magazine* of that year. During mounted drill on Southport Sands one day, an Airedale terrier got itself entangled among the Troops and 'was three times bowled over by the horses' hoofs'. Miraculously escaping injury and not a whit deterred, the dog insisted on trotting back to camp with the Regiment, where he was given 'a good dinner with the troopers'. Since he was obviously a stray, the Bolton Troop adopted him, housed him in their Riding School and presented him with a handsome silver-mounted collar. Regrettably, 'Jack's' subsequent military career is not recorded.

Between 1893 and 1897 all Yeomanry were issued with an improved carbine to replace the Martini-Henry. This was the rifled Martini-Metford, lighter (6 lb. 11 oz.) than its predecessor, and for the first time introducing the .303 in. calibre that was to remain standard for all British Army rifles and machine guns until the 1960s. It was sighted to 2,000 yards, but the maximum range for annual classification was still 600 yards. When mounted, the trooper carried it barrel down in a leather boot secured to the rear offside of the saddle.

By now the War Office had stressed that **musketry** was an essential element of the cavalryman's training. On 22 April 1897, the Commander-in-Chief, Lord Wolseley, issued a Special Army Order addressed to 'Commanding Officers of the Regiments of Yeomanry Cavalry'.[7] After declaring that 'complicated manoeuvres in regimental drill are on no account to be attempted', the Order went on:

> As the United Kingdom is probably the only country in which regiments of Yeomanry Cavalry would be called on to meet an enemy, it must be borne in mind that the carbine is the weapon upon which the most reliance must be placed. Dismounted work must therefore receive the greatest attention, and the necessity for proficiency with the carbine, and strict attention to fire discipline, cannot be too strongly impressed on all ranks.

Two years later such precepts were to be borne out in South Africa – only to be apparently confounded by the Yeomanry's swords in Palestine during the First World War.

With RHQ still at Worsley, The Duke of Lancaster's was now organised in three Squadrons, each with two Troops of 40-odd rank-and-file. What we should today term the ORBAT was thus:

> A Squadron: Oldham and Rochdale Troops
> B Squadron: Broughton and Worsley Troops
> C Squadron: Bolton and Blackburn Troops

The Army and Navy Gazette of 10 September 1898 listed officers as follows:

> Colonel C. M. Royds, MP, in command; Major P. Hargreaves, Second-in-Command; Major J. Rutherford, MP (*Blackburn Troop*); Captains G. Kemp, MP (*Rochdale*), A. E. Lees (*Oldham*), R. H. Tilney (*Broughton*), W. L. Bourke (*Worsley*) and H. M. Hardcastle (*Bolton*); Lieutenants J. R. Ormrod (*Bolton Troop*), A. W. Huntington (*Blackburn*), Hon. F. W. G. Egerton (*Rochdale*), T. A. S. Shepherd-Cross (*Blackburn*), A. E. J. Reiss (*Worsley*), E. A. J. Johnson-Ferguson (*Oldham*); 2nd Lieutenants W. E. Royds (*Rochdale Troop*), E. Johnson (*Broughton*), C. H. Bibby (*Broughton*). The Adjutant was Captain E. W. N. Pedder (13th Hussars).

With one exception, the Annual Camps from 1892 to 1899 were held at Southport, where on occasions the Regiment in Full Dress afforded the townspeople a splendid spectacle as they rode along the gracious thoroughfare of Lord Street, accompanied by their Band. The exception was the more remote location of Carlisle (in June 1896), this being chosen as Brigade Camp with The Westmorland and Cumberland Yeomanry. Before break-up the Brigade paraded for inspection by its commander, Colonel the Earl of Lonsdale, and the

---

7. PRO WO 83

Carlisle Patriot had some interesting comments to make: 'The men presented a fine appearance. Those of the Duke's Own, with the exception of one squadron, wore their new white burnished helmets with white plumes and brass facings (sic) . . . which are the same as those worn by the Inniskilling Dragoons . . . and looked quite brilliant in the sunshine. The Regiment have also been provided with white gauntlets which cover the blue facings on the cuffs.' The odd one out among the squadrons was B Squadron, whose Broughton and Worsley Troops had not yet received their helmets, so that they must have rather spoilt the effect by parading in their forage caps.

The new helmet, introduced for Regular regiments in 1871, was of white metal with brass regimental device and chinscales. While it may have been similar to 'those worn by the Inniskilling Dragoons', it was common to all Dragoon Guards and Dragoons, though the former had a brass skull instead of white metal.

There was now a welcome change in the manner of carrying the sword when mounted. Instead of being slung from the man's waist-belt (and clouting the horse's flank at trot or gallop) it was secured to the nearside of the saddle in a leather frog – a method which survived until the cavalryman exchanged his horse for an armoured fighting vehicle (and still seen today in The King's Troop RHA). However, in dismounted Review Order sword-belts and slings as before were retained. The 'sword-on-saddle' change came about in 1891.[8]

The year 1897 saw the celebration of the Queen's Diamond Jubilee, when almost every regiment in the British Army (and Colonial and Indian forces) sent detachments to line the London streets and to take part in the Procession. The Duke of Lancaster's Own Yeomanry was represented by a mounted detachment of RSM J. Darvell and twelve troopers commanded by Captain Walter Bourke of the Worsley Troop. All of course were in Review Order.

In its 100-odd years of existence the Regiment had performed its statutory duties, sometimes distasteful, occasionally with pomp and ceremony, but generally humdrum – all with the spirit of selfless 'volunteer' dedication that was the hallmark of the Yeomanry Cavalry. But never had it been asked to draw sword or fire carbine or pistol in defence of its Sovereign and country. In 1899 events far from Lancashire had moved to a climax and The Duke of Lancaster's was soon to suffer its first casualties on active service overseas.

---

8. It was said to have been the inspiration of Lord Roberts, who in his Indian campaigning had witnessed unhorsed cavalrymen encumbered with useless swords in one hand (or dangling, to trip them up) and rifles in the other.

South Africa 1899-1902

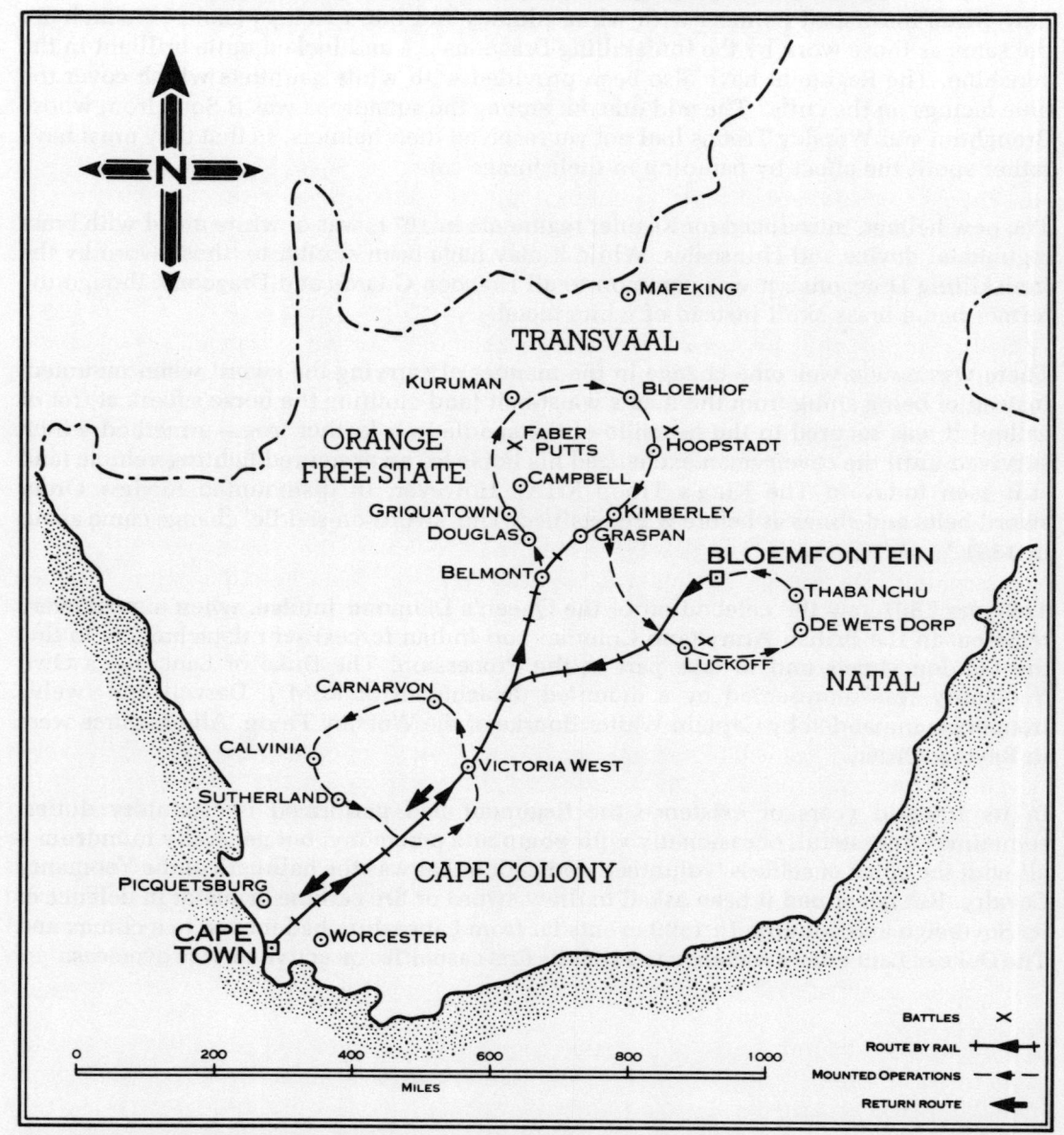

Route followed by 23rd (Duke of Lancaster's Own) contingent of the Imperial Yeomanry 1900-1901

CHAPTER IV
Imperial Yeomanry
1900–1902

In October 1899 Paul Kruger, President of the semi-independent republic of the Transvaal, launched a force of some 24,000 Boer commandos across the frontier into British-held Natal, while others rode south to bring out their brethren of the Orange Free State and Cape Colony.

Whether or not the Boer War of 1899–1902 was 'the last of the gentlemen's wars', it was certainly the first in which British soldiers had confronted a white enemy since the Crimean conflict, and the first to expose the outdated training and tactics of the British Army. After the jingoistic public at home had been stunned by news of the disastrous 'Black Week' in December when General Buller lost nearly 2,000 men killed and wounded, and 800-odd taken prisoner, Whitehall recognised that this was to be no 'bush fire' clash with a rabble of untrained, undisciplined farmers, but a major campaign against a well-organised, highly-trained and highly mobile foe. Unlike the British field force which was essentially infantry, the Boer commandos were all expert horsemen, adept not with sword or lance, but as mounted guerillas relying entirely on their modern Mauser and Martini rifles. In other words, they were all mounted infantrymen, a type of arm to which Britain had so far given little attention.

Resulting from Buller's demands, the War Cabinet (or Committee for National Defence as it was then termed) agreed that to oppose such an enemy in the vast expanses of the veldt, a similar force was urgently needed. In fact, immediately on the outbreak of war the Yeomanry and Volunteer infantry had offered their services, but these had been declined by the War Office, which was confident that the Regular forces were quite competent to deal with Boers unaided. The shock of the 'Black Week' brought a hurried change of views. On 23 December a special Act of Parliament was promulgated, authorising the formation of a mounted infantry force of volunteers, to be designated 'Imperial Yeomanry' and organised in 20 battalions. The same Act enabled existing Yeomen and Volunteers to serve overseas, while provision was made for civilians to be enlisted.

To organise and administer the Imperial Yeomanry, a Yeomanry Committee was set up, consisting of senior Yeomanry officers and including Colonel the Earl of Lonsdale of the DLOY's Brigade partners, the Westmorland and Cumberland. By mid-January 1900 the scheme was fully in operation, and enthusiastic volunteers were flocking to Yeomanry headquarters to register. Age limits were from 20 to 35 and preference was given to unmarried men. Rates of pay were as for Regular cavalry. Horses, saddlery and uniforms were to be provided by the individual units, the War Office supplying arms, ammunition, camp equipment and regimental transport (two-wheeled horse-drawn carts).

The Battalions were raised by each of the existing Yeomanry Brigades, each component regiment raising a Company. It might have seemed logical for these companies to retain their own regimental identities, but this was too logical for Authority. Instead, numbers were allotted and in most cases regimental titles disappeared. And so, for their first experience of active service, volunteers of The Duke of Lancaster's Own Yeomanry found themselves saddled with the uninspiring label '23rd (Lancashire) Company, 8th Battalion IY.' But it was at least fitting that their comrades of The Westmorland and Cumberland Yeomanry should make up the '24th Company' in the Battalion. The other Company was formed from Volunteer Battalions of the Manchester Regiment which, with an odd numerical leap, was designated '77th Company'. The Lancashire Hussars, with four Troops and RHQ at Ashton-in-Makerfield, raised the 32nd (Lancashire) Company, which with Warwickshire and Cheshire Yeomanry companies made up the 2nd Battalion IY. Why two 'Lancashire' Companies should not serve in the same Battalion was another quirk of War Office reasoning.

When the call came for volunteers in December and early January, The Duke of Lancaster's was still based with RHQ at Worsley, under Lieutenant-Colonel Clement Royds, and deploying three Squadrons of six Troops — at Oldham, Rochdale, Broughton, Bolton, Blackburn and Worsley itself. Officers and men registering for overseas service were asked to report to Manchester Town Hall, where they were formally enrolled as members of the 23rd Company. Not all of the Company were existing Yeomen: some were recruits straight from civilian life, some came from the Volunteer infantry, but there is no record of the proportions. The Company was commanded by Captain George Kemp, MP, who was a true member of the Regimental 'family'. Not only had he served in the Regiment since 1889, but in 1896 he had married the daughter of the Earl of Ellesmere, Commanding Officer.[1]

The complete roll of officers was as under:

    Captain G. Kemp, *Commanding*
    Lieutenant J. A. B. Heap, *Cmdg A Troop*
    Lieutenant H. M. Hardcastle, *Cmdg B Troop*
    Lieutenant C. H. Bibby-Hesketh, *Cmdg C Troop*
    Lieutenant A. W. Huntington, *Cmdg D Troop*
    Lieutenant J. J. Brocklebank, *Cmdg Gun Section*
    Surgeon-Captain Charnley-Smith, *Medical Officer*
    Lieutenant H. G. Westgate, *Veterinary Officer*

It will be noticed that although the Imperial Yeomanry had adopted infantry designations with their 'Battalions' and 'Companies', the DLOY contingent still preferred 'Troop' for sub-units. The other ranks included seven sergeants, seven corporals, two buglers (erstwhile trumpeters) and 117 privates. A nominal roll of all ranks was included in one of two published accounts of the contingent's services in the Boer War: *The Duke of Lancaster's Own Yeomanry Cavalry, 23rd Co. IY*, compiled by Trooper L. H. Johnson of B Troop and printed at Bolton in 1902. What is listed as the 'Gun Section', commanded by Lieutenant J. J. Brocklebank, consisted of two Colt automatic machine guns of .45 in.

1. George Kemp, of Beechwood, Rochdale, represented the Heywood Division of Lancashire in Parliament. Surviving the Boer War, he was elevated to the Peerage in 1913 with the title Baron Rochdale of Rochdale.

calibre, mounted on horse-drawn carriages with a detachment of 17 other ranks. Brocklebank's second-in-command was Sergeant Charles Storey, member of the Bolton Troop and son of Sir Thomas Storey of Lancaster.

Once complete, the Company concentrated at Blackpool for issue and fitting of new service dress, allotment of horses and a month's intensive training in their novel role as mounted infantrymen. And here they were introduced to the khaki attire that, with some modifications, was to become the regulation service dress for the British Army. It consisted of drab serge tunics, Bedford cord breeches and – novelty of novelties – puttees, which were regarded with mixed feelings. Although providing excellent protection to the lower limbs, they were irksome to wind neatly round and round the calves, while the tapes were apt to work loose in the saddle.[2] However, in South Africa these were replaced by the more practical leather leggings. The dress was completed by a rather unmilitary type of felt slouch hat, with one side of the brim turned up. With the 'exigencies of the service' (and weather) this article soon lost its original shape, becoming anything but 'uniform'. Trooper Johnson probably expressed the general feeling about the dress when he wrote: 'The new khaki uniform and slouch hat were undoubtedly serviceable and fairly comfortable, but when one has been accustomed to see the regulation smart-fitting uniform familiar to us for home service, khaki does not seem quite soldierly' . . . The men had been issued with boots costing 13s. 6d. a pair, but Major Kemp considered these of such poor quality that he sent the lot back and ordered a new consignment at 25s. a pair. He paid the difference out of his own pocket.

Not only a new uniform, but a new weapon appeared. This was the 'long' magazine-fed Lee-Enfield rifle of .303 in. calibre which had become the standard infantry weapon in 1895, and was the prototype of the renowned 'SMLE' (Short Magazine Lee-Enfield) familiar to all British, Indian and Colonial soldiers through two World Wars, and after. An accurate weapon, sighted to 2,000 yards and taking ten rounds in its magazine, the 'long' pattern was bulky and heavy (9 lb. 4 oz.) compared with the handy little Martini-Metford carbines the men had been accustomed to, and which now seemed 'like toy guns', said Johnson. Moreover, in their wisdom the Weedon Ordnance Depot had omitted to provide any means of carrying the weapon – no buckets, not even slings. So on mounted drills ' . . . it was no easy matter to ride and manage a horse and hold a rifle in one hand at the same time'. Slings were eventually issued in South Africa, and later, short butt-buckets appeared, to be secured to the offside of the saddle. Live firing with the new rifle was carried out on the range near Rossall School, Fleetwood, the men being transported part of the way by the Blackpool Electric Tramways.

The horse strength was made up from various sources, since few of the men owned mounts judged suitable for campaigning. As soon as the DLOY Company was formally raised, many of the local gentry and farming community generously presented animals, while others came from Army remount depots.

2. In the early days all soldiers, mounted and dismounted, applied the puttees from the ankle upwards, finishing with tapes just below the knee, where of course they were chafed by the saddle-flap when mounted. Later all mounted arms reversed the mode of application, to give the 'cavalry style', with tapes neatly wound above the ankle.

While the bitter January weather of gales, sleet, snow and ice did little to endear the Yeomen to this exposed part of the Lancashire coast, they enjoyed comfortable free billets in the many hotels and boarding houses, and the warm-hearted townsfolk of Blackpool did much to make them welcome, with free entertainments at music halls, the Winter Gardens, the Tower and suchlike attractions.

When the time came to leave Blackpool for embarkation, the Mayor and Corporation laid on a splendid Farewell Dinner in the Alhambra ballroom, at which the whole Company and some 200 guests were wined and dined. There were patriotic speeches, 'Mr Bosanquet's orchestra discoursed an enjoyable programme', and the Toast 'The Queen, The Duke of Lancaster' was proposed by the Mayor and drunk with musical honours. On 12 February 1900, the Company attended a service in St Paul's Church, Blackpool, when again the Mayor was present and the sermon was delivered by the Revd A. A. Slack, who happened to be a cousin of Captain George Kemp.

These details, and much that follows, are derived from a booklet entitled *South African War. With the 23rd Imperial Yeomanry (Duke of Lancaster's Own) from Blackpool to Fabers Putt*. This very scarce account of the DLOY's doings up to 30 May 1900 lacks author's name, publisher and date, but it is believed to have been compiled and published by the family of Lance-Corporal G. E. M. Barry, who was killed at Fabers Putt, and whose full-length portrait in Imperial Yeomanry kit forms the frontispiece. The work is essentially a compilation of newspaper extracts and letters from Yeomen, and forms a valuable complement to Trooper Johnson's account.

On 11 February 1900, the DLOY Company (as we shall now call it) arrived at Liverpool docks and (in a raging blizzard) embarked in the hired transport, the White Star liner SS *Afric*: 143 all ranks and 120 horses, commanded by Captain Kemp. Present to see them off were Colonel Royds, CO of the DLOY, and the Commander of their Yeomanry Brigade, Colonel the Earl of Lonsdale who 'intended to follow us out in a short time' (Johnson). But as the Earl was appointed Assistant Adjutant-General of the Imperial Yeomanry in London, his Lordship remained at home. Also present was the Chairman of the White Star line, Joseph Bruce Ismay, whose patriotism was such that all accommodation and messing on board was granted free of charge.

The departure of Lancashire Yeomen for their first overseas service was naturally an event of due import for the local Press. In its issue for 13 February 1900 the Blackpool *Gazette and News* devoted five columns to an account by its reporter who accompanied the contingent to Liverpool. Horses were embarked up a ramp to the lower deck and some proved 'very frisky', a trooper being badly injured by a kick in the stomach. The men were warmly clad in thick greatcoats and encumbered with kitbags, saddlery and rifles, but no swords. There was 'renewed vigorous cheering' when the Westmorland and Cumberland Yeomanry contingent (24th Company) arrived, and the reporter could not forbear to draw comparisons between the two bodies of men. The Westmorland and Cumberland were 'sturdy sons of the soil, used to the open air, the gun and the horse – real Yeomen. The Duke's Own, we must confess, are not, for they do not all come from the land, but from the more enervating callings of life.' The 'sons of the soil' mustered 121 all ranks, commanded by Captain W. H. Parkin.

The voyage to Cape Town was largely uneventful; only nine of the 300-odd horses on board succumbed to the then common hazards of sea transport. But there was a minor flurry of excitement when a stowaway was discovered lurking in one of the lifeboats. He turned out to be a member of the DLOY who had been rejected for service on account of his age, but was nevertheless determined to accompany his Regiment. The name of this dedicated Yeoman, and his subsequent fate, are not revealed.

On 4 March 1900 the *Afric* dropped anchor in Table Bay, and on the following day the troops disembarked, the DLOY and Westmorland and Cumberland marching to the huge base camp at Maitland, some twelve miles from Cape Town. Here they remained to acclimatise themselves and horses, until 15 May, when they moved up country.

The two contingents were now posted to a Column of all arms under Lieutenant-General Sir Charles Warren, tasked to suppress rebellious Boer factions in the Griqualand West district across the Orange River, west of Kimberley. After a week's march which saw a minor brush with some Boers, the Column arrived at the township of Douglas on the Modder River some 60 miles from Kimberley. In addition to the 24th (Westmorland and Cumberland) Company, the force included a squadron of Paget's Horse,[3] a battalion of The Duke of Edinburgh's Own Volunteer Rifles (raised in the Cape) and E Battery of the Canadian Field Artillery.

During the next few days patrols were sent out to search neighbouring farmsteads for arms and lurking guerillas, and though the DLOY Company made no finds or contact, a patrol of the 24th Company was involved in a brush with a strong party of Boers, when Captain Parkin (Westmorland and Cumberland) was wounded. This was the Column's first casualty.

The routine in camp and on patrol is described by a Trooper 'Ernie' of the DLOY (otherwise unidentified) in a letter dated 1 May 1900 and reproduced in the anonymous booklet quoted above:[4]

> The Camp rises at 5.30 a. m.; at 6.0 we turn out to stables and clean horses; 6.30 we mount bareback and take them about 1½ miles to water at the river; 7.30 we return and feed;...8.0 breakfast-up is sounded and at 9.0 we saddle-up and parade for drill. We get back at all times, and dinner sounds at 1.0 o'clock. At 2.0 we have rifle or saddle inspection; 4.0 o'clock we have bathing and watering parade, back again for tea at 6.0 Clean up tent, mess, etc. at 7.0 and then until 9.0 o'clock is our own ... Of course the above routine is varied ... word will come that the rebels (and they swarm about here) are holding meetings and arming; and away we go then for one or two days, sometimes for only 10 miles, and sometimes as much as 60. When we get on these long marches the worst thing is the heat and dust. It's awful. Every rag we have is wet through, and our faces and hands might have been smeared with red clay.

3. Known by some as 'Piccadilly Horse', by others as 'Perfectly Harmless', this unit was raised in London by Major George Paget, grandson of the first Marquess of Anglesey. The ranks were largely filled by 'young men of good social position and public school education'.
4. *South African War. With the 23rd Imperial Yeomanry ... from Blackpool to Faber's Putt*

Logistics seemed to be overlooked in this initial campaigning. A three-mile round trek to water horses thrice daily indicates a curious siting of camp, while on one 30-mile patrol the men were sent out 'with nothing in our haversacks or waterbottles'. Although no enemy had yet been contacted, there were casualties from sickness: 50 men were down with the prevalent dysentery, and one died. The Duke of Edinburgh's Rifles suffered more severely, losing eight and 80-odd ineffective.

By 22 May intelligence sources had reported between 1,000 and 2,000 armed Boers roaming within a 50-mile radius, and General Warren planned to advance his column from Douglas to an abandoned farmstead called Faber's Putt,[5] which was to form his base for an attack in force on a Boer position at Tweefontein. The name Faber's Putt meant nothing to the Yeomen as they rode up to the deserted buildings and kraals on 27 May, but it was to be remembered by their successors in The Duke of Lancaster's Own Yeomanry down to the present day.

From Trooper Johnson's account of the action that took place here three days later, we gain the impression that the DLOY company was the only unit engaged, but the reality was very different, as is made clear by General Sir Charles Warren's despatch to the Field Force Headquarters at Pretoria, on 29 June. Not surprisingly, this despatch was unseen by Johnson, but it is reproduced in full in the other published source (. . .*From Blackpool to Faber's Putt*). Since the despatch runs to seven pages, only extracts can be given here.

> From Lieut-General Sir Charles Warren, Military Governor of Cape Colony, North of Orange River, to Chief of Staff, Head-Quarters, Pretoria. 29th June, 1900. . . .
>
> 3.-The only good position that could be selected as a base for an attack on Tweefontein was that of Faber's Put, where there was plenty of water, and a hollow surrounded by hills where horses could be kept more or less secure from musketry at long ranges.
>
> 4.-I began to concentrate my force at this place on the 27th May, about 10 miles east of Tweefontein, and was unable to move forward owing to delay in transport of food which did not arrive until the night of 29th of May, accompanied by an escort of 50 Infantry. This convoy must have arrived shortly before the enemy, on their way to attack us at Faber's Put, passed across the road.
>
> 5.-Ridges encircle Faber's Put to the north-east and west, while a shallow valley runs from the water through the garden to the south. The north and north-west is the front of the position, and the south is the rear, facing on the Vaal River. There are two farm houses about 800 yards apart at north-east and north-west, and the Infantry picquets occupied the whole of this front, the Infantry being bivouacked near the north-east farm house, where were also my head-quarters; the men of the Intelligence Branch and Warren's Scouts and some infantry were at the north-west farm house, while the Yeomanry and Artillery were in the hollow occupying the kraals around the

---

5. This name appears variously as 'Put', 'Putt', 'Putts' and 'Spruit', the latter being the true version.

water and northern portion of the garden, providing the picquets on the ridges south-east and south-west.

Daylight was at this time 6 a. m. reveille being at 5.30 a. m.

6.-On the night of the 29th the rebels collected at Campbell from several points, and arranged for an early morning attack on Faber's Put, in three parties. One party, under Forster, to attack the Infantry camp and head-quarters farm house ...; the second party of crack shots, under Commandant-General De Villiers, from the country about Campbell and Griquatown, to steal into the garden and attack the Yeomanry and Artillery; and a third party, who were to take possession of the western ridge and fire into the kraals and Artillery.

8.-I was up that morning at reveille, making up a good fire, as the thermometer was below freezing; and some minutes before 6 a. m. heavy firing commenced from the east upon our head-quarters and The Duke of Edinburgh's Own Volunteer Rifles' camp. The Duke of Edinburgh's Own Volunteer Rifles were all on the alert, and at once moved out two companies in the direction of the firing. I stopped one company to act as a reserve, and the fourth company went off to hold our front and north. Some of the enemy crept up through the bush to within 250 yards of my head-quarters, which could not be prevented in this very thick bush by any number of picquets, and were driven back by the Maxim Gun Detachment and the two companies, under Captain Twycross, moving out to meet them. These two companies drove the enemy right back to the eastern ridge and thence, in an easterly direction, right away over the bushy plain. This took about half-an-hour, and the fire from this quarter was over about 6.30 a. m., but while it lasted it was exceedingly heavy and well directed ...

9.-After placing a company of The Duke of Edinburgh's Own Volunteer Rifles in readiness in reserve, I mounted and went across with my Staff close to the main farm house to see that the Yeomanry were on the alert and the Artillery were getting ready to come into action whenever it was necessary, for it was still dark and it was impossible to conjecture the exact point where the fire was coming from. Major F. Heath, C.S.O., and my two Aides-de-Camp were with me, and in returning across the open space when it was almost daylight, we were subjected to an exceedingly heavy fire, which was directed with such precision that I came to the conclusion that it must be at very short ranges; it proved to be less than 400 yards. Both Major Kelly, A.D.C. and Lieut. Paton, A.D.C. were wounded, and Major Heath had his horse shot under him. . .

12.-No. 2 party [of Boers], who went to the garden, appear to have arrived there in the early morning, and their numbers, as given to me by a considerable number of Boers from different parts, was 56, out of which they say only four returned unwounded. Many of these were known to be among the noted shots of Griqualand West, many of whom were killed; they were under Commandant De Villiers, who is stated to have threatened that he would shoot any man who attempted to retire from the gardens; they were mostly men who knew the farms intimately, which alone accounts for their being able to occupy and line the edge of the garden without being seen . . .

13.-They appear to have commenced their fire from this garden at about 6 a.m.; they commenced their fire upon a kraal where the Colt gun was with a party of Yeomanry, and upon some of Paget's Horse who were exposed on the left. Two or three of their men got into the blockhouse, but the Artillery and a great part of the Yeomanry were quite secure in their bivouacs from fire from the garden; subsequently they fired on a party of the Yeomanry under Col. Crawley, moving out to the ridge towards the west to support the picquet at that point, while another party in the gardens fired on anybody moving on the open space between the gardens and upon the reserve company of The Duke of Edinburgh's Own Volunteer Rifles in position near their Camp.

14.-When the firing commenced, Colonel Crawley, commanding 8th Battalion of Yeomanry (not knowing that the enemy were in the garden close to him), finding firing from four different directions and having seen his horses stampeded, judged the best defence would be to make an offensive movement, southwest to reinforce his picquet on the ridge, and from there direct a fire into the garden, or on to the enemy further along on the ridge. He took thirty men with him, and thirty followed shortly afterwards; it was during this advance across the open that nine men of the Yeomanry were killed. This detachment under Colonel Crawley reinforced the picquet, and forced No. 3 party, under Ventner, to retire from the diamond diggings on the ridge.

While Colonel Crawley was making this advance, Lieut. Huntington, 23rd Company, Imperial Yeomanry, whose bivouac was close to the garden, covered his left flank by firing at close range into the garden while under a heavy fire. This, no doubt, saved Colonel Crawley from suffering heavier loss.

15.-This rebel party under Ventner had the duty of occupying the diamond diggings so as to fire at long ranges into our camp, and some of the more daring of the men were directed to occupy a stone cemetery about 600 yards from the large kraal, and to go right down to the kraal itself, fire into it, and stampede the English horses of the Yeomanry which Colonel Crawley had placed there and which he had omitted to ring. It is not certain whether two or more rebels got so far as the kraal, but it is certain they fired into the kraal in the dark, and that the English horses at once surged up against the wall of the kraal, pushed it over, and stampeded in all directions.

17.-The picquet on the hill which Colonel Crawley went to reinforce under Corporal Wilson, 23rd Company, gallantly held its own against a superior force until relieved. A section of Yeomanry with two Colt guns under Lieut. Brocklebank, 23rd Company, Imperial Yeomanry, in the kraal near the garden, were under a heavy fire for a considerable time, and the shields to the guns were smashed to pieces; they were joined by a party of Yeomanry under Sergeant Fowkes (24th Coy.) and made a most gallant defence at close range.

18.-The whole attack did not take more than an hour, and as soon as the enemy cleared off I pushed out the available mounted men, two guns and two companies of Infantry across the veldt to the north to endeavour to intercept the enemy, but there were not sufficient horses left to do more than scouting, and though some shells were fired very close to the retreating enemy, both east and west, I was unable to intercept them. I then proceeded to collect together the stampeded horses, but some of them stampeded for over 20 miles, and they have not yet been all got together.

Several acts of gallantry occurred during the attack, mostly in cases where the firing was at very short ranges, which I will bring forward.

Since the action of Faber's Put, the rebels in all directions have continued to surrender in increasing numbers, and with one consent the whole of the rebels say that the repulse at Faber's Put and great loss they sustained there caused a sudden collapse of the rebellion . . .

I have not been able to estimate the number that attacked us, but from general information they cannot have been less than five to six hundred.

At the conclusion of the despatch General Warren permitted himself to observe: 'It was fortunate that our troops were not taken by surprise in this attack as otherwise the loss would have been far greater.' In fact, as will be seen from what follows, most of the Column was taken completely by surprise, having allowed a force of some 600 enemy to surround the position during the night, and in some sectors to approach within less than a hundred yards. 'There is no doubt we were caught napping . . . the men are very bitter about it,' wrote Trooper Brownrigg of the DLOY Gun Section. But of course, to admit such a failing in an official despatch would not have redounded to the Column Commander's credit.[6]

We must now look a little more closely at the part played by the DLOY Company. Their campsite lay on a completely open expanse of ground, the only form of cover being two small kraals about 200 yards apart, each surrounded by a low stone wall. The south-eastern sector of the perimeter was bounded by a dense, tall hedge of cacti (prickly pears), behind which lay what had been the farmstead's orchard. The site was overlooked to the west by a series of low scrub-covered kopjes. Having off-saddled and watered their horses from a nearby stream, the men picketed them inside the kraals and then the four Troops disposed themselves in tight circles between the kraals, each position being surrounded by saddles as a form of makeshift 'breastwork'. The Gun Section lay within 50–odd yards of the belt of cacti, and only 30 yards from a small stone building which had been a stable. Nearer still to this was a section (eleven men) of Paget's Horse.

Meanwhile the 24th (Westmorland and Cumberland) Company had camped a few hundred yards to the east, with the Canadian 4–gun battery behind them; The Duke of Edinburgh's Volunteers were about 500 yards to the north-east. They provided three 10–men pickets posted several hundred yards outside the perimeter, but nothing was done to watch that potential threat, the cactus hedge and orchard.

---

6. Sir Charles Warren had the reputation of being a prickly, quarrelsome character. Although he was successful in 'cleaning' Griqualand of the rebels by July 1900, his methods came in for criticism by Lord Roberts and he was replaced and sent home in August.

The anonymous compilation *From Blackpool to Faber's Putt* includes several letters to relatives from men who were in the thick of the fighting, the most graphic and detailed being one from Trooper F. Brownrigg, mentioned above. Addressed to his parents in Manchester, it was originally published in *The Manchester Weekly Times* of 3 August 1900. Here, an edited abstract must suffice:

> I suppose you know of our little scrap with the Boers at Faber's Spruit [sic]. The Boers, unknown to us, had taken up position during the night all around us, and even got into a garden and hut, only 52 yards and 25 yards respectively from us ... They opened fire on us about 15 minutes before daybreak, and many were killed and wounded as they lay asleep in their saddle rings ... We were in a very bad position, on a large round piece of ground, absolutely without cover, and flat as a billiard table, and all close together ... We awoke by heavy firing and found bullets literally raining on us as we lay in our saddle rings. The 23rd and 24th Yeomanry (DLO, and W and CY) made for cover on the right and lost heavily in covering the open ground (200 yds about). The Artillery dare not fire plump at the enemy because they would have shot down our own men also.
>
> The D.E.O.V.R. (Cape Volunteers) opened fire, and also their Maxim, but the Maxim did not fire at first because they could not readily locate the enemy, and when they did, some fool told them to stop as they were firing on their own men ...
>
> The Colt Gun Section had undoubtedly and admittedly the hottest corner of the whole column. We measured the distance by strides and found the garden to be about 52 yards from our Colt guns and the hut about 25 yards. Seventy-two Boers were planted in the garden and concentrated their fire on our two guns, and the hut was full also, and these men had absolute safe cover and fired through the windows. Paget's Horse (11 of them) lay within 20 yards of the hut, the Colt Gun Section lay about 25 yds off it, and D Troop (DLOY) 30 yds off it, and those men in the hut did crack shooting to our cost.
>
> At the first alarm the Colt gunners grabbed their revolvers (had no rifles then, but have now) and rushed to their guns. God knows why we were not all killed who crossed the few yards of open ground from our ring to the guns. Inside 10 minutes both Colts were pumping bullets into the garden at a rate of 400 a minute, but not for long. Bang, bang, crash on the shields came the heavy Martini bullets and smash into pieces went No. 2 gun shield, and immediately after No. 1 shield was knocked off unbroken, and Gunner (sic) David Rew killed stone dead by a bullet through the temple ...
>
> One gun was inside the kraal at the corner angle, and the other outside at the other corner. I thought, now if I get a rifle and go to the far corner, I may be able to draw the fire ... and give 'em a chance to start, and by jingo! I got what I wanted. I lay flat on the ground and opened fire. My first man was kneeling in the act of firing, partly covered by a large cactus. Bang! Up went his arms, and he rolled over. Then I was spotted, and don't forget it Dad, that things did get lively round me. It was a good job I lay as flat as a fluke, for by jove! the bullets splashed the wall just a few inches above my head ...

Both guns were momentarily out of action. However, Mr. Brocklebank, our officer, got down to us from the other extreme end of the camp (the officers' quarters, at least 250 yards off), and scatheless too, which was a marvel . . . I shall never forget seeing him come up to his own little Colt Gun Section (14 of us). He simply rushed into us at a wild run . . . and as he came he shouted 'Colt Section, Gun Section, stand to your guns!' I replied, 'We are at them now Sir, with Sergeant Storey.' He smiled and said, 'Good, I thought you would be.'

If ever there were two brave men on the face of the globe, those [were] our young officer and our Sergeant Storey. They were simply superb . . .

Away I went to my corner and rapidly emptied my magazine, when suddenly I saw a crowd of men stand up and begin to run down the garden. It was the enemy retreating. I gave a holy yell and . . .shouted to the gun boys to get the guns [firing] again as the rebels were on the run. Then I commenced firing as quickly as I could till the rebels reached the scrub. Then I went into the garden and took three Martini rifles and six bandoliers off three wounded Boers. All our horses stampeded, or else we should have followed the rebels. The horses were nearly all brought in after a few days; I got mine back the third day after the fight.

The total British casualties at Faber's Putt amounted to twenty killed and thirty wounded, three of the latter subsequently dying. In view of the surprise attack and intense enemy fire, this seems a remarkably light toll for a force numbering some 800 all ranks.

Since this battle saw the first active service casualties of The Duke of Lancaster's Own Yeomanry, the names should be recorded.[7]

CASUALTIES AT FABER'S PUTT
23rd Company (DLOY) Imperial Yeomanry
30 May 1900

KILLED

Corporal W. Coulston	D Troop
Lance-Corporal G. E. Barry	,,
Private J. W. Derbyshire	C Troop
,, F. W. Hackforth	D Troop
,, P. Orrell	B Troop
,, D. Rew	Coy HQ

---

7. This roll is compiled from General Warren's Despatch, supplemented by the two Regimental accounts quoted above. The rank of Private is given since at that date the commonly used 'Trooper' was unofficial.

WOUNDED

Lieutenant	A. W. Huntington	D Troop
Sergeant	C. B. C. Storey	Gun Section
,,	W. Mason	D Troop
Corporal	W. Lupton	Gun Section
Lance-Corporal	E. Poole	B Troop
Private	P. R. Agnew	C Troop
,,	C. H. Brunner	,,
,,	R. P. B. Carter	D Troop
,,	T. Gibbs	,,
,,	W. Looker	,,
,,	J. Turner	,,
,,	A. E. Wright	C Troop

With six killed and twelve wounded, the DLOY Company suffered the heaviest of all units engaged. Their Yeomanry comrades of the Westmorland and Cumberland lost five killed but only six wounded.

If the action saw the Regiment's first campaign casualties, it also brought the first decorations for bravery. On 27 September 1901 the *London Gazette* announced the awards of the Distinguished Conduct Medal to Sergeant R. Fairclough and Privates D. Elce and W. Looker. Earlier (4 September) these names, together with those of Captain George Kemp and Lieutenant Arthur W. Huntingdon, had been Mentioned in Lord Robert's Despatch. The same Gazette announced the awards of the DSO to Arthur Huntington (now Captain) and Lieutenant John Jasper Brocklebank.

Faber's Putt might justifiably be claimed as a victory, for the attack was repulsed, while the enemy survivors were later rounded up and captured. But the action raised some disturbing questions: why was a body of some five or six hundred commandos allowed to surround the whole camp during the night without being either spotted or heard by sentry or picquet? Why was there no attempt at any form of defences, such as trenches or sangars? Ample stone lay around; picks and spades were part of the camp equipment. Indeed, excellent 'sangars' were already available in the two stone kraals which would have offered adequate protection for riflemen. But these were occupied by the DLOY horses, for which the low, 3ft. stone walls afforded little or no cover.

Trooper Brownrigg had some pertinent comments:[8]

> Although we were there from Saturday to Wednesday, yet no entrenchments were made, nor any walls built for cover, and I am sure the pickets were too far apart, and too close in to camp, or else the Boers could never have got so close unobserved ... How they got so close is a mystery, and speaks badly for the positions chosen ... After the fight, guards were doubled, and stone walls built round the saddle rings ... every morning every man was wakened and lay with his arms under cover till daylight. But of course, all this should have been done before.

8.   ... *From Blackpool to Faber's Putt* (op. cit.)

The fact is, neither General Sir Charles Warren nor any of his subordinates were experienced in this type of warfare, with the result that the Column was 'caught napping', as Trooper Johnson admitted.

The DLOY's fatal casualties and those of the other units together with some Boers, were buried in the orchard from which the initial attack had come, the Trumpeter (now 'Bugler') of the Regiment sounding 'Last Post' and 'Reveille'.

From this date of May 1900 until twelve months later when the DLOY Company was posted home, we have to confess that their services, though essential, were unremarkable for any major battles or actions. Some Imperial Yeomanry, however, saw action which did little for their morale or prestige. On Christmas Day 1901 the 11th Battalion (Kent and Middlesex) was surprised at Tweefontein by some 1,000 burghers and almost destroyed, losing 145 killed and wounded and 200 captured. Earlier, in May the 13th (Irish) Battalion was overwhelmed at Lindley and after losing 61 killed and wounded, the remaining 390 surrendered.

There was no such trauma for the 8th Battalion and its DLOY Company, for whom the remainder of the Campaign saw them riding continuously over some thousand miles of veldt. The 'Great Trek' commenced, in fact, after Lord Roberts (who had succeeded Buller) entered the Transvaal capital of Pretoria on 5 June 1900. This was the opening of the 'guerilla war' stage in which attempts, seldom successful, were made to round up the elusive commandos and deny them provisions by raiding and destroying their farmsteads and capturing their livestock.

In September 1900 the DLOY Company joined a column under Brigadier-General H. H. Settle, which included their comrades of the 24th Company (Westmorland and Cumberland), together with Paget's Horse, battalions of Somersetshire Light Infantry and the Royal Munster Fusiliers. With supporting arms of British and Canadian artillery and a 'tail' of ox wagons, Cape carts, ambulance wagons and miscellaneous vehicles straggling back for more than two miles, the unwieldy column of about 5,000 troops was expected to out-manoeuvre the highly-mobile bands of guerillas who could gallop up to commanding kopjes, fire a few volleys and disappear again before Yeomen or infantry had time to deploy. Leaving the base camp of Vryborg on 19 September, the column took three days to cover the 38 miles to their first objective of Schweize-Reneke in the Transvaal, where, not surprisingly, the Boer garrison had vanished.

While the succeeding treks and patrols brought no death-or-glory actions – or even actions – the strain on men and horses tried the physique of both. Trooper Johnson of the DLOY:

> We marched all night through a steady downpour of rain, about as miserable a march as any we experienced, many of the fellows being so thoroughly weary that they slept as they rode, starting up with a jerk if the horse happened to change its gait . . . It is not possible for anyone who has not actually experienced the overpowering weariness to appreciate it fully – the fatigue of marching slowly through a country with absolutely no variety or distractions, not only all day, but through the night as well, with but little rest and little to eat, soaked through and through with continual rain.

The issued rations consisted only of hard biscuits ('hard tack') with tea and/or coffee, and, when supplies could catch up with the columns, canned meat ('Bully Beef') and Quaker Oats – 'the most choicest additions to our food supply as we could stow them comfortably in our saddle wallets,' wrote Johnson.

By now all the Yeomen (and Regulars) were hardly distinguishable from the burghers with their worn and patched attire which had not been replaced since landing in South Africa. Opportunities for bathing were infrequent, with the result that fleas and lice added to the discomforts. 'Every man in South Africa belonged to the same brigade namely the C.I.V. or 'Covered in Vermin' Contingent.' (Johnson)[9] However, on arriving at Hoopstad, south of the Vaal river, the Company were glad to receive a complete new issue of tunics, breeches, slouch hats and boots, so that they once more resembled British soldiers.

On the approach to Hoopstad, on 20 October, the Column became engaged in one of the rare brushes with the enemy who, as usual, appeared unexpectedly and attempted to cut off the rearguard. The Duke of Edinburgh's Volunteer Rifles dropped into action and with their Maxim guns kept the burghers at a respectful distance, while Lieutenant Hardcastle brought his B Troop of the DLOY galloping to their aid. 'We opened a hot fire at eight hundred yards,' wrote Trooper Johnson, 'the enemy's bullets dropping thickly amongst us as we lay on the open ground without any sort of cover ... After about an hour's hard shooting we had the satisfaction of driving the enemy off and preventing them carrying out their object.' This sharp fire-fight cost the Column 23 killed and about 80 wounded, most of these being suffered by The Duke of Edinburgh's contingent. Hardcastle's Troop had two men wounded.

In early November the 23rd Company enjoyed a week's rest at Kimberley, where they received a batch of much-needed remounts to replace the jaded, sore-backed and done-up animals that they had ridden since landing at Cape Town. The new mounts were a motley herd of Cape ponies and imported Australian Walers, Hungarians and Argentines. Trooper Johnson was allotted a 'pretty, wild, fat little mare, apparently of native stock crossed with English, not over-blessed with intelligence, and who took a mad delight in bolting with me on the slightest excuse, the curb bit having about as little effect on her mouth as spurs and curses elsewhere'.

While at Kimberley the DLOY Company was sad to see the break-up of their staunch Gun Section under Lieutenant John Brocklebank, which had performed such valiant service at Faber's Putt. Brocklebank was now granted a Regular commission and transferred to the 1st (King's) Dragoon Guards; his Troop was disbanded, the men being distributed among the other Troops. The carriages of the Colt guns had become unserviceable, and the two guns themselves were added to the armament of an armoured train at Kimberley. This meant that the Company no longer had any automatic weapons: for reasons unclear, no Maxim guns were issued as replacements.

9. The true C. I. V. were the City of London Imperial Volunteers, a mixed force of artillery, mounted infantry and infantry raised in London in December 1899.

Leaving Kimberley in mid-November, the Company resumed the endless routine of march, patrol, camp and the occasional skirmish with would-be ambush parties lurking on kopjes. One such incident enlivened the monotony near the little dorp of Luckoff (for which the soldiers coined an alternative name). Here a commando of some 700 men under the redoubtable leader, Judge Herzog, had occupied a line of kopjes, hoping to pounce on the rearguard and baggage train. But, assaulted by shrapnel from the Royal Artillery 15-pounders, followed by a bold infantry advance with bayonet, the Boers as always, preferred discretion to valour, retreated to their ponies and galloped off, leaving a few dead and wounded behind them. The British column reported only minimal casualties of two men killed and ten wounded, among the latter being Sergeant R. Fairclough of the DLOY's B Troop.

By 20 December the Column had reached Bloemfontein, camping outside the town in high hopes of a Christmas respite with all the civilised amenities of the first large township they had seen since leaving Kimberley. But on the 22nd came orders to entrain at the railway station (on the main line from Port Elizabeth to Pretoria), and after a cramped journey of two days with men and horses herded in open trucks, they arrived at Victoria Road in Cape Colony, to spend a cheerless Christmas Day in a barren campsite alongside the railway line. However, thanks to some clever 'foraging' on the part of their officers, the men of the DLOY Company were able to enjoy 'a present of Christmas puddings, pipes and tobacco and a bottle of beer to each man.' (Johnson)

Some 50 miles west of Victoria Road lay the township of Carnarvon, which was reported to be threatened by a strong force of commandos, so that on Boxing Day all the mounted troops of the Column were hastily despatched to occupy the town and hold it until the rest of the Column could arrive. The 23rd DLOY Company, with their 24th Westmorland and Cumberland comrades and Paget's Horse, rode hard for two days, to find the town still free of enemy. But it had been a 'close-run thing', for another column under Colonel (later General Sir Beavoir) de Lisle had outstripped them, just in time to deter any attack. For the next two days the Yeomen were put to work strengthening defences, building stone walls, digging entrenchments and erecting barbed-wire entanglements all round the position (lessons had been learned since Faber's Putt). Before setting out for Carnarvon they had been told that one of the infrequent arrivals of home mail would await them there, but alas, on arrival they learned that the mail convoy had been ambushed by the Boers 'who had amused themselves by reading our correspondence and then destroying everything.' (Johnson)

While at Carnarvon the DLOY Company was reinforced by a draft of 35 men under Lieutenant H. Erwood, recently arrived from England. On the arrival of the rest of the Column, now under Colonel Sir Charles Parsons, the defences were handed over to de Lisle's infantry, and two days later the Column marched out to resume their 'sweeps', or endeavours to intercept and capture the elusive bands of guerillas. Detached from the Column, the DLOY Company rode 70 miles in two days to search and occupy a farmstead named Achterkop, reputed to be held by Boers. This lay on a high, rocky ridge or kopje, the only track being so steep and narrow that the men had to dismount and lead their horses. Then occurred an unhappy incident of mistaken identity. As the leading Troop reached the crest, a volley of rifle fire burst upon them, wounding a sergeant. With two-thirds of the Column still struggling up the track, unable to turn horses round, the little force was in a parlous position: to continue the advance in the face of heavy fire seemed suicidal. Bullets smacking and ricocheting all around, the men took what cover they could among the rocks. As they did so, one bold Yeoman crawled forward in an attempt to pinpoint the source of the firing. What he saw caused him to leap to his feet waving his slouch hat and yelling 'Yeomanry, Yeomanry!' a cry quickly taken up by his comrades. Firing ceased and the 'enemy' turned out to be another Troop of fellow-Yeomen who had occupied the position the previous day. Having driven off a party of Boers attacking up the same track that very morning, they had not been over-careful about identifying the newcomers in the fading evening light. It was fortunate that the only casualty was the sergeant (unidentified), with a bullet through his arm.

It was now March 1901, and although they did not know it, the DLOY Company were nearing the end of their campaigning. There followed two months in the mountainous region of the south-eastern Cape Colony, during which there was no serious confrontation with the wily guerilla bands, but days and weeks of hard marching in the difficult terrain, Boer farms raided and destroyed – in fact, operations as before. All these were carried out as an element of a column commanded by Colonel A. Henniker, RE, and including besides the Westmorland and Cumberland Yeomanry, a Company of the 2nd Coldstream, the 65th and 71st Companies IY, three Squadrons of Australian mounted rifles known as 'Bushmen', and one section (two guns) of M Battery RHA. One might imagine that such a force of some 1,200 all arms would be a match for any guerillas, and so it would have been if the enemy were bold enough to stand and fight. But as always, they melted away on the approach of the column with its lumbering 'tail' of baggage wagons.

> So we started on the march again [wrote Johnson] trekking around those parts and dodging from one place to another after the wily enemy, frequently coming in touch with parties of their rearguard and scouts, but they never showed any inclination to make a stand against us; as they had no wagons or impediments of transport, and depended on the support given to them by the farmers or what they could commandeer from stores, it was not difficult for them to keep out of danger.

In early May 1901 Colonel Henniker's Column had come to rest at a small railway station called Thorngrove on the Port Elizabeth–Pretoria line. Here Captain George Kemp, commanding the DLOY Company, received orders to leave the column and entrain his command for Cape Town and posting home. 'Of course the fellows went nearly mad at this good news, and were quite satisfied to get any sort of conveyance to take us on our last African railway journey.' (Johnson)

The journey, in the now-familiar open trucks, took five days, first up north to the junction at De Aar then south again to Cape Town.

It so happened that there was a serious epidemic of plague in the district, and immediately on detraining the Company was marched straight to the docks and embarked on the hired transport *Avondale Castle*, together with some 1,200 other details. Three weeks later the troops were landed at Southampton and despatched to their several depots.

During their fourteen months' campaigning the 1st DLOY Contingent of Imperial Yeomanry had marched (or ridden), and camped, in all weathers over a total distance of some 5,000 miles, always with threat of ambush or sniping, often under conditions which tried to the extreme the endurance of man and mount. Except for their staunch fight at Faber's Putt they had not been able to show their mettle in serious actions, or to boast of resounding victories, but this was no fault of their own. Rather, it was attributable to the hidebound tactics of senior commanders who could not adapt to the novel form of fluid, guerilla warfare, but attempted to defeat an elusive highly-mobile enemy by pursuing him with unwieldy, baggage-encumbered columns reminiscent of Wellington's day.

Hostilities dragged on for another twelve months after the return of the DLOY's 1st Contingent, and now it must be confessed that this record of the Regiment's services in the Boer War is incomplete. Nearly all Yeomanry units (or 'Companies') sent out 2nd Contingents in the spring of 1901, as did the 23rd (DLOY) Company.

A brass wall plaque in the former Regimental Headquarters at Chorley lists a complete nominal roll of the 'Relieving Draft Joined the Company During 1901'. This is in fact the 2nd Contingent, of whom the first draft of 25 other ranks commanded by Lieutenant T. B. Forwood arrived in early May. These had all enrolled specifically for the DLOY, but shortly afterwards they were followed by another four officers and 151 other ranks who had joined for the Imperial Yeomanry and were posted to the 23rd Company. Command of the Company, now numbering five officers and 176 other ranks, was given to Captain A. W. Huntington, who had been wounded with the 1st Contingent at Faber's Putt. In addition, another nine DLOY troopers had volunteered and went out with the draft, but these were posted to their erstwhile Brigade comrades in the 24th (Westmorland and Cumberland) Company.

There is no record of the 2nd Contingent's activities in the final year of the war: all that exists is a nominal roll of casualties, inscribed on the above plaque. From this we find that one officer (Lieutenant H. O. Spratt) and four other ranks were killed, and one officer (Lieutenant J. A. Bingham) and ten other ranks wounded, one of the latter subsequently dying of his wounds. In addition, two other ranks succumbed to enteric.

Thus, during the two years that The Duke of Lancaster's were represented in South Africa the total losses, including those of the 1st Contingent, amounted to eleven killed and 25 wounded, plus six died of fever.

As so often, the sufferings of those essential elements of a Yeomanry unit – the horses – receive not a mention. All that can be said is that during the four years of war out of 52,00 remounts, the appalling figure of 35,00 cavalry and yeomanry horse succumbed to bullet, disease or privation.[10] Within twelve years both mount and man were to suffer even more dreadfully.

---

10. Smith, Maj-Gen. Frederick *A Veterinary History of the War in South Africa 1899–1902* (1919)

DLOY Officers enjoying amateur theatricals at Regimental Camp at Hightown in 1902; (*left to right*) the Officers are 2nd Lieut J. A. B. Heap, Captain E, Johnson and 2nd Lieut A. M. Lees-Milne.

CHAPTER V

Last Days of Summer
1902–1914

For the first time in 63 years the throne of Great Britain was occupied by a King, and the brief Edwardian era began. This was the zenith of the British Empire, upon which the sun truly never set. In the rose-tinted spectacles of hindsight it also seems perpetual summer: halcyon days of peace and plenty; of straw-hatted holidays on the seashore (Southport, Blackpool, Morecambe for Lancashire folk); cricket on the village green, tennis and croquet at the Manor – and of respect for law and order, when caps were doffed to 'the Squire and his relations' and everyone knew their proper stations.

When a young Lancashire lad enrolled in The Duke of Lancaster's Own Yeomanry in Edwardian times, he had no reason to believe that his Regiment in the foreseeable future would be called upon for any other tasks than the weekly mounted or dismounted drill sessions, the periodic visit to the rifle ranges, and that culmination of the year's programme, the Annual Camp at Southport, Penrith or wherever.

Resulting from South African experience, military pundits in Whitehall were in dispute about the true role of the mounted arm in any future conflict, but although musketry training was now intensified, to most Yeomen it seemed inconceivable that the old order could change within their lifetime. And so the Troops and Squadrons continued to practise their time-honoured drill of 'Stand to your horses!' . . . 'Prepare to mount – Mount!' . . . 'Eyes centre, draw swords!' . . . 'Sections right, walk march!' And that exhilarating climax on parkland or seashore: 'Line will attack – Gallop! . . . Charge!'

The month of June 1902 was a busy one for The Duke of Lancaster's Yeomen. On the 2nd the Regiment less one squadron entrained at Worsley for Camp and Annual Inspection at Hightown, between Liverpool and Southport. At the same time an unusually strong squadron of 140 all ranks under Major Albert Lees went by rail to Aldershot, there to parade in Full Dress for a review by the Prince of Wales accompanied by Major-General Lord Chesham, Inspector-General of Imperial Yeomanry. The latter expressed himself 'much pleased with the turn-out and general bearing of the squadron'. Meanwhile, the other squadrons had been put through their paces at Hightown under the eyes of Colonel E. R. Courtenay, Inspecting Officer for the North-Western District. *The Lancaster Guardian* of 18 June 1902 revealed that on the day of the inspection the men were 'virtually in the saddle and hard at it for eleven hours'. The inspection report on men, drill and horses was 'eminently satisfactory'. No fewer than eight special trains were needed to transport 434 men and 380 horses from Worsley to Hightown and back.

June the following year saw the Regiment in camp at Altcar when the squadrons competed for a silver cup presented by Lieutenant-Colonel George Kemp, who had commanded the DLOY contingent in South Africa. In that campaign the Yeomanry had been criticised for the time it took the men to get saddled and mounted in an emergency, and so Kemp suggested a simple inter-squadron competition. This was really a variant of what became familiar in military tattoos and displays as the 'Reveille Race'. Horses were picketed in line, saddlery behind them and men a hundred yards or so further back. On a trumpet call, the men rushed forward, saddled up and mounted. The squadrons were then inspected and the one completing the drill in the shortest time, with no faults in saddlery or equipment, was adjudged the winner.

On 19 July 1904 there was royal ceremonial when King Edward VII and his Queen-consort visited Liverpool for the laying of the foundation stone of the city's new Anglican cathedral. Commanded by Lieutenant-Colonel Percy Hargreaves, the entire Regiment of 350 all ranks, in Full Dress, provided two Guards of Honour: at Lime Street Station A and B Squadrons saluted the arrival of Their Majesties, while C and D Squadrons paraded at St James' Mount where the actual laying ceremony took place.

Prior to this date, the Blackpool Troop, raised by Captain T. A. S. Shepherd-Cross in 1899, had been labouring under the disadvantage of lacking a permanent headquarters and drill hall. All office work had to be done in a small store-room rented from the Winter Gardens, while drill sessions (dismounted) were held in the old Ballroom at Raikes Hall Gardens. The Permanent Staff Sergeant-Major was obliged to live in one of the town's boarding houses. Thanks to the efforts of Colonel Hargreaves, supported by the Hon. Colonel, the Earl of Ellesmere, and several other notabilities of the county, this unhappy situation was resolved in 1903 by the aquisition of a purpose built drill hall in Talbot Road, Blackpool. The corporation leased the site on very generous terms and much of the work was carried out by members of the Troop, Sergeant F. M. Wilding and Lance-Corporal J. C. Derham acting as Clerks of the Works.

The buildings contained a complete residence for the Sergeant-Major Instructor, an Armoury, an Officers' Room, a Non-Commissioned Officers' Room, a Recreation Room and Lecture Room (plus 'ample lavatory accommodation'). The Drill Hall included a miniature range for musketry practice, 'the apparatus being the gift of Col. P. Hargreaves'. On 17 July 1903, the new Troop Headquarters was formally opened by none other than Field-Marshal Earl Roberts, Commander-in-Chief of the Army, accompanied by the Rt. Hon. Lord Chesham (Inspector-General of Yeomanry) and other personages of note. The Blackpool Troop, in dismounted Review Order, found a Guard of Honour. Lord Roberts paid tribute to 'the generous way in which the Corporation of Blackpool had assisted an object of such national importance'.[1]

In 1907, C Squadron under Major Ernest Johnson was based with RHQ at Lancaster House, Whalley Range, Manchester, and with two local Troops was known as the Manchester Squadron. In November of that year Major Johnson published his 'C Squadron Orders', a little cloth-bound booklet running to seven pages, a copy of which survives in the Regimental Museum[2] and is worthy of a few extracts.

1. The above details are derived from 'The Duke of Lancaster's Own Imperial Yeomanry, Blackpool Troop.
2. Ref. LANOY 416.10.

Every Yeoman of the Squadron 'must remember that on him depends the honour and good name of his Regiment. He can only hope to maintain this by ready and willing obedience, careful attention to duty, and smartness in his turn-out, whether on or off duty.' NCOs were to study the temper and disposition of the men under them and to perform their duty 'with tact, impartiality and firmness'. The old Army slogan 'obey first and complain afterwards' was duly trotted out: 'If any Yeoman receives an order which he considers unjust, he must remember that it is his duty to obey, and if he desires to do so, complain afterwards.' Good horsemastership and stable management were stressed. Any evidence of a horse losing condition or being off his feed was to be immediately reported to the Troop Sergeant. No grey or white horses were allowed in the ranks, and any member hiring a horse should have it inspected and accepted by the Squadron Commander. When 'walking out' in uniform the men were to wear (white) gloves and carry a whip, while all officers, of any regiment, were to be smartly saluted 'if recognised'.

The programme of training for the year was detailed as under:

DRILLS 1907–8
Commencing November 11th 1907

Squad Drills each MONDAY, Recruits only WEDNESDAY, all Ranks from 1st Jan, 1908 MONDAYS & WEDNESDAYS, Recruits half an hour previous to each Drill. Also *Recruits* ONLY, each Tuesday evening at 7.30.

Riding Drill each Thursday at 7 pm, Hulme Barracks . . .

The *first and last Wednesday* in each month will be for Troop and Squadron Drills. N.C.O.s and men are requested to attend these drills as strong as possible.

The *second Tuesday* in each month is the day when new articles of clothing will be fitted and any articles put forward for renewal should be available for inspection by the Quarter Master at 7.45 pm.

A note added that 'By the kindness of Colonel Hargreaves, [Commanding Officer, 1902–1906] a shooting hut has been erected for the use of the Regiment on Altcar Rifle Range,' where members could be accommodated when firing their annual musketry classification.

In 1910 appeared a book by Erskine Childers entitled *War and the Arme Blanche*, with an introduction by Field-Marshal Lord Roberts. Childers, an Irishman, had served in a CIV Horse Artillery battery in the Boer War, had also written a volume of *The Times History of the War in South Africa*, and was the author of a best-selling mystery yarn, *The Riddle of the Sands*, which prophesied the threat of German naval might.[3] *War and the Arme Blanche* was a diatribe against 'traditional' cavalry, urging the abolition of the sword ('dead as the Dodo'), and the immediate conversion of all cavalry regiments to mounted

---

3. Erskine Childers went on to serve in the Royal Naval Air Service and the Royal Flying Corps in WWI, wherein he gained Major's rank and the DSC. Later he became more hazardously involved in Irish politics and as a member of the Irish Republican Army, was executed by Free State soldiers. His son, also Erskine, died in 1974 as President of the Irish Republic.

infantry, relying solely on the rifle. Predictably, this created a furore among die-hard cavalrymen such as Haig and French (in Britain) and Von Bernhardi (in Germany), and Childers was vehemently attacked in the columns of the newly-founded (and traditionalist) *Cavalry Journal*. Lord Roberts had already expressed his radical views about the cavalry's role when he took the unusual step of writing a preface to the 1904 issue of the *Cavalry Training* manual. In this he categorically asserted that with the introduction of the long- range, low-trajectory magazine rifle and the machine gun, it was clear that 'instead of the firearm being an adjunct to the sword, the sword must henceforth be an adjunct to the rifle, and cavalry soldiers must become expert rifle shots and be constantly trained to act dismounted'. But the traditionalist lobby dismissed Boer War lessons as 'abnormal', maintaining that future wars were likely to be fought in the European theatre where professional armies, such as those of Germany, Russia and France, were steadfastly adhering to the sword. In Britain the anti-reform faction seemed to have won the day when a revised edition of *Cavalry Training* was issued in 1907. Effectively reversing the principles laid down in the previous edition, this included a stirring passage of rhetoric that must have been hailed with glad cries by all true horse-soldiers:

> It must be accepted as a principle that the rifle, effective as it is, cannot replace the effect produced by the speed of the horse, the magnetism of the charge and the terror of cold steel. For when opportunities for mounted action occur, these characteristics conspire to inspire such dash, enthusiasm and moral ascendancy that cavalry is rendered irresistible.

Meanwhile, the internal combustion engine was to be seen functioning here and there on the roads; soldiers at Aldershot were making some irreverent comments at the spectacle of their GOC being conveyed to and from his HQ in his horseless carriage. This had been allotted by the War Office so that the General 'could assess the military potentialities of the mechanically propelled vehicle . . .' A few years later (in 1909) it seemed that such potentialities were recognised, for in that year fifteen motor cars were issued to each Cavalry Division, for employment in 'long-distance reconnaissance and despatch carrying'. The machines were to be driven by carefully selected officers who had to be not only 'first-class car-masters' but good linguists and expert map-readers. This early attempt at a 'reconnaissance corps' died a natural death. Contemporary mechanical horsepower was no match for the live animal, while the cars' cross-country capabilities were of course nil, and they were thus road-bound.[4]

During the large-scale autumn manoeuvres of 1910 on Salisbury Plain the troops were startled by a strange kite-like contraption propelling itself above their formations. This was one of three aircraft purchased by the War Office for 'experiments in military aeroplaning'.[5]

These innovations were of course portents of a future that was to have profound effects on the cavalryman, and on warfare itself. But they were largely unnoticed at the time, both

---

4. *The Cavalry Journal* October 1909
5. The primitive Bristol machine was piloted by Captain Bertram Dickson, Royal Artillery, and his reconnaissance flight (on 24 September 1910) is recorded as the earliest military use of aircraft in Britain.

by Yeoman and Regular horseman, and apart from some more serious dismounted training in musketry, and with the stuttering Maxim machine gun now issued to the Yeomanry, life went on much as before.

In August 1907 the Secretary for War, Richard Haldane (later Viscount), introduced far-reaching reforms with his creation of an Expeditionary Force ready to take the field in the event of war, and a properly organised second-line army in the shape of the Territorial Force (later Territorial Army). The latter comprised all the 56 Yeomanry regiments, who were organised in 14 Cavalry Brigades, while the Volunteers formed 14 Infantry Divisions.

As far as the Yeomanry were concerned, there was nothing novel in the brigading of regiments, for as we have seen, this had been introduced in 1893 (p. 35), although just as in South Africa, it was largely ignored when war came again in 1914, most regiments being committed piecemeal, regardless of brigades.

However, the new *Territorial and Reserve Forces Act*[6] directed that the organisation, training and administration of the Yeomanry should now become solely the responsibility of the County Associations (virtually committees), headed by the Lords Lieutenant as *ex officio* Presidents, with officer-members of the Territorial Force appointed by the Army Council. Some Commanding Officers were suspicious of this move, suspecting a loss of independent authority, but as before, in practice they were still allowed wide discretion in the management of their commands.

The Act allowed a maximum establishment of 25 officers and 449 other ranks for each regiment. Pay and allowances (when on duty) corresponded to Regular cavalry rates, as under:

Yeomanry Rates of Pay (Daily) 1909[7]

Lieutenant Colonel	21s. 6d.
Major	15s. 0d.
Captain	13s. 0d.
Lieutenant	7s. 8d.
2nd Lieutenant	6s. 8d.
Adjutant (if Captain)	18s. 0d.
Quartermaster	10s. 6d.
Quartermaster Sergeant	4s. 4d.
Squadron Sergeant-Major	4s. 4d.
Sergeant	2s. 8d.
Corporal	2s. 0d.
Trumpeter	1s. 4d.
Private	1s. 2d.

There were sundry allowances. In camp (if 'under canvas') an officer was allowed four shillings a day for messing, other ranks one shilling for rations. On Embodiment of the Force every officer and man would receive a gratuity of five pounds.

6. 7 Edward VII, Cap. 9 (2 August 1907)
7. *The Territorial Yearbook* (1909)

The new Act included a titular change. The rather grandiose term 'Imperial Yeomanry' adopted at the outset of the Boer War, was modified and the force once more became simply 'Yeomanry'.

The officers and other ranks of The Duke of Lancaster's Own Yeomanry probably felt that their emergence as a unit of the new Territorial Force was little more than academic. They still owed respect to Frederick Arthur, 16th Earl of Derby, as Lord Lieutenant of Lancashire and now President of their County Association. Their Honorary Colonel was still Francis Egerton, 3rd Earl of Ellesmere, who represented their interests as a member of the County Association. The Commanding Officer was Lieutenant-Colonel John Rutherford who had taken over from Lieutenant-Colonel Hargreaves in 1906. Their 'orbat' comprised RHQ and four sabre squadrons, whose locations were as under:

RHQ and C Squadron	Manchester
A Squadron	Oldham and Rochdale
B Squadron	Bolton and Liverpool
D Squadron	Preston and Blackpool

As already noticed, Regimental Headquarters had been removed from their long association with Worsley in 1903 when the location became Lancaster House, Whalley Range, Manchester.

The total enrolled strength of the Regiment amounted to 19 officers and 433 other ranks.[8] Their role in the Territorial Force was as divisional cavalry regiment to the 42nd East Lancashire (Territorial) Division. And it was thus roled that they experienced their first Annual Camp and training on the vast expanse of Salisbury Plain. This was in June 1909, and while in camp at West Down North they also suffered their first experience of a phenomenon that sometimes afflicted even the best-managed cavalry regiment – a stampede of horses. What caused this one, in the lines, is not known – possibly a violent thunderstorm, but it took all ranks several hours to round up the hundreds of strays, when it was found that many had injured themselves so badly that they had to be destroyed.

A novel feature of these Divisional Camps on the Plain was the opportunity to work with other arms. Hitherto, all field training had been hidebound and parochial to a degree: very rarely did a Yeomanry squadron set eyes on, let alone co-operate with, a battery of artillery or a single company of infantry. 'We each of us look upon the other arms with mild toleration; we dine with them, play polo with them, and affect a polite interest in each other: but as for combining to practise our joint work – it is not the custom of the army.'[9] This was written by a Gunner officer, *circa* 1907, but obviously it held equally true for everyone else, and except for the occasional all-arms camp, continued to do so down to 1914.

Apart from realistic exercises, the 42nd Division camp of 1909 and again the following year 1910, no doubt resulted in meetings with many friends from home, for the

8. *The Territorial Yearbook* (op. cit.).
9. Quoted in Headlam, Maj-Gen Sir John *The History of the Royal Artillery* ... Vol 2 (1937).

Territorial battalions of the East Lancashire and Manchester Regiments and the Lancashire Fusiliers hailed from centres such as Wigan, Blackburn, Rochdale, Oldham and Manchester itself – as did, of course, the majority of The Duke of Lancaster's ranks. But A Squadron could not foresee that they were to become more closely associated with these battalions when they sailed to Egypt as the Divisional Cavalry Regiment in 1914.

In the old days all movements to and from Camp had to be performed by 'March Route', on horseback, which is why convenient locations such as Southport were favoured, to limit marching time. But with the development of the railway network the whole Regiment, men and horses, could be speedily conveyed further afield – Lowther Park, for instance, and of course, Salisbury Plain. In the 1890s, and later, the London & North Western Traffic Superintendent at Manchester was quite accustomed to providing special trains to transport some 300 Duke of Lancaster's Own Yeomen and an equal number of horses from Worsley and other stations to Penrith, or Rhyl, or elsewhere. Yeomen of today who have only to mount their pre-packed vehicles to be ready for a drive of 200 miles or more to Annual Camp, might spare a thought for their predecessors labouring to entrain horses, baggage, tentage and the rest at a railway siding. As always, many horses would obstinately decline to be led into a cattle truck without expenditure of much physical coercion (and troopers' language) on the part of four or more strong men – two at the head and two more with rope round hindquarters. On such occasions the horse-soldier's traditional affection for his mount was sorely tried.

The railway companies were obliged to provide special concessionary fares for all troops. Officers (1st Class) and men (3rd) were allowed return fares for the price of a single; 50 or more horses were charged $1^{1/4}$d. per horse per mile. These rates were laid down in the 1910 *Regulations for the Territorial Force*.

Previously to the 1909 Divisional Camp on the Plain, the DLOY had held their Regimental camps in the more familiar locations of Lowther Park (1905) and Brackenber Moor, near Appleby (1906). In 1907 they ventured for the first time into Wales, at Caerwys (near Holywell), while the following year saw them by the Welsh seaside at Rhyl. On the first night at Caerwys a violent gale blew up and flattened two of the squadrons' messing marquees.

On 6 July 1909 the Regiment was honoured by a visit to Worsley Park from the Colonel-in-Chief, King Edward VII, who presented a new Guidon on a ceremonial parade. Later His Majesty was fittingly entertained by Lord Ellesmere and the officers. This Guidon continued in service until 1961 when it was replaced by a new one presented by Her Majesty Queen Elizabeth II (p. 143).

By this date the splendid Full Dress, or Review Order, uniform had been superseded by the more mundane, but practical, Khaki Service Dress, first donned during the Boer War, and to remain the British soldier's normal attire until in turn superseded by the Battledress of 1939. Prototype of the modern Number Two Dress, it consisted of khaki or 'Drab Mixture' tunic (quaintly termed 'Frock' in the *Dress Regulations*),[10] Bedford cord

---

10. The first issue of *Dress Regulations* to specify Khaki Service Dress was that published in 1900.

riding breeches with leather strappings, puttees and ankle boots with steel spurs ('Spurs, Jack'). The other ranks' tunic was buttoned up to the neck with a stand-up collar displaying collar badges. Officers of course had superior-quality material, known as barathea, with turned-back lapels revealing shirt and tie, while their breeches were of the 'cavalry twill' material still preferred by civilian riders today. For leg attire they could adopt either brown leather leggings or knee-boots, but the Regulations demanded that 'all officers of a unit [should be] dressed alike'. Head-dress was the now familiar peaked cap with chinstrap, which was always worn 'down' when mounted.[11] A distinctive feature of the cavalryman's dress was the pair of burnished steel-link shoulder-chains embellishing the tunics. These had originated for a purely practical purpose in the Indian Cavalry during the Mutiny, when they were adopted to afford protection from sword-cuts. While today they still glisten on the shoulders of all regiments of the Royal Armoured Corps and Yeomanry in Number One Dress, The Duke of Lancaster's Own Yeomanry is the only Regiment permitted to wear them in Number Two Dress. [see next chapter].

Saddlery had evolved into the pattern that was to remain unchanged until the mounted soldier abandoned his horse for tank or armoured car. All of brown leather, the trooper's saddle was the 'Universal Pattern Steel Arch' article, immensely strong but commensurately heavy, weighing all of 40 lb. complete. Secured by both leather girth and surcingle, it was not padded, but rested on a numnah and folded saddle-blanket. The lighter officer's pattern had padded seat and flaps, and no blanket. These were the regulation patterns for the regular cavalry, but as always, the Yeomanry were the last to receive the latest issues.

The bridle carried the single, dual-purpose bit known as 'Portmouth Reversible', which in the Regulars had superseded the bridoon-and-curb bits of the double bridle in 1900. By means of two pairs of reins buckled to the cheeks, this combined the action of the old double bridle. A steel-link curb-chain controlled leverage. Civilian horsemen still know this type of bridle as a Pelham. The cavalryman was always taught to ride with reins in the left hand only – the other being needed for his weapon – hence the term 'bridle hand'. A useful feature of the Army bridle was the ease with which it could be converted into a temporary stable headcollar simply by unbuckling and slipping off the headstall complete with bit and reins: convenient when feeding in the field.

Passing round the horse's neck and secured to the jowl-piece of the bridle was a white hempen headrope (formerly a steel chain). As the name implies, this was primarily intended for tethering the animal on the picket lines, but, laboriously blancoed, it added a touch of panache on drill and ceremonial parades. All this tack can still be seen in service with The King's Troop RHA, and the mounted police forces.

Like the modern St John's Wood Horse Gunner, the Yeoman of the 1900s was burdened with hours of soaping, polishing, burnishing and blancoing to achieve a smart turnout on parade – in addition of course to the strapping and grooming of his mount and attention

---

11. Although there was no official ruling, it became de rigueur for cavalry and Yeomanry to wear the chinstrap on the point of the chin when mounted. The Gunners, always a law unto themselves, wore it firmly under the chin, against the throat.

to his own kit and arms. The firms of Wren (boot-polish) and Propert (saddle-soap) enjoyed a steady profitable market among the cavalry and Yeomanry. There were no 'staybrite' buttons and badges in those days: all brasswork had to be shined with those 'soldiers' friends', Brasso or Bluebell, all plain steelwork to be brought up with a chain-link burnishing pad. After rainy days' manoeuvres in camp the once-glistening sword scabbard could have broken out in a dismaying rash of rust-spots, as could the stirrup irons.

If some Yeomanry recruits felt they would have done better to join the Territorial infantry who had only their personal kit and rifles to bother about, it speaks volumes for the enthusiasm and dedication of the majority of those part-time horse-soldiers that all such time-consuming chores were not only accepted as part of their voluntary obligations, but, unlike the Regulars, had to be performed in addition to their civilian duties. The term 'yeoman service' had acquired other connotations, but it surely originated in the Yeoman regiments of the British Army.

The Regular cavalry were now armed with the sword still carried by The King's Troop, and known as the '1908 Pattern'. As already noted, it was carried (when mounted) in a steel scabbard secured in a frog on the spare horse-shoe case on the near-side of the saddle. For dismounted Review Order parades the old sword-belt and slings were retained. But as with saddlery, the Yeomanry lagged behind the Regulars, and photographs in the DLOY archives show the old pattern (slightly curved) sword in use in 1913.

On the off-side of the horse a full-length leather bucket held the Short Magazine Lee-Enfield, or SMLE, rifle which was to continue as the British soldier's chief personal firearm until after the Second World War.[12]

It was no simple business for a trooper to mount his horse encumbered with his rifle. On the command 'Prepare to mount!' he heaved the weapon over the saddle to the off-side, there grasping it (together with two pairs of reins) in his left hand. Having mounted, he transferred it to his other hand and thrust it muzzle down into the bucket – all the while attempting to control a possibly restive 'part-time' horse. Since the rifle was never to be left in the bucket when dismounted, the order 'Prepare to dismount – dismount!' involved the drill in reverse.

The trooper's ammunition was carried in a leather bandolier slung over the left shoulder. With five pouches in front and four at the back, each containing two five-round clips, this could provide 90 rounds of .303 in. ammunition 'on the man'. When war came it was the practice to sling a second bandolier round the horse's neck.

The pattern of Full Dress, reserved solely for ceremonial duties, underwent some changes after 1902. All ranks still wore the white-metal helmet with white horsehair plume, but the former tunic was replaced by a scarlet patrol jacket with blue collar, steel

---

12. Yet again there is uncertainty about the date when the 'short' Lee-Enfield was issued to all Yeomanry regiments. Museum photographs show the old 'long' model in a short butt bucket in use as late as 1912.

shoulder-chains and gold-braid arm badges for NCOs. As already mentioned, sergeants and warrant officers wore in addition to their badges of rank the unique Regimental arm badge of a gold ducal coronet – the Duke of Lancaster's. The attire was completed by drab Bedford cord breeches with scarlet piping, leather leggings and ankle boots, and tan gloves. For dismounted ceremonial, the breeches were replaced by blue overalls with broad yellow stripes, Wellington boots and swan-necked box spurs (locking into the heels of the boots). For both mounted and dismounted Review Order, officers continued to wear the former scarlet tunic with gold pouch-belt. Although 'authorised', all this finery was no longer Government issue, so all this expense had to be found by the Regiment (and the County Association).

In those brave times of overt, unashamed patriotism, the soldier was proud to wear a smart uniform in public, just as his girlfriend was proud to be seen with him. For this purpose the aptly-named 'Walking Out Order' was approved for other ranks. The Duke of Lancaster's pattern was similar to the Dismounted Review Order, with scarlet jacket, blue overalls and Wellington boots and spurs, but in place of the helmet a peaked blue cap was worn. Altogether a very smart and soldier-like attire – particularly with those gleaming shoulder-chains and broad yellow stripes on the overalls. In 1909 brass shoulder-titles were issued, to be affixed to the shoulder-chains, those of the Regiment reading 'D of Lancasters' surmounted by a 'T' and a 'Y' ('Territorial' – 'Yeomanry').

The Annual Camp of May 1910 was again held at West Down North, Salisbury Plain, together with the 42nd East Lancashire Division. On 6 May the Regiment learned the sad news that their Colonel-in-Chief, King Edward VII, had passed away, and the state funeral was fixed for 20 May at Westminster Abbey, at which all regiments of the British Army were to be represented in the solemn ceremony. The Duke of Lancaster's hastily organised a contingent of 24 NCOs and troopers in Full Dress, commanded by Major Henry Bibby. Since they had arrived at Aldershot expecting only field training, none of these had Full Dress with them, but it so happened that the Home Headquarters of the 1st (Royal) Dragoons and their QM stores were also based at Aldershot, and some very friendly co-operation resulted in the loan of 25 sets of Full Dress. The Royals' dress was similar to The Duke of Lancaster's – scarlet with blue facings – and all that remained to be done was to change shoulder-titles and collar-badges.

There was ceremonial of a joyous nature in June 1911, for the Coronation of HM King George V (who was of course the new Colonel-in-Chief). In pomp and pageantry the Coronation outshone even Queen Victoria's Diamond Jubilee of 1897, with every regiment of the British, Colonial and Indian forces being represented, while for the first time in their history, all 56 Yeomanry regiments sent detachments to London, each of one officer and 25 other ranks. The Duke of Lancaster's were commanded by Captain L. G. S. Molloy and dressed in dismounted Review Order – plumed helmet, scarlet jacket (with shoulder chains), blue overalls and Wellington boots. There was a curious mixture of dress among the 56 Yeomanry contingents: most were able to produce sufficient sets of Full Dress, others could only afford walking-out attire (some adding a rather incongruous leather bandolier), while yet others appeared in drab service dress. All 1,400-odd Yeomen were accommodated in a vast tented camp in Kensington Gardens, and on Coronation Day (22 June) they lined the street in Piccadilly, performing the same duty on the following morning when Their Majesties made their Royal Progress through the city.[13]

Following the creation of the Territorial Force in 1910 the War Office issued a manual entitled *Regulations for the Territorial Force and County Associations*, which with some amendments in 1912, formed the 'bible' for Yeomanry and other 'Terriers' until after the Great War.[14] Essentially resulting from Viscount Haldane's proposals, this dictated significant changes in the organisation and administration of the whole Territorial Force, only some of which can be noted here. First, as we have seen, the County Associations became entirely responsible for the recruiting, organisation, administration and funding of their own County Territorial units. This seemed to usurp the authority previously enjoyed by the Lords Lieutenant, but as they were now *ex officio* Presidents of their County Associations they still had considerable say.

The Regulations directed that an Association would 'be required to provide the necessary drill halls, headquarters, . . . and to provide saddlery for their horses and the ranges for instruction in their shooting, and to arrange for their attendance at drills &c. outside the annual training in camp'. Thus a great measure of the administrative (and financial) burden of a regiment was shifted on to its County Association, which in addition to its own funds was entitled to several Government grants, as approved by the Army Council. For example, to meet the general expenses of administration, an annual grant of £160 was allowed for each Yeomanry squadron on its rolls; £300 per regiment was allowable for expenses in hiring horses; the sum of £4. 10s. could be claimed for each man's initial clothing issue.

The County Association was responsible for the approval of all candidates for first commissions. Such aspirants were to be no younger than 17 years of age and [should be] acceptable to the Commanding Officer and to the Lord Lieutenant as President of the Association, who would forward the names to the War Office for submission to the King.

An officer's steps up the promotion ladder were regulated by proficiency examinations, as in the Regulars, exemptions being made in the case of ex-Regular officers who had already qualified. All Yeomanry officers were required to attend at least 40 drills per year besides the annual training in Camp. The latter (no longer termed 'Permanent Duty') was to extend for at least eight and not more than eighteen days – most regiments opted for fourteen – and where a regiment was chiefly recruited in rural areas it should be arranged so as not to interfere with haymaking or harvest. From 1 May to 30 September was the normal season for Camp. If a man were unable to produce his own horse for Camp, he could claim a grant of £5 for the hire of one.

Like the officer candidate, the rank-and-file recruit was to be at least 17 years of age, not under 5 ft. 3 in. in height, to be passed medically fit, and approved by his County Association. Officers and other ranks willing to serve overseas 'in time of national

---

13. A full account of Yeomanry at the Coronation is given in *The Uniforms of the British Yeomanry Force 1794–1914. No. 10: The Yeomanry Force at the Coronation* by R. J. Smith and R. G. Harris (1988). Replete with many contemporary photographs, this contains descriptions of all 56 detachments.
14. The provisions of this manual are conveniently summarised in *The Territorial Yearbook (op. cit.)* which although published in 1909, pre-empted the regulations.

emergency' were required to sign an agreement to that effect. Other ranks enlisted for a period not exceeding four years. As before, they could terminate the engagement at any time (except when embodied) by giving written notice to the CO, though they now had to pay £5 for the privilege.

The subject of discipline received due attention. First, after reminding a Commanding Officer that he was responsible to His Majesty 'for the discipline, efficiency and proper management of his unit', he was enjoined to 'discountenance any disposition in his officers to gamble or extravagance. He is also to check any tendency among his officers to practical jokes . . .' (No fun and games in the Mess Tent, or dunking an unpopular subaltern in the horse trough?) Officers were subject to Military Law at all times, other ranks only when under training, when embodied, or when called out for service under the Territorial Forces Act. In their dealings with the men NCOs should 'avoid the use of intemperate language or the adoption of an offensive manner'. Since most of the NCOs were well known to the trooper in civilian life and there was always a strong 'family' atmosphere in a Yeomanry unit, such caution was largely academic.

Other ranks' offences were still largely punishable by fines or dismissal. Thus a Yeoman failing to attend the prescribed drills or Annual Camp would 'be liable to forfeit to His Majesty' a sum not exceeding £5, according to the number of such offences. Repeated absences, without due cause, would incur dismissal from the regiment. However, the graver offence of absence on embodiment would be regarded as desertion, and on conviction by a court martial the offender might 'be taken into military custody', or in other words, suffer a term in a military prison. All fines were now credited not to the regiment, as formerly, but to the County Association.

The authorised peacetime establishment of a Yeomanry regiment remained at 25 officers and 449 other ranks, in four squadrons with one machine gun section (of two horse-drawn Maxim guns), but of course not all regiments were up to full strength. The Duke of Lancaster's now came under Western Command (Headquarters, Chester), No. 4 District, and were 'attached for training' to the Welsh Border Mounted Brigade which also included Cheshire, Denbighshire and Shropshire Yeomanry, the Lancashire Hussars and the Westmorland and Cumberland Yeomanry.

Although by 1913 Armageddon was looming near, there was nothing to suggest it as the final year of peace passed uneventfully enough for the Regiment, occupied with routine drill sessions at Manchester, Bolton, Preston and elsewhere. In June 1913 the last Annual Camp for many seasons was spent at Greystoke, near Penrith, where the Regiment was commanded by Lieutenant-Colonel Robert Tilney, who had succeeded John Rutherford the previous year. May 1914 brought a final flourish of ceremonial when all the Lancashire 'Terriers' assembled in Liverpool for a church parade and marched past the Lord Lieutenant and the Lord Mayor. The Duke of Lancaster's was represented by a detachment of 30 NCOs and troopers from B Squadron.

On 13 July 1914 the Regiment suffered the loss of their Honorary Colonel, Francis Egerton, 3rd Earl of Ellesmere, who died at his home, Old Hall, Worsley, aged 67. Son of the 2nd Earl, Lord Ellesmere had succeeded his father in 1862, and took over the

Colonelcy from his uncle, the Hon. Algernon Fulke Egerton, in 1891. At the same date he also became Honorary Colonel of the 4th (Volunteer) Battalion of The Manchester Regiment and held both appointments until his death. One of the wealthiest landowners in Lancashire, with some 13,000 acres,[15] Lord Ellesmere was not only a dedicated Yeoman (he had served as Captain and Major in the Regiment), a much-respected and benevolent employer, a keen racing man and cricketer, but, unusually for his circle, he also dabbled as a novelist. His published corpus included lively yarns with such titles as *A Broken Stirrup-Leather*, *Sir Hector's Watch* and *A Sapphire Ring*. Though none of these might be hailed as classics of English literature, at least the 3rd Earl of Ellesmere is noteworthy as the only member of The Duke of Lancaster's Own Yeomanry to achieve authorship.[16]

Lord Ellesmere's death marked the end of the Regiment's remarkably long association with the Egerton family who had provided Honorary Colonels and Commanding Officers since the 1850s. The successor as Honorary Colonel was Lieutenant-Colonel Percy Hargreaves, who was not appointed until March 1915. This officer had commanded the Regiment from 1902 to 1906 and was the grandson of Captain James Kearsley who was Commandant of the Bolton Troop when it was re-raised in 1819.

In the sun-blest summer of 1914 the Regiment had been looking forward to the culmination of their year's training, the Annual Camp with the East Lancashire Division on Salisbury Plain, fixed for late July. However, events on the Continent dictated otherwise. In June the Press carried reports of the assassination of an Austrian Archduke and his Consort at somewhere called Sarajevo in the Balkans. This seemed of no concern to officers and soldiers of The Duke of Lancaster's engaged in their normal part-time drills and annual musketry qualification. But it was a prelude to a convulsion that embroiled the Regiment, and the British Army, in the bloodiest conflict they had yet endured, and was to prove a *fin de siècle* for contemporary society.

---

15. The Egerton wealth stemmed from Francis, 3rd Duke of Bridgewater, who had settled at Worsley in 1759, there to develop the coal resources. His construction of a canal from Worsley to Manchester greatly reduced transport costs, and hence the cost of the product.
16. That is, until 1973, when the then Commanding Officer, Lieutenant-Colonel Desmond Bastick, published his *Trumpet Call* – a short history of the Regiment.

Route of A Squadron in Egypt and Palestine 1914-1918

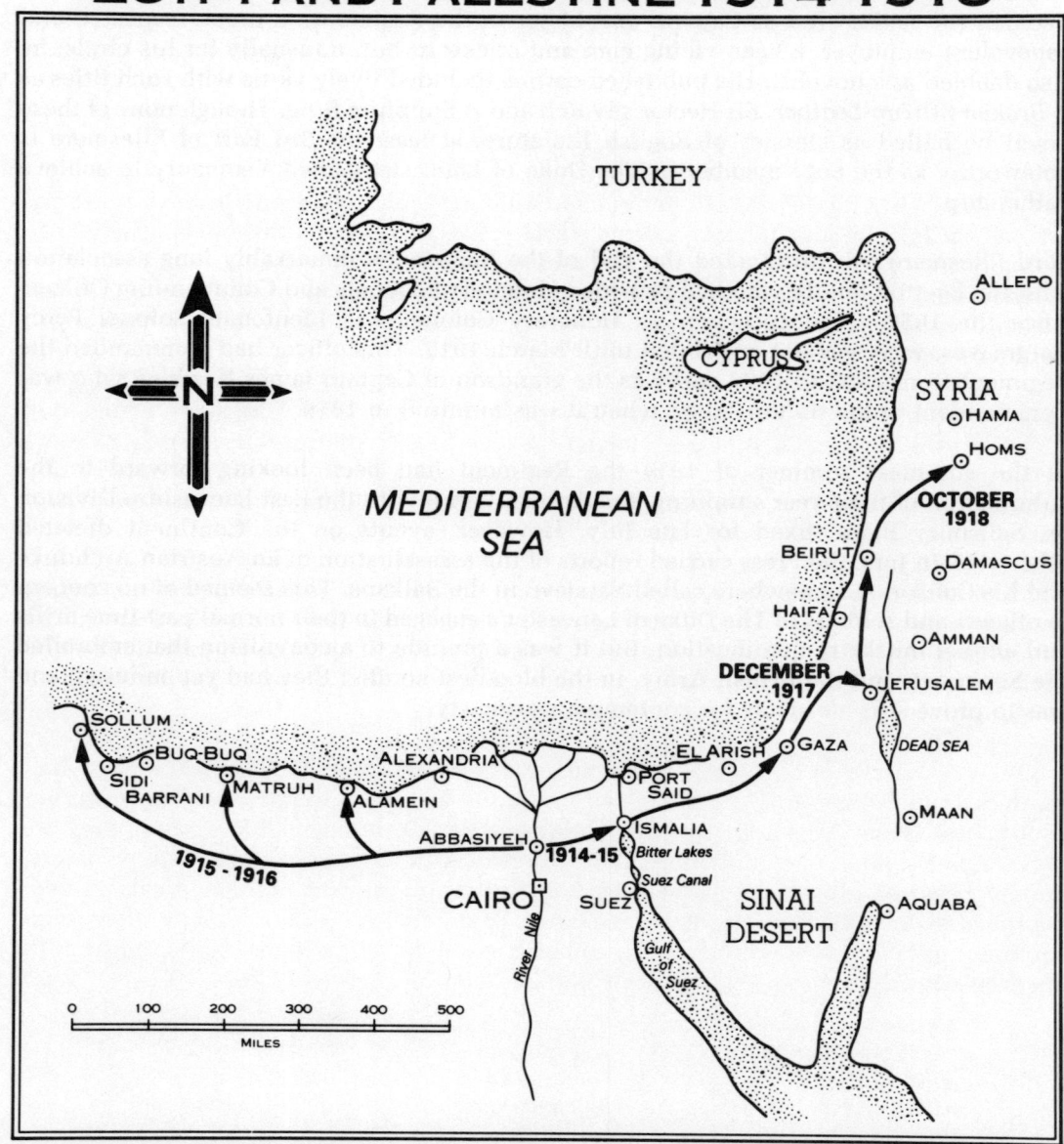

Unlike the Squadrons in France and Flanders, A Squadron remained mounted throughout.

[72]

CHAPTER VI

The Great War 1914–1919

Part 1. Egypt and Palestine

On 3 August 1914 The Duke of Lancaster's deployed their squadrons in the Knutsford environs of Cheshire for a tactical scheme with the Earl of Chester's Yeomanry. The latter, mounted on bicycles, acted as enemy, but the outcome between horsemen and cyclists is not recorded. This was the last time for five years that either regiment was able to indulge in such diversions. On 4 August Britain was at war with Germany and the Yeomanry faced more serious tasks.

The Foreign Secretary, Viscount Grey, was heard to say: 'the lamps are going out all over Europe; we shall not see them lit again in our lifetime'. But such gloomy foreboding was not shared by the cheering crowds outside Buckingham Palace, or by the patriotic throngs of young men in Manchester, Liverpool, Bolton and elsewhere when General Mobilisation was ordered.

At this momentous date The Duke of Lancaster's were still based at Whalley Range, Manchester, where RHQ and C Squadron were located. A Squadron deployed Troops at Oldham and Rochdale, B Squadron at Bolton and Liverpool, and D Squadron at Preston and Blackpool. In command was Lieutenant-Colonel R. H. Tilney, TD,[1] and the total strength numbered 25 officers and 432 other ranks.

By the very nature of a Yeomanry regiment's part-time status, with Squadrons and Troops widely dispersed, its mobilisation naturally took longer than its Regular counterparts. Nevertheless, all Squadrons of the Regiment were able to report complete to War Establishment in men and horses by 17 August. Although there are no records of any 'dummy runs' or practise mobilisations, the Squadrons had in previous years issued 'Mobilisation Instructions' to their members, detailing all clothing, kit, arms and equipment to be brought with them on embodiment. The following is an extract from D Squadron's Instructions issued by its OC, Major T. A. S. Shepherd-Cross.

> Members will assemble wearing their Service Dress, viz. – Khaki cap, Jacket, Pantaloons [breeches], Puttees, Jack spurs, and bring with them Great Coat and Haversack, Waterbottle, Pocket Knife and Lanyard, Mess Tin and Strap, Kit bag, Bandolier, Brown Waist Belt and Pouches, Rifle (with Oil Bottle and Pull-through), Rifle sling, Sword, Grooming Kit (Horse sponge, Comb, Brush, Rubber, Stable Bag and Hoof-picker), Saddlery, Field Dressing, Identity Disc. Sergeants to bring Whistles.

---

1. Robert Henry Tilney had been serving with the Regiment for 24 years, thus earning his Territorial Decoration, for which at least 15 years' continuous service was required. He had been promoted Lieutenant-Colonel in 1912, assuming command the same year, and was to remain in command throughout the war.

On 10 August Lord Kitchener issued a circular to all Territorial units, inviting them to volunteer for service overseas, and by the end of the month all 56 Yeomanry regiments had complied. At the same time all were ordered to raise a home-based second-line regiment to train recruits and provide drafts for their overseas, or first-line partners. Thus for the duration the parent regiment was officially designated '1/1st Duke of Lancaster's Own Yeomanry', the second-line unit being '2/1st . . .'

Another Army Order of the same month directed that Yeomanry regiments should deploy no more than three sabre squadrons, a move to simplify administration and ensure that all three were fully up to strength. Since The Duke of Lancaster's had four squadrons, and B was the weakest, this was broken up, officers and men being absorbed by the other three, who still retained their lettering, A, C and D. Having completed mobilisation the Regiment concentrated its squadrons at Clitheroe on 17 August.

Colonel Tilney had been instructed that his Regiment would form the Divisional Cavalry Regiment of the 42nd (East Lancashire) Division – logical enough, since this had been its role in peacetime training and at recent annual camps. But early in September came revised orders: only one squadron would accompany the 42nd Division overseas, the others, with RHQ, to remain behind for home defence pending further instructions. There was nothing unusual in Divisional Cavalry being limited to a single squadron: the seven regular infantry divisions of the 1914 Expeditionary Force had only one each.

And so on 8 September, A Squadron entrained at Bolton for Southampton, where on the following day they embarked men and horses to join the 42nd Division's convoy sailing for Egypt. This East Lancashire formation was the first Territorial division to sail for active service, and its fleet of 15 transports and escorting warships was the largest yet assembled. Totalling some 15,500 men of the County Palatine, it included four Territorial battalions of The Lancashire Fusiliers, two of The East Lancashire Regiment, six of The Manchester Regiment, together with the Blackburn and Bolton Brigades, Royal Field Artillery.[2]

Commanded by Major H. L. Bibby,[3] A Squadron, The Duke of Lancaster's Own Yeomanry mustered six officers and 132 other ranks, with 142 horses. The Squadron was of course proud to be the first representative of the Regiment to see active service in 1914, but it was by no means the first Yeomanry unit to do so. Pride of place was achieved by The North Irish Horse whose A Squadron landed in France at the remarkably early date of 19 August, while the entire Oxfordshire Hussars followed on the 22nd.

The Great War story of The Duke of Lancaster's Own Yeomanry is a fragmented one, like the Regiment itself. A Squadron remained estranged in Egypt and Palestine throughout the conflict. D Squadron went to France in May 1915, followed by C Squadron with RHQ in August of that year. But these two saw nothing of each other until May 1916 when, with a squadron of the Surrey Yeomanry, they came together as the III Corps Cavalry

---

2. A full (and very readable) history of the Division's services was compiled by Frederick P. Gibbon and published in 1920: *The 42nd (East Lancashire) Division 1914–1918*.
3. Henry Leigh Bibby was commissioned 2nd Lieutenant in the Regiment in 1899 and had risen to Major in 1908.

Regiment. Later the two Duke of Lancaster's Squadrons lost not only all yeomanry, or cavalry, semblance, but their identities, when in September 1917 they were dismounted and absorbed as infantrymen in the 12th Battalion, The Manchester Regiment, with which they finished their active service.

But since A Squadron was the first to confront an enemy, it is fitting that they should receive prior attention. On 23 September 1914 the Squadron disembarked at Alexandria and marched to Cairo, where it went into Abbasia Barracks with the Lancashire Fusiliers. Here all ranks were issued with the tropical kit that was to become familiar to British soldiers in the East until the Second World War: khaki drill tunic, light cord breeches and the cork helmet (or topi). All Yeomanry (and Regular cavalry) were now armed with the Short Magazine Lee-Enfield rifle – the SMLE – and the 1908-pattern straight sword. As a single squadron, the DLOY had no medium machine guns: a complete cavalry regiment was allowed only two Maxim guns. But they had four Hotchkiss light machine guns.

If A Squadron imagined that they would quickly draw swords, or rifles, to confront the Turks, they were as quickly disillusioned. Although Britain was well aware of the potential Turkish threat to the Suez Canal and Egypt, no formal state of war existed at that date, and the role of the 42nd Division was one of a watching brief. Thus the DLOY Squadron spent the first couple of months on intensive training in the vast expanse of open desert which was ideal terrain for mounted manoeuvres. The Divisional Commander, Major-General Sir William Douglas, 'paid close attention to the Squadron, not only in work, but in the general welfare of the men, earning him the nickname of Father . . . and this sobriquet stuck to him until he was replaced'.[4]

It was only on 5 November 1914 that war with Turkey was officially declared, and by now it had become common knowledge that the Turks were preparing for an attack on the Canal. However, the attack did not materialise until the following February when, as an element of the Canal Defence Forces, A Squadron joined with squadrons of The Hertfordshire and County of London Yeomanry to form the Yeomanry Mounted Brigade. The attack, on 3 February 1915 was easily repulsed by the 42nd Division's infantry and artillery, the Yeomanry only being let slip after the retreating enemy, to capture stragglers and abandoned arms and ammunition. They suffered no casualties in this affair, and the total British losses were no more than 150. But the Turks had been given a bloody nose. Losing more than 1,500 killed and wounded, they withdrew to their Sinai bases.[5] There then followed a lull during which the Yeomanry withdrew to Cairo for further training in company with Australian and New Zealand mounted units newly arrived in Egypt.

In the spring of 1915 the controversial plan for an invasion of the Gallipoli peninsula was evolved, and in May the 42nd (East Lancashire) Division was withdrawn from Egypt to take part in the operations. But A Squadron DLOY was retained for the defence of the Suez Canal and so escaped the carnage of that disastrous campaign.[6]

4. *The Wanderings of a Yeomanry Squadron.* 'A Squadron The Duke of Lancaster's Own Yeomanry', anonymous unpublished MS in DLOY Museum.
5. Throughout this narrative casualty figures, and much else, are derived from: *The Palestine Campaigns* by Colonel A. P. Wavell (1928) and *The Desert Mounted Corps* by Lt-Col. R. M. P. Preston (1921).
6. No fewer than 27 (dismounted) Yeomanry regiments took part and suffered crippling casualties. The abortive operation cost a total of 28,200 killed and 89,344 wounded, the East Lancashire Division losing 8,547 all ranks.

Meanwhile, the Squadron had confronted another enemy. Aided and abetted by Germany and Turkey, the powerful Senussi tribes of the Western Desert had risen against the British and were posing a diversionary threat to Cairo and the Canal. In December 1915 the Squadron joined the Western Frontier Force at Mersa Matru, forming a Yeomanry Mounted Brigade with the Dorsets, Royal Bucks. Hussars and Berkshires. After exhausting marches in pursuit of an elusive guerilla enemy reluctant to stand and fight, the tribesmen were at length brought to battle on 26 February at Agagiya, a few miles east of Sidi Barrani, where the Dorset Yeomanry put in a gallant charge, routed the enemy, and captured their General.[7]

The DLOY Squadron could take no part in this battle, for they had previously been withdrawn, 'to refit', at Alexandria. But they had proved their endurance. 'The outstanding feature of this excursion into Western Egypt' (wrote the author of *The Wanderings of a Yeomanry Squadron*) was the number of long distance treks ... The record march of the Squadron was a trek of 122 miles in 4 days, with the last 55 miles in 22 hours.'

In March 1916 the survivors of the 42nd Division returned from the Gallipoli fiasco and the Squadron was reunited with its Lancashire comrades, to become once more part of the Canal Defence Forces. On 24 July 1916, the Squadron Leader, Major H. L. Bibby, was stricken down with typhoid and shortly afterwards was evacuated home. In May 1917 Henry Bibby had recovered and sailed from Southampton to rejoin his command. But a few days later his ship, HMT *Transylvania* was torpedoed by a U-boat in the Mediterranean and he, with many other officers and soldiers, was drowned.

> To Major Bibby, beyond all others, the Squadron owed its efficiency and morale. As O.C. in pre-war days he never spared himself in the interests of the Squadron ... A born leader of men, he commanded his Squadron by love rather than power of authority, and by his death the Squadron suffered an inestimable loss.[8]

After Major Bibby's evacuation, command of the Squadron was assumed by Captain D. H. Bates, who proved a worthy successor, and was to lead it until the Armistice.

In July 1916 the Squadron was attached for patrol and reconnaissance duties to the 127th (Manchester) Brigade. Meanwhile command of the Turkish field force had been assumed by the able German General Kress von Kressenstein, while his force was stiffened by German and Austrian staff and artillery units. The first clash came on 4 August at Rumani when Kressenstein's advance was met by the 42nd, 52nd and 53rd Divisions. This pitched battle, only some 20 miles east of Port Said, was chiefly a slogging match between opposing infantry, while the Yeomanry, acting as 'long stop' on the route to the Canal, were not engaged. Nevertheless, since six complete regiments were present in the battle zone, they later received the Battle Honour 'Rumani'.[9] But as the DLOY were

7. The Queen's Own Dorset Yeomanry became the only regiment in the Army to bear the Battle Honour 'Agagiya'. The Senussi General, Jafar Pasha, later sided with the Allies, to become Prime Minister of Iraq.
8. *The Wanderings of a Yeomanry Squadron, op. cit.*
9. They were: Ayrshire, City of London, Gloucestershire, Scottish Horse, Warwickshire, Worcestershire.

represented only by the single squadron, with no RHQ, they did not qualify – a circumstance that applied throughout the campaign.

Having lost nearly half his 16,000 men, Kressenstein withdrew along the coast to regroup. The battle of Rumani was a turning- point in the campaign. The threat to the Canal was finally removed and the British were able to prepare for the offensive in Palestine. This did not get under way until the following spring, by which time there had been organisational changes. In January 1917 the 42nd Division was ordered to France, its place being taken by the 53rd (Welsh) Division. Thus A Squadron DLOY bade farewell to their many Lancashire friends when they were transferred as Divisional Cavalry to the 53rd, being attached to 158 Brigade. Here they found the familiar Lancashire speech supplanted by the Welsh lilt of three Territorial battalions of The Royal Welch Fusiliers. In March (1917) 17 Yeomanry regiments were deprived of their horses to become infantrymen of the 74th (Yeomanry) Division, aptly known as 'the Broken Spur Division'. But A Squadron was spared this trauma as Divisional Cavalry, and in fact were proud to remain mounted until the end of hostilities.

The British offensive opened with unsuccessful attacks on Gaza in March and April 1917, when the 53rd Division lost heavily. A Squadron, however, were employed on patrol and reconnaissance and the inglorious tasks of digging trenches, so that they had no chance to distinguish themselves. One of the incidental problems now, and for most of the campaign, was that of watering horses from the only desert sources, the infrequent wells or *birs*. Many of these proved so brackish that the animals refused to drink, with the result that often they went 48 hours or more without a smell of water and began to lose condition. And the men suffered likewise. The actual business of watering was laborious and time-consuming. The canvas water-buckets (each holding one gallon) were lowered down the deep wells on lengths of field telephone wire, heaved up again, and carried to the thirst-crazed horses, which spilt much of the contents as they plunged their muzzles in. The Squadron's War Diary records that on one occasion it took three hours to water their 140 mounts.

In June 1917 General Sir Edmund Allenby arrived from France to take over as C-in-C from General Sir Archibald Murray. A thrusting cavalryman by instinct and training, Allenby was determined that his mounted arm should be given full opportunity to display the mobility and aggression expected of it, and within a month he had created the renowned Desert Mounted Corps from the Anzac and Yeomanry horsemen, which was to fight the last full-scale mounted campaign in history.[10] In all, 20 Yeomanry regiments were represented.

Having exchanged their fellow-Lancastrians of the 42nd Division for the Welshmen of the 53rd, only seven months later (in August) they found themselves among Londoners of the 60th (London) Division, still as Divisional Cavalry. If this was a largely unrewarding role, worse was soon to follow. On 1 September General Allenby ordered that all Divisional

---

10. Hitherto, all the Australian and New Zealand Light Horse had been armed only with rifle and bayonet – they were in fact, mounted infantry. But Allenby issued them with swords, impressing upon them that they were now true cavalrymen.

Cavalry squadrons were to be abolished, each to be joined with others for form 'Corps Cavalry Regiments'. Thus on 10 September 1917 A Squadron DLOY suffered a loss of identity when they merged with A Squadron, Hertfordshire Yeomanry and C Squadron Royal Glasgow Yeomanry, to become part of the XXI Corps Cavalry Regiment, commanded by Lieutenant-Colonel G. G. M. Tyrell (ex–5th Lancers). Under this undistinguished title they fought the remainder of the campaign, although within the new Regiment they were still known as A Squadron, DLOY. All these transformations prompted the author of *Wanderings of a Yeomanry Squadron* to recall 'it became a standing joke that divisions, etc. might change, but the DLO went on for ever'.

The Corps Cavalry Regiments were regarded as little more than general dogs-bodies. Often split into detached squadrons, even troops or less, they were given no death-or-glory opportunities but were submitted to such humdrum tasks as routine patrolling, despatch riding, escorts to senior commanders and herding prisoners to the rear.

After the third, and victorious, battle of Gaza on 7 November 1917, the XXI Corps Cavalry Regiment was dispersed, the DLOY Squadron being attached to yet another Division, the 52nd (Lowland). On the 8th this Division was heavily engaged at Wadi Hesi, between Beersheba and Jerusalem, repulsing the enemy only with severe casualties. This action was one of the few when A Squadron was able to show its mettle. It had been ordered to dismount and occupy a position on the Hesi ridge, which it did without serious opposition. But then a strong enemy counter-attack developed and after a gallant fire-fight with overwhelming numbers the Squadron was forced to withdraw on the advancing infantry of 157 Brigade.[11] In this action the Squadron lost its Second-in-Command, Lieutenant P. J. Crook and two men killed and five men wounded. On the following morning Captain Bates received congratulations from the three Brigade Commanders of the Division for his Squadron's 'energetic activities'.

With the capture of Gaza and Beersheba, the Turks were steadily pushed back and Allenby began the marathon pursuit that was to continue until the final surrender. A Squadron DLOY continued its essential but unrewarding tasks of reconnaissance and patrolling which, in soaring temperatures and difficult terrain of sandhills and scrub-covered rocky outcrops, tried the stamina of mount and man. The War Diary reveals that in one period of ten days in September the Squadron rode more than 170 miles. There were occasional skirmishes with Turkish counterparts 'who were nicknamed rabbits, as they always scuttled away to the wadis as soon as they were attacked'. (*Wanderings of a Yeomanry Squadron*). But, even a rabbit may sometimes turn, and on 19 June an unusually daring body of Turkish cavalry made an attack on one of the Squadron's dismounted standing patrols. Covered by two machine guns, they galloped boldly for their enemy, but were brought up sharp by rapid fire, and dismounted under cover. 'If this attack had been pressed home the DLO position would have been untenable, but after a two hours' scrap the Turks withdrew to a discreet range. Shortly afterwards two Troops of Australian Light Horse cantered up, with apologies for being too

---

11. The wisdom of employing a cavalry unit to act dismounted was always tactically dubious, for with one man in three acting as horse-holder in rear, only two-thirds of the strength was available as riflemen.

Muster Roll of the Bolton Light Horse Volunteers for June 13th 1805, now on display at the Regimental Museum, Preston.

The Memorial Tablet to **Thomas Gardner, Drill Sergeant** to the 'Furness Cuirassiers' killed in a fall from his horse in 1821.
This memorial is on the south wall of the parish church at Great Urswick, Nr. Ulverston.

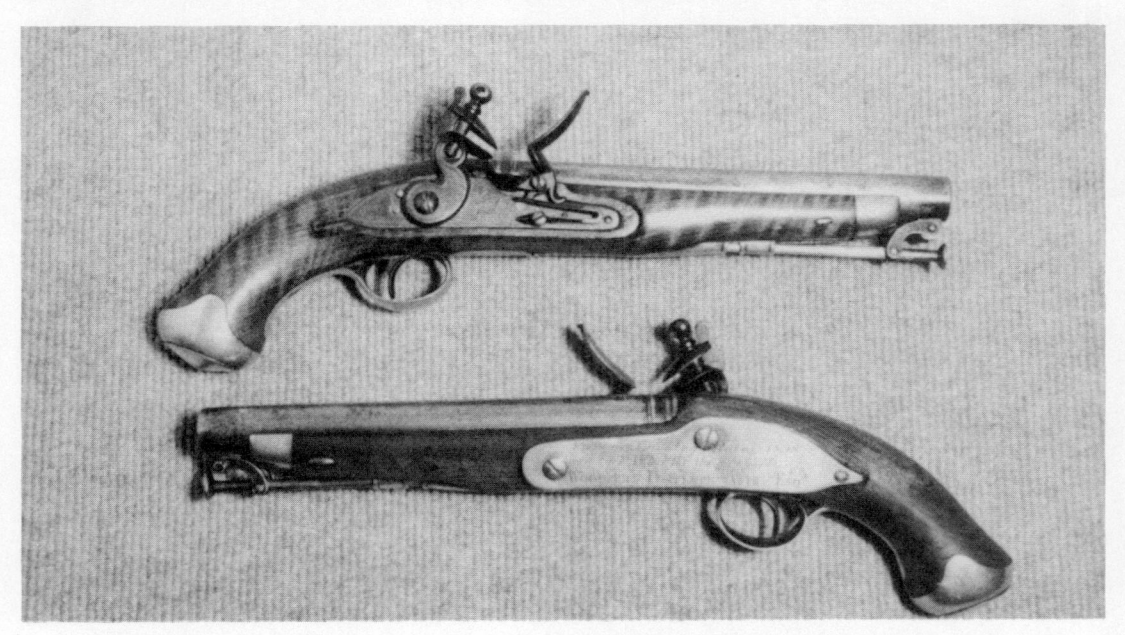

A pair of New Land pattern flintlock pistols *c.* 1810. These pistols were used as prizes in the Furness Cavalry Races for 1828 when they were won by Paul Pry. Previously, the pistols had been the property of Woodburn Postlethwaite, the Quartermaster of the Furness Yeomanry Cavalry. These pistols are in the regimental museum.

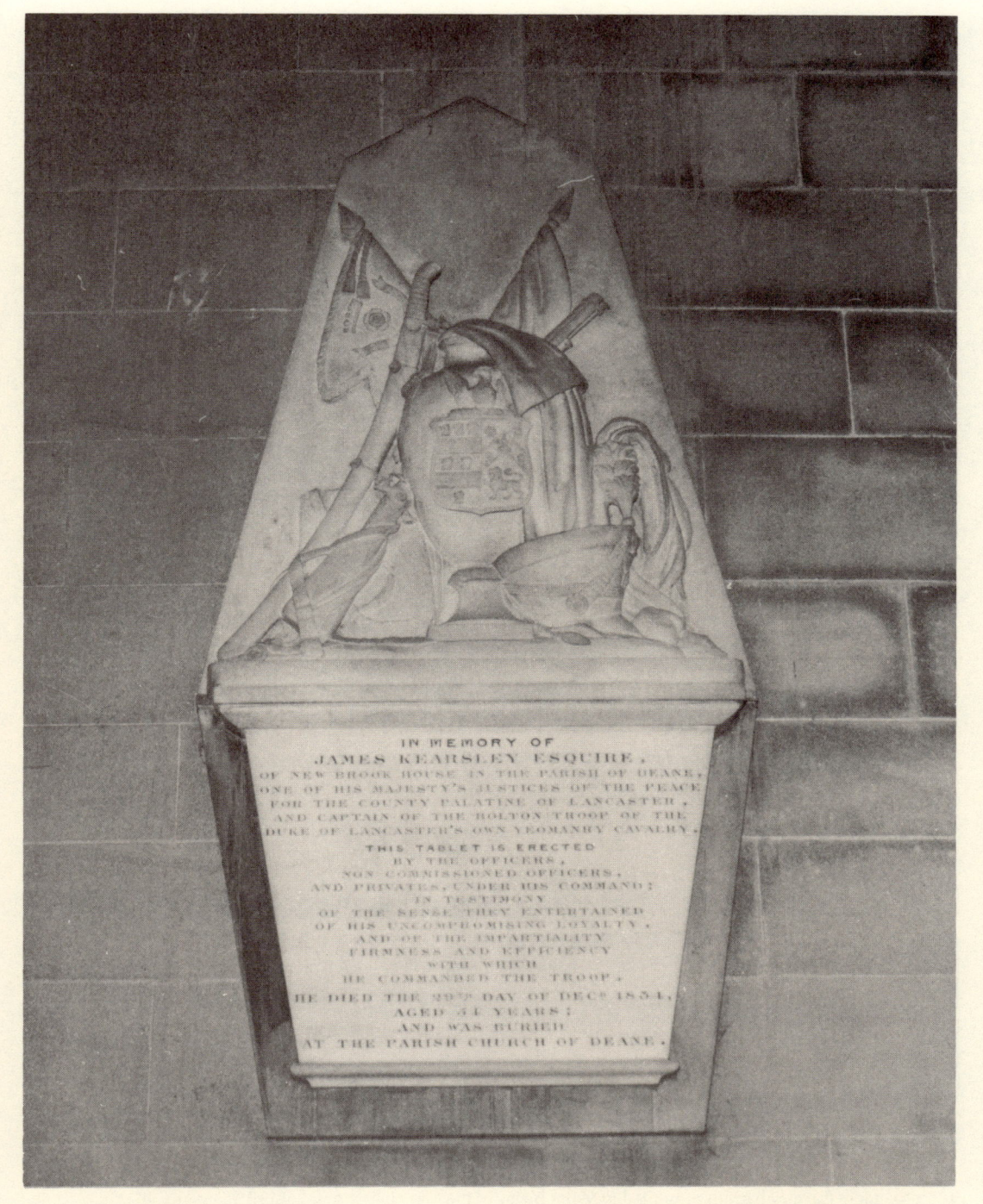

This Memorial Tablet to James Kearsley is to be found in the porch of Bolton parish church and was erected by former comrades in arms in 1834.
The military trophies surrounding the coat of arms show the contemporary bell-topped shako, 1796 pattern Light Cavalry sabre, carbine and Troop or Regimental Guidon.
(Picture by kind permission of the Churchwardens and Vicar of Bolton parish church)

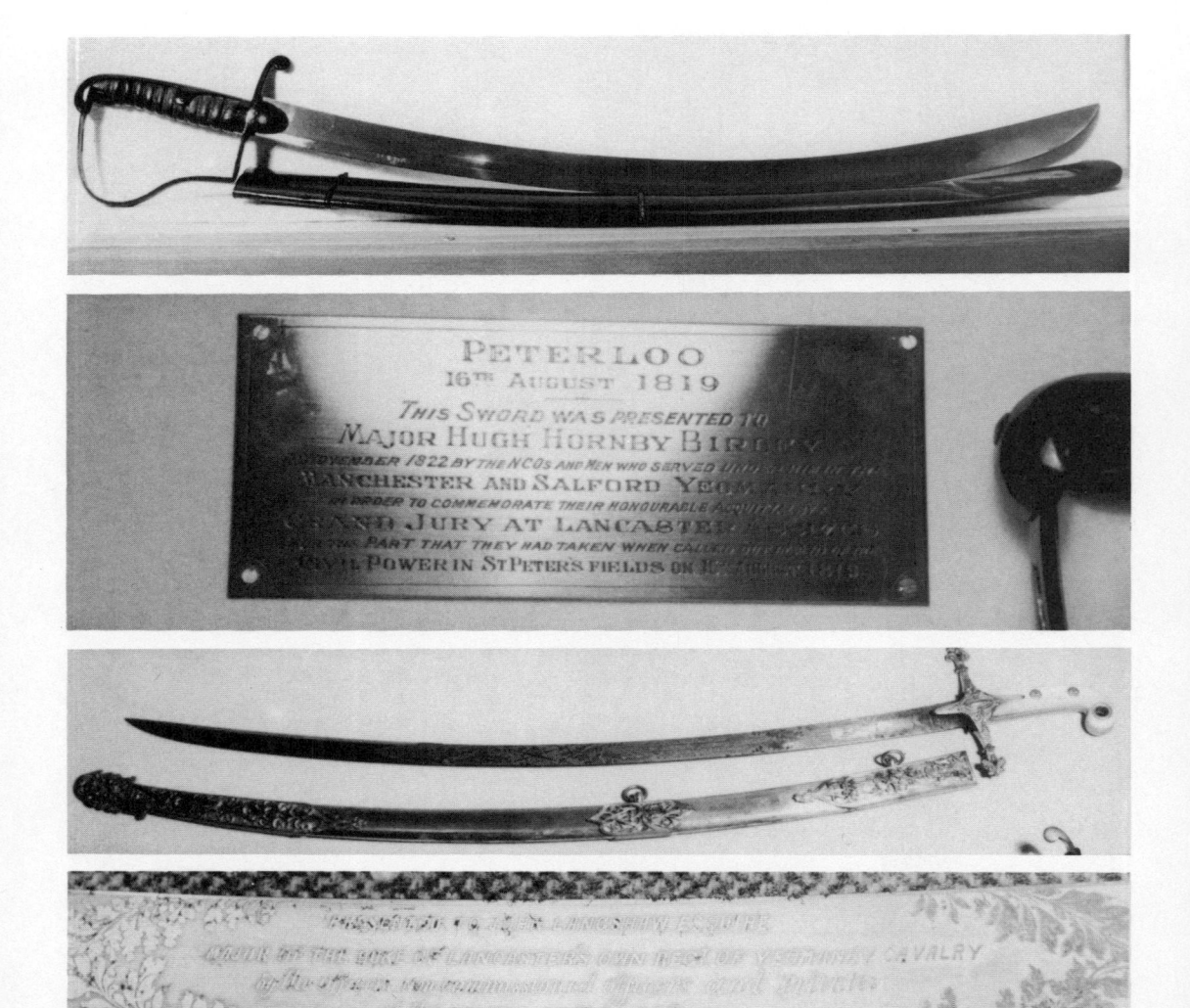

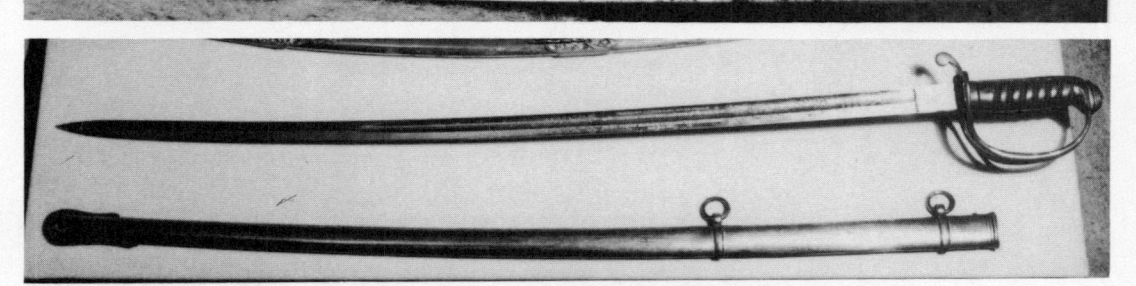

Presentation Yeomanry Swords on display in the Regimental Museum.

1. 1796 Light Cavalry pattern presented to Major Birley of the Manchester and Salford Yeomanry after his acquital at the Lancaster Assizes following the Peterloo Massacre.

2. Mameluke Sabre presented to Major Langshaw by the Bolton Troop in 1856.

3. 1822 Light Cavalry Officers sword present to Sgt. Major Williams by the Worsley Troop in 1877.

Sepia and grey wash drawing by the Earl of Ellesmere showing the Duke of Lancaster's Own Yeomanry escorting Queen Victoria's carriage along the drive to Worsley Hall during Her visit on 10th October 1859. This drawing originally came from one of Queen Victoria's souvenir albums.
(Reproduced here by kind permission of the Royal Collection. © 1994, Her Majesty the Queen.)

a.   b.

A   Victorian Regimental Carbine Medal now on view in the Regimental Museum.
B   Obverse and reverse of two Victorian Regimental Long Service Medals. That on the right was awarded by the Bolton Troop in 1861.

This is the earliest known photograph of the Regiment and is believed to date from 1863. The four officers are: (*left to right*) Capt. Le Gendre N. Starkie, Capt. John Jacson, Lieut. Lord Frederick Cavendish, Capt. C. B. Molyneux. All are wearing undress dark blue frock coats with black mohair braiding, dark blue overall trousers with gold lace stripe and Wellington boots with box spurs. Swords are the Light Cavalry officers 1822 pattern and the dark blue soft-topped forage caps with gold lace bands, gold topped button and gold braided peaks were introduced *c.* 1850.

This is a continuation of picture 1 and the officers are: (*left to right*) Lieut. J. N. Fazakerley, Major J. Langshaw, Lieut. R. H. Ainsworth, Lt. Col. A. F. Egerton the Earl of Ellesmere, Capt. J. Fletcher, T. Howitt, Surgeon.
Lieut. Ainsworth is dressed for Mess with his scarlet stable jacket open to show a dark blue waistcoat with gold braid figuring.

A further continuation shows the final picture of the officers who are: (*left to right*) Capt. The Hon. A. F. Egerton, Lieut. C. Patrick, Lieut. J. P. C. Starkie, Capt. W. E. Royds, Capt. S. C. Cavendish. the Marquis of Hartington, Cornet C. M. Royds.
Lieut. Starkie and Cornet Royds are shown wearing the Lancer-style full dress tunic introduced *c.* 1857; the tunic was scarlet, double breasted, with gold laced blue collar and cuffs, the buttons were gilt.
Cornet Royds is carrying the black first 'Albert' pattern helmet with white plume.

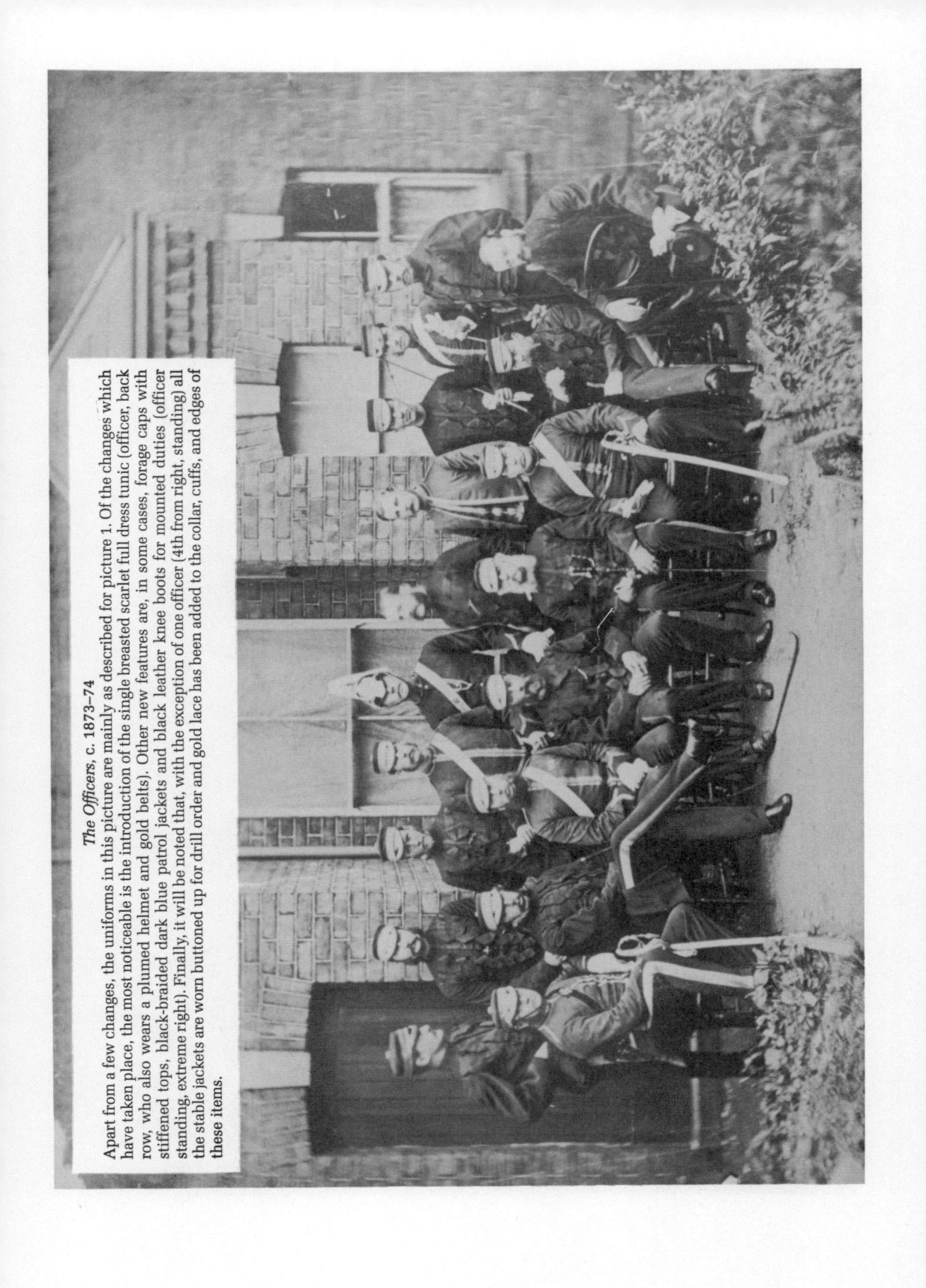

The Officers, c. 1873–74

Apart from a few changes, the uniforms in this picture are mainly as described for picture 1. Of the changes which have taken place, the most noticeable is the introduction of the single breasted scarlet full dress tunic (officer, back row, who also wears a plumed helmet and gold belts). Other new features are, in some cases, forage caps with stiffened tops, black-braided dark blue patrol jackets and black leather knee boots for mounted duties (officer standing, extreme right). Finally, it will be noted that, with the exception of one officer (4th from right, standing) all the stable jackets are worn buttoned up for drill order and gold lace has been added to the collar, cuffs, and edges of these items.

This shows the Regimental Sergeants' Mess in front of the Queen's Hotel, Southport at Camp in 1897. Note that the RSM and Trumpet Major Batley (*third from right centre row*) are both wearing Officer's style mess kit jackets whilst the RQMS (*third from left on centre row*) is wearing the short ribboned black frock. The Corporals at each end of the rear row are presumably Mess orderlies or Acting Sergeants.

A regimental detachment parading for the High Sheriff of Lancashire outside Manchester Cathedral in 1898.

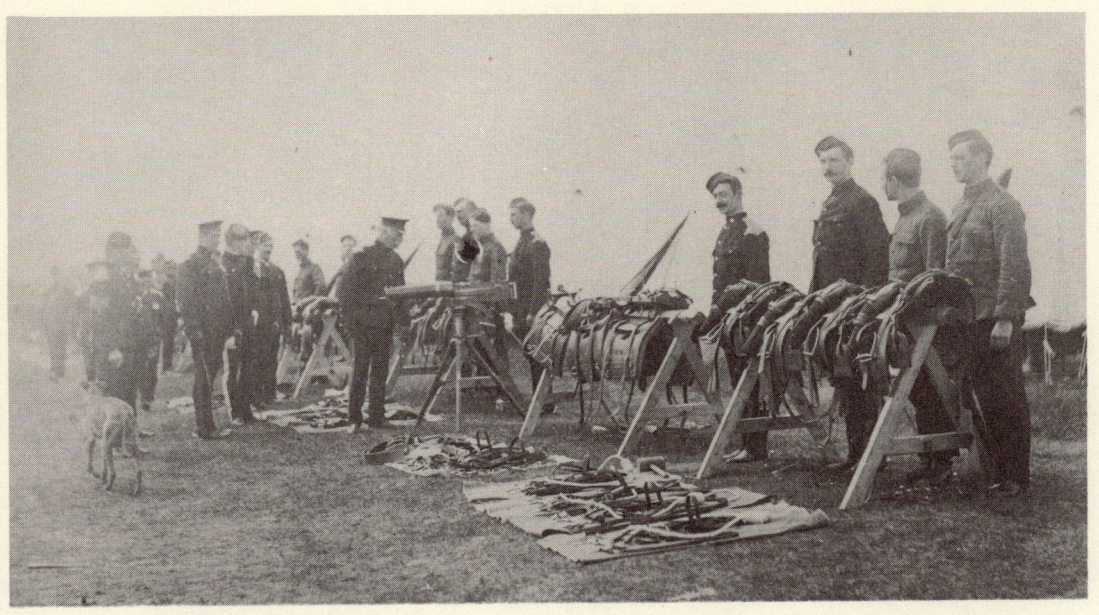

The Quartermaster, Major Hanbridge inspecting a machine gun together with saddles and tack at camp *c.* 1900.

The Regiment crossing the river Alt at Hightown near Southport c. 1900. Note that the headdress is the slouch hat worn for the whole of the Boer War.

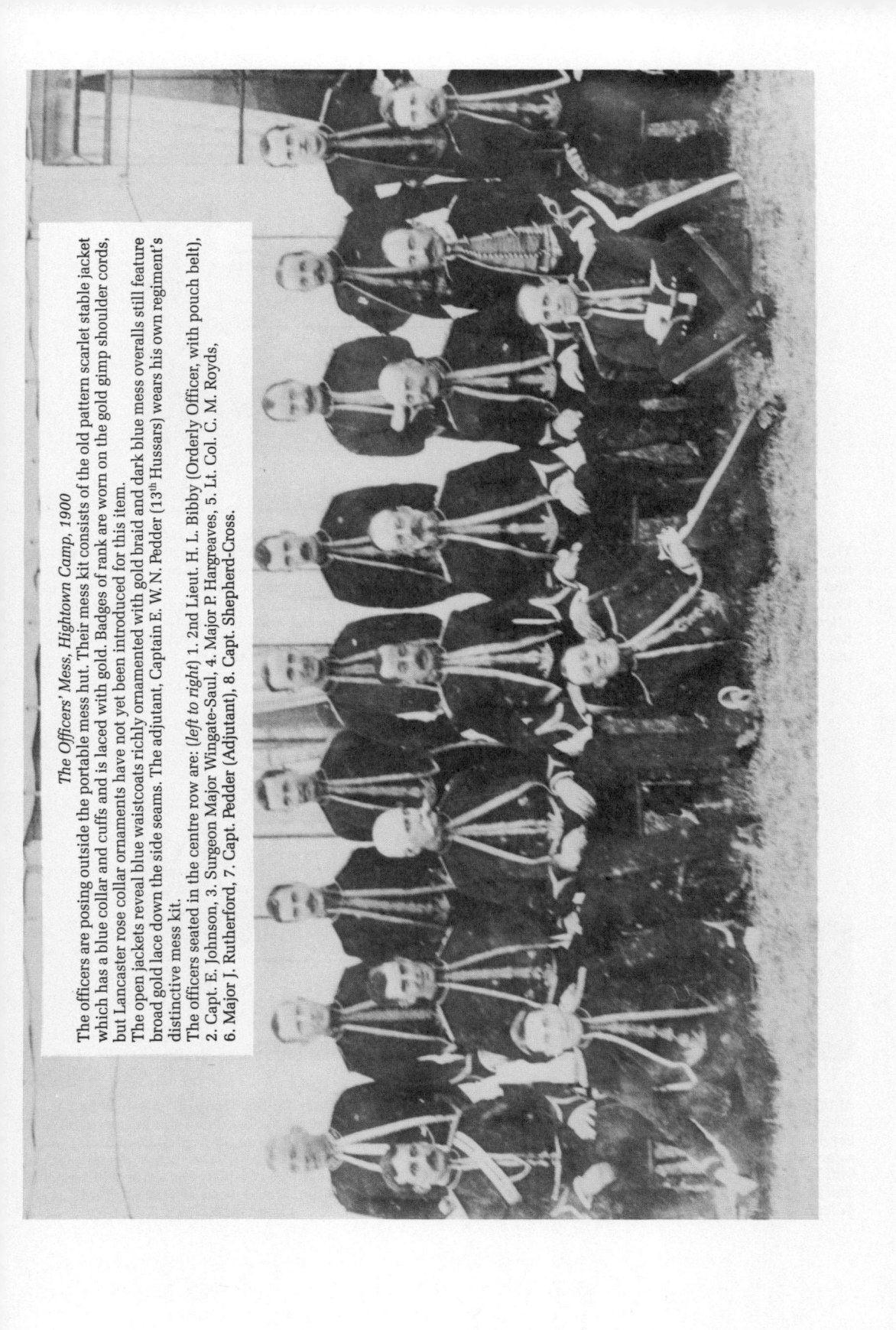

The Officers' Mess, Hightown Camp, 1900

The officers are posing outside the portable mess hut. Their mess kit consists of the old pattern scarlet stable jacket which has a blue collar and cuffs and is laced with gold. Badges of rank are worn on the gold gimp shoulder cords, but Lancaster rose collar ornaments have not yet been introduced for this item.
The open jackets reveal blue waistcoats richly ornamented with gold braid and dark blue mess overalls still feature broad gold lace down the side seams. The adjutant, Captain E. W. N. Pedder (13th Hussars) wears his own regiment's distinctive mess kit.
The officers seated in the centre row are: (*left to right*) 1. 2nd Lieut. H. L. Bibby (Orderly Officer, with pouch belt), 2. Capt. E. Johnson, 3. Surgeon Major Wingate-Saul, 4. Major P. Hargreaves, 5. Lt. Col. C. M. Royds, 6. Major J. Rutherford, 7. Capt. Pedder (Adjutant), 8. Capt. Shepherd-Cross.

Officers Group, 23rd Company (D.L.O.), 8th Battalion Imperial Yeomanry, 1900

This photograph was taken prior to the embarkation of the 23rd Company, I.Y. to the South African War; they sailed from Liverpool on 11th February 1900. The Officers are: (*left to right*) Capt. H. M. Hardcastle, Capt. G. Kemp (*seated*), 2nd Lieut. J. A. B. Heap and Capt. A. W. Huntingdon. Their uniform and equipment consist of drab felt slouch hats, khaki serge jackets and drab coloured riding pantaloons which are worn with tan leather leggings and ankle boots fitted with jack spurs. Web ammunition bandoliers are carried over the left shoulder, while there are rolled-up haversacks and binocular straps over the right. Additionally, the leather waist belts carry revolvers in holsters on the right and leather ammunition pouches can be seen, together with bayonets, on the left.

Guard mounting, Hightown Camp, 1900

At this, the first annual training of the D.L.O. under canvas, members of the Bolton Troop of 'C' Squadron parade for guard mounting. The pill-box forage cap, which was dark blue with a yellow band and top button (gold lace band and button for sergeants and officers) is worn by all ranks, while Lieut. Ormrod (*in front of the parade*) wears a dark blue frock coat and overalls with yellow stripes. The men are in their full dress scarlet tunics, overalls, white buff leather pouch belts, sword belt, slings and sword knots. White wrist gloves complete the kit. It will be noted that SSM Kearney (*far left of photograph*) has a four bar gold lace chevron, Ducal Coronet and Royal or Crown proper.

RSM Dalyell wearing **mess kit** *c.* 1900; note the Ducal Coronet immediately above his **rank** chevrons surmounted by the Royal Crown.

The Hon. F. Egerton in 1901 He is wearing a mourning band for the late Queen Victoria.

Squadron stables of B (Manchester) Squadron in 1901 at Hightown Camp near Liverpool. The Officer is Capt. Johnson and, to his right is Sergeant Major Campbell.

Major George Kemp, later Viscount Rochdale, photographed in 1901.

Trooper 2672 David Elce of 23 Coy Imperial Yeomanry in a posed studio portrait. Trooper Elce won the DCM for his role in the engagement at Faber's Putt.

Members of 23 Coy Imperial Yeomanry in Field Dress in South Africa: Major George Kemp (*centre*) is wearing a mourning band as are the officers on either side to mourn the death of Queen Victoria.

A trooper of 23rd Company Imperial Yeomanry on duty in the field during the Boer War which appears in Trooper L. H. Johnson's History published in 1902 by Tillotson Press; the picture is believed to be that of Trooper Johnson himself.

Members of 23 Coy Imperial Yeomanry on active service in South Africa during the Boer War.

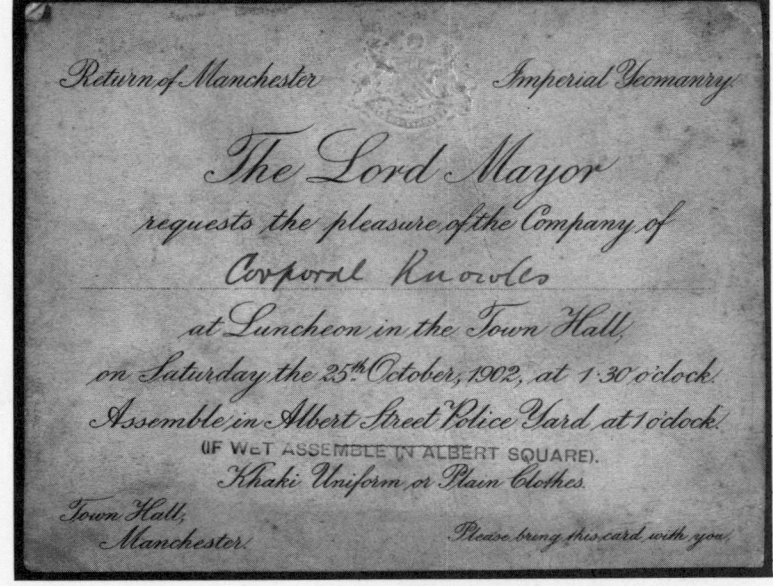

The central figure in the topee is Corporal Knowles of the Worsley Troop on duty in South Africa. On return of the Imperial Yeomanry from South Africa they were fêted by the municipality and friends; shown on this page is an invitation to luncheon at Manchester Town Hall.

ORs' Khaki Field Service Dress c. 1903–9

The correct method of wearing the kit is demonstrated by Permanent Staff Sergeant Major Campbell, 4th (Royal Irish) Dragoon Guards, *c.*1905. The sergeant major's kit consists of a drab felt slouch hat, a khaki mixture serge frock or jacket, dark shade drab cord riding pantaloons with red piping down the seams, tan leather leggings and ankle boots with jack spurs. He is equipped with a web ammunition bandolier for single rounds over both the left shoulder and around the waist. Also featured is a water bottle over the right shoulder and a folded haversack carried over the left shoulder. He is armed with a bayonet carried in a frog on his left side. The rifle is the earlier or long Lee Enfield magazine rifle which was replaced in 1909. The sergeant major's arm badges are interesting; before *c.* 1900 the Ducal Coronet appears to have been worn above the chevrons to distinguish staff sergeants and above. From *c.* 1900, however, the Coronet assumed the role of a regimental arm badge for all sergeants. The Royal Crown or Crown proper was then introduced as the badge distinguishing staff sergeants and above, in conjunction with, and surmounting, the Coronet.

The main photograph shows Field Marshal Lord Roberts together with the Mayor of Blackpool at the opening of the Blackpool Troop Drill Hall in Talbot Road, July 1903: The insert shows the carved stone tablet over the main entrance.

Regimental signallers with signal lamps at Hightown Camp 1904.

Machine gun section training at camp in Lowther Park, 1905.

Watering horses at camp, Lowther Park 1905.

Early regimental transport believed to have been taken in 1908.

Chaff cutting party at Regimental Camp, probably 1908

The Officers, Rhyl Camp, North Wales, 1908

The officers are in Camp Church Parade Order. The dark blue forage caps introduced in 1903 have scarlet bands and piping and the black leather peaks have gold-braided edges for field officers, while all have gilt badges and buttons. Also introduced in 1903 were the scarlet serge patrol jackets which had dark blue collars with crimson and gold Lancaster Rose badges, pointed blue cuffs, shoulder chains and gilt buttons. The dark blue overall trousers have broad yellow cloth stripes and the kit is completed by Wellington boots with box spurs, tan wrist gloves and walking sticks. Sam Browne belts were also generally worn in this order. In 1909, plain all-blue caps were substituted for those described above.

The D.L.O. Coronation Detachment, B Camp, Kensington Palace Gardens, London, June 1911.
On the 22nd and 23rd June 1911 this smart dismounted party of 25 ORs under Capt. L. G. S. Molloy paraded at Hyde Park Corner to carry out street lining duties during the Coronation celebrations of King George V and Queen Mary. Capt. Molloy is wearing the complete pre-1900 dismounted review order with the gold laced scarlet tunic with blue facings and gold laced belts and sword knot. The ORs seen are wearing the uniform described previously with the exception here that tan gloves are worn instead of white.

The D.L.O. Guidon and Escort c. 1912–13

The Guidon was presented at a mounted parade reviewed by King Edward VII on 6th July 1909 at Worsley Park, Manchester. This party wears dismounted review order, consisting of the helmet with white plume; the scarlet serge patrol jacket with blue collar and cuffs, steel shoulder chains and gilt collar badges and buttons; the dark blue overalls have broad yellow side stripes and are worn over Wellington boots with box spurs. Note the white leather sword knots and slings, the latter from under the jacket. White wrist gloves complete the uniform. The original photograph notes the party as being: (*left to right*) 1. SSM Wheeler, 8th (Kings Royal Irish) Hussars permanent staff; 2. SSM Drew, 15th (King's) Hussars, permanent staff, bearer; 3. SSM Hilton 'C' Squadron. It is though that SSM Drew was acting Regimental Sergeant Major at this time.

Watering Horses, Lowther Park Camp, 1912

The officer on the right of the photograph is Capt. T. B. Forwood, who can be distinguished by the drab badges of rank and braiding on his cuffs and the blue dress forage cap which is fitted with a khaki top cover for service dress; he also wears a Sam Browne belt and tan knee or field boots. The ORs wear plain regulation khaki service dress with putees throughout. They are equipped with the 50 round 1903 pattern bandoliers and the short magazine Lee Enfield rifle which were issued to the yeomanry between 1909 and 1910. It will be noted that the rifles are carried in short butt buckets on the offside, mounted infantry fashion, as was the practice before the First World War.

Group of ORs, Fatigue Duties, Lowther Park Camp, 1912

These yeoman are engaged in the hard work of cleaning horse kit. A mixture of khaki service dress and unofficial civilian attire is worn. Note the figure in the back row who wears a plain dark blue dress peaked forage cap, as does the seated private (*2nd row, 2nd from left*), who is probably ready to walk out of camp as he also wears his scarlet patrol jacket with shoulder chains.

Private Edwards, wearing **Walking Out dress**, 1913. Tunic: Scarlet with blue collar and cuffs; Overalls: Blue with single scarlet stripe; Cap: plain blue; Gloves: brown.

This photograph shows the Commanding Officer's Rover in 1913. Captain Royds is in the rear off-side position and the Commanding Officer, Colonel Tilney, in the front nearside. Greystoke Camp 1913.

An officer together with 3 other ranks training on a recently issued radio in 1913. Radio has always been of vital importance to the Yeomanry.

The Guidon and Escort with Guard of Honour, Blackpool, 1913
Both the Officers, Capt. L. G. S. Molloy (*centre*) and Lieut. H. R. Hornby (*right of picture*) wear the pre-1900 (1883 pattern) full dress tunics with gold lace, gold lace belts and white gauntlets. The uniform of the men is as described earlier. Note the gold laced chevrons, gold embroidered Ducal Coronets and Royal Crowns on the sleeve of the guidon bearer and escort.

late to see the show.' Enemy casualties were not recorded, but A squadron's men suffered none.

On 13 November was fought the splendid Yeomanry action of El Mughar in which squadrons of the Dorsets and Bucks. supported by the Berks. Battery RHA, galloped a commanding ridge, sabred some 600 Turkish infantrymen and took 1,100 prisoners. The DLOY Squadron with the supporting 155 Brigade must have chafed as they sat their horses in a wadi, to watch their fellow-Yeomen earning a renowned Battle Honour.[12] They were even more frustrated when a week later the whole Squadron was temporarily dismounted to serve briefly as infantry with 155 Brigade covering approaches to Jaffa.

General Allenby entered Jerusalem on 9 December 1917, and there now followed a lengthy pause for much-needed recouping, refitting and improvement of rear communications. During this period A Squadron's attachment to the 52nd (Lowland) Division was ended when in April 1918 the Division was withdrawn to embark for France. Before leaving, the Divisional Commander, Major General Hill, sent a kind message to Captain Bates, saying 'Scotland is not a little proud of the little bit of Lancashire which has been temporarily attached to it'. The Squadron still formed an element of XXI Corps Cavalry Regiment, and as this formation now included two Indian infantry divisions to which Troops were periodically attached, the men were able to make first acquaintance with their sepoy brothers-in-arms. During the reorganisation process the Squadron's four Hotchkiss light machine guns were taken from it, to be fitted to four Rolls-Royce armoured cars, the unit being designated No. 2 Light Armoured Car Battery. One DLOY lance- corporal and six men were attached as part of the crews.

Allenby's final offensive was launched on 18 September 1918. During the next week XXI Corps and the Desert Mounted Corps captured Haifa, sending the Turks in full retreat to Beirut and Damascus. But for A Squadron there was only the interminable patrolling and reconnaissance, with no action of consequence. About a month earlier, Lieutenant Neville Percival had joined, posted in from C Squadron in France, and his MS diary affords a few glimpses of the Squadron's arduous but largely uneventful existence.[13]

> Sept. 19. Our Squadron was much divided up, one Troop being sent to each division. No. 4 Troop under [Lieut A. L.] Paramor had the most exciting time jumping trenches and barbed wire with the infantry attack and by ill luck just missed capturing a battery of Turkish guns. [This was during the initial advance on Haifa.] All ranks employed escorting back prisoners . . . the Turkish field cashier was caught with £10,000 in gold.
>
> Sept. 26. Our scattered Troops return . . . and the Regt [XXI Corps Cav. Regt.] is ordered to proceed at once to Acre with a view to advance on Beirut. We march at 1300 due north through a desolate country and enter the pass of Megiddo at dusk. Many dead horses lying about. Reach Lejjun at far end of pass at 2100. Distance 23 miles.

12. Only six days earlier, at Huj, weak squadrons of the Warwickshire and Worcestershire Yeomanry had performed a truly Balaclava-like charge to capture a complete battery of field guns and rout two battalions of infantry.
13. Lieutenant N. F. Percival's diary, which also includes some account of his services in France, forms part of a bulky scrapbook preserved in the Regimental Museum. (ref. LANOY 29/20).

> 27 Sept. Sqdn march through plain of Esdraelon at daybreak ... Terrific heat and dust and no water. At Midday halt I go on ahead to Haifa and pass Sherwood Rangers who are off to Damascus. Find water in a spring, but polluted by dead horses. We camp at Haifa. Distance 21 miles.

On 30 September, XXI Corps Cavalry Regiment was ordered to form an independent 'Cavalry Group' with the Light Armoured Car Battery and the 1/8th Gurkha Rifles, tasked to advance along the coast to Beirut. There was no opposition, and with A Squadron as advance guard Beirut was reached on 8 October. The inhabitants, who had no love for their Turkish overlords, gave the British soldiers an enthusiastic reception.

> Oct 9. Infantry Bde with 1st Bn Seaforths arrive after heavy marching and we line the streets while they march through the town. I buy whisky and soda for 8s! At Beirut our racehorse 'Tango' dies of colic. He was one of the horses bought by Major Bibby for Yeomanry work before the war. [He was one of the very few English horses who had survived thus far.]

By this time Squadron Headquarters had marched 181 miles since 19 September, but individual Troops had covered much longer distances. According to the War Diary, the horses (now mostly Australian Walers) had stood up well and only two were broken down and had to be destroyed.

> Oct 12. Regiment [XXI Corps] plus two armoured cars and with 48 hours rations (on horse) marched 0600 with orders to reach Tripoli, distant about 70 miles, in two days. Stifling heat. No water. Continue marching until 1900 when we reach Madfan. No water ...

> Oct 13. Halt at Sheik Aatik, midday, very hot and several men bad with fever. In afternoon we trek across side of mountain, very rocky and I lose two hind shoes. After about six miles of this we halt, men absolutely dead beat. Then we have better going flat ground ... The DLO Sqdn and C Sqdn Herts reach Tripoli about 2000.

> The inhabitants express much delight at our arrival, but no material assistance is forthcoming and we sleep on market square and buy coffee at 2s per cup.

On 26 October elements of the 5th Cavalry Division entered Aleppo to find that the Turks, harried by pro-British Syrians, had withdrawn. Thus the campaign's last objective was secured without a shot being fired. Now completely demoralised (and largely deserted by German and Austrian allies) the Turkish High Command sued for peace and the Armistice was signed on 1 November. Lieutenant Percival estimated that in their final advance commencing on 19 September, A Squadron had ridden more than 400 miles, including the constant patrolling 'so that everyone was rather pulled down and easy victims to malaria'. On 12 November the War Diary reported that sickness had reduced the effective strength from 114 rank-and-file to 64. Ten days later the depleted Squadron was withdrawn to Beirut, where officers and men went into a pleasant camp in a nearby pine forest, there to await orders for repatriation.

The four-year campaign had seen several changes of officers with postings in and out (and two deaths), but at this final date the roll was as under:

>Captain D. H. Bates (*Commanding*)
>Captain N. F. Percival (*2nd-in-Command*)
>Lieutenant A. L. Paramor (Bedfordshire Yeo. – Attd)
>Lieutenant J. C. S. Malcolm (Lancashire Hussars – Attd)
>Lieutenant A. Byford
>2nd Lieutenant T. Davies

Of those who had embarked with the Squadron in September 1914, only Captain Bates remained.

It took nearly three months for repatriation to be completed, as successive drafts were despatched according to their length of service overseas. Captain Percival and his draft of 100 men did not reach Southampton until February 1919, while one detachment were even longer in seeing home. In December 1918 30 men and horses under 2nd Lieutenant Davies were sent north to act as mounted police in the Taurus Mountains of Turkey, where there was sporadic guerilla activity. There is no record of their doings, but they remained out there until August 1919.

Men might be repatriated but horses were not. To the shame of the British Government, the 20,000–odd which had survived the campaign were ordered to be cast and sold off in Egypt, thus saving the expense of transport home. The great majority ended their days as beasts of burden in the bazaars of Cairo or in stone quarries, lame, galled, half-starved, and treated as Orientals are wont to treat their domestic animals. This scandal prompted Mrs Geoffrey Brooke, wife of the Brigadier commanding the post-war cavalry brigade in Egypt, to organise the 'Old War Horse Fund' which secured a hospital and rest home for the still surviving horses which could be bought back from their callous owners. Some 5,000 ex-Army horses were thus rescued, many in such dreadful condition that they had to be put down, but the rest were able to end their lives in ease and comfort. Dorothy Brooke died in 1955, but her foundation lived on, and since 1961 has become widely known as the Brooke Hospital for Animals, Cairo, which continues its work of mercy to this day.

In view of their continuous campaigning from 1914 to 1918, A Squadron DLOY suffered relatively light casualties. As already mentioned, Major H. L. Bibby was drowned when the troopship carrying him back from sick leave was torpedoed in the Mediterranean. Lieutenant P. J. Crook was killed in action, and 16 other ranks were killed or died of wounds or sickness.

Honours and Awards were as under:

MC

Captain D. H. Bates
Lieutenant A. L. Paramor (*Bedfordshire Yeo. – Attd*)

DCM

Sergeant T. B. Hindle
,, J. S. Meredith

MM

Sergeant E. W. Jackson
,, A. L. Jarvis
Private P. H. Abbot

In addition, Captain Bates, Lieutenant Paramor and Lieutenant C. R. Hartley received Mentions in Despatches, while Lieutenant C. F. Clark was awarded the Croix de Guerre.

A total of 23 Battle Honours were granted to complete regiments or battalions which fought in Egypt and Palestine, but as observed above, since The Duke of Lancaster's Own Yeomanry contributed only the one squadron while Regimental Headquarters was elsewhere, in France, their applications for certain Honours were refused by the War Office Committee. And so today the Regiment has none to display for those four years of campaigning.

Part 2. France and Flanders

We have seen that when A Squadron embarked for active service in Egypt in September 1914, B Squadron was broken up and C and D with RHQ, were retained in England where they continued until the following year.

In September 1914 a young Oxford graduate, Basil Sanderson, had been unsuccessfully endeavouring to enlist as an Army despatch rider (he was a keen horseman), when he received a letter from his brother 'Winchy', then a 2nd Lieutenant in The Duke of Lancaster's.[1]

> Winchy wrote to me with his colonel's approval, asking whether I would accept a commission in the Duke of Lancaster's Own Yeomanry, to which I immediately answered 'Yes' ... To my delight I received orders to join the Regiment at Scarisbrick in Lancashire and duly arrived about 20 September ... The Regiment was recruited solely from Lancashire and its peacetime headquarters was in Manchester. C Squadron to which I was posted was largely composed of clerks from Manchester and district, and I personally have never seen a finer or more intelligent body of men.

---

1. Basil Sanderson later became Lord Sanderson of Ayot and as such wrote his autobiography *Ships and Sealing Wax* (1967) from which, and his unpublished diary, much of the following is derived. His brother was named Harold Winchester but within the family he was always known as 'Winchy'.

Within a month C and D Squadrons and RHQ said farewell to Lancashire for the duration of the war when they were moved south to Sussex, going under canvas in Buckhurst Park, Withyham, near Crowborough. Here, under Lieutenant-Colonel R. H. Tilney, TD, Commanding, they commenced intensive training for an eagerly expected posting to join the Expeditionary Force in France. But no such posting arrived, and when another move was ordered, in October, it was merely one of a few miles, to Maresfield and a hutted camp. This was certainly an improvement on canvas during the cold and wet December and January, but the 260-odd horses were picketed in the open. 'Anyone with experience of open horse lines during winter months in this country will understand my saying that gumboots were regularly sucked off the wearer while going round the lines.' (Sanderson) If the Yeomen were inconvenienced, their horses were even more so. Permanently over fetlocks in mud, they inevitably suffered cracked heels and mud fever which no amount of treatment could cure in the absence of dry standings. The lines were constantly moved, but with only temporary improvement, for they quickly became as poached as ever.

In March 1915 came relief with yet another change of scenery, to Forest Row near East Grinstead and 'a lovely camp with huts and stalls . . . and we began to look clean for the first time for months'. And with horses under cover their condition soon picked up.

All this while, fellow-Yeomen had been in action and earning Battle Honours at Messines, Ypres, Neuve Chapelle and elsewhere on the Western Front. But The Duke of Lancaster's two squadrons could only chafe as they carried out training much as they had done in peacetime camps, together with the old routine of 'stables', exercise (of horses), kit and saddlery inspections, camp fatigues and the rest. It seemed that they were forgotten by High Command.

But at last came the long-awaited orders. In April D Squadron was sent off to join the 14th Infantry Division at Aldershot, to function as their Divisional Cavalry regiment, and in June RHQ and C Squadron were posted in similar role to the 13th Division, also at Aldershot but destined for the Middle East. Now with A Squadron remote in Egypt, the Regiment was completely dismembered: C and D were not to meet up again for another year, while of course, A was not seen until after the war. C Squadron's expectations of desert warfare were quashed when in August they were ordered to leave the 13th Division and join the 23rd, under orders for France. The Division was commanded by Major-General J. M. Babington, 'an elderly but fearless man who was universally popular', wrote Sanderson. The General was an ex-cavalryman (16th Lancers), and during the intensive spell of divisional training he was wont to bestow embarrassing attention on his only mounted unit. 'Whenever he had a moment to spare he gave way to his homing instinct to come and inspect the "Yeoboys" as he termed us. This may have been good for our souls but was rather trying in other ways.' (Sanderson)

Since D Squadron preceded C across the Channel, we must attempt to follow their fortunes first. And at once it has to be admitted that records of their services are scant in the extreme; in fact, the sole extant source is the official War Diary manuscript, which is little more than a barren chronology of movements, fatigues and other duties, with not a single reference to any action of consequence. However, we learn that the Squadron disembarked at Le Havre on 23 May 1915, still as Divisional Cavalry to the 14th Division.

The strength was seven officers, 129 other ranks (plus two RAMC orderlies attached) and 140 horses. The officers were as under:

        Major F. C. A. Hurt[2] *Commanding*
        Captain J. W. Fitzherbert-Brockholes *Second-in-Command*
        Lieutenant J. Stanning
              „   J. A. Grierson
        2nd Lieutenant P. Boddington
              „   C. Gwyer
              „   H. Tatton

Just as A Squadron had discovered in Palestine, Divisional Cavalry regiments in France tended to be regarded as general dogsbodies, subjected to humble if necessary tasks more fitting for a labour battalion than a cavalry squadron. And since the combatants had now burrowed into trenches in battle zones dominated by artillery, machine guns and barbed wire, even mounted reconnaissance patrols were not in the order of things. Thus, for the first year of their active service D Squadron found themselves acting as little other than a pool of personnel for fatigues and other inglorious chores, as a few extracts from the monotonous War Diary will show.

30/5/15	Found digging party 5 officers and 80 men improving trench at Zillebeke
4/6/15	1 officer 24 OR making dugout at 13 Bde HQ
7/6/15	2 officers 59 OR entrenching E of Zillebeke
29/6/15	1 officer 60 OR to Ypres to dig cable trench
23/7/15	1 officer 30 OR relieved Salvage party of Cyclist Coy.[3]
3/9/15	1 officer 110 OR relieved Salvage Squad
24/9/15	4 officers 25 OR to trenches as escort for prisoners
1/10/15–1/12/15	[Parties of] 30 OR working parties for 6 Corps RE park
23/12/15	53 OR bringing remounts (mules) for Field Remount Dept.
1/2/16–21/2/16	14 OR Police patrol 33 OR Salvage work
1/3/16–13/3/16	NIL
20/3/16	25 OR Coal fatigue at Saultey 22 OR Fatigue at Hauteville
19/5/16	1 officer 28 OR Police Duties 34 Div. 50 OR Squadron training

Such unheroic activities do not warrant a detailed itinerary of D Squadron's wandering across the Western Front during this period. But what the jejune War Diary unaccountably fails to record, is that on 14 May 1916 the Squadron was pulled back to a base camp near Boulogne, where it met its erstwhile comrades of C Squadron, likewise withdrawn. The two were then joined with C Squadron of the Surrey Yeomanry to form III Corps Cavalry Regiment – as related later.

2. Francis Hurt was a newcomer to the Regiment, having been posted in only in September 1914. His previous service had been with The Royal Welch Fusiliers.
3. Cyclist Companies were largely dismounted Yeomen, and 'Salvage' duties included the grim task of recovering dead bodies, identifying and burying them.

We must now revert to August 1915 with C Squadron at Aldershot as Divisional Cavalry to the 23rd Division. On the 27th of that month they embarked with the rest of the Division at Southampton ' . . . for the distant war which most of us thought we should never see', as Sanderson scribbled in his diary.[4] Accompanying the Squadron was Regimental Headquarters: Lieutenant-Colonel R. H. Tilney, CO, Major L. G. S. Molloy, Second-in-Command, and Captain E. W. Love, Adjutant. Commanded by Major W. E. Royds (late 7th Hussars) C Squadron mustered six officers, 139 other ranks and 144 horses.

Disembarking at Le Havre on 28 August, men and horses entrained for St Omer, and arriving the next morning, the squadron rode through pelting rain to their first French billets at a nearby village.

By now the bloody battles of Second Ypres had been fought, with heavy Allied losses and there was a period of stalemate, neither side prepared for another major offensive. The 23rd Division was holding a sector between Armentieres and Neuve Chapelle, and as the Divisional Cavalry, C Squadron (with RHQ) were moved up to the village of Steenwerck, about five miles west of Armentieres, where they were based throughout the winter. Like D Squadron they were given no chance of action, mounted or otherwise, but instead had to submit to fatigues and odd jobs: unloading coal barges on the Lys river and brick wagons at a railway siding; escorts to ammunition and rations columns, the occasional jog to forward positions to herd back prisoners. All very necessary tasks, but hardly those for which horse-soldiers had been trained.

However, there were compensations. There were weatherproof billets in a market garden complex, officers comfortable in the proprietor's house, men in heated greenhouses and even horses under cover – in former potting sheds. On the principle of 'all work and no play . . .' the officers devised a novel form of mounted sport. It all began with Basil Sanderson, who with a few others organised exhilarating gallops across country in pursuit of hares with which the locality abounded. 'We would go out across the fields, extended to about 50 yards apiece, until we put up a hare and then try and gallop him down.' Soon The Duke of Lancaster's 'meets' attracted fields from neighbouring Gunners, and eventually the men were allowed to join in, so that whole Troops were to be seen thundering madly after a jinking 'puss'. Though 'we never caught a hare of course, it was great fun'. But there was an unusual hazard of the chase in the lengths of field telephone cable snaking across the terrain, ready to entangle a horse's legs and send him and rider crashing down. After Captain Greenall had suffered a purler that put him into hospital with a broken collar bone (and subsequent awkward questions from Divisional HQ), it was deemed prudent to call a halt to such diversions.

Soon there was activity of a more martial nature. Since it was now accepted that mounted cavalrymen had no place on the present battlefield, all Yeomanry were committed to

---

4. Not to be confused with his autobiography *Ships and Sealing Wax* (op. cit.), Sanderson's voluminous diary records his doings until January 1917 (the final pages were unfortunately lost). Though much of it is concerned with his detached duties away from C Squadron, it is a lively narrative and does much to amplify the bald pages of the War Diary. The original typescript was presented to the Churchill Archives Centre at Cambridge, but the DLOY Museum holds a copy.

spells as infantrymen in the trenches. At first selected officers were sent up 'to get the hang of things', wrote Sanderson, who in October did a week's tour of duty with the 11th Northumberland Fusiliers in the line near Bois Grenier. Here he distinguished himself by leading night patrols across the wire, to bring in much valuable intelligence. His reputation in this infantry role was such that on returning to base he was somewhat unkindly received by his Squadron Leader. 'I really don't know why you are here at all,' grumbled Major Royds, 'you ought to be a bloody infantryman!'

On 20 November Colonel Tilney was ordered to send successive parties of two officers and 50 men each for duty with the 9th Yorkshire Regiment, also around Bois Grenier. Sanderson led the first, which remained with the Yorkshiremen until December when they were relieved by Lieutenant Neville Percival and his 50 men. Another similar detachment under Sanderson's brother Harold ('Winchy') did a spell with the 69th Infantry Brigade around Chapelle d'Armentieres. This period saw heavy fighting in the battles of Loos in which six Yeomanry regiments earned that Battle Honour in the trenches. The Squadron's War Diary is unenlightening as regards actions and casualties, but since only detachments were in the line, no Battle Honours were forthcoming.

Nevertheless, during their spells in the trenches the Yeomen learned the true meaning of the term 'Poor Bloody Infantry': bitter cold, knee-deep mud, waterlogged and rat-infested dugouts, constant 'hates' by enemy guns and mortars, incessant chattering of machine guns, the recurrent cry of 'stretcher bearers!' and the hazardous tasks of night raids to capture prisoners. At least the Lancashire Yeomen were for the first time able to fire their rifles in anger ' . . . an opportunity of which they took full advantage', wrote Lieutenant Percival.

At any one period about half of C Squadron's strength was thus committed at 'the sharp end', while other details were labouring on the numerous fatigues in rear. But the 150–odd horses back at Steenwerck still had to be watered, fed, groomed and exercised: 'We were always below strength in men, but never in horses,' said Sanderson. So that it was quite common for one trooper to be burdened with the demanding care of ten or more animals, not to mention saddlery. Yet another facet of the questionable policy of employing cavalry as infantry while still retaining the horses. Although admitting that there was no useful role for horsemen under present conditions, High Command (led by Haig, an ex-cavalryman) fondly believed that the mounted arm would eventually gallop through 'the G in Gap' to achieve the cavalry breakthrough. As we have seen, such a consummation was indeed achieved – but far from the Western Front.

As with D Squadron's War Diary, that of C's is less than enthralling, noting only movements, postings in and out, personnel to and from leave, and suchlike domestic details, with no record of serious action, nor even a mention of casualties. In fact, had it not been for Lieutenant Basil Sanderson and his diary, this account would be barren of interest.

On the assumption that all Yeomanry officers were intelligent, well-educated types, and trained to observe, record and accurately report, many of them were now detached from their units to become Observation Officers in the firing line. Their duties were to report back enemy movements, to liaise between own troops and to record the progress of attacks. Thus in March 1916, Sanderson was selected as Observation Officer for the 23rd Division.

By the end of June 1916 the Allies had committed themselves to the Somme offensive, along a front extending from Gommecourt in the north to Foucaucourt south of the Somme river. But meanwhile C Squadron (with RHQ) had been given another role – or rather title, for the role was to remain much the same. On 12 May 1916, they said farewell to the 23rd Division and marched back to a base camp at Beaucourt, near St Omer, where they renewed acquaintance with the long-lost D Squadron, recently arrived. GHQ had now ordered that Divisional Cavalry squadrons were to be combined with others to form complete three-squadron Corps Cavalry regiments, directly under the orders of Corps commanders.

C Squadron's War Diary for 21 May has the laconic entry: 'C Squadron Surrey Yeomanry arrived to complete 3rd Corps Cav. Regt'.

But the transformation was not as simple as that. On arriving at Beaucourt, Sanderson found 'a fine old muddle in progress'. The War Diary omitted to record that the original plan was for the two DLOY squadrons to be joined by one of the Royal Wiltshire Yeomanry, already present. The Wiltshires as a Regiment were of course much senior to The Duke of Lancaster's (actually first in order of Yeomanry precedence), while the Squadron had with them the Commanding Officer, Lieutenant-Colonel Ulrich Thynne. When it was ordered that Thynne should take command there was resentment among the DLOY, and a lengthy domestic wrangle began. It was pointed out to GHQ that although the Wiltshires enjoyed pride of place in the Army List, they were represented only by one squadron and no RHQ, while the DLOY contributed two squadrons, plus their RHQ. 'It was obviously wrong', wrote Sanderson, 'that we should be under command of their Colonel who was also junior by two years to ours . . . The whole affair seemed a damned muddle by some fool at GHQ, who must have put all the Squadrons in France in a hat, and drawn them out regardless.' It so happened that Colonel Tilney was absent on local leave at the time, but an urgent signal brought him hurrying back to add his weight in the dispute.

After about a week of suspense in all, orders came at last. 'Ulrich was to go and take his squadron with him to XV Corps, where two squadrons of South Irish Horse completed his regiment. We stayed where we were, and got a squadron of the Surrey Yeomanry to complete us. They arrived soon after, and proved a very nice lot.' And so, on 24 May the III Corps Cavalry Regiment was formed from C and D Squadrons DLOY and C Squadron Surrey Yeomanry, with Lieutenant-Colonel R. H. Tilney in command.[5]

The first action for the combined Regiment came with the long- rumoured 'Great Push', or the British-French offensive of the Somme. This opened on 1 July 1916 with the dreadful loss of 57,000 men for the gain of about half a mile of frontage. But the Regiment was

---

5. Strange that C Squadron's War Diary should make no reference to The Royal Wiltshire dispute, since all entries were signed by Colonel Tilney himself.

spared the carnage of the initial attack, being ordered to take over a sector of support line trench near La Boiselle (having left their horses back at Dernancourt). The position was 'not alluring', wrote Sanderson. On their front the 34th Division's attack had been repulsed with crippling casualties and a German counter-attack seemed inevitable. As usual, the Regiment's strength was severely depleted, with men left behind in the horse lines and two whole Troops being detached on police duties in rear. All they could muster for the firing line were three officers and 60 men with six Hotchkiss guns. They were to be joined in the trenches by a battalion of the Lincolnshire Regiment, but on arrival they found that this comprised just two officers and 87 men, all that remained of the 600-odd who had gone over the top that morning. This puny force of 150 men was expected to 'hold' nearly a mile of trenches against the threatened attack. Fortunately, however, no such attack developed, for the Germans were otherwise occupied. Subjected to heavy shelling, the Yeomen saw the infantry of the 19th Division advancing on their left as part of Haig's second assault. Said Sanderson: 'I watched the first three lines move over No Man's Land. After going a couple of hundred yards they suddenly went down one after another, just as if they had been mown with a scythe. It made me feel absolutely sick.' The next few days brought other sickening experiences:

> The left of the line was always a nasty place in those days. For about 400 yards SE of Munster Alley all our trenches got shelled night and day with 5.9s, very heavily at times, and the result was that one day you found a trench in a certain spot and the next there wasn't a sign of it ... The smell round this portion of the line was perfectly appalling. What with the Bosch and us, several hundred men had been killed at one time or another. Some of these had been buried, some not. Not that that mattered much, as the shells blew up all those who had been buried and buried those who hadn't, alternatively. And what was worse, any bit of decaying flesh anywhere on the surface was always covered with large green bluebottles; so covered that you could not see any sign of the leg, arm, head or whatever it was. These rose in clouds when you got up to them, and invariably flew into your face. Ugh! ...
>
> When I went round the Intermediate line the next day I wondered how they [6th Camerons] had ever stuck it. It was like Munster Alley at its worst: arms, heads, legs and trunks lying everywhere.

Surprisingly, the constant shelling with HE by the 5.9 in. (15 cm.) howitzers caused little damage, other than to trenches, for the few men were widely dispersed along the line, but air-burst shrapnel was another matter, serving to highlight a serious defect in equipment – no steel helmets. These had already been issued to infantrymen but not to Yeomanry, who were always the last to receive new issues. When two of his men had suffered fatal head wounds, Sanderson bravely led a foraging party of volunteers across the wire to strip helmets off dead infantrymen, and managed to collect sufficient for the DLOY squadron.

After four days and nights in the trenches, the III Corps Cavalry Regiment was pulled back to Dernancourt and here it had the novel (and not entirely welcome) experience of witnessing a huge railway-mounted gun hurling its 12 in. shells at Bapaume in the German rear. Every time the monster fired, the blast ripped off tiles in Dernancourt village, flattened the tents of some Sappers encamping nearby, and caused their horses to bolt in panic.

Having been puzzled to learn that the gun detachment amounted to 70 men, and unable to imagine what they could all do, Lieutenant Sanderson went to observe a shoot.

> ... Two men opened the breech, one checked the dial [sight], while two more operated the elevating gear. Then a trolley was wheeled along from the next coach to the breech of the gun, with a shell on it. That took eight men. Eight more men came along with a long ramrod & pushed the shell into the breech. The trolley rolled back again, and pushed by four fresh men, reappeared with three colossal slabs of cordite. This was pushed in in its turn & the breech closed, when all the other various men assisted in the laying of the gun. I was standing on top of one of the coaches in the rear, with my fingers in my ears, & even then when the thing did fire, the shock I got nearly toppled me off.

A friend of his in the 9th Yorkshires nearby told him that every time the gun went off his camp bed jumped six inches in the air.[6]

The third offensive of the Somme took place in September 1916, and this saw the first appearance of the 'secret weapon' that was to banish the cavalryman's horse – the tank. Haig over-ruled wiser counsels by prematurely demanding 40-odd of these 'caterpillar machine-gun destroyers' to support his assault of 15 September. Still not thoroughly proven, and with half-trained crews, they were launched into battle in driblets instead of being massed as originally proposed. They were largely unsuccessful. As a horsed cavalryman, Sanderson had scant respect for these new-fangled mechanical monsters.

> [The Somme, 15 Sept. 1916] As regards the tanks, the ones on our front didn't do very much. The female[7] never got to the starting point at all, and the male tank got stuck about every 20 yards. Eventually, in the afternoon, it got as far as Martinpuich and rolled into the remains of a house, which it knocked down; and then, seeming to be satisfied with this, waddled home again. Here it was caught and made to carry up some ammunition, which was the only useful thing it did that day. We had a good laugh, however, at about 12 o'clock as we got a report that a tank had been seen waddling into Flers, followed by a crowd of Tommies walking along the main road, waving their hats in the air and cheering. It seemed such a ridiculous idea.

Ridiculous or no, the report was true. Tank D17 (Lieutenant Hastie) drove straight through the German-held village of Flers spreading panic among the defenders, who were mopped up by the following infantry.[8]

6. Sanderson, of course, did not know that this British railway gun was one of only two in service in France. The first was built in 1915 by the Vickers concern, the second in 1916 by the Elswick Ordnance Company. The latter was probably the one seen by Sanderson. (Ian Hogg: *The Guns 1914–18* (1971))
7. The 'female' of the species (Tank Mark I) was armed only with five machine guns. The more potent 'male' had two 6-pounder QF guns in sponsons and four machine guns.
8. This incident, remembered by the present Royal Tank Regiment, is described in Captain Basil Liddell Hart's *The Tanks: The History of The Royal Tank Regiment* (Vol. I, 1959).

In October 1916 Sanderson left III Corps Cavalry Regiment for further staff duties, first with the 23rd Division, then with the 42nd, finally with the 41st, and from now on his diary though interesting enough, has nothing to say about the DLOY squadrons. Which is sad, for as seen, it has done much to enliven this account, and in the inexplicable absence of the War Diary after May 1916 little can be said about the Squadron's activities until it became part of the 12th Manchester Regiment in 1917.

But before our Regimental diarist departs these pages he warrants a valedictory. Basil Sanderson was undoubtedly one of the DLOY's finest wartime officers, although never achieving high rank. Conscientious and utterly fearless, he was also modest, and as his writings make clear, tended to laugh off his many hazardous observation exploits as 'great fun'. But these were to earn him the MC and Bar, to become the only DLOY officer so doubly decorated. The Citation for his Bar in the *London Gazette* of 16 September 1918 reads:

> For conspicuous gallantry and devotion to duty. During a heavy engagement this officer went forward with complete disregard for his own safety under heavy shellfire to clear up the situation which at the time was obscure. He returned with very valuable information. He performed his staff duties under the most trying circumstances cheerfully and with cool and skilful precision on all occasions.

Sanderson was also awarded the Belgian Croix de Guerre. Finishing the war as Captain, 41st Division, he retired in 1920 to embark on a distinguished civilian career in shipping and finance: Chairman of the Shaw Savill line, Director of the Bank of England, President of the International Shipping Federation, High Sheriff, County of London. In 1960 he was created Baron Sanderson of Ayot, the only 20th-century member of the DLOY to be raised to the Peerage. Lord Sanderson died at his home of Ayot Bury near Ayot St Peter in 1971, aged 77. In the same year his son, Dr Alan Sanderson, disclaimed the title.

To revert to the Western Front, the year 1917 saw the fierce and costly battles of Arras, Messines and Third Ypres, which after three terrible months floundered to an indecisive halt in the shell-torn mud and blood around the ruins of Passchendaele. During these struggles the III Corps Cavalry Regiment was, as usual, frittered away on various familiar tasks: Troops for mounted police duties, escorts for prisoners, detachments relieving infantrymen in the trenches. The DLOY element served thus during the Ypres battles, thereby earning another Battle Honour for the Regiment. Since their Surrey comrades comprised only a single squadron and no RHQ, they did not qualify. The climax of the year's fighting came on 20 November with Haig's attempt to smash through the Hindenburg Line around Cambrai – a name now chiefly remembered as the first battle in which massed tanks were employed. It also brought the opportunity for which the cavalry had long been waiting: to ride through 'the G in Gap'. No fewer than five cavalry divisions were present (all of them Regular), but owing to the failure to follow up and consolidate initial gains (and with conflicting orders), the horsemen were unable to achieve a breakthrough, and after a massive German counter-attack the offensive petered out on 4 December, when the British Third Army had lost some 44,000 killed and wounded, for no gains.

Neither the DLOY squadrons nor their III Corps Cavalry Regiment had any share in the Cambrai offensive, for in June of that year the Regiment had ceased to exist as such. On 27 June, at Dernancourt, the three component squadrons were informed that they were finally to lose their horses and convert to infantrymen - a traumatic decision for them, but one which was not entirely unsuspected. The horses were sent off to remount depots, whence some were absorbed by units remaining mounted in France, while others were shipped out East to join General Allenby's Yeomanry and Anzac horsemen in Palestine. Officers and men were then withdrawn to the Base Depot at Beaucourt for a course of intensive infantry training, at the end of which their fate was announced. In August C and D Squadrons of the DLOY were ordered to join the 12th (Service) Battalion The Manchester Regiment; C Squadron of the Surrey Yeomanry was to be absorbed by the 10th (Service) Battalion The Royal West Surrey Regiment. At least if such a metamorphosis had to be, both Lancastrians and Surreys would now serve with friends from their native counties.

On 24 September 1917 the 12th Manchesters, having suffered heavily in the Ypres battles, were recouping behind the lines at Hauteville near Avesnes, and on that date their War Diary included the following entry:

> A Draft of 7 officers and 125 OR from the 1st DLOY and another of 59 OR from Manchester Regt. joined Bn.

The seven officers were later named as under:

> Major W. E. Royds (late OC C Sqn)
> Captain T. B. Forwood
>   ,,   J. E. Greenall
> Lieutenant C. Gwyer
> 2nd Lieutenant H. Jameson
>   ,,   M. F. Drinkwater
>   ,,   N. G. Hill

On 27 October two more DLOY officers joined the Battalion: Lieutenant P. Boddington and 2nd Lieutenant J. H. Holdridge.

From now on, and until after the Armistice, The Duke of Lancaster's lost not only their cavalry status, but their title as a distinctive regiment. But there was a sop to their pride when shortly after their arrival the title of the Battalion was altered to '12th (D.L.O.Y.) Battalion The Manchester Regiment' and remained thus to the end of hostilities. The Commanding Officer was Lieutenant-Colonel T. W. Bullock (Manchester Regiment). Lieutenant-Colonel Robert Tilney of the DLOY was recalled home to take command of the 2nd Line Regiment in Ireland. At the age of 52 he was considered somewhat elderly for a regimental or battalion command in the field. But his services earned him a DSO (gazetted 6 June 1917), and nominally he continued to be listed as Commanding Officer of the DLOY until he retired in 1919.

While we have seen that the Manchester Battalion absorbed nine DLOY officers and 125 other ranks, it is obvious that the total strength of C and D Squadrons (and RHQ) must have numbered considerably more than that, so the question arises, what became of the others? Although perhaps not the definitive answer, a clue is provided by the Regimental Roll of Honour. In addition to those of the 12th (DLOY) Manchester Battalion, this lists 42 NCOs and men who fell while serving with various other battalions between June 1917 and November 1918. It thus seems reasonable to assume that the 'missing' remainder were dispersed among these other units.[9]

The 12th Manchesters were an element of the 52nd Infantry Brigade, their comrades being the 10th Lancashire Fusiliers and 9th Duke of Wellington's Regiment. The Brigade was under command of the 17th (Northern) Division, which also included the 50th and 51st Brigades, so that all the ex-DLOY members were now serving in the same Division.

The only sources for the 12th (DLOY) Battalion's services until the Armistice are the War Diaries and an unpublished typescript history.[10] The latter consists almost entirely of verbatim extracts from the former, and although recording movements, casualty figures and reinforcements, it is scarcely more readable than the official document.

During the previous fierce fighting at Arras, Scarpe and in Third Ypres the 12th Manchesters had been severely mauled, suffering more than 460 killed and wounded, and they were now withdrawn to Proven in order to recoup. But the respite was short-lived, for in early November the bloody battle of Passchendaele saw all reserves hastened up to the front. On 9 November the Battalion relieved the 6th Northumberland Fusiliers in the line near the Turenne crossing, to be greeted by heavy shelling from the fearsome 5.9s. At the ironically-named Tranquille Farm C Company suffered the brunt, losing one officer and eight other ranks killed and three officers and 23 wounded, while one officer and 16 other ranks were missing, believed killed. On the next day another seven men were killed and 23 wounded.

The first offensive of Cambrai (with its historic massed tanks attack) was fought out between 20 November and 4 December, the British losing all ground gained in the initial assault. But the 12th (DLOY) Battalion was not engaged, being on the support line south of Flesquieres, and so suffered no casualties. January 1918 found the Battalion still with 52nd Brigade between Havrincourt and Flesquieres, repulsing enemy attacks without loss to themselves, and, less gloriously, providing working parties to carry up RE material (wire, trench boards and the like) to the trenches. On 10 January D Company were caught by a German 5.9 'hate', which killed and wounded several, among the latter being Lieutenant P. Boddington, their first officer to be positively identified as ex-DLOY.[11] In February the Battalion went into Divisional Reserve at Havrincourt, to indulge in much-needed baths and a general clean-up, but as the War Diary records, there were chores to be performed: 100 men were sent up to the forward area 'for burying cable'. Also, 2nd Lieutenant J. H. Holdridge (DLOY) was selected to take up duties with 17

9. They were: Lancashire Fusiliers, Border Regiment, South Lancashire Regiment, Sherwood Foresters, East Lancashire Regiment, The Manchester Regiment (50th, 51st, and 52nd Brigades).
10. '12th (Service) Battalion The Manchester Regiment in France and Flanders', compiled by H. C. Bardsley and now held by the Tameside Archive Service, Stalybridge.
11. In recording officer casualties neither the War Diary nor Bardsley's unpublished history identifies ex-DLOY members.

Division HQ as 'Divisional Agricultural Officer'. What such unlikely tasks involved is not revealed, but they were evidently deemed appropriate for a Yeomanry officer.

Back in the line again forward of Havrincourt, the Battalion was subjected to repeated attacks during March, all of which were repulsed, but not without casualties. On 22 March four successive attacks were beaten off, for the loss of one officer and 30 other ranks. On the following day shellfire killed another officer and 25 men, and worse quickly followed. At 2.15 p. m. on the 24th the CO of the 20th London Regiment reported that the battalion on his right had broken and the enemy were following through in force. While the Londoners withdrew, the DLOY Battalion stood fast to protect the right flank, which they gallantly did for more than an hour, enfiladed by machine-gun fire and heavily shelled by a 5.9 battery which had unlimbered in full view to their front. The position was critical: having been constantly in action for three days, the men were exhausted, ammunition was running short and casualties were mounting. The whole of the 52nd Brigade was now ordered to withdraw to Flers, and at 3.50 p. m. the depleted DLOY Battalion struggled back, joining up with the rest of the Brigade after a gruelling five-hour march during which more casualties were suffered. There followed a series of moves and actions to plug gaps in the line, until on 31 March the 52nd Brigade were concentrated around Albert. The War Diary of the DLOY Battalion recorded that the last ten days' fighting had cost the Battalion one officer killed, six wounded and two missing; 17 other ranks were killed, 102 wounded and 108 other ranks were missing, some of the latter subsequently being reported prisoners-of-war.

By this date the Germans were preparing for their final attempt to break the Allied line and their attack on the Albert sector fell on 4 April, to be repulsed after heavy fighting. But the Battalion was not in action here, for on 2 April it was withdrawn to V Corps reserve, first at Villarsbocage and then Canaples, where it welcomed much-needed reinforcements of seven officers and 283 men, chiefly from the South Lancashire and Manchester Regiments.

Although the War Diary dutifully records the activities of the Battalion during the final months of the war, it is bald indeed (like so many others), and it would be tedious and unrewarding to follow suit. However, in October 1918 when the Allies drove back the Germans beyond their vaunted Hindenburg Line, the Battalion distinguished itself at the crossing of the Selle river. This obstacle, defended by MG emplacements, was more than twenty yards wide and four feet deep. All the bridges had been destroyed by the retreating enemy. The Battalion was ordered to get across as best as it could. Under heavy fire from machine guns and 5.9s, the Battalion bravely struggled across with some Sappers, and while the latter attempted to erect a temporary bridge the remainder pushed forward across a railway to their first objective of high ground near the village of Neuville. The War Diary continues:

> On the right the D of W[12] did not get further than the Rly; thus our right flank was very much in the air all day and we were in great danger of a serious counter attack. The Bn detailed to mop up the village were not able to clear it of the enemy entirely, and this fact made our position even more delicate.

12. 9th Bn Duke of Wellington's Regiment.

In addition the enemy accurately shelled our forward positions and made things very uncomfortable. 2 Coys of 7th East Yorks were placed at disposal of our CO as well as one Coy of 10th LFs . . . The former were on their way to a position East of the village when the enemy put down a very heavy box barrage . . . Our troops in front were no longer able to hold the hill crest and were literally blown out of the small trenches where they had consolidated. This unfortunately involved a withdrawal to the level of the troops on our right (9th D of W) who had still failed to cross the Rly. Many casualties were caused during the withdrawal and previous bombardment.

After retiring further to a position on the River Selle, almost back to the start line, the sadly mauled force held off German attempts to overrun it, until in the evening the whole were relieved by the 51st Brigade and withdrawn to Inchy. As the War Diary recorded, it had been 'one of the most strenuous days in the history of the Battalion'. And also one of the most costly. Eleven officers and 269 men had been killed, wounded or captured and the effective strength was now down to four officers (CO, Adjutant, MO and one Company officer) and 300-odd men. But one German officer and 49 other ranks had been captured.

Fierce fighting along the line of the Selle continued to 25 October, when after losing Le Cateau the Germans were pushed back to Valenciennes, which was taken on 2 November. But the DLOY Battalion's losses at the first Selle crossing rendered it scarcely capable of playing an active part until it had a chance of recouping. Back at Inchy, and then Orvillers, several reinforcements were received from home, many of the men being 'green' young soldiers with no more than three months' service, while some were drafted from Labour battalions.

November 1st found the Battalion still at Orvillers, and here the 17th Division Commander visited to present medals awarded since 25 August. These included one DSO, six MCs. two DCMs and 41 MMs (one with Bar). Frustratingly, neither War Diary nor Bardsley's *History* specifies names.

From now until the Armistice the repleted DLOY Battalion was fully committed to the final Allied offensive which saw the Pursuit to Mons and the German surrender. The Battalion's last action of consequence occurred on 4 November, when together with the 10th Lancashire Fusiliers and 9th Duke of Wellington's it successfully carried the attack on Mormal Wood, though in doing so it lost six officers and 100-odd other ranks. By the 10th the 52nd Brigade had reached Beaufort, expecting further fighting and casualties. But on that day, said the War Diary, 'it was officially reported that the Kaiser had abdicated, and there was not a sound of war all day'. Nor was there the next day.

And so on the eleventh hour of the eleventh month of 1918 the four years of carnage were ended. On the hour the Regimental Band paraded in the village square and after the buglers had sounded the 'Cease Fire', the bandsmen performed British and French National Anthems followed by the Regimental March.[13]

There was no immediate repatriation. The Battalion and its 52nd Brigade spent the next five months on sundry tasks of salvage and releasing German prisoners, and it was not

13. So recorded in the War Diary. This is the first (and only) reference to a band, which must have been one of the Manchester's.

until April 1919 that the remnants of 12 (DLOY) Battalion were posted home to Southampton and demobilisation.

The Great War had cost the 12th Manchester Battalion 124 officers, 2,710 other ranks killed and wounded.[14] In its varied roles as Divisional Cavalry, Corps Cavalry and infantrymen, The Duke of Lancaster's Own Yeomanry lost nine officers and 119 other ranks killed or died of wounds. These are detailed in Appendix I.

The Decorations awarded to A Squadron during their service in Egypt and Palestine have already been noted, but the following is a complete Regimental list.

DSO

Lieutenant-Colonel R. H. Tilney, TD (CO)
Major L. G. S. Molloy (RHQ)

MC

Captain D. H. Bates (A Squadron)
Captain J. W. Fitzherbert-Brockholes (C Squadron)
Major F. Green (RAMC, attd)
Lieutenant B.W. Heaton (D Squadron)
Lieutenant B. Sanderson (C Squadron – also Bar)

DCM

SQMS T. B. Hindle (A Squadron)
L/Cpl J. O'Hara (12 DLOY Bn)
Sgt J. S. Meredith (A Squadron)
Cpl H. Ware (attd 23rd Manchester)

MM

Pte T. Allen
Sgt A. Blythe
Pte J. N. Buckman
Farrier E. Catterall
Cpl C. H. Hay
L/Sgt E. Jackson
Cpl A. L. Jarvis
Sgt G. Reed
Pte E. H. Roberts
Cpl A. Sutherland
Pte R. Whitham

CROIX DE GUERRE (French)

Captain C. F. Clark (A Squadron)

CROIX DE GUERRE (Belgian)

Lieutenant (A/Captain) B. Sanderson MC

14. Bardsley, op. cit.

ITALIAN MEDAL FOR MILITARY VALOUR

SQMS T. B. Hindle DCM (A Squadron)
Sgt W. Sullivan

Part 3. The Reserves

On 31 August 1914 the County Associations of the Territorial Army were ordered to duplicate their units with 2nd Line regiments and battalions. These were to provide reinforcements for their 1st Line partners overseas and also to form a home defence force. In March and April 1915, 3rd Line units were raised, with similar roles. Details of The Duke of Lancaster's two reserve units are scant, so that only a summary of their services is possible.[15]

The 2nd/1st DLOY, as it was known, came into being at Whalley Range, Manchester in September 1914. Like the 1st Line, it was composed of three squadrons, but where these were located is not known. In March 1915 all the 2nd Line Yeomanry were grouped in brigades, and 2 DLOY joined with the 2nd Lines of their peacetime comrades The Lancashire Hussars and Westmorland and Cumberland Yeomanry to form the Western Mounted Brigade. During the following year 2 DLOY sent drafts totalling some 80 men to C and D Squadrons in France. By March 1916 the Western Mounted Brigade had moved north to Cupar in Fife, and in that month the Brigade was redesignated 21st Mounted Brigade, though there was no change in its role. But the following July brought drastic reorganisation for most of the 2nd Line units. These were ordered to hand over their horses and take to the humble bicycle, so that the 21st Mounted Brigade was yet again retitled, as the 21st Cyclist Brigade. Apart from the trauma of parting with their flesh-and-blood mounts, this change involved some intensive retraining (and novel drill), for it was found that no more than about a third of the men had ever bestridden the new steel mounts.[16] But at least bicycles did not need mucking out, feeding, grooming and all the other chores of stable management (did the Farriers become adept at mending punctures?).

During the war a total of fifty-one 2nd and 3rd Line Yeomanry regiments were converted to cyclists. Some of the horses thus released were 'demobbed' and returned to their former owners, many were sent to suffer in France and Flanders, others joined Allenby's mounted units in Egypt and Palestine.

15. This is largely derived from the invaluable work *British Regiments 1914–1918* by Brigadier E. A. James (1978).
16. In August 1916 the Duke of Connaught inspected the troops at Newcastle-upon-Tyne and the recently 're-mounted' Cheshire Yeomanry was selected to represent the Cyclist units. Since no ceremonial drill had been laid down for cyclists 'and as no one could tell it how to manoeuvre a bicycle on a ceremonial parade, it had to invent its own drill. At least no one was able to criticise it.' (Lieut-Col Sir Richard Verdin: *The Cheshire (Earl of Chester's) Yeomanry 1898–1967*(1971).

The 2nd DLOY remained at Cupar with The Lancashire Hussars and Westmorland and Cumberland until the end of 1917, sending out drafts to their 1st Line regiments and dutifully pedalling around the coast of Fife on 'mounted' patrol. This period saw the fourth change of Brigade title when in October 1916 it became 10th Cyclist Brigade. In January 1918 there was a move south to Lincolnshire, 2 DLOY being based at Skegness and Alford. By now most of the reserve Yeomanry units had been relocated in southern Ireland, and in May 1918 2nd DLOY and their Cyclist Brigade joined the others, with the DLOY element posted to the Kerry coast around Tralee. Here they ended their war.

The 3rd Line DLOY was formed in March 1915 – where we do not know, for its records are even sketchier than those of the 2nd Line. But the authority quoted above asserts that in the summer of 1915 it went with the 3rd Line Lancashire Hussars and the Westmorland and Cumberland to Ireland, stationed on the Curragh, where in 1916 it was affiliated to the 10th Reserve Cavalry Regiment. Unlike the 2nd Line, it retained its horses to the end.[17] Here it remained until early 1917, when it moved back to England. And unlike the 2nd Line, 3 DLOY suffered casualties in action, though not against the Germans.

In April 1916 the virulently anti-British faction, the Irish Republican Brotherhood (precursors of the IRA) rose in open revolt in Dublin, and the 'Easter Rising' saw much of the city in flames. The troops on the nearby Curragh were called to put down the outbreak, 3 DLOY being among them. Regrettably, there are no details of their actions, but *The Times* in its issues between May and June 1916 reported several Yeomanry casualties. One of only two officers listed was Lieutenant H. H. Thompson of 3 DLOY, wounded. Three other ranks were killed and nine wounded, but as these were shown merely as 'Yeomanry' it has not been possible to identify those who may have been DLOY members. In January 1917 the Regiment was withdrawn from Ireland and posted to Tidworth, where it was absorbed by the 6th Reserve Cavalry Regiment of the 2nd Reserve Cavalry Brigade. And there its services ended with disbandment in early 1919.

---

17. These Reserve Cavalry Regiments had been formed in 1914, primarily to provide reinforcements for the Regular cavalry. But in June 1915 certain Yeomanry units were affiliated.

Operations of C and D Squadrons DLOY France and Flanders 1915-1918

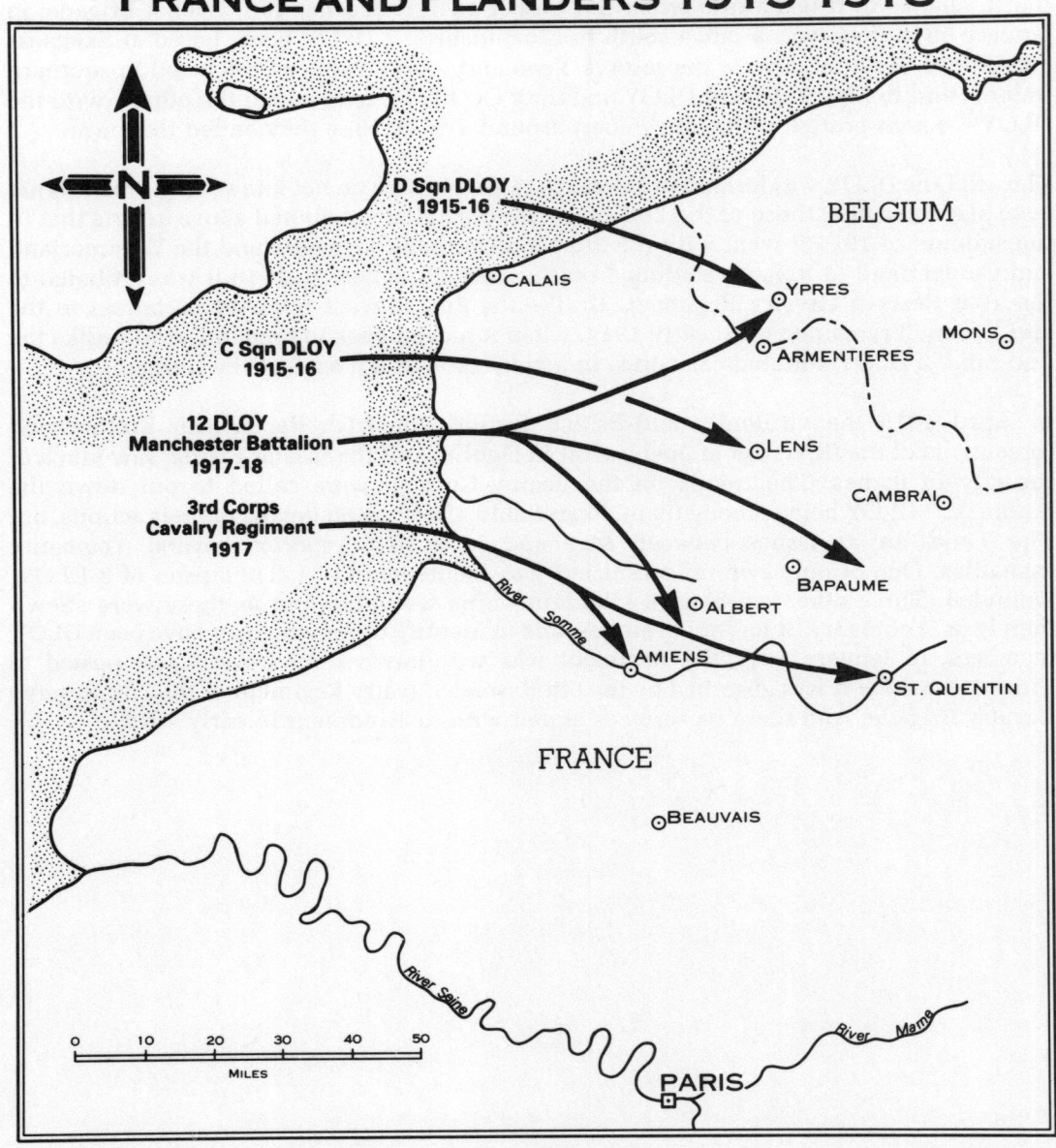

[98]

CHAPTER VII
'Peace In Our Time' 1919–1939

The formal end of hostilities in 1919 saw the virtual extinction (if only temporary) of The Duke of Lancaster's Own Yeomanry. Together with other wartime units, the 12th (DLOY) Battalion of the Manchester Regiment was disbanded, ex-members of the Yeomanry were demobbed, while the Territorial Force itself was placed in 'suspended animation' pending decisions on its future role and organisation. Lieutenant-Colonel R. H. Tilney, DSO, TD, was still nominally Commanding Officer of the DLOY, but all he had to command was a so-called 'cadre' of himself and two Permanent Staff NCOs at the Whalley Range headquarters in Manchester.[1]

It was not until March 1920 that the Territorial Force was reconstituted, with the new designation of Territorial Army, and with radical changes in organisation, especially among Yeomanry. In February of that year a representative committee of Yeomanry Honorary Colonels and commanding officers, under the chairmanship of Lieutenant-General Sir Charles Harington, met at the War Office to debate the future of their regiments.

As we have seen, the pre-war establishment had allowed for 56 distinct regiments, representing practically every county in Great Britain. Of these, 25 were now to be transformed as brigades of the Royal Field Artillery; eight were to become armoured car companies of the Royal Tank Corps, one would convert to infantry, one to a Signals unit. Six regiments would be disbanded or relegated to suspended animation.

Two of those destined to become Gunners were The Duke of Lancaster's Own and the Lancashire Hussars, though it was not until March 1921 that they received their unwelcome orders. The two regiments were combined to form 2nd (Lancashire Yeomanry) Army Brigade Royal Field Artillery under Lieutenant-Colonel Hon. F. W. Stanley, DSO, of the Hussars. With Brigade HQ at Manchester the formation would consist of two 18–pounder gun batteries from the DLOY and three batteries from the Hussars. Naturally, this aroused much heart-searching and not a little dismay among the existing officers who, apart from having to transfer their loyalties to a completely new unit with unfamiliar technical skills to be acquired, deeply resented the loss of their Regimental identities. However, they were all given the option of resigning or transferring to the Territorial Army Reserve, and Lieutenant-Colonel R. H. Tilney chose the former, leaving Lieutenant-Colonel H. M. Hardcastle to take command of the DLOY element of the Brigade.

---

1. In this Chapter all figures for Regimental strengths are derived from the relevant files in the Public Record Office (Ref. WO73/115–143).

Captain D. H. Bates, MC (ex-A Squadron, DLOY), was worried. In a letter to Colonel Stanley he explained that 'however efficient or otherwise I may have been during the War as a Squadron Leader, I know absolutely nothing of the technical side of artillery', besides which, his demanding civilian employment as an executive of the Cunard shipping line would leave him little time for military duties. However, he forbore to resign, eventually to become Commanding Officer and then Honorary Colonel.

Recruiting for other ranks went ahead in Manchester, Bolton and Rochdale, but very few of the original Regiments signed on, while the Adjutant, Major K. M. Agnew (a Gunner) reported in a letter to Bates on 23 March that 'officers are non-existent at the moment'.[2]

However, before the new artillery brigade was fully established and equipped, the War Office underwent a change of thinking, and in May 1921 Colonel Hardcastle received the glad news that his DLOY batteries were to be disbanded and reconstituted as a mounted Yeomanry regiment in their own right. They were one of the fourteen senior regiments so selected, and were to remain mounted until 1941. The complete roll was as under:

1 Royal Wiltshire
2 Warwickshire
3 Yorkshire Hussars
4 Nottinghamshire (Sherwood Rangers)
5 Staffordshire
6 Shropshire
7 Ayrshire
8 Cheshire (Earl of Chester's)
9 Yorkshire Dragoons
10 Leicestershire
11 North Somerset
12 Duke of Lancaster's Own
13 Lanarkshire
14 Northumberland Hussars

The Duke of Lancaster's Own were now the only representatives of the County Palatine to remain as Yeomanry cavalry. Their Lancastrian brethren, The Lancashire Hussars, suffered yet another metamorphosis, this time as 106 (Lancashire Yeomanry) Brigade RFA, with two batteries. By special permission from the War Office, any former officers and men of the Hussars so wishing were allowed to transfer to the reformed DLOY. Many did so. Among the Hussars officers switching allegiance to the DLOY was Major H. A. Bromilow, soon to become Commanding Officer.

The Regiment's role was exactly what it had been in 1914: Divisional Cavalry to the 42nd (East Lancashire) Division, whose headquarters were now at Preston. Reversion to the old familiar duties as mounted cavalry brought a gratifying response from officers and soldier-recruits, so that when the Regiment undertook its first Annual Camp since the war, in July 1922, it mustered thirteen officers and 232 other ranks, with 215 horses.

The Camp was held at Dinarth Hall near Rhyl. A scribbled note in the Regimental archives reveals that 'it poured with rain on most days, but this didn't prevent us from putting in some useful mounted drill and exercises'.

While on training all ranks received Regular rates of pay: a trooper got 2s. per day, a corporal 4s., a sergeant 6s., while the RSM enjoyed 14s. – four shillings more than a 2nd Lieutenant on only 10s. A major received 33s. 6d., the Lieutenant-Colonel 43s. In addition, the horse allowance was £5, unchanged since 1901.

2. The above letters and many others, are extant in the DLOY Museum.

A minor, but welcome, change affecting Regular and Yeomanry private soldiers came with Army Order 222 of 1923, in which the rank designation 'Private' was altered to 'Trooper'. The latter had of course been in common use, unofficially, ever since 1788 when the prestigious Regiments of Horse had been 'demoted' to Dragoons (or Dragoon Guards) and were required to term their men 'Privates'. Now at last the mounted soldier was officially distinguished from the foot-slogging infantryman.

By 1924 the Regiment had increased its strength to 19 officers and 255 other ranks, commanded by Lieutenant-Colonel H. A. Bromilow, TD, with Colonel Sir John Rutherford, TD, as Honorary Colonel.[3] Regimental Headquarters was located at Lancaster House, Whalley Road, Manchester, in premises presented to the Regiment by the former Honorary Colonel, Colonel Percy Hargreaves. There were three Squadrons: the combined A and C Squadrons were based at Whalley Road, B Squadron was dispersed between Bolton and Rainhill (near Liverpool), while D was at Preston and Liverpool. Also at Liverpool was the Machine Gun Troop of one subaltern and 30 men with four Vickers guns carried on pack-horses.

In July-August 1925 the Regiment of 290 all ranks concentrated for Annual Training at Oulton Park, near Tarporley, and hard by at Delamere was the Cheshire Yeomanry, likewise assembled. At once a very friendly liaison developed between the two Regiments, with officers and sergeants entertaining each other in their respective Messes, while Major R. Barbour of the Cheshires threw a ball for all the officers at his nearby country seat. Before break-up there was non-military rivalry in a day of inter- regimental mounted sports, when the Cheshires roundly defeated the DLOY by winning nine of the ten events. Perhaps this reflected the different make-up of the two Regiments. Whereas the Cheshire ranks were almost entirely country lads, bred and born to the saddle, as we have seen the DLOY had recruited from the manufacturing districts of Lancashire and not all the men were yet fully horsewise.

Meanwhile, it was during the early 1920s that The Duke of Lancaster's Own Yeomanry acquired its coveted, and unique, dress distinction. Any one observing the Regiment on ceremonial parade in their Number Two Dress could hardly have failed to notice the glistening chain-link shoulder chains on their tunics. While today all Regular regiments of the Royal Armoured Corps (except the Royal Tank Regiment) wear these embellishments on their blue Number One Dress, The Duke of Lancaster's Own is the only unit permitted to display them on the khaki Number Two Dress (formerly Service Dress).[4]

And at once it has to be confessed that the true origins of this unique distinction are shrouded in mystery. Readers will recall that the Regiment's A Squadron fought as

---

3. Sir John, as Lieutenant-Colonel, had commanded the Regiment from 1906 to 1912.
4. Shoulder chains originated for a strictly utilitarian purpose. During the Indian Mutiny some British officers of the Indian cavalry took to affixing spare curb chains on their shoulders to ward off sword cuts. Later the practice was adopted by the British cavalry, when the 'do-it-yourself' articles were superseded by official issues of purpose-made shoulder chains, very similar to those of today. These were abolished on the outbreak of war in 1914, only to be reintroduced in 1922 – but only for wear on what was then termed 'Blue Patrols', the modern Number One Dress.

mounted cavalry throughout the war in Egypt and Palestine. But as only a single squadron (with no RHQ present) they did not qualify for any of the 22 Battle Honours awarded to more complete units.[5]

Strong Regimental tradition has it that as some recognition of A Squadron's doughty mounted services in four years of campaigning, in lieu of those Battle Honours, the whole Regiment was granted the distinction of wearing shoulder chains on Service Dress.

But despite exhaustive research in Regimental and public archives (including the Public Record Office) the incomprehensible fact remains that the original official authorisation has eluded all attempts to trace it. After the First World War when the Regiment was reduced to a cadre, most documentary material was lost (or destroyed); the first organised depository of Regimental archives was not established until 1987, with the opening of the DLOY Museum in Preston, by which date much of the earlier records had also been dispersed and lost.

However, photographs of the 1920s–1930s in the Museum clearly show that the shoulder chains were certainly in wear throughout that period. And, with successive annual inspections and subsequent reports to the War Office, it seems highly improbable that these conspicuous embellishments could not have been queried if unauthorised.

Surprisingly, it was not until 1953 that the question of authorisation surfaced, with an enquiry from Major Arthur Jones, DLOY, to Colonel D. H. Bates, MC, TD, the then Honorary Colonel (who as Captain had led A Squadron in Palestine). Bates replied as follows:[6]

> Chorlton Hall
> Malpas
> Cheshire
> 27th March, 1953
>
> *My dear J,*
>
> ... I have no record, but I think it was in 1925 that the War Office, who had always been sympathetic to Colonel Tilney's plea for some recognition of 'A' Squadron's service, officially authorized as a 'Special Distinction' the right to wear shoulder chains on our service dress because 'A' Squadron D.L.O.Y. had remained mounted the whole of the war.
>
> I cannot give the precise wording at this interval, but I am sure this was authorized on the above grounds – it was meant to be a kind of consolation prize!

Colonel Bates added that if the question were to be raised by the War Office he would gladly sign a statement testifying to the above. But apparently, no such query arose, which seems to add weight to the Colonel's assertion.[7]

---

5. In 1922 the Honours and Distinctions Committee of the War Office laid down that in order to qualify for a specific Battle Honour a unit must have been present with at least 50 per cent of its effective strength, plus headquarters. Two years later this was modified for a cavalry regiment to two squadrons and RHQ.
6. MS letter in Regimental Museum.
7. In June 1924 a War Memorial window was unveiled in Manchester Cathedral, one pane of which clearly depicted the shoulder chains. (This seems to conflict with Colonel Bates's date of 1925.) The window was destroyed by Luftwaffe bombing in World War II.

There is now a hiatus of some 20 years in the story. In January 1972 the Army Dress Committee met to debate sundry matters within its aegis, including regimental 'Embellishments'. Among these was, of course, the DLOY's right to their shoulder chains. Despite the undisputed fact that they had been wearing them unchallenged since the 1920s, and despite representations for continued wear from the Honorary Colonel (Lieutenant-Colonel M. A. A. Birtwistle, TD), the Committee was cold in its response. Having noted that 'the practice of wearing shoulder chains on No 2 Dress had now ceased [exactly 50 years ago!], there was now no precedent, and to approve this item would cause unnecessary proliferation of other requests', the Committee therefore resolved 'Not to approve the wear of shoulder chains on No 2 Dress by officers and soldiers [of the DLOY]'.

Thus, after nearly half a century The Duke of Lancaster's Own was to forfeit its cherished distinction. But happily this proved only a temporary hiccup. During the following year Colonel Birtwistle continued to press his case, to such effect that on a subsequent meeting of the Dress Committee, on 23 October 1973, the following Minutes were recorded:

> SHOULDER CHAINS. Wear by officers and soldiers of The Duke of Lancaster's Own Yeomanry.
>
> *Item 18* The Secretary said that at the above meeting the representative of the D.L.O.Y. had asked if the proposal for the wearing of Shoulder Chains on No 2 Dress by officers and soldiers, which was not approved at the 208th Meeting, could be recognised. Following a discussion, the Chairman had instructed PS12 (Army) to carry out further research. Subsequently DPS (Army) [Director of Personal Services] had given the Regiment interim permission to wear Shoulder Chains, pending consideration of the case by the Honours and Distinctions Committee . . .
>
> PS12 (Army) said the Honours and Distinctions Committee had recently recommended the continued wearing of Shoulder Chains by D.L.O.Y.
>
> The Chairman said that the Committee would consider that proposal, but only because this particular Embellishment was in use prior to the submission presented at the 208th Meeting, when it had been turned down.
>
> The Committee agreed, and decided: *To approve the wearing of Shoulder Chains on No 2 Dress by officers and soldiers of The Duke of Lancaster's Own Yeomanry.*

An addendum noted that provision of the chains was to be 'at Regimental expense', while the approval 'did not create a precedent for the future'.[8]

Thus at long last the Regiment could quote chapter and verse for its unique dress distinction, never since disputed. But one facet emerging from the above is that apparently neither Regiment nor Dress Committee could discover proof of the original authorisation in the 1920s, and neither has subsequent research.

8. Copies of the above Dress Committee deliberations are preserved in the DLOY Museum.

To revert to the inter-war period – this saw the usual peacetime routine of weekly drills, at Manchester, Bolton, Preston and other Squadron locations, interspersed with Annual Camps. For the record, the latter were held at the following venues:

1926	Torrisholme, near Morecambe
1927	Stainton, near Penrith
1928	Kinmel Park (North Wales)
1929	Stainton
1930	Hornby (north of Lancaster)
1931	Hornby
1932	(No camp)
1933	Dinarth Hall, Rhyl
1934	Kirkoswald (near Penrith)
1935	Windmill Hill, Tidworth
1936	Black Pill, near Swansea
1937	Welbeck Abbey, Worksop
1938	Lowther Park, Penrith
1939	Garndale, Catterick Camp

In 1930 Lieutenant-Colonel D. H. Bates, MC, TD took over command from Colonel Bromilow (retired) and in February 1932 he compiled and issued to all officers a booklet entitled *Some Hints for Training*. These were obviously based on the author's personal experience in war, and are worthy of a few extracts.

First, the Colonel reiterated a truism that had always applied: 'The spade-work for a successful Yeomanry Camp is all done in the drill hall. The fortnight's training is so short that we must aim at giving every man sufficient individual training *before* Camp to allow him to take his place in the Squadron immediately on arrival at Camp.' Here lay the main responsibility of the Permanent Staff Instructors . . . 'Such matters as drill, points of the horse, saddlery, parts of the rifle, the sword, riding school &c.' Variety could be introduced with sand table exercises, map reading tests, compass work, competitions on the miniature range. All officers should make every effort to attend drills: Squadron Leaders should attend at least once a month.

In Camp, the Squadron Leader was entirely responsible for his command, not only as regards discipline, drill and turnout, but for the proper care of men and horses. The Squadron Orderly Officer of the day should always go round the horse lines last thing at night to ensure that orders re haying-up, rugging, etc. had been carried out. 'Remember that men shout loud enough if not fed or if they are cold: horses cannot do more than kick!'

> 'The position of S.S.M. is always difficult, as he is responsible to you and yet is junior to your Troop Leaders. When you give him an order that affects a Troop Leader in any way, see that the latter is advised direct, and *vice versa* . . .
>
> TROOP LEADERS. You are the father of your troop under all circumstances.

In Stables. See that your men are not wearing spurs, caps or sweaters &c (unless with a cold), and have their braces down.

Your Troop Sergeant should report to you at once re shoeing and injured horses.

You should know the characteristics and temperament of all your horses. Which horses are bad feeders. What horses need reshoeing or a remove.[9]

Ask your men simple questions re horses and saddles, and try to get them interested.

Troop Leaders should remain five minutes after feed off, to see the bad or delicate feeders.'

All this focus on stable management merely reflects the traditional priorities in a mounted regiment: care of horses was paramount; men could look after themselves. But Colonel Bates evinced a true understanding of the Territorial soldier:

'Always remember that the Yeoman is a civilian learning a military job voluntarily. Hence you cannot drive him, but you can lead him anywhere if he is interested.'

There were detailed hints and tips about various aspects of field training in camp, among which are the following:

'To my mind the undermentioned points are critical on a field day:

(a) A Squadron Leader not concentrating on the job in front of him, but distracted about such things as how far his main body is behind him, or what formation they are in. *He should know his Second-in-Command is carrying out his orders.*

(b) A Squadron Leader surrounded by a jabbering set of Troop Leaders.

(c) Troop Leaders in reserve coffee-housing amongst themselves without watching their Squadron Leader.'

By 1934 Lieutenant-Colonel Bates had become a senior executive with Cunard in their Liverpool headquarters, and this of course made it difficult for him to devote adequate attention to his command. On 31 October he issued a Farewell Order to his Regiment from which the following is an extract:

'I have now served the Regiment continuously for over 25 years, including 4½ years mobilized overseas. During that war period I purposely avoided service on the Staff or with other units so that I could remain with my own Regiment and the men I loved. I now retire from the position of your Commanding Officer with personal feelings of pride and regret – pride in the achievements and position you have gained for yourselves as a Regiment; regret over the cessation of my own active service with the Duke of Lancaster's Own Yeomanry and the inevitable partial break in **valued** associations.'

9. For the benefit of non-horsemen, a 'remove' was (and is) the removal of the part-worn shoe, paring down the growth of hoof, and replacing the shoe.

The break was indeed only 'partial', for Colonel Bates continued to take an active interest in the Regiment, and in due course was to become its Honorary Colonel. He was succeeded in command by Lieutenant-Colonel John Heaton who had served since 1915.

In 1935 the Regiment, under Colonel Heaton, travelled (by rail) to Annual Camp at Windmill Hill on the outskirts of Tidworth. By now the strength was 20 officers and 269 other ranks. In addition to training in their role as 42nd Divisional Cavalry, they were entertained with demonstrations by the newly-formed 'Mechanised Force, of tanks and armoured cars. An amateur snapshot in the present Museum shows a group of DLOY officers curiously viewing a Light Tank Mk II. On the back an unidentified officer has scribbled 'Many of us went for a ride, but personally I'd stick to four legs every time.'[10]

In January 1936 the nation was plunged into mourning for the death of King George V. The State funeral was attended by representatives of the Regular and Territorial forces, and among them were five NCOs and WOs from the DLOY, headed by SSM F. H. Knowles. Edward, Prince of Wales now became King Edward VIII and, *ipso facto*, Colonel-in-Chief of The Duke of Lancaster's Own Yeomanry. But his tenure of that appointment proved the briefest in the history of the Regiment, for on 10 December of the same year he stunned the public world-wide by abdicating to marry his American divorcee, leaving his brother to ascend the throne as King George VI – and to become the new Colonel-in-Chief.

The Regiment's 1937 Annual Camp at Welbeck Abbey (Worksop) was marked by a triumph. For some years previously *The Daily Telegraph and Morning Post* had been offering a trophy for the Territorial unit with the strongest attendance at Annual Camp. In the previous year this had been won by the 10th Battalion The Manchester Regiment, with a percentage of 107.34 of total establishment. Now the DLOY beat this with 117.72 per cent. The official establishment of a Yeomanry regiment was then 23 officers and 279 other ranks, but the DLOY could parade 24 officers and 315 soldiers.

During the whole of the 20 year inter-war span the Regiment saw little change in dress, arms, saddlery or training. In fact, the squadrons on mounted parade in their Service Dress looked much as they had done in 1914, except that their tunics were now embellished with those unique shoulder chains. But the Regular cavalry had suffered a transformation that altered it out of all recognition. By 1938 all regiments except the Royal Dragoons and Royal Scots Greys had held sad 'Farewell Mounted Parades', after which their horses were exchanged for tanks or armoured cars. In the following year they became units of the newly-formed Royal Armoured Corps. However, mechanisation had not yet smitten the fourteen mounted Yeomanry regiments, and officers and soldiers of The Duke of Lancaster's Own continued to study the time-honoured cavalry drill and practise that exhilarating climax, the charge with 'sword in line'. When in September 1938 Neville Chamberlain, Prime Minister, returned from his meeting in Munich with 'Mr Hitler', waving his piece of paper and triumphantly announcing that there was to be 'peace in our time', few of the Regiment were able to foresee that there was

---

10. Mechanisation of the British Regular cavalry had begun as early as 1928 with the conversion of the 11th Hussars and 12th Lancers to armoured car units, but another decade was to pass before the process was completed.

any reason for the old order to change during their tour of service. Even the contemporary issue of the official manual, *Cavalry Training*, devoted all its pages to mounted drill, sword exercises, tactics and field training on horseback. Although admitting that 'owing to the power of fire', opportunities for shock action with the sword might be less frequent, '... they will still present themselves, particularly in bodies up to and including the size of a squadron ... The defeat of a demoralized enemy can often be completed by a mounted attack, and in minor actions a cavalry charge which comes as a surprise will often achieve success.' In other words, the hallowed *arme blanche* was not yet defunct.[11]

Thus in July of that fateful year of 1939, the DLOY under Lieutenant-Colonel W. M. Musgrave-Hoyle carried out Annual Training at Garndale Camp near Catterick. Armed with the venerable .303 in. SMLE rifle[12] introduced in 1903, and the 1908 Pattern 'thrusting sword', attired in Service Dress of khaki tunics, breeches and puttees (brown riding boots for officers), they performed mounted evolutions and exercises in conformity with the Manual.

This camp was the last that the Regiment was to undertake for nearly ten years, and it was the last that many of its soldiers would ever see. By the time all had returned from Catterick and dispersed to their homes, early in August, events on the Continent were moving to a climax. Confounding the British Prime Minister and others, Hitler had already raped Austria and Czechoslovakia, and after signing pacts with Stalin and Mussolini was now threatening Poland, whose sovereignty was guaranteed by Britain and France. None but blind optimists could fail to recognise that war was inevitable, and by the last week of August Lieutenant-Colonel Musgrave-Hoyle and his command at Manchester, Liverpool and Preston were daily expecting orders for General Mobilisation.

11. *Cavalry Training (Horsed)* of July 1937 was the last such manual to be issued.
12. Short Magazine Lee-Enfield.

SECOND WORLD WAR

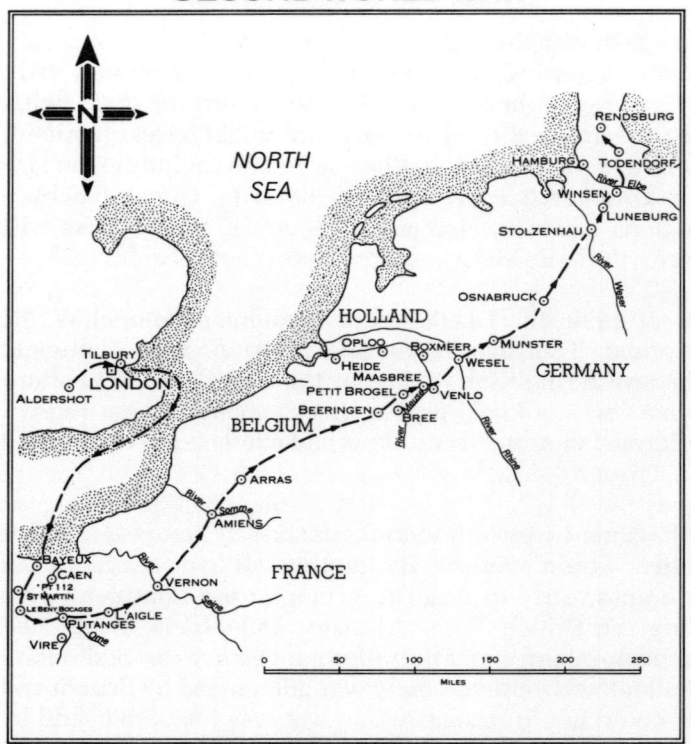

ROUTE OF 77TH (DLOY) MEDIUM REGIMENT RA,
JUNE 1944-FEBRUARY 1946

SECOND WORLD WAR

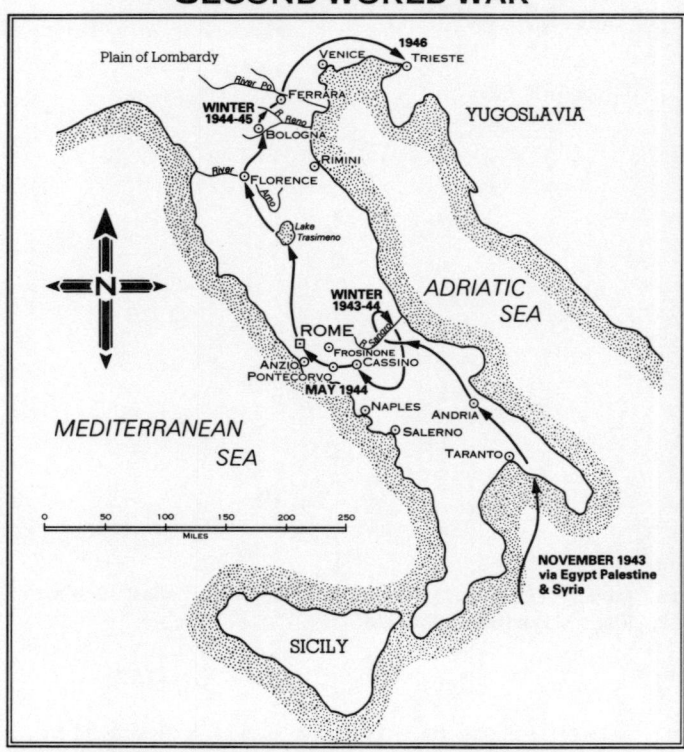

ROUTE OF 78TH (DLOY) MEDIUM REGIMENT RA, ITALY 1943-1946

CHAPTER VIII

The Second World War 1939–1945

Part 1

At 7.30 p.m. on 1 September 1939 Lieutenant-Colonel W. N. Musgrave-Hoyle commanding The Duke of Lancaster's Own Yeomanry received a telegram from Western Command Headquarters. It contained a single word: 'Roberts'. This was the code for 'Mobilize'.

As in 1914, all ranks knew exactly what they had to do. Alerted by telephone or personal contact, they reported to Regimental or Squadron headquarters, kitted out with Service Dress, equipment and 'necessaries' as detailed in the Embodiment notices issued to everyone a year previously at the time of the Munich crisis. On 3 September Prime Minister Neville Chamberlain's tired voice on the BBC announced that Britain was at war with Germany.

By 5 September the Colonel was able to report that his Regiment was fully mobilised: excluding attached personnel, it mustered 30 officers and 635 other ranks, of whom many were newly joined.

At this momentous date the following officers were serving with the Regiment:

Lieutenant-Colonel Commanding

W. M. Musgrave-Hoyle, MC

Majors

E. J. Pyke
R. F. Fleetwood-Hesketh
W. R. Palmer
J. E. Palmer

Captains

J. R. Reynolds
C. B. Clegg
C. P. F. Fleetwood-Hesketh
R. T. Sanderson

Lieutenants

G. G. Ley
T. M. Hesketh
C. P. Shaw
T. M. Heaton
G. G. Beazley
B. Greenwood
F. C. B. Fleetwood-Hesketh

2nd Lieutenants

R. E. Heaton
J. D. M. Wilson
T. J. L. Rushton
J. P. Crump
J. H. M. Shaw
W. F. Reynolds
R. C. Walker
A. C. Cropper
J. M. Hesketh
R. H. Bowring
H. J. Gillow

Adjutant

Captain D. O'B E. Blake (13/18th Royal Hussars)

Quartermaster

H. A. Townsend, DCM

The Regiment now deployed four Squadrons: RHQ and HQ Squadron were located at Ramsbottom (for which the men had a coarser term which cannot be reproduced here); the combined A/C Squadron was at Hawkshaw, B at Walshaw and D at Edenfield.

Like the other Yeomanry regiments remounted in 1921, the DLOY seemed destined to go to war on horseback: they were still roled as Divisional Cavalry for the 42nd Division. But as yet no horses had arrived, and the first week of war service was perforce spent on foot drill, weapon training, map reading classes, and frequent route marches, interspersed with that venerable Army pastime 'interior economy' – cleaning and maintenance of accommodation.

Although the CO and many of his officers had brought their own hunters (for which they received £60 each from the Government), the official provision of horses for the mounted Yeomanry was organised by the Army Remount Service which had the daunting task of inspecting and purchasing from civilian owners nearly 8,000 animals for the mounted regiments. As just intimated, £60 was paid for one likely to make an officer's charger, but £40 was the sum for a troop horse. While the majority came from the same dealers and contractors who had hired them out for peacetime Annual Camps, a large number originated from private owners, reluctant to part with well-loved, perhaps home-bred, animals. There were many instances of poignant little notes tied to head-collars on receipt by the new soldier-owners.[1]

The DLOY's first batch of 150 horses arrived from depots at Bicester, Kingham and Banbury on 11 September: 'a very high class lot as a whole', commented the War Diary. During the next fortnight successive intakes were received and by 1 October the Regiment was fully mounted with 587 chargers and troop horses. Inevitably, these were a somewhat motley collection, ranging from aristocratic blood animals which had galloped in the Shires to humble 'hairies' which had spent their days between the shafts of a milk float or farmer's cart. Performance was thus equally varied. Some would take a five-barred gate in their stride; others could not be persuaded to negotiate a 2-foot ditch. One of the latter was named 'Blouse' by its rider. On being asked the reason for this odd choice, the trooper replied, 'Well, sir, he ain't no bloody jumper, like.'

There now followed intensive mounted training, with sundry schemes, lectures on horsemanship, mounted dummy-thrusting sessions with the sword, besides more realistic dismounted activities, such as live-firing with the SMLE rifle and the Lewis LMG on the

---

1. The present author may here be permitted a personal aside. In September 1939, when in billets with the Shropshire Yeomanry near Market Drayton, he was allotted a well-bred bay mare whose head-collar note bore the following: 'Besides a splendid hunter, never put a foot wrong, Lizzie has been a family pet. Please look after her and bring her back safe. Thank you!'

Altcar ranges.[2] There were also demanding mounted route marches. On one November day D Squadron rode 40 miles from their headquarters at Edenfield to Southport, where they carried out exercises on the sands and rode back again two days later. This was the first time that Southport had seen the DLOY since 1898, when the Regiment went into camp there.

One of the problems in mounted training was the fact that most of the new recruits (if not officers) had never sat in a saddle before, so that they needed the most elementary instruction. Paradoxically, however, this proved less serious than might be imagined. An anonymous typescript in the Regimental Museum has this to say:[3] 'Although lads from the cotton mills and collieries . . . seldom knew one end of a horse from the other, strangely enough our permanent staff instructors used to say they were better raw material, for it was easier to teach a man to ride from scratch, rather than the country boy who had ridden all his life and acquired bad habits . . . the style demanded by Weedon[4] was very different from that used in riding round the farm or even in the hunting field.'

As with horses, the newly-enlisted rank-and-file were of all sorts and conditions. Captain James Reynolds of D Squadron recalled that 'the best Section was led by a certain Cpl Baldwin who in civilian life was a farm labourer. He had under him five solicitors, most of whom were public school types, and in addition he had two Stonyhurst lads . . . Cpl Baldwin was beloved and respected by them all. By the time the war ended he was a Captain in the Regiment and one of our most efficient officers.'[5]

And so with all this effort, by the end of November 1939 The Duke of Lancaster's Own Yeomanry was fully capable of confronting the King's enemies – on horseback with drawn swords. But though other Yeomanry regiments were soon to do so, in Palestine and Syria, the DLOY's exertions proved in vain.

On 29 November the War Diary recorded, 'verbal information received from HQ 66th Div [to which the DLOY had been transferred] that *the Regt is to lose its horses*'. This was a scarcely credible bombshell; but on the next day came official confirmation with War Office Letter 79/2964. This ordered that all the unbrigaded mounted Yeomanry regiments were to convert to mechanised units of the Royal Artillery, with their own choice of Medium, Field or Anti-Tank roles. On 1 December Colonel Musgrave-Hoyle summoned a conference of Squadron Leaders to debate the choice. On a show of hands it was decided that the Regiment would become Medium gunners, and accordingly Divisional Headquarters was informed.

Even in wartime, such radical transformations are not effected within less than months, and meanwhile, since no one could offer even an elementary knowledge of gunnery, while neither instructors nor manuals materialised, the Regiment could only occupy its

2. Although the Bren had superseded the Lewis gun in the Regular Army by 1939, the Yeomanry and most of the Territorial infantry still had to make do with the vintage Lewis, dating from the First World War.
3. '78 (DLOY) Medium Regiment RA Regimental History'.
4. Since 1920 the Army Equitation School had been located at Weedon, Northamptonshire, and its precepts were sacrosanct among cavalrymen.
5. Unpublished MS in Regimental archives: 'Memoirs of the 1939/45 War', by Major James R. Reynolds.

time with tending and exercising the horses it was about to lose, weapon training as before and sundry other tasks which now seemed rather pointless. Some 30 other ranks 'unlikely to make gunners' were posted to regiments remaining mounted, 19 going to the Cheshire Yeomanry, the remainder to the two Cavalry Training Regiments at Colchester and Edinburgh.[6] It was not until 24 January 1940 that some intensive training in the new role became possible with the posting in of Major Arnold Forster, RA as Instructor Gunnery and the issue of the first instalment of *Artillery Training* manuals. As Captain Reynolds wrote, for most of the officers this was tantamount to becoming schoolboys again. 'The strain of trying to learn the technicalities of gunnery was appalling. Many of us had been unfamiliar with long division, let alone trigonometry and all the other horrible things we had to cram into ourselves in the autumn of our youth.' Although as yet not a single piece of ordnance was to be seen, at least they could ponder the mysteries of such arcane devices as dial sights and clinometers.

At the end of December the Regiment began to say farewell to the horses they had just got to know, when the first batch of 250 were sent off to remount centres. Some were destined for the 1st (Mounted) Cavalry Division under orders for Palestine, but others went to a Royal Artillery battery reconverted from mechanised to horse-drawn role. To the Regiment this seemed an odd quirk of War Office mentality when they learned that 95 per cent of this battery had never bestridden a horse. 'We wondered why we, a regiment of fully-trained horsemen, had not been so converted.'(Reynolds)

January and February of the new year saw the worst winter for decades, with snow and ice disrupting all forms of communication and transport. The few horses still remaining were put to good use as pack-animals for distribution of rations, and as mounts for orderlies carrying orders and messages during the breakdown of telephone communication. There was also an errand of mercy, as ex-BSM Jack Wilson recalls:

> Word came to us that a number of young children evacuated from Manchester were in a Convent at Greenmount. They were completely cut off, and food was running short. Each of the four Troops in the Squadron had a Bren Gun section, which had two pack-horses ... The eight pack-horses and their pack saddlery, together with one or two other mounts were pressed into service, and it was a case of ride one, lead one ... We battled our way to the village of Tottington, which was as far as the train from Manchester could get, loaded food, including 'goodies' such as apples and oranges on to the packs and battled to Greenmount Convent. And I mean battled: the snow at times was up to the horses' chests. When we rode into the courtyard at Greenmount, all the kids were at the first floor windows cheering like mad. When we got back to Hawkshaw both horses and men were dead beat.[7]

Having parted with the last batch of horses, the Regiment (still without any guns) moved by rail to Pembroke Dock, concentrating there on 14 April 1940. Since February, it had

6. These two units continued to turn out horse-soldiers until 1941, while the Army Equitation School at Weedon, which became the 110th Cavalry OCTU, was training some 230 officer-cadets for a mounted role which few of them were to see when commissioned.
7. Letter to author from Mr J. Wilson of Salford (ex–77th DLOY Medium Regiment RA).

been organised in two Batteries, thus:

A Battery
A Troop (A/C Squadron)
B Troop (HQ Squadron)

B Battery
C Troop (B Squadron)
D Troop (D Squadron)

With Lieutenant-Colonel Musgrave-Hoyle continuing in command, the strength as reported in the War Diary was 32 officers and 539 other ranks.

So far, the DLOY had retained its cohesive identity as a single Regiment, but on 15 April came a radical reorganisation which saw it split into the two distinct units under whose titles it was to fight the war. On that significant date the Regiment emerged as:

77th (DLOY) MEDIUM REGIMENT ROYAL ARTILLERY (TA)

78th (DLOY) MEDIUM REGIMENT ROYAL ARTILLERY (TA)

The 77th was made up of the former 'A Battery', the 78th of 'B Battery'. Command of the 77th was assumed by Lieutenant-Colonel Musgrave-Hoyle, that of the 78th by Lieutenant-Colonel R. F. Fleetwood-Hesketh (who had joined the DLOY as 2nd Lieutenant in 1922). Now officially Gunners, all ranks had to adopt the RA 'Gun' badge on their head-dress, but their origins were proclaimed by The Duke of Lancaster's 'Rose' on their collar dogs.

At long last, the two Regiments were able to get down to some practical training as Gunners. Qualified RA officer-instructors arrived, together with NCOs and other ranks from the Royal Regiment; officers and men were sent on intensive gunnery courses at the Larkhill School of Artillery and at Llandrindod Wells in Wales. All ranks now began to put classroom study into practice, but both armament and vehicles were somewhat makeshift. The former were 6in. howitzers and 60-pounder guns of First World War vintage, mounted on wooden, iron-tyred wheels. One of the howitzers bore a plaque revealing that it had been the 'Property of City of Birmingham Parks'. Vehicles were a commandeered civilian assortment. One flat-backed lorry had a huge board behind the driver's seat with the word PERSIL in foot-high letters. Another was a large covered van, announcing on its sides that it had belonged to 'W. E. Evans Suppliers of High Class Furniture. Distance No Object'.

However, the 78th were able to indulge in some warlike activities. The anonymous author of its early history:

> The great moment came when we were to fire six rounds from each gun into the sea at Fishguard, for which extensive preparations had to be made ... warnings to the Admiralty, Air Ministry, Western Command, the local Town Council; the hiring of a tug to pull a target at the end of a very long line. Incidentally, we do not know why we ever asked for a towed target, as in those days we had only just seen dial sights and we do not even remember what method of laying was employed. However, the shells eventually arrived in the sea after what seemed an interminably long time of flight, and

not too indecently close to the towing craft. After the first shot or two the boat and target parted company, but we never discovered whether this was due to (1) mechanical defect, (2) a shell severing the towing line, or (3) the tug master deeming it expedient to rapidly increase the distance between tug and target. But the shoot whetted our appetites . . . and we felt well on the way to becoming competent gunners.

In June (1940) both Regiments were obliged to suspend training to act as hosts for 500 survivors of the Dunkirk evacuation ('very tired and short of equipment') who had been sent to Pembroke to recuperate and refit.

The Battle of Britain between the 'Few' of the RAF and the Luftwaffe was now in full spate, and August and September saw bombing raids on Pembroke Dock. In early September a bomb fell near the 77th's Officers' Mess, causing no structural damage but killing one soldier. Gunner P. Jenkinson is thus recorded as the first wartime casualty of the DLOY. The War Diary of the 77th did not fail to report that on 5 September one HE bomb exploded in a nearby field and 'killed 3 cows and 7 more had to be put down'.

Previously on 19 August there had been a heavy raid on the oil tanks near Pembroke Dock, which left fires raging for 21 days. All this while the only AA defence available to the Regiment was one Lewis gun mounted on a tripod and manned 24 hours a day. There is no record of any downings of enemy aircraft, but one day the CO of the 77th received a message from the local RAF Station Commander congratulating the Lewis gun team on their alertness, 'but would you please confine your firing to enemy planes only, as one of my Blenheims had a few holes in it'.[8]

In October 1940 the two Regiments left Pembroke for live-firing practice camps, first at Pontypridd in South Wales and then on the vast Sennybridge Training Area near Brecon.

Thus far 77th and 78th had remained in close contact with each other, but in November they parted company and never again came together. The 77th was posted to Northern Ireland, arriving at Gosford Castle, Market Hill, Co. Armagh on 30 November, while the 78th went to a training area near Bude in Cornwall. For nearly four years the 77th were kept at home: it was only after D Day that they were able to fire their guns in action – but this period saw them transformed from what was admitted to be a not markedly efficient body into a first-class battle-worthy unit of the Royal Artillery. Much of the credit for this was owed to Lieutenant-Colonel F. H. C. Rogers, MC, a Regular Gunner, who replaced Lieutenant-Colonel Musgrave-Hoyle as CO in November 1940. By dint of his wide experience as an Instructor Gunnery, coupled with firmness and tact, Colonel Rogers soon brought his command to its peak of efficiency. Colonel Musgrave-Hoyle was given responsibility for the airfield defences at Bramcote, near Nottingham, and did not rejoin the DLOY. At the same time several other Yeomanry officers were replaced by Gunners.

Meanwhile, the 78th had also seen a similar change of command when in August 1940 Lieutenant-Colonel R. Fleetwood-Hesketh was replaced by Lieutenant-Colonel V. A. Young, MC, Royal Artillery.[9]

8. Private letter to author from ex-Bombardier Harry Hartill of the 77th.
9. Having dropped his hyphenated prefix, Colonel Roger Hesketh became a senior staff officer in Planning at the War Office, and as such played a crucial role in devising the bogus 'Operation Fortitude' which misled Hitler into believing that the D Day landing was to take place in the Pas de Calais.

Since the two DLOY Regiments were now completely divorced, henceforth their stories must be likewise separated, and as the 78th were the first to confront the enemy they must be given precedence.

Part 2

78th (DLOY) Medium Regiment RA

Like their counterparts in Ireland, the 78th spent a lengthy span at home, mostly in southern England in locations such as Bodmin Moor and the Dartmoor ranges. This span brought not only changes in command, but a rather confusing succession of equipments. On being posted to Bude in December 1941 they were ordered to exchange their antiquated 60-pounder guns for 4.5in. howitzers – a somewhat puzzling decision since the latter were Field rather than Medium ordnance. However, on arrival at Bude they found no howitzers, only the 'Quads', or towing vehicles.[10] A week later the weapons arrived, but instead of the expected 4.5 howitzers they proved to be the heavier 6 in. types (post WWI). Someone had blundered. The Quads were quite incapable of towing such loads, so a quandary arose: either guns or Quads must be replaced. Eventually it was decided that the 6 in. howitzers would be retained, as appropriate for a Medium role, and the Quads would be exchanged for the more powerful AEC 'Matador' gun-tractors with four-wheel drive. Properly equipped at last, the Regiment's batteries hurled their 6 in. shells over the ranges of Bodmin Moor and Dartmoor, and by the end of 1942 all were fully confident of pinpointing indirect fire targets, engaging mock 'opportunity targets' and sending HE shells to burst safely ahead of advancing infantry. But as will be seen, before living targets were engaged there were further changes in equipments.

Between 1941 and 1942 the Regiment also underwent changes in command. In March 1941 Lieutenant-Colonel V. A. Young, MC departed to a Heavy AA unit, being replaced by another Regular Gunner, Lieutenant-Colonel E. M. Tyler,MC. But his tenure lasted only a year: in April 1942 he was posted to GHQ RA Home Forces as GSOI, and the Regiment's Second-in-Command, Major W. R. Palmer, was promoted Lieutenant-Colonel in command. Thus, after a spell under Royal Artillery COs, the 78th was again commanded by a true member of the DLOY 'family'. Colonel Bobby Palmer had joined the Regiment as 2nd Lieutenant in 1923, and was to lead the 78th throughout their campaigning.[11]

Although both 77th and 78th now had other matters on their minds, some of the older members of the original DLOY were probably interested to learn that, on 11 May 1942, Colonel D. H. Bates, MC, TD, had taken over from Colonel Hardcastle as Honorary Colonel. As we have seen, Denis Bates had distinguished himself as Squadron Leader of A Squadron in the Palestine campaign of 1917–18, which resulted in that unique

---

10. Officially 'Gun Tractor Field Artillery', the popular name 'Quad' was said to be derived from its equine predecessor, the quadruped. The covered vehicle's somewhat bloated appearance resulted in the troops' nickname 'Pregnant Frog'.
11. His son became Major-General Sir Michael Palmer, KCVO, who at the time of writing is Honorary Colonel of the DLOY and of the 14th/20th King's Hussars.

distinction of shoulder chains on Service Dress. Although long retired, he had always maintained an active interest in his Regiment. Three days after his appointment he visited the 78th at Bude, met all the officers, chatted with the soldiers and attended a field-firing exercise the following day.

In October 1942 the 78th received the newly-developed equipments with which it was to perform such 'Yeoman' service in the Italian campaign. These were the 5.5in. gun-howitzers, throwing 100 lb. shells nearly nine miles, and remaining in service as standard weapons for Medium RA for the rest of the war. Mounted on pneumatic tyres and with a split trail which allowed maximum elevation, the 5.5 was an excellent weapon, proving itself in Europe and the Middle East. Its ammunition was also 'split': first, the 100 lb. HE projectile itself, with fuse that could be set to explode the shell on impact or as air-burst, creating an effect similar to the obsolete shrapnel; then came the separate propellant, or charge, in a cloth bag; finally, to ignite the charge there was a small brass cartridge, rather like a blank .303 round. To serve it the gun needed a detachment ('crew' to the layman) of ten soldiers commanded by a Number One, or sergeant. To load and fire a round was quite an involved business. First, No. 2 on the right of the breech, opened it; Nos. 4 and 5 then heaved the shell on to the sliding tray in rear of the breech, lifted it to engage the breech and, with a rammer, shoved the round into the chamber; next No. 6 pushed in the charge behind the round, and No. 2 inserted the cartridge into a small lock in the breech. Having been layed by No. 3, on the left, the gun was now ready to fire, and on the command from the No. 1, all stood clear and No. 2 jerked the firing lanyard attached to the cartridge.

After two months of such training, with practice shoots on Bodmin Moor, the long-awaited orders for an overseas posting arrived. The destination was supposed to be 'secret', but the Bude shopkeepers and publicans assured all that it was the Middle East. This seemed to be confirmed when the QM was inundated with 500-odd suits of tropical khaki drill shirts and slacks.

And so, on 15 January 1943 the 78th embarked at Liverpool for Egypt, to become the first representatives of the DLOY to see active service in World War II.

After a lengthy voyage round the Cape and up the Red Sea, the Regiment arrived at Qassassin, near Alexandria, on 14 March. The strength was now 27 officers and 522 other ranks, with Lieutenant-Colonel Palmer commanding and Major D. W. Seddon-Brown Second-in-Command.

At this date the British and US commands were planning the landing in Sicily as the necessary prelude to the invasion of Italy, and the 78th were confident of imminent action. But frustration followed. In May they were ordered to hand over their sixteen 5.5s to the 80th Medium Regiment RA (Scottish Horse), receiving in exchange just eight 25-pounder guns. The next five months were spent on such inglorious tasks as escorting German prisoners from the Western Desert and guarding shipping and stores at Alexandria.

In August the 78th were sent even further from the theatre of war in Italy when they were ordered to undertake a 400-mile trek (or drive) from Alexandria to the Syrian-Turkish border. Since the Vichy French had been ejected from these parts a year ago and all was peaceful, this exercise seemed rather pointless – especially when a large number of the Regiment was stricken down with sandfly fever, 'which more or less put us out of action for a week', as Captain Catterall noted.[12] However, while at Slenfe, north of Tripoli, in September, the 78th was able to take part in a demonstration of Divisional artillery concentration on a 'Mike' target (all divisional guns). This was 'terrific and most impressive,' wrote Catterall, 'I have never seen anything like it. The target area was covered with bursts and our 5.5 shells were easily seen and heard.' (By now, Catterall's 105 Battery had acquired 5.5s, 106 Battery making do with 25-pounder field guns.) In October 1943 the Regiment was posted back to Alexandria and the marathon march was executed in reverse.

At long last those demanding years of training, the nomadic wanderings, the humdrum duties, were over, and the 78th (DLOY) Regiment was about to fire its guns at an enemy. Sicily had now been occupied and the invasion of Italy was to follow. The Regiment formed an element of 6 AGRA (Army Group Royal Artillery), allotted to the 8th Army in XIII Corps. In conformity with the rest of AGRA, the two batteries had now been redesignated, P Battery becoming 105 Battery and Q, 106 Battery.

Sailing from Alexandria in early November, the Regiment concentrated at Taranto on the 22nd, to shiver in tropical KD kit, which, however, was soon exchanged for serge battle dress. By this date the Italians had capitulated, but the occupying Germans under Marshal Kesselring were to prove more implacable enemies. The first couple of months in Italy proved almost a *dolce far niente* existence for the Regiment. On 23 November they travelled by train some 90 miles north to the coastal town of Barletta (north of the 8th Army's port of Bari), then by road to Andria, and here in billets they remained until the New Year. There was no fighting in this area, and apart from schemes, training and inspections, life was very little different from the days in England. The officers saw to it that Yeomanry traditions were maintained. On 9 December Captain Catterall noted in his diary that there was a 'Grand dance in our Mess – large room decorated and good band – 25 nurses (Canadian) from the hosp. in Andria – Terrific success.'

There was still a mixture of guns in the Regiment – eight 5.5s and eight 4.5 howitzers. Nearby were fellow Yeomen-Gunners, the 76th (Shropshire Yeomanry) Medium Regiment, who were likewise equipped. When the CRA of 6 AGRA decreed that there were to be no 'mixed' regiments in his command, it fell to the two Commanding Officers to determine between them which was to have which calibre. 'Neither wished to give up his 5.5s, and rumour has it that after long deliberation the matter was decided by a game of poker. Be that as it may, the 76th gave up its 5.5s and a quarter of a million pounds worth of equipment changed hands without a hitch in twenty-four hours on December 11th.'[13]

---

12. Captain (later Major) Catterall, who died in 1988, kept a detailed diary of his experiences with the 78th. Through the kindness of his widow and son a copy of this, together with his photographic record, is now preserved in the Regimental Museum.
13. Gladstone, E. E. *The Shropshire Yeomanry. The Story of a Volunteer Cavalry Regiment* (1953).

Thus finally equipped, on 1 January 1944, the Regiment was routed north to the battle area between San Eusanio and Castel Frentano. In raging blizzards gun pits were dug and OPs established, and on the 9th the 5.5s of 105 Battery were the first in action. The targets for concentration and harassing fire were German positions at Orsogna and Guardiagrele: '3 direct hits on Orsogna tower', noted the War Diary. There was constant enemy counter-battery annoyance, and on the 17th RHQ suffered a 'stonk' which killed two gunners and wounded a third – the Regiment's first battle casualties.[14] During the ensuing period officers were given experience of working with the Sherman tanks of the 14th Canadian (Calgary) Armoured Regiment, using the tanks as a very 'Forward' OP at 'the sharp end'. Major L. A. H. Riddett was attached to a tank squadron of the Calgary Horse for a time . . . 'Space in a Sherman tank being somewhat limited, our OP party consisted of one officer (technically in command of the tank) and one Signaller – I think he had to double as a gunner. Communications were complicated as we had to be tuned in to the squadron net as well as our artillery net, and at the same time control the tank on the intercom. I hope we did some good in this role, but I don't remember much about it.'[15]

After the first couple of months of action Colonel Palmer issued a Special Order of the Day in which he praised the efforts of both Batteries' gun detachments:

> The speed with which guns are reloaded and relayed between ranging rounds is magnificent, so much so that CRA 4 Ind Div, when observing a shoot the other day, said to me 'Your fellows are too damned quick between ranging rounds – they don't even give me time to take my glasses down'. The Regiment has shown it possible to fire with accuracy 5 rounds per minute – a rate which proves a very high standard of training and efficiency. But owing to the extra wear imposed [on barrels] these feats must be reserved for special occasions, when we shall show the infantry that, with crack detachments the 5.5 is in reality a field gun firing 100lb shells.

On 16 March the Regiment was ordered to move west across the waist of Italy to an area near Caserta, there to come under command of the 5th US Army. Having handed over their Orsogna sector to the 58th Medium Regiment – Regular Gunners – the 78th arrived in their new concentration area on the 18th.

The stage was now set for the most ferocious and crucial battles of the Italian campaign. With the failure of the Allies to exploit the Anzio landing, the 5th US and 8th British Armies planned a thrust up the Liri valley and Route 6, to force the Gustav Line and capture Rome.

Some 70 miles south of the capital this route was barred by the formidable German strongpoint of Cassino, with its Monastery Hill towering 1,700 feet above the Liri and Rapido valleys. Kesselring had concentrated nearly 26 divisions between Cassino and the coast, and between January and April three successive assaults by Americans, British, New Zealanders and Indians had been beaten off with appalling casualties. Devastating bombing and artillery fire had reduced the Monastery itself and most of the town below it to ruins, but amid the rubble the tenacious Germans were still in strength.

14. Gnrs Smith, S. S. and Green, G. C. killed; Gnr Leathley, J. wounded.
15. MS notes provided by Major Riddett.

Put very simply, General Alexander's plan for the fourth – and final – offensive was thus:[16] on the left the 8th Army was to 'clean' Cassino and its Monastery and then advance along Route 6 – the Rome highway. Further left, the 5th Army would push up the other highway, Route 7, while at the appropriate moment the Anzio divisions would break out of their perimeter and cut off the retreating Germans. Specifically, the capture of the Monastery was entrusted to the Polish II Corps; the British 4th and Indian 8th Divisions were tasked with crossing the Rapido river and outflanking Monastery Hill. Meanwhile, in an attempt to deceive Kesselring and draw forces away from the Cassino area, Alexander mounted a fictitious landing operation north of Rome. Such was the plan for Operation DIADEM: but in war events do not always conform strictly to plans.

By 28 March – a week after the failure of the previous assault – the 78th (DLOY) had moved up to the Cassino sector. The offensive was to open on 11 May and the intervening weeks were spent in calibrating guns, dumping ammunition, registering targets and responding to calls for shoots on enemy batteries. On the eve of 'D Day' the two batteries were in position behind the prominent 1,200 feet whaleback ridge of Monte Trocchio, from the crest of which there was a clear view across the Rapido to Cassino Monastery and town, thus affording excellent OPs. The 5.5in. gun-howitzers of the Medium regiments[17] had no difficulty in clearing the crest, but for reasons which they never discovered, between the two 78th's Batteries was a huge 240 mm. American gun, whose elevation was more limited. For a period Captain Riddett was acting as FOO on Mte Trocchio, and he recalls that the shells screamed over his head with only feet to spare, while their driving bands, ' . . . great coils of copper, used to come off the shells and whistled about in all directions'.

There were casualties in the 78th before the initial attack. On 30 April a 105 mm. shell scored a direct hit on RHQ's cookhouse, killing two gunners and wounding another.

Zero hour on 11 May was 2300, and precisely at that moment the night was shattered by the thunder of 1,600 guns and the reverberations and almost continuous glare of explosions on the battered Monastery Hill. While most OP parties were on the Mte Trocchio vantage point, some had the more hazardous task of going forward with the infantry of the 4th Division in their attack across the Rapido. One of these parties joining a battalion of the East Surreys, was led by Captain Riddett, and as they set off, laden with wireless sets, batteries and arms, the bombardment opened. 'All hell broke loose over our heads. Wireless communication became chaotic – or non-existent. With so many frequencies, so many units using them, to say nothing of jamming by the Germans, very little contact could be made.' The rear-link set, the bulky No. 19, could not be operated on the move, but Riddett carried a small 38 set, similar to the modern 'walkie-talkie' and used for close-range work with the infantry. Twiddling the knobs as he strode along, he at first could get nothing but atmospherics. Then suddenly, loud and clear, came the astonishing strains of familiar dance music. 'This was soon identified as the BBC, and we marched into battle to the music of Carol Gibbons and his Savoy Orpheans, coming straight from the hotel. Little did those dancers know who was listening to them! This

---

16. General Sir Harold Alexander was GOC 15th Army Group, which included 5th US and 8th British Armies.
17. Among whom were the 78th's fellow-Yeomen, the 76th (Shropshire Yeomanry) Regiment RA.

must have been some quirk of the airwaves.' On the lifting of the barrage his signaller was able to get through to 106 Battery and, with pre-recorded map references, numerous calls for fire from the infantry were effectively dealt with.

On that same night Captain S. E. Catterall took an OP party to join the 2nd Bedfordshire and Hertfordshire Battalion who, like the others of 4 Division, were involved in the attack across the Rapido. Having crossed the river in canvas boats, hauled by ropes, the party dug in and made contact with Battalion HQ and with their 105 Battery away behind Mte Trocchio. The infantry attack met fierce opposition, one battalion (2nd King's) losing nearly 50 per cent of its strength. And for nearly 48 hours the OP party, lurking in their hole in the ground, sent back targets and corrections, assaulted meanwhile by enemy shells and Nebelwerfers. On the next day two badly wounded infantrymen were brought in by stretcher bearers, together with two German prisoners. Two of the OP party, Gunner E. White and Signaller F. Crocker, were deputed to evacuate these across the Rapido. Half way across in their canvas boats, they got into difficulties in the fast current ('rapido') and it was only with the willing help of the prisoners that the wounded men were safely landed.

May 13th was unlucky for Captain Catterall. While outside the foxhole he was hit in the thigh by a shell or mortar fragment which rendered him almost immobile. Supported by Bombardier B. Richardson he managed to hobble towards a Bailey bridge which the Sappers had just put across the Rapido. Here the two rested for half-an-hour until there was a lull in the shelling. Then they managed to struggle across and reach an Advanced Dressing Station, when Richardson returned to the OP. Throughout this episode, the NCO had not only supported Catterall, but carried all his kit and 38 set, plus his own kit and Tommy gun: 'He was bloody good,' wrote Catterall in his diary.[18]

Captain Catterall was evacuated to the base hospital in Naples and was not able to rejoin until 20 July.

Meanwhile the 78th had suffered more casualties. In their gun positions behind the bulk of Trocchio they were not immune to counter-battery annoyance, and on 12 May one of the gun pits (A4) suffered a direct hit, wreaking death and destruction. As ill luck had it, the Second-in-Command, Major D. W. Seddon-Brown, Lieutenant Straker and BSM Turner had chosen this moment to visit the gun: all were killed outright, together with six gunners of the detachment. The Number One, Sergeant Williams, had a miraculous escape, being blown clean out of the gun pit with only cuts and bruises.

During the next two weeks while the infantry were battling against ferocious opposition and suffering horrendous casualties, the 78th continued to fling percussion and air-burst shells on registered targets. 'During the period 11–25 May we fired more than 22,380 shells, of which owing to our fwd posn we were enabled to shoot a high percentage with Charge 1,' reported the War Diary.

---

18. Subsequently Mentioned in Despatches, Brian Richardson had joined the Regiment as a gunner in 1940. Having survived the war (and numerous OP adventures) he rejoined the reconstituted DLOY in 1951 and rose to become RQMS. He retired in 1973 after more than 30 years' service.

It was only on 25 May that Kesselring authorised the staunch remnants of his 1st Parachute Division to evacuate Monte Cassino, and the final battle was an end. With the following pursuit until 5 June, the struggle for Cassino cost the Allies nearly 45,000 killed and wounded – more than any other offensive in the Italian campaign.

After Cassino Lieutenant-Colonel Palmer issued a Special Order of the Day to his 78th, which gives a summary of its tasks[19]

> Although the Regiment had been in the line more or less continuously for the previous six months, the Battle of Cassino gave its first opportunity of taking part in a large scale action. The role assigned to its Medium guns was firstly to take part in the bombardment of hostile batteries prior to the attack, and secondly to give close support to the 10th Brigade of 4 British Infantry Division in the crossing of the Rapido and subsequent advance. This necessitated more or less continued firing for six hours at a time. Then as operations became more fluid ... opportunity targets were the Regiment's chief responsibility ... the targets then being generally either strong points of enemy resistance, or the areas where the enemy was forming up for counter attacks ...
>
> Calls for fire from FOOs often caused anxious moments for those responsible for the protection of our forward troops from our own shells. Under normal circumstances the 100lb shell of the Medium guns should not be fired less than 500 yds from our own troops, owing to the greater lethal area of the burst compared to the 25pdr, but during the attack of the Beds & Herts on Pt. 55 near Cassino, fire was called for within 200 yds of the forward infantry. The situation was critical, for although the objective had been gained, only one officer and 20 ORs remained to hold the position against the inevitable counter attack ... The surviving officer called on his wireless for defensive fire from all artillery, including the Mediums, whose heavier shells were particularly needed to deal with tanks. The risks were pointed out, but accepted, and it was arranged that the Regiment should fire one round salvo from the 16 Medium guns. After which the CO of the Beds & Herts was anxiously asked over the wireless whether the shells had fallen too close. 'Bloody close', came the reply, 'but don't let them go any further away.' Ten minutes' gun fire was then put down ... and the objective was held.[20]

With the 'cleaning' of Cassino Alexander planned to encircle the German 10th Army with his own 8th and General Mark Clark's 5th US Army. But the flamboyant American had other ideas and marched straight for his triumphal entry into Rome, thereby allowing the Germans to withdraw towards their Gothic Line.

On their own advance towards Rome the 78th were repeatedly called upon for infantry support or destructive fire. On one occasion Captain Riddett was again ahead with his OP party:

'We found a good OP in a ruined house, and as there was little doing I agreed that Bdr Graham [signaller] would man the OP for the first part of the night while I had a rest ...

19. Included in 78th's War Diary.
20. 'Salvo': all guns firing simultaneously. 'Gun fire': each gun firing independently.

He woke me up about midnight to say that there was to be a 'William' target which we were required to observe . . . '[21] The target proved to be an airfield, and when the guns opened up there was a spectacular display in roughly the right direction. On an enquiry as to whether the 'stonk' was on target, Riddett left Graham to reply, and was somewhat alarmed to hear the young NCO order over the wireless 'Right 400, repeat'. This meant that some hundreds of guns and tons of ammunition were being switched 400 yards: 'I hardly thought it would be authorised, but it was and Graham duly reported "Spot on".'

The Allies' next objective, the strongly defended Gothic Line, extended some 200 miles from La Spezia on Italy's west coast to near Rimini on the Adriatic. Much of it ran through the formidable heights of the Appenine mountains with their natural as well as constructed defences. By July the 8th Army, with the US 5th on their westward flank, had reached Florence. Still under command of the 4th British Division, whom they had supported at Cassino, the 78th (and their Yeoman-comrades, the 76th) were almost continuously in action laying down defensive fire, supporting infantry attacks, and occasionally opening up on a 'William' target. On 28 July the War Diary recorded that in four hours both 105 and 106 Batteries fired 200 rounds in support of the Royal West Kents who carried a strongpoint just south of Florence. A few days later they were aiding a Gurkha battalion assaulting a mountainous position. Seventy-odd German prisoners were captured, and on being passed back through the 78th's gun positions they 'repeatedly mentioned the devastating accuracy and weight of our artillery fire'.(War Diary) During this period one of 105 Battery's guns was disabled by a mine when moving to a new position. Luckily, the detachment in the tractor escaped unhurt. But a little later 106 Battery's A Echelon was shelled, with two gunners killed and one wounded.

On 11 August Kesselring's forces evacuated Florence, and the 4th Division was withdrawn for a much-needed rest. The 78th was now transferred to the 1st British Infantry Division, but before leaving the former, its staunch support (during which it had fired some 50,000 rounds) was acknowledged by the Commander, Major-General A. D. Ward, who wrote thus to Colonel Palmer:

> HQ 4 Brit Inf Div
> 8 Aug 44
>
> *My dear Palmer*
> Now that your Regiment is to pass from my command, I want very much to let you know how grateful I and the whole Division are for the splendid co-operation that we have received from you, both at the Cassino battle and during this last seven weeks of hard fighting from STRADA to FLORENCE.
>
> I am sending you a stencil of a small version of my Divisional sign and we should all be very pleased if you, on your own car, jeep or other command vehicle, would wear this sign of the 4th Division in some convenient place as a continual reminder of the Yeoman service that you have rendered to us. My very best thanks and the best of good luck to you and your Regiment.
>
> Yours ever,
A. D. Ward, Maj-Gen

21. There were code names for the various concentrations of fire. M or 'Mike' required only regimental guns; U or 'Uncle' was for all Corps artillery, while W or 'William' demanded the whole army artillery.

Colonel Palmer accordingly had a replica plaque made by his REME craftsmen, and was proud to display it on his jeep for the rest of the war.

On 21 August an unhappy incident occurred in 105 Battery, when fire destroyed two 3-ton lorries, one of which was the Officers' Mess truck: 'This reduced the Mess property to NIL for the second time in three months.' (War Diary)

Having crossed the Arno river near Florence on 2 September, the Regiment was temporarily taken out of action in the Vicchio area for well-deserved recuperation and refitting. At this date the War Diary showed a strength of 22 officers and 541 other ranks. With Lieutenant-Colonel W. R. Palmer in command and Major E. H. L. Fisher as second in command, 105 Battery was commanded by Major T. M. Heaton, 106 by his brother, Major R. E. Heaton. The adjutant was Captain J. D. M. Wilson.

During the rest period, 1–9 October, all ranks were granted leave to sample the varied amenities of the city of Florence, cultural and otherwise. There was also much essential maintenance on guns and vehicles, replenishing ammunition and stores, checking wireless sets and so forth: the 'rest' was not a period of idleness.

With the advent of the Appenine winter of rain, mud and snow, there followed a stalemate of static warfare with neither side able to mount any major offensive. Still in the Vicchio area, the men of the 78th groused about 'sunny Italy', as they endured not only periodic enemy shelling but the assaults of the elements. Roads became virtually impassable to all but 4×4 or tracked vehicles, and even the 6×6 gun tractors often had to employ their powerful winches to drag a 5.5 from a mud-bound gun pit. However, for some, there were still opportunities for leave, and during November Captain Catterall exchanged the privations of gun positions for the more urbane ambiences of Florence and Rome. In the latter he indulged in some culture with visits to performances of 'La Traviata' and 'La Boutique Fantasque'.

Back in the line, now at Cuirola, there was more military activity, especially for the FOOs. In the mountainous terrain there were problems beyond human muscle-power. 'For short distances one can hump a wireless set and all the gear, and if there are roads one can use a truck or a jeep, but where there are no roads and where the OP party may be out for a week or more, mules are needed. Three of us with our ordinary packs, a 19 (or 21) set, two batteries (like car batteries) and a petrol generator to charge them, plus rations, blankets etc., need two mules.' Thus laden Captain Riddett's OP party did 'Yeoman' work with a Guards battalion and later with the Gurkhas ... 'I felt safe with them – they used to boast about chopping off heads with their kukris'.

From November 1944 until April 1945 the campaign remained bogged down. But the Regiment's 5.5s were constantly in action with harassing and counter-battery tasks and the occasional call for fire on opportunity targets. Their German counterparts were active too, inflicting casualties on gun positions. On 12 January 1945, a 105 mm. shell landed squarely in one of 105 Battery's gun pits, killing all the detachment and putting the gun out of action.

The Allies' spring offensive opened on 9 April. Alexander assured his forces that the Germans were now 'very groggy indeed and need only an almighty punch to knock them out for good'. This was no exaggeration, for the enemy knew that in North-West Europe the Allies were over-running their homeland, and as the hordes of dejected German prisoners confirmed, morale was fast ebbing.

In the advance to the capture of Medicina 106 Battery supported a squadron of the 14th/20th King's Hussars. This was the first contact with the unit that was later to become the DLOY's affiliated regular cavalry regiment.

When some less thrusting types had joined the Regiment in England they fondly imagined that Medium Gunners were a fairly safe crowd to be with – always well back from the front line and out of harm's way. 'Not so as it turned out!' recalls Major Riddett. 'Bobby [Colonel] Palmer's idea was not to stay back and shell the German front line, but to get well forward and shell their backsides . . . in spite of the weight and size of our guns and tractors, we were more often than not up with the field artillery, and at one stage even amongst the anti-tank guns.' With the pursuit now in full spate, the 'groggy' Germans pulling back from position after position, the 78th kept well up with the units of XIII Corps, dropping into action, pulling out, rumbling forward, into action again and 'banging away all day'.(Catterall) On 28 April they crossed the Senio river near Faenza in support of 6 RTR and then thrust forward to the Adige river some 50 miles north of Bologna.

A week earlier the Regiment had learned that Lieutenant-Colonel Bobby Palmer had been awarded a well-merited DSO. It was typical of his selfless nature and intense regard for his Regiment that he promptly issued a Special Regimental Order:

> I wish all of you to realise that the D.S.O. given me is a decoration towards the earning of which every man who has served the Regiment through these many months of battle has vitally contributed: it is the official recognition of the part we have played since coming into action, particularly I understand, during the advance from CASSINO to FLORENCE.
>
> I am only too well aware that such results have only been achieved by team work; and the loyalty, resolution and cheerfulness, under every condition, of all ranks of the Regiment have been a constant inspiration in helping me carry out my part.
>
> You know that I carry on my Jeep the 4 British Divisional Sign given to the Regiment by its Commander. I ask you all to regard in the same light my wearing of this award.
>
> (Sgd) *W. R. PALMER*
> Lieut-Colonel, DSO, TD, RA

By 28 April New Zealand forces had entered Venice, while the US 5th Army were through Verona. 'Gen. Mark Clark declared organised resistance practically ceased – we may have fired our last round!' enthused Captain Catterall in his diary. On 2 May he waxed more excited: '*Terrific news!* The German Army in Italy surrendered unconditionally to

Alexander!!! Terms signed on Sunday – all on BBC news . . . Terrific relief to realise that the war is over for us. Now we are sure we shall go home!'

Indeed, the arduous 18 months' campaigning was at an end for the 78th, though months were to pass before anyone saw home. The Regiment remained in position on the south bank of the Adige river, near Padua until 7 May, when it was routed to the Trieste area. During this brief period Colonel Palmer was able to exhibit typical Yeoman resourcefulness. While the Regiment had been 'resting' in a charming Italian Marquesa's estate between Florence and Pisa, they learned that the lady was lamenting the loss of all her farm horses, commandeered by the Germans. Now, it so happened that on their perambulations around the position on the Adige, Colonel Palmer and RSM Miller discovered a herd of ex-German transport horses grazing in the meadows. Here was an opportunity for some off-the-record horse dealing. A number of selected animals were boxed in 3-tonners and motored the 150-odd miles to the estate. The gracious Marquesa proved not only delighted, but generous; so generous indeed, that the sum she handed over was sufficient to form a Regimental fund for entertainment and sporting events, and for officers to cash cheques.

On 7 May the Regiment moved via Padua, Treviso and Portogruara to the environs of Trieste. RHQ and 106 Battery were located in a pleasant site at Monfalcone across the bay from Trieste itself, where was 105 Battery. At first the situation in these parts was tense, for Marshal Tito and his Yugoslav forces had over-run Istria and were seeking to occupy Trieste much against the will of the Italians. Fortunately there was no serious confrontation and the issue was peacefully decided later in the year when Trieste was formally ceded to Yugoslavia. Nevertheless, there were occasional demonstrations and clashes between rival factions, so that the Regiment had to provide armed patrols in the Trieste streets and guards on shipping in the docks.

Commanding XIII Corps, with responsibility for the whole area, was Lieutenant-General John Harding, and in June he directed that a mounted military police unit should be formed to assist in maintaining law and order. The choice fell on the 78th, since they were a Regiment that had commenced the war as horsed cavalry, and many of the older members were experienced horsemen. There was no problem about mounts, for the Germans had been using vast numbers for transport purposes and these had been handed over to the British after the surrender; forty of these were co-opted for the police unit. Forty of the ex-horsemen were selected, to be commanded by RSM Harry Miller. This excellent Warrant Officer was not only a fine horseman, but enjoyed a great natural personality, and had even taught himself Italian.

The Mounted Police Troop was allotted quarters and stabling in the Italian barracks above Trieste and after some weeks of training, both men and horses were judged competent to patrol the streets in pairs. And very smart and cavalry-like they looked: Service Dress tunics with white waist and cross-belts, breeches and spurred riding boots, peaked caps (with green band in place of the MP red, in deference to Italian national colours); saddlery decked out with embroidered shabraques and white-blancoed headropes. For those former horse-soldiers the wheel had turned full circle: it was just like the good old days. In due course orders were received that Italians should gradually replace the British ranks so that the latter could be released for demobilisation. For a period, therefore, the patrols consisted of one DLOY and one Italian. The *Venzia Giulia Polizia* as it was known, continued thus, under RSM Miller, for another year, when it became all-Italian.

The Cheshire Yeomanry proudly boast that they were the last British soldiers to fight on horseback. This is true, but the DLOY members of that unique body, though they never had to fight, could equally well claim that they were the last to serve mounted overseas.

By January 1946 the 78th Regiment had become known as '78 Regiment (DLOY) (Auxiliary Police)'. In March orders were received that the Regiment was to be disbanded on 15 April 1946. In his valedictory order of 31 March, Lieutenant-Colonel W. R. Palmer wrote:

> In bidding farewell to those of you still serving, I wish to express my special gratitude for the very worthy part you have played in our exploits. Most of you came to us at an early stage of our gunner training and by immediately assuming our traditions, contributed so materially to the building up of that unbeatable team spirit which was the outstanding factor in our success. Many of you would have enjoyed much quicker promotion had you been in a non-Territorial unit, but you accepted the delay unselfishly, and never allowed it to detract from your efficiency. Since becoming Auxiliary Policemen, you have maintained the Regiment's reputation by your discipline, common sense and good humour ... I hope we shall all meet again at many a reunion.

Part 3

77th (DLOY) MEDIUM REGIMENT RA

We have seen that in November 1940 the 77th were divorced from their 78th (DLOY) comrades and posted to Gosford Castle, Market Hill, Northern Ireland, where they underwent intensive training under their new Gunner officer, Lieutenant-Colonel F. H. C. Rogers, MC. This entailed not only live-firing on local ranges, but large-scale operations in support of mock infantry attacks in the Mourne Mountains, while specialist training in wireless, MT driving and maintenance, and MG firing went ahead. In 1941 the 6 in. howitzers were replaced by the standard Medium equipments of the war, the 5.5 in. gun-howitzers with which the Regiment fought throughout the North-West Europe campaign.

In September 1942 Colonel Rogers was posted as commander HQ 2 AGRA 1st Army, and another Gunner, Lieutenant-Colonel F. G. Wintle, MBE, assumed command of the 77th. He was to lead it for the rest of the war. At this date the Second-in-Command was Major J. E. Palmer (brother of Lieutenant-Colonel W. R. Palmer who commanded the 78th). When he was passed over by Wintle, the latter generously offered to step down, but the War Office refused. Eric Palmer was a devoted Yeoman, his sole ambition being to command his own

Regiment. He expressed this view when later offered another command, to be curtly informed by Authority that an officer 'was not in a position to express his wishes or pick and choose as to command'. And so in due course he was severed from his DLOY to take command of the 63rd Medium Regiment RA.

During the Regiment's tours at Pembroke and in Northern Ireland its ranks included a 35-year-old Gunner named Arthur Lowe, who had joined the DLOY as Trooper in 1938. Transferring to the REME in 1942, he served in the Middle East, achieving the rank of Sergeant-Major. But in his subsequent civilian career he was to become better known as 'Captain Mainwaring' of 'Dad's Army'.

In June 1943 the 77th left Ireland for Yorkshire, where they were based at Scriven, near Knaresborough, coming under command of 8 AGRA, with which they were to see most of their subsequent campaigning. After sundry other moves – up to the Otterburn ranges in Northumberland, down to Newark, up to Catterick and Lockerbie – May 1944 found them at Aldershot in Mandora Barracks, and here they remained for the next month.

By now, despite strict security, it was common knowledge that the long-awaited Second Front was about to be launched with the invasion of Normandy, although as yet no one except High Command knew exactly when and where this would take place. The whole of southern England was virtually a huge armed camp with troops, guns and vehicles massed in their concentration areas.

In their Aldershot area, as an element of VIII Corps, the 77th were busy with the laborious and messy tasks of waterproofing guns, tractors and vehicles, loading ammunition, checking stores, in preparation for what had become known as D Day.

However, that momentous date of 6 June passed without any move, and it was not until the 12th that orders came to concentrate in Marshalling Area A, at Portsmouth. On arrival there the Regiment was immediately rerouted to Marshalling Area B, at Tilbury, and after a thirteen-hour drive in convoy, they reached the docks that evening. On the following morning, all were embarked on two American LSTs (Landing Ships Tanks), and at 2100 hours on 14 June the 77th (DLOY) Medium Regiment RA at last left the shores of Britain for what Montgomery had dubbed 'the Great Crusade' or Operation Overlord. After delays due to heavy seas, the convoy made 'Mike' Beach on the Normandy coast (between Courseulles and St Aubin) on the evening of the next day.[1]

By now the fighting had moved inland and, apart from wrecked landing craft, 'drowned' tanks and vehicles, there was little evidence of the D Day assault and no enemy opposition. But the landing was not without its hazards. As Bombardier Hartill recalled, 'the Captain ran the LST into shallow water and lowered the ramp. The first vehicle down

---

1. The following account is based largely on the privately printed history *The 77th (Duke of Lancaster's Own Yeomanry) Medium Regiment RA. North West Europe Campaign. June 1944–May 1945* This was published anonymously (c. 1947) but the author was Lieutenant-Colonel L. J. Thomas, MC, who served with the Regiment throughout the campaign and became its last Commanding Officer.

the ramp was a Bedford 3-tonner which promptly vanished in deep water, as the ramp had been lowered at the edge of a bomb crater.'[2]

Having disembarked without further incident, the Regiment first came into action on 16 June on the outskirts of Lantheuil, where defensive fire was put down. The Luftwaffe were still bombing the shipping on the beaches and, wrote Colonel Thomas, 'we could see the red balls of Oerlikon fire filling the sky behind us as they drifted apparently lazily to meet the planes . . . Our only discomforts were the AA shell splinters which pattered around us like hail and occasionally bounced off a vehicle with a most disconcerting clang.' A little later the two Batteries were firing concentrations in support of 44 and 46 Infantry Brigade between Cheux and St Mavieu, and on 26 June the Regiment suffered its first battle casualty. Major P. T. Hollins was up front in a tank directing fire for his 104 Battery. Says Bombardier Hartill, 'I still picture our Battery Commander, Major Peter Hollins, still only 23 years of age, shot through his steel helmet by a sniper while standing in the turret of his tank to direct fire on a concentration of enemy tanks. A small wooden cross at the roadside, with his helmet and khaki scarf, showed how far he had advanced into the Normandy countryside.' The tank threat was repulsed.

On the advance across the Odon on 28 June, the Regiment supported 11th Armoured Division: 'We moved up to a gun area between Norrey-en-Bessin and Cheux. Here we found ourselves in a very exposed position . . . with the enemy within 1,500 yards of our left flank. A 15 cm. battery in the Carpiquet area proved particularly troublesome and shelled us at intervals through the day. The enemy counter-attacked several times and we had a busy time shelling his forming up areas. The guns were firing extremely accurately and rapidly, and on several occasions observed shoots were taken on within 100 yards of our leading tanks with great success.'

On 17 July the Regiment was tasked with support of 'Operation Goodwood', the break-out on to the Falaise plain. Colonel Thomas continues:

> Our new gun area was centred on the village of Gruchy about three miles north of Caen. The village was nothing but untidy heaps of rubble and occasional walls and shells of houses. The road through had been cleared by a bulldozer, which had piled rubble with pathetic scraps of furniture and household goods on either side. The surrounding fields were littered with burnt out tanks and vehicles and abandoned guns . . . Many of the dead had not been cleared. Some still remained in their burnt out tank traps and craters, while yet more were concealed in the hedges and ditches . . . The air was warm and moist, and with the occasional breeze the stench of mortality was wafted over us in sickening waves as we prepared for our next action.

On the following day the guns were continuously in action in support of the advance, and in the course of some twelve hours the two Batteries engaged 31 targets and expended 3,412 rounds. During that afternoon Captain H. W. Dimbleby was acting as FOO with 3rd Royal Tanks. At 1500 hours he radioed back that his tank had been hit and the crew were

---

2. A Gunner reservist, Bdr Harry Hartill was called up in 1939. Joining the 77th in 1940, he served with the Regiment throughout the campaign.

trying to extricate it. Nothing further was heard about him until the damaged tank was recovered, with Dimbleby's body. He had been killed by Spandau fire.

On 22 July the Regiment advanced through the devastated town of Caen to support 2nd Canadian Corps who were pushing towards Falaise, and there followed numerous calls for concentrations on enemy armour. On 30 July 103 Battery Command Post suffered a direct hit which killed two Gunners and wounded one officer and another Gunner, besides destroying instruments.

While still in the Falaise pocket, the Regiment underwent some very tense moments, as recalled by ex-Sergeant N. J. Sharp:[3]

> We had left our position near Caumont when everything was very fluid and the Germans were trying to escape from the Falaise pocket. The column was halted and news got around that we were cut off and surrounded. We had apparently driven into a no mans land area. We were ordered into a field . . . to go on full alert and await the possible arrival of Tiger tanks, the most feared of the German weaponry. We camouflaged up and waited. Soon we heard the roar of tank engines, obviously very powerful machines.
>
> This field of ours fell away down to a road running west to east. The squadron of Tigers moved slowly across our front at about 5mph, at a distance of some 2–300yds – uncomfortably close. Our gunners had the barrels of the 5.5s depressed to their limit and were ready to fire over open sights . . . But nothing happened. Whether those Germans saw us, we will never know, but I think if they had opened fire with their 88s at that range we would have been blown out of that field. Our rate of fire would have been quite inadequate to cope.

August 6th saw the Germans making a last desperate effort to extricate themselves from the Falaise pocket, with a massive attack by 10 Panzer SS Division. This was an occasion for 'Uncle Target' – all available guns in action – and concentration after concentration was fired to halt the attack.

'The guns were now showing signs of the enormous strain put on them during the past weeks,' wrote Colonel Thomas. 'Some had been put out of action for unreliable firing; others dropped at intervals through mechanical defect, to be brought back again as rapidly as the fitters could improvise a repair . . . at one stage we could only muster four guns in the Regiment.'

After being in action continuously for 46 days, the 77th was pulled back to a hide area near Bayeux for a much-needed refit and rest. Here in the 2nd Army base workshops new barrels were fitted to guns, damaged gun carriages and vehicles repaired, defective or lost instruments replaced.

Meanwhile the Falaise pocket had been 'cleaned' with the Germans suffering crippling losses: 240,000 killed and wounded and 21,000 prisoners besides hundreds of guns, tanks

---

3. Norman Sharp had joined the DLOY at Pembroke in 1940 and became Survey Sergeant. He served throughout the NW Europe campaign and was demobbed in 1946.

and other material destroyed or captured. 'Operation Overlord' had fully justified its planners, and the way was now open for what the troops dubbed the 'Great Swan', the advance through France and Belgium.

It was not until 17 September that the 77th were ordered forward again to join in the advance as support of 11 Armoured Division. The drive through liberated France took on the nature of a triumphal progress rather than a military operation, the only 'opposition' being the cheering hordes of locals in towns and villages who blocked progress to embrace embarrassed gunners and press on them offerings of fruit and flowers. Harbouring for a night near Bapaume, 'we had a busy time chasing children out of our vehicles and cookhouses . . . As we entered Belgium our welcome became even more tumultuous, and our drivers found it difficult to avoid running down the cheering crowds who overflowed the pavements in every village' (Thomas). Crossing the Escaut Canal and entering Dutch territory with little annoyance but an occasional Spandau, the Regiment was greeted as before ' . . . soon vehicles were bedecked with orange rosettes and ribbons'.

But more serious business was imminent. On 21 September the Regiment came into action supporting 159 Brigade at the crossing of the Wilhelmina canal opposite Asten. This bridgehead was secured after a fierce enemy counter-attack. Crossing the canal the Regiment established an OP in Asten church tower, whence at one juncture the FOO signalled back to the unbelieving Gun Position, 'Target cavalry'. It turned out that the 'cavalry' was a posse of escaping Germans who had commandeered local farm horses.

There was now fierce opposition from the enemy who had regrouped after their Normandy debacle, and the Regiment was daily in action with counter-battery and defensive fire and the frequent 'opportunity target'. By early October they had moved up to a position near Overloon in support of 3 Infantry Division's attack. Here on the 12th, 103 Battery came under heavy fire from artillery and the fearsome Nebelwerfers (multi-barrelled mortars) which killed two Gunners and wounded one officer and eleven other ranks, and damaged two guns. 'In spite of this', noted the War Dairy, 'the guns continued to be served. The high sense of duty displayed by all ranks was remarkable.' For their gallantry in keeping the guns in action, Captain Charles Harrison and Lieutenant Edward Bailey were awarded the MC, while Lance- Bombardier E. Galbraith, medical orderly, received the MM for his bravery in tending the wounded under fire.

By 18 October the infantry had captured Venraij just west of the Maas, and in their position outside the town the Regiment put down counter-battery fire, being themselves subjected to periodic reply by 122 mm. guns, which fortunately 'did us no harm'. For these shoots the OP parties had the novel experience of sharing their post with lunatics. The OP was established in the Venraij Asylum whose inmates were still in occupation. They were later evacuated, 'but caused great confusion during the fighting, as they ran about aimlessly, terrified by the shelling and the showers of glass that descended from the enormous glass roofs of the asylum.'(Thomas)

During October and November 1944 the Regiment was engaged mainly on counter-battery shoots, with a few observed shootings. But, one of the more popular pastimes was the destruction of enemy OPs in church steeples across the Maas. For this a 'roving gun' (i.e.

detached) was employed, to avoid giving away the main gun position by prolonged firing. Such fellers of church steeples may have done sad damage to local ecclesiastical architecture, but they no doubt contributed their mite to the felling of the Third Reich.

In support of 3 British Division near Venlo, the Regiment now had other enemy opposition to contend with. 'Our gun area was most uncomfortable. It was impossible to dig in the guns as water lay about six inches below ground level. Building up gun pits was a poor substitute as a pond appeared wherever we excavated. The gun positions were between quarter and half a mile away from the main road and the mud tracks which led to them were soon unusable to all but four-wheel drive vehicles, and these latter frequently stuck.'(Thomas) Unlike the 78th Regiment in Italy, with their 6X6 American 'Mack' gun tractors, the 77th had AEC 'Matadors' with only four driven wheels (plus low-ratio transfer box). In the bitter winter, gun detachments had to 'bivvy' as best they could in makeshift shelters contrived from odd planks and charge cases with a tarpaulin over the top. Others might enjoy the amenities of farm buildings. 'At one time we were billeted at a farm', recalled ex-Trooper/Gunner Bob Nuttall, 'and some of us slept in a byre with cattle on one side, our bedding on the other and a stye with a sow due to farrow next to us. Whiffy – but oh so warm!'

Between November and December the Regiment was in action supporting attacks by units of the 15th (Scottish) Division west of the Maas. By 1 December the two Batteries were in position at Sevenum, some five miles west of Venlo. The latter, or its suburb, Blerwick, was the next objective of the 15th Division, and all guns of 8 AGRA were to support with a massive barrage. This opened at first light, with Field, Medium and Heavy guns blasting the enemy positions for two hours. During that time the two 77th Batteries each contributed some 300 shells. And here for the first time they witnessed 'mattresses' in action. These were multiple rocket projectors, each firing a salvo of 26 missiles. 'We had over fifty of them in action, and the roar of their discharge drowned all other sounds of battle. The effect at the target was devastating, and highly unpopular with the prisoners who soon began to come in.'(Thomas). By nightfall Blerwick was taken and the whole of the west bank of the Maas was now in Allied hands.

On 9 December the Regiment moved ten miles south to a new area near Maasbree, where they viewed with misgivings the waterlogged fields and mud-bound gun positions. The winter spell of static warfare now set in and the Regiment itself remained static until the end of February, in conditions of much tribulation. Colonel Thomas:

> During this period we appreciated to the full the boredom and discomfort of static warfare under winter conditions. The mud was only conquered by frost, and frost in its turn brought us a host of other problems, particularly when we had 30 degrees of it. During acute frost we would light fires under the recoil systems of the guns to keep them ready for action, using tarpaulins to shield the glow from any hostile aircraft. All day fuel cutting parties worked in the pine forests . . . We suffered occasional counter battery and harassing fire, but with very few casualties. The hostile fire was usually heralded by an air burst over the position; having seen this we knew for certain that the 'hate' would arrive in half an hour, and took precautions accordingly. When a troop was well spotted it moved, leaving dummy guns

in the original position ... We heightened the illusion by using flash simulators at night, but never succeeded in drawing enemy fire by this method, though a hostile aircraft was once persuaded to shoot up a dummy position, much to our satisfaction. We had at our disposal sound ranging and flash spotting sections, radar troops and air OPs.

The main object of the winter artillery battles was to drive back the enemy batteries, which we did most successfully with these aids ... Air photographs showed us the results of many of our concentrations, which were most satisfying, revealing many direct hits on gun positions and complete devastation of hostile battery areas. Wherever possible we administered a dose of a hundred shells to each enemy gun spotted.

With sixteen 5.5s in constant action, the weight of HE delivered must have been enormous. On 17 February of the New Year fire was called for on three enemy batteries across the Maas, which were molesting the forward infantry. 'After a total of 1,100 shells had been sent over, the three batteries lapsed into silence.' (War Diary)

All this colossal amount of ammunition – shells, charges, cartridges – had to be lorried up to the gun positions from rear dumps, along routes blasted by enemy fire, often deep in mud or under water, and the exertions of the A Echelon drivers (who never had the satisfaction of firing a shell at the enemy) won admiration from those in the gun pits.

By early March (1945) the Germans had been driven back across the Rhine, and only their bridgehead at Wesel remained to be liquidated. After a spell of 'rest' in Belgium, spent in re-calibrating guns and essential maintenance, on 16 March the 77th moved up to a concentration area opposite Wesel and, together with the whole of Montgomery's 21st Army Group artillery, prepared their gun positions.

The stage was now set for Operation PLUNDER. Ebullient as ever, Monty promised in his Order of the Day that '21st Army Group will now cross the Rhine . . . and having crossed the Rhine, we will crack about in the plains of Germany, chasing the enemy from pillar to post'. The Rhine crossing was the most massive operation yet mounted since D Day, with 1.25 million British and Canadian troops, 2,000 guns, 600 tanks and 32,000 assorted combat and other vehicles. Several days were spent preparing and camouflaging gun positions, dumping ammunition and drawing up fire plans. The Germans – troops and civilians – had fled to the opposite bank of the river, leaving abandoned farmsteads and livestock. Many of the latter were put to good use: some of the DLOY gunners were ex-farm lads and proved adept at milking cows; others rounded up poultry, so that fresh milk, free range (very 'free') eggs and chicken were on the daily menu. One-time DLOY Trooper, now TSM Wilson, appropriated an abandoned horse on which he rode round his gun pits.[4]

On the morning of 23 March all 2,000 guns opened up with a preliminary bombardment that exceeded even that of El Alamein. This was followed by 'cab ranks' of bombers, and

---

4. Jack Wilson joined the DLOY, aged 17, in 1937, following in his father's footsteps (or hoof prints) who had served from 1920 to 1934. Jack became BSM and left the Regiment at the end of the war, when he joined the Lancashire Constabulary.

as Colonel Thomas wrote. the 77th in their position ready to support 1st Commando Brigade, had a grandstand view:[5]

> First came the pathfinders, dropping their flares in a circle round the town. Soon afterwards we saw dull orange flashes of the sticks of high explosive bombs, every one of which fell right across the target area ... soon the burning town glowed red behind the thick smoke that covered it. As the sounds of the departing planes died down there were a few moments of unearthly quiet, an awestricken silence at the obliteration of a town. Then the crack of our guns again filled the air as they supported the Commandos in their advance into the town ... We fired a heavy anti-flak programme to support the airborne landings, and as we were firing the first planes passed overhead ... As we looked our own 6th Airborne Division was dropping slightly to our left, while 17 American Airborne dropped to our immediate front.
>
> We felt a tremendous but impossible desire to help as we saw the intense flak through which many of them fell, and watched helplessly as planes crashed in flames, many of them landing in and around our own gun area.
>
> Then came the gliders, casting off their tow ropes immediately above us ... The flak had diminished by now under the combined assaults of counter battery fire and parachutists, but still planes and gliders were being hit as they came in. All round us plumes of black smoke indicated a wrecked aircraft.

By nightfall on 24 March the Wesel bridgehead had been secured, and Monty's 'crack about' in northern Germany was to follow. After continued shoots in support of the advancing infantry, the 77th made their own, unopposed, crossing of the Rhine by a Bailey bridge erected rapidly by the Sappers and again came into action a few miles east of the shattered Wesel. Rumbling through the devastation they found it difficult to understand how the defenders had managed to put up any resistance in the face of the artillery and air bombardment. 'Newly captured prisoners were still removing bodies from the smoking ruins.'

The Regiment now came under command of the 6th Guards Tank Brigade[6] with the capture of Munster as their objective. This role entailed rapid dropping into action with no time to prepare gun pits or even slit trenches, and equally rapid moves forward. The drill was a 'leap frogging' performance: while one Troop, or Battery, continued in action, another advanced to the next position. Often the leading unit was no more than a few hundred yards behind the Brigade spearpoint of armour. Very 'forward' for Medium artillery! By 29 March they had pushed through Dorsten to the town of Dulmen, 20 miles west of Munster, and the guns went into action just 2,000 yards short of the defended strongpoint. The first Battery to open up was 104, which suffered immediate retaliation from SP guns lurking in a nearby wood.[7] One registered a direct hit on a gun tractor,

---

5. And so did Winston Churchill who, against all advice, had flown out to witness the operation and was on a vantage point behind the guns.
6. 1 Coldstream, 3 Scots Guards, 3 Recce Regiment, 6 Field Regt RA and one American Parachute battalion.
7. The German Self-Propelled (SP) gun was the fearsome 88 mm. which, since the Western Desert fighting, had proved the most dreaded threat to British and American armour.

destroying it, killing the driver and wounding several detachment numbers. The explosion also damaged the gun and showered debris over a large area. Promptly, 105 Battery engaged the SPs and silenced them.

Continuing with 6 Guards Tank Brigade the Regiment moved forward until 31 March when they took up position just west of Munster. The Guards Group were now tasked to seize the bridges over the Dortmund-Ems Canal. This they did, and as the War Diary recorded, 'with the guns covering the city of Munster and its environs, it may be that the surrender will be demanded from the Burgomaster tomorrow morning'. The surrender indeed followed on 2 April, and moving into the town, the 77th occupied vacated German barracks on the north-western outskirts.

All fighting in this sector had now ceased, and the Regiment moved forward to Osnabruck, already 'cleaned'. Guns were now taken out of action and for the next three weeks fire tasks were replaced by more peaceful duties, when detachments were detailed to assist the British Military Governor by sorting out and administrating the hordes of DPs (Displaced Persons), guarding German prisoners and mounting guards and patrols to preserve law and order in the town, and arresting German service personnel. TSM Jack Wilson was one of those given this task, and he writes:

> After a few days I was allotted the job of rounding up all the fit German service personnel . . . I was given the services of a certain Herr Tiermann as interpreter. Tiermann was over 60 years of age and had been the headmaster of a school in Osnabruck. He had been vetted by the Army and it was said that he had been kicked out of his school for refusing to indoctrinate the children with Nazi idealism . . . I used to go off with Tiermann in my jeep at 9 o'clock in the morning and warn about 25 men to be ready to move with their equipment at 2 o'clock. A three- tonner would follow me to collect the bodies, which were then lodged for the night in the cells of the barracks which we were occupying. My brief was not to take anyone who had his discharge papers or anyone not fit in my opinion to bear arms or to actively engage in subversive activities.
>
> The very first person I called on was about 25 years of age . . . married and living with his father. As soon as I saw him I knew I wouldn't be taking him because he was on crutches, having only one leg. He hadn't got any discharge papers, but it was obvious they had been lost in the post. However, I wasn't letting on too soon that he was in the clear, and through Tiermann and my broken German I began to question him. His father interrupted, saying, 'I have told my son he will be well treated by the English . . . I was a prisoner in the last war and was well treated by the English.' I asked him where his camp had been, and he said Manchester. Now I was born in Manchester and often heard my parents talking about the POW camp which was on the site of the present Christie Cancer Hospital on Wilmslow Road. I told the father I came from Manchester, to which he replied 'You know Platt Fields?' That was the large park near where I lived. An amazing coincidence! I then told them that since the father had said so much good about the English, I wouldn't take the son away.

Moving on into Munster, the **Regiment** was involved in striving to maintain peace between roving armed gangs of violently anti-German DPs and the local inhabitants. 'Our released allies, though scorning any law aimed at protecting the German population were most friendly. Generally the sight of a British uniform was sufficient to disperse any DP riot, but was unfortunately no guarantee that the rioters would not move off to the next street to recommence operations where British eyes would not be offended.' (Thomas).

By this time hordes of dejected German prisoners seemed to indicate that victory could not be far off, but the death throes of the Wehrmacht were not yet over, and staunch pockets of SS units and Paratroops were still holding out along the route to Hamburg. On 28 April the 77th were once more assigned to their proper job with guns, again in support of the 15th (Scottish) Division who were pushing up the Elbe river towards Hamburg. Resistance was almost non-existent, and they were called upon for only one concentration to clear the forest of Sachsenwald. On 1 May came a BBC news flash on the wireless that Hitler had committed suicide amid the ruins of Berlin. Two days later the Regiment was ordered to cease all firing while German emissaries came through the position to negotiate the surrender of Hamburg. Now entire enemy units were surrendering and the roads were jammed with marching columns making their way into captivity. 'The enemy troops were a mixed lot,' wrote Thomas. 'Some were good Wehrmacht units, well dressed, disciplined, and marching smartly. Others were ill-clothed, shambling creatures reminiscent of the Volksturm and medically unfit who had opposed us in the early days of our fighting in Holland. We saw no signs of SS or Panzer troops.'

The 77th had now fired their final rounds of the war. On 4 May they drove through the bombed-out suburbs of Hamburg to an area near Todendorf, some 20 miles north, where they harboured peacefully, awaiting the momentous signal that everyone was expecting. This came from Divisional HQ at 2040 hours the same day:

> Germans surrendered unconditionally at 1830 hrs. STOP Hostilities on 2nd Army fronts will cease at 0800 hrs tomorrow 8 May STOP No repeat no advance beyond present positions until further orders from this HQ STOP

Thus ended the Second World War for the 77th (DLOY) Medium Regiment RA. Since landing in Normandy eleven months before they had driven some 900 miles, fired incalculable tons of high explosive in support of infantry and armour, and suffered inevitable casualties.

Although VE Day of 8 May 1945 marked the final overthrow of the Third Reich, there was no immediate repatriation and demob for the 77th and their 2nd Army comrades. The war in Europe might be over, but in Burma General Slim's 'Forgotten Army' (14th) was still fiercely contesting the road to Rangoon with a more savage enemy. Meanwhile in Germany there remained multifarious security, administrative and other tasks to be undertaken by the occupying forces.

On that memorable day of 8 May the 77th was ordered to Rendsburg on the Kiel Canal, about 20 miles west of Kiel itself, there to occupy former German barracks. Together with other units of 8 AGRA it shared administrative responsibility for some 1,800 square miles of territory with its thousands of DPs, German prisoners and released Allied prisoners of numerous nationalities.

Still in command of the Regiment was Lieutenant-Colonel F. G. Wintle, MBE, who had led throughout the campaign. The daunting nature of his own responsibilities is disclosed by the War Diary: besides an unspecified number of Wehrmacht and other prisoners, he had to organise and administer 1,169 Poles, 798 Italians, 738 Russians and 89 Romanians – all either DPs or released prisoners. In addition, guards had to be found for important buildings and installations, roads had to be patrolled and, not least of the tasks, members of the SS and Gestapo had to be hunted down and arrested.

On 8 June the 77th said farewell to the 5.5s that it had served so nobly: all the guns were withdrawn to a base ordnance depot and for the remainder of its existence the Regiment was 'Medium RA' in name only, becoming virtually an infantry unit. At the end of June Colonel Wintle was posted home, his place being taken by Lieutenant-Colonel (later Brigadier) J. F. Lindner, MC. However, in August he too departed and Lieutenant-Colonel L. J. Thomas, MC, became the last Commanding Officer of the Regiment.

As with the 78th in Italy, the succeeding months of 1945 and early 1946 saw the Regiment progressively depleted as officers and men went home or were drafted to other units destined for the Far East. By March 1946 the strength was down to little more than a skeleton, and in that month came the finale, with 'Suspended Animation'. There was no emergence from this limbo, so that after six years' Yeoman service the 77th (DLOY) Medium Regiment RA ceased to exist.

The Second World War had cost the Regiment seven officers and 38 other ranks killed, as recorded in the Role of Honour. It also brought the following awards for distinguished service and gallantry.

Distinguished Service Order
Lieutenant-Colonel W. R. Palmer, TD
Lieutenant-Colonel F. H. C. Rogers
Lieutenant-Colonel F. G. Wintle

Member, Order of the British Empire
Lieutenant-Colonel F. G. Wintle

Military Cross
Lieutenant-Colonel J. F. Lindner
Major J. Arrowsmith
Major S. E. Catterall
Major R. E. Heaton
Major G. Lawson
Major L. A. H. Riddett
Major L. J. Thomas
Captain C. Harrison
Lieutenant E. W. Bailey

Military Medal
Bombardier A. Baker
Lance-Bombardier E. Galbraith

CHAPTER IX

Resurgence 1946–1973

With the euphemistic 'suspended animation' of the 77th and 78th (DLOY) Medium Regiments RA in 1946, The Duke of Lancaster's Own Yeomanry temporarily ceased to exist. But, as will be seen, the hiatus was a brief one.

Meanwhile, the indefatigable Colonel Denis Bates, as Honorary Colonel, was determined to keep alive some semblance of the Regimental 'family' in the form of an Old Comrades Association. Under his chairmanship a meeting of past and present officers and ex-NCOs was held in The Queen's Hotel, Manchester on 14 August 1946, when it was unanimously resolved to create such an Association. Oddly, there was some objection to the title 'Old Comrades' and the organisation emerged as the 'DLOY Association'. With Headquarters in Manchester, and branches in Bolton, Blackpool, Preston and Liverpool, this was the nucleus of the present Old Comrades Association.

By this date the Labour Government under Clement Attlee had announced the reconstitution of the Territorial Army, which took effect on 1 January 1947. A total of 50 Yeomanry regiments were reformed after their suspended animation. Twenty-four of these lost their pre-war cavalry roles to become Field, Medium, Heavy or AA units of the Royal Artillery; twenty-six reassumed their original cavalry role, now of course with tanks or armoured cars as Territorial members of the Royal Armoured Corps.[1] One of the latter was The Duke of Lancaster's Own Yeomanry, roled as Divisional Regiment for its old pre-war formation, the 42nd (East Lancashire) Division. Regimental Headquarters was re-established in Whalley Road, Manchester, and the task of reforming was undertaken by an officer well qualified to do so. As we have seen, Lieutenant-Colonel W. R. (Bobby) Palmer, DSO, TD had not only led the 78th (DLOY) Medium Regiment throughout the Italian campaign, but was a dedicated member of the Regiment, having served in it since 1923.

The contemporary (1947) issue of the Army List showed the officers serving with the reformed Regiment as under:

Lieutenant-Colonel
W. R. Palmer, DSO, TD

Captains
M. A. A. Birtwistle
B. Greenwood
D. R. Poynton
J. J. Thwaites, OBE
R. C. D. Walker, DFC

---

1. The Royal Armoured Corps had been created in April 1939 to embrace the 18 mechanised regular cavalry regiments and the Royal Tank Corps, henceforth renamed Royal Tank Regiment (one could not have a 'Corps' within a Corps). Then as now the Headquarters and training centre were located at Bovington, Dorset.

Lieutenants
S. Gorst
P. G. Clemence, MC
J. N. B. Cardwell
A. C. D. Spence
B. S. Bourne

Squadrons (still nostalgically termed 'Sabre Squadrons') were located at Bolton, Preston, Chorley and Blackpool. As a Divisional armoured regiment, the DLOY was supposed to be equipped with the then obsolescent Cromwell tank mounting a 75mm. gun. But as always with Territorial units, issues were minimal, so that when the Regiment went to Annual Camp they had to rely on loans from regulars, as they did at Tilshead in 1953 when the 3rd Carabiniers obliged.

After the post-war reorganisation all Yeomanry regiments were affiliated to regular cavalry regiments. The latter provided Training Majors, Adjutants, Permanent Staff Instructors (or PSIs) and occasionally, Commanding Officers. In 1947 the DLOY formed an affiliation with the 14th/20th King's Hussars, which continued until the Regiment ceased to exist.[2]

Shortly after the Regiment's rebirth, the Commanding Officer, Lieutenant-Colonel W. R. Palmer and the Honorary Colonel, Denis Bates, agreed on some minor modifications to the cap badge, which was considered too large to be worn on Battle Dress. Accordingly on 7 May 1947, Colonel Bates submitted suggested alterations to the Under Secretary of State at the War Office. Little could he foresee the hornets' nest he was stirring up. Specimens of the existing badge and the modified version were supplied, as demanded, to the Director of Ordnance Services, and after cogitating on these for more than two years, in November 1949 that functionary raised the objection that the design of cap and collar badges 'includes the Garter without the Garter Motto (*Honi soit qui mal y pense*), and such arrangement is contrary to the policy announced by Army Order 232 of 1901'. Unless the Honorary Colonel could quote authority for this departure, the badge would need to be redesigned to conform. Piqued, Colonel Bates retorted that 'the right to wear the Garter without the Motto on our Regimental badge and button is one of the *most* cherished and ancient privileges of The Duke of Lancaster's Own Yeomanry,' stemming from 1834 when King William IV granted that cherished title and the 'plain' garter to the badge of the Regiment. Unhappily, Colonel Bates had to confess that documentary proof was lacking, since during the First World War all records were deposited in the Cavalry Records Centre at Canterbury – only to be lost. The obdurate Director of Ordnance Services now referred the matter to the Heraldic authority, Sir Gerald Wollaston, Garter King of Arms. His reply (of 7 December 1949) was uncompromising. 'The rule that nothing can be inscribed on the Garter other than the Motto of the Order 'Honi Soit qui mal y pense' is always to be strictly observed . . . The Badge as now used is not a plain Garter, but a Garter with an inscription on it which is foreign to the Order . . . I cannot conceive that any Sovereign would allow it to be used encircled by a Garter which was not the insignia of the Order.'

2. With their Home Headquarters in Fulwood Barracks, Preston, the 14th/20th have long been Lancashire's regular cavalry regiment. They share their Museum at Preston with the DLOY and The Queen's Lancashire Regiment.

But the valiant Honorary Colonel was not to be beaten. On 3 January 1950 he played his trump card. Writing to the Director of Ordnance Services, he declared: 'if you still desire to persist in this challenge, I will lay the correspondence, together with the letter from the College of Arms, before His Majesty The King, our Colonel-in-Chief, for his gracious consideration and command.'

This did the trick. On 15 May 1950 the DOS conceded defeat, so that thanks to Colonel Bates, the Garter with its 'foreign' inscription remained a distinctive feature of the Regiment's Badge.

A couple of months later (on 2 July) the Honorary Colonel was on parade for the ceremony of unveiling a War Memorial at RHQ, Manchester for all who fell in the two World Wars. A full turn-out of the Regiment was commanded by Lieutenant-Colonel E. B. Studd (14th/20th Hussars), and the service was conducted by Major the Revd P. A. Patrick, Senior Chaplain to the 42nd Division.

June 2nd, 1953 saw the Coronation of Her Majesty Queen Elizabeth II and, as was customary on such occasions, a Coronation Honours List was prepared for publication in *The London Gazette*. This included Her Majesty's appointments as Colonel-in-Chief or Honorary Colonel of the several regiments so honoured. Now it is scarcely necessary to remind readers that ever since 1834 the Sovereign, as *ipso facto* The Duke of Lancaster, had been graciously pleased to head The Duke of Lancaster's Own Yeomanry as its Colonel-in-Chief. Thus on 2 May Colonel Bates was dumbfounded by the contents of a 'Personal and Confidential' letter from the Director of Personal Services, Major-General M. B. Dowse. This bombshell informed him that *The London Gazette* of 1 June would announce that Her Majesty was graciously pleased to assume the appointment of 'Honorary Colonel of The Duke of Lancaster's Own Yeomanry'. This was scarcely credible. Was the 119-year-old privilege of a Royal Colonel-in-Chief to be abolished without a word of explanation? How could he, Colonel Bates, continue as Honorary Colonel? Must he step down? The position became confused when in reply to a congratulatory telegram from the Regiment to the Queen on her Coronation, he received sincere thanks from Her majesty for the loyal message 'which as Colonel-in-Chief I much appreciate'.

There now followed a flurry of correspondence between Colonel Bates, the Director of Personal Services, the Chancellor of the Duchy of Lancaster, the Secretary of State for War and the Queen's Private Secretary. This bulging file, now preserved in the Regimental Museum, cannot be reproduced here, but the outcome, though never admitted, was that someone had blundered.

On 1 September 1953 the Supplement to *The London Gazette* announced:

> The QUEEN has been graciously pleased to assume the appointment of Colonel-in-Chief of The Duke of Lancaster's Own Yeomanry (T.A.), 18th August 1953.
>
> The appointment notified for this Regiment in Gazette (Supplement) dated 1st June 1953, is cancelled.

Once more, the noble Denis Bates had preserved his Regiment's traditions.

Just over a year later, in October 1954, the Regiment was able to welcome the Colonel-in-Chief to its home territory when Her Majesty visited Lancashire and, in Wigan, opened the Wigan and District Mining and Technical College. Lieutenant-Colonel D. B. Stewart, Commanding Officer, was in attendance, and Major M. A. A. Birtwistle commanded a Guard of Honour.

In the 1950s the Regiment included many National Servicemen who, after their eighteen months' (later two years') service with regular regiments were obliged to carry out a total of 60 days' training with Territorial units, spread over three-and-a-half years. In practice, the NS men did little more than attend annual camps, and the obligation ceased in 1957.

In June 1953 the Regiment was joined by a 24-year-old Lieutenant who had just completed his NS stint with the 12th Royal Lancers. His name was David Waddington and no one, least of all himself, could imagine that 30-odd years later he was to become Secretary of State for the Home Department in Her Majesty's government, and a QC into the bargain. Despite the cares of his high office, in 1990 he found the time to recount the following incident during his DLOY service.[3]

> We went to Kirkcudbright for the annual camp in the summer of 1954. I was given a job at Headquarters doing precisely nothing and quite enjoying it, but disaster struck half way through the second week. A General arrived and demanded to be driven to where the Regiment was performing. My heart sank into my boots. I didn't know the way. Having driven round in circles for nearly an hour under the increasingly suspicious gaze of the General, I was obliged to make an abject confession. It didn't seem very funny at the time, but as the years go by one sees things differently!

In 1955 the Annual Camp was held in the Thetford training area (Norfolk), when B Squadron was subjected to an air attack. The Squadron Leader, Captain J. A. Peake, a qualified pilot, managed to borrow an Auster light aircraft from a nearby Air OP Squadron, and having 'bombed up' with a full load of toilet rolls, made several low-level attacks on his Squadron lines. But he had not reckoned with defence measures. The Squadron PSI, Sergeant-Major Hardwidge, gathered a few men with Very pistols, and on his last run the attacker was received with a volley which caused him to retire to the airfield 'with a very pale face'. He was later obliged to pay for repairs to holes in one of the plane's wings - 'which taught him not to bomb B Squadron'.[4]

The year 1956 saw a far-reaching reorganisation in the Territorial Army. Henceforth only two TA divisions (43rd and 53rd) would remain at full scale ready to support the regulars in NATO commitments, the remainder were to undertake Home Defence only. This meant that several Yeomanry regiments were axed or amalgamated, while others were given new roles.

3. Letter, 29 March 1990 from Rt. Hon. David Waddington, QC to Lt. Col. M. T. Steiger, TD, commanding DLOY.
4. This incident is recalled by ex-SSM Hardwidge and ex-RQMS Richardson, both of whom helped to repel the attack.

The DLOY was relieved to learn that it was to remain intact, but the role was to change from Divisional Armoured Regiment to Light Armoured Reconnaissance (Home Defence). It would remain in the Royal Armoured Corps. Theoretically it would be organised on the basis of three squadrons, each of one troop of Daimler armoured cars and three troops of Daimler scout cars (or 'Dingos'). But in fact the armoured cars never materialised and the Regiment had to make do with the little open-topped two-man scout cars, plus a fleet of Land Rovers.[5] In June 1956 the DLOY under Lieutenant-Colonel M. A. A. Birtwistle, trained for their new role on Salisbury Plain where 'their scout cars and jeeps [sic] covered hundreds of miles from their base at Tilshead,' reported *Lancashire Life*.

Meanwhile, the indefatigable Honorary Colonel, Denis Bates, had become involved in another tussle with Authority, this time over Battle Honours. In January 1956 the Army Council, in consultation with the Battles Nomenclature Committee, issued their recommendations for Second World War Battle Honours, and on the 24th of the month Colonel Bates received a communication from the Director of Personal Services relaying a Special Army Order[6] in which it was laid down that ' . . . units of Yeomanry and infantry regiments, which were converted to other Arms during the War, but which have since resumed their original status within their regiments, may be awarded an Honorary Distinction in the form of a Badge in place of Honours, to denote their war service in another arm'.

This implied that the DLOY would not be able to claim any of the several Battle Honours awarded to other unconverted units for service in Italy and North-West Europe. At once Bates went into action. In a lengthy and somewhat impassioned letter to the Under Secretary of State at the War Office he emphasised the point that although his Regiment had been converted to artillery during the war, it retained its Yeomanry origins and traditions, as was confirmed by the initials 'DLOY' in its titles . . . 'Indeed I will go so far as to say that in the last War the Yeomanry tradition prevailed throughout and ALL the Gunners who joined us regarded themselves as YEOMEN and were proud to do so'. He appreciated that the Royal Artillery had never borne Battle Honours, but while intending no slight to the Royal Regiment, he had to reiterate that during the war, as now, they were essentially The Duke of Lancaster's Own Yeomanry, and as such they should be entitled to the appropriate Battle Honours.

But alas, despite protracted correspondence over three months, this, Colonel Bates's last battle with Authority, ended in defeat. On 7 March 1956 he received the following letter from Major-General C. E. A. Firth, Director of Personal Services:

>THE WAR OFFICE LONDON, S.W.1
>7th March, 1956
>
>Sir
>I am directed to refer to your letter of the 20th February, 1956, regarding Battle Honours for the 1939–45 War. As it appears from your letter that there may be a possible misconception of the meaning of the words

---

5. The long-serving Land Rover (or Landrover as the Army prefers) was then a relative newcomer. Originally developed for civilian use in 1948, the short-wheelbase (½ ton) model was accepted by the Army in 1950, the 'long' (¾ ton) following in 1953.
6. A.O. 1/1956

Honorary Distinction, I should say that this is the official term for a Battle Honour which takes a pictorial as opposed to a written form. There have, in the past, been many instances of this practice: viz. the Bengal Tiger for services in India and the Naval Crown for services as Marines with the Fleet, among others.

It should, therefore, be apparent that no slight is involved to any regiment which has the honour to be awarded an Honorary Distinction by the Sovereign.

As regards the case of your regiment, it is traditionally not the custom to award Battle Honours to regiments of the Royal Artillery, and it was decided, and approved by Her Majesty the Queen, that regiments converted for service as artillery, should conform to this long standing custom. This ruling, of course, affects many infantry battalions as well as yeomanry regiments. To have made an exception to this rule could only have provided cause for grievance in the Royal Regiment of Artillery.

You will appreciate that those regiments which have not been converted, as your regiment has been, to their original status will be unable to claim either battle Honours or Honorary Distinctions. On the other hand, since those regiments which had been reconverted would again carry guidons and Colours, and might have no specific Honours to show on them because of their service as artillery regiments, it was decided to revive for their benefit the old custom of the award of Honorary Distinctions, and thereby make good a gap in Honours which would otherwise have appeared.

I am, Sir,
Your obedient Servant,
(Sgd) C. E. A. Firth
Major General
Director of Personal Services

Colonel D. H. Bates, M.C., T.D.,
Colonel, The Duke of Lancaster's Own Yeomanry,
Chorlton Hall,
Malpas,
CHESHIRE.

And so today all the Regiment has to display on the Guidon for its arduous services in the Italian and North-West Europe campaigns is the Honorary Distinction of a small 'Gun' Badge of the Royal Artillery (less Crown and Motto) with the dates '1944–45' and two scrolls, 'North West Europe' and 'Italy'.

In 1958 it was resolved to present to Her Majesty the Colonel-in-Chief a diamond, ruby and emerald brooch in the form of the Regimental Badge. This was duly made up (in London) and on 11 March 1959, the presentation was made by the then Honorary Colonel, Colonel R. F. Fleetwood-Hesketh and the CO, Lieutenant-Colonel M. A. A. Birtwistle, TD, at a private audience in Buckingham Palace. Afterwards a luncheon was laid on at the Cafe Royal for those who had travelled to London for the occasion. Among those present, in addition to the Honorary Colonel and CO, were the late Honorary

This picture shows 'A' Squadron after their arrival in Egypt in September 1914. The squadron leader, Major Dennis Bates is the third officer from the left.

The wedding of a DLOY SQMS. This picture comes from a collection of photographs relating to the service of SSM W. Sudell who appears to be the third swordsman on the right moving away from the camera. The picture was taken in 1916 when Sudell, together with the bridegroom was serving with 2/1 DLOY in Scotland under the command of Lt Col. H. M. Hardcastle. The swords in use appear to be the 1899 pattern and sharp-eyed readers will note the combination of leather gaiters and puttees.

These cartoons appeared in the *Westmorland Gazette* on 1st January 1916. At the centre of the cartoons is the Commaning Officer of 2/1 DLOY, Lt. Col. H. M. Hardcastle with his dog 'Duchess'; it is believed that the officer at the top right chasing the chicken is a cartoon of Major A. W. Huntingdon DSO; the officer beneath him wearing spectacles is 2nd Lieut. J. G. Fair and the officer to his left with the monacle Lieut. H. L. Rushton. For serious students of the officers of 2/1 DLOY see Lanoy 281.1 in the Regimental Museum showing the officers at Annsmere Camp, Ladybank 1916.

'C' Squadron crossing the River Somme at Brie Bridge on 20th March 1917 during the British advance.

This photograph shows members of A Squadron on the march south towards Beiruit in November 1918 somewhere in the vicinity of Tripoli. The Squadron spent Christmas at Beiruit.

Regimental Cooks at annual camp at Stainton near Penrith 1927. The modern reader will note how little the utensils of military cooking have changed over the intervening 65 years.

Regimental Cooks standing in front of field ovens at camp at Kinmel Park near Rhyl in 1929.

SSM S. H. Knowles wearing service dress. Note the boots with leather leggings and 1908 pattern cavalry sword secured to the saddle.

THE DUKE OF LA

OCdt RHF Williams   OCdt PA Whittingham   OC
        Lt MA Carnell   Lt SGJ Norman
Maj HCD Laing   Capt EN Ryder   Capt RA Koss   Capt M
       Maj JJ Escott   Capt TH Lovell JP   Capt BG Stocker
Maj C Godby   Maj F Baier   Maj BJ Fowden TD   Lt Co
      Maj E Sheen MBE   Maj AJ Hammersley   Maj J Eastham TD J

OWN YEOMANRY

   OCdt JWD Roe   OCdt J Baier   2Lt H Rieger
Schmidt   OCdt AJ Pearson   OCdt T Ripley
4/20H Capt AP Berry Capt GO Fulton OCdt JN Ashworth
Maj AJC Best RTR Lt W Stehr Capt VL Colborne
 Maj J Tustin Maj JDA Patterson TD Capt JD Steven MBE
Steiger TD Maj ME Hammersley TD Rev T Vaughan

Sgt Harris photographed between the wars and later a member of 77 Medium Regiment R.A.

Major W. R. Palmer leading 'B' Squadron on a road march at an inter-war camp.

A group of regimental officers taken at Buckingham Palace levée, 9th June 1936. The officers are all in mourning for the death of King George V and are as follows: (*left to right*) Front row – Lt. Col. J. Heaton CO, Col. H. M. Hardcastle TD Hon. Colonel, Major E. J. Pyke. Back row – Lieut. Peter Fleetwood-Hesketh, Capt. Eric Palmer, Capt. James Reynolds, Lieut. Gerald Ley, Lieut. Robert Sanderson.

Vol. 3. No. 2. FEBRUARY, 1938

THE TERRITORIAL

Lancashire's Lead — the Duke of Lancaster's Own Yeomanry have set up a new record in winning the *Daily Telegraph and Morning Post* Cup awarded to the T.A. Unit with the best attendance at Annual Training. In 1936 the trophy was won by the 10th Manchesters for the third time with a percentage of 107·34. Now the County Yeomanry secure first place for 1937 with the high figure of 117·72 per cent. .
Here we see a spectacular jump by a Trooper at the Duke of Lancaster's Own Yeomanry Camp at Welbeck Park, near Worksop.

DLOY Officers at Lowther Castle Camp, 1937

Rear row: (*left to right*)
Lt. J.H.M. Shaw, Capt. C.P. Shaw, Capt. Guy Gardner, Lt. T.M. Heaton, Lt. T. Hesketh, Lt. Basil Greenwood, Lt. G. Beezley, Lt. J.D.M. Wilson, Lt. T.J.L. Rushton, Lt. R.E. Heaton, Lt. P. Crump.

Front row: (left to right)
Capt. Sir Gerald Ley Bt, Major J.R. Reynolds, Major J.E. Palmer, Major E.J. Pyke, Major Musgrove-Hoyle, Lt. Col. J. Heaton, Major Ffrench-Blake, (Unknown), Major Roger Fleetwood-Hesketh, Major W.R. Palmer, Capt. Fleetwood-Hesketh, Capt Sizzling.

A group of DLOY NCOs believed to date from the early days of the Second World War showing Cpl. Arthur Lowe (*extreme left*), later well-known as the TV personality, Captain Mainwaring of "Dad's Army".

Trooper J. B. H. 'Baggy' Hide, Lumb Mill, Ramsbottom, after mobilization during the bad winter of 1939/40.

77TH (D.L.O.Y.) MEDIUM REGT. R.A.
SERGEANTS' MESS, 1943

77th (D.L.O.Y.) Medium Regiment, R.A.Sergeants, Mess, 1943.
Top Row: Sgt. L.R. Alderson, L/Sgt.C. Hill, L/Sgt. F.A.Wignall, BQMS T.E. Cain, Sgt. J.A. Aston, Sgt. T.N. Watt, L/Sgt. E.C. Stevens, Sgt.G.F.Spicer, L/Sgt. J. Tomlinson.
Second row: L/Sgt. A. Parker, Sgt. J. Tinker, Sgt. J. Parkin, L/Sgt G. Bell, L/Sgt. W. Bedford, Sgt. J. Lawrence, L/Sgt. J. Pearson.
Third row: L/Sgt. D. Rogerson, L/Sgt. W.A. Watkins, Sgt. L. Etches, L/Sgt. G, Crossley, Sgt. F. Leaman, Sgt G.O'Hare, Sgt.P. Burdett, L/Sgt. R.V. Lloyd, Sgt.R.Nowell.
Fourth row: RQMS J. Ashworth, Sgt. C.W. Long, Sgt. W.H. Welch, L/Sgt. W. Wills, L/Sgt G. Jones, Sgt. A.D. Angus, Sgt. E. Cook, L/Sgt. H. Garner.
Seated: BSM J. Wilson, BSM T. Corfield, BSM G. Hewitt, Capt. L.J. Thomas, RA.,RSM L.O.Bellis, ASM F. Holt, BSM A.E. Tonks, BSM G. Lloyd.

Gun Crew demonstrating ramming and firing From the collection of Sgt Arthur. Harris 77 Med Regt RA

Members of 78 (DLOY) Medium Regiment RA, relaxing in Italy late in the war, in front of a 5.5 Howitzer.

Members of 77 (DLOY) Medium Regiment RA, on VE Day.

The Queen inspecting a guard of the Regiment on the occasion of her opening the Wigan Mining Technical College on 21st October 1954. She is accompanied by Lt. Col. M. A. A. Birtwistle who later became Hon. Colonel. Note that the troops are wearing battledress with blancoed gaiters and belts and the NCOs wear the Ducal Coronet above their chevrons. The rose arm badge is that of the 41st (East Lancashire) Division TA.

The Guidon being marched past Her Majesty The Queen at Belle Vue, Manchester, on 24th May 1961 after its presentation. The guidon party consists of (*left to right*) SQMS Johnson, WO2 Holdship who carried the Guidon and Sgt. Torkington. Immediately behind the guidon party is the Regimental Sergeant Major, RSM E. Sheen of 14/20th Kings Hussars and to his right can be seen Capt. Condon the Regimental QM. To the left of The Queen on the Royal Dais can be seen His Royal Highness Prince Phillip and the Honorary Colonel, Colonel Roger Fleetwood-Hesketh.

The TA Centre at Devonshire Road, Chorley which was the Headquarters of the Regiment between 1982 and 1992. Before 1982 this building had been the home of 'B' Squadron and it is presently occupied by 101 Bn REME (V).

The TA Centre at Manchester Road, Clifton. This building was the home of RHQ after Lancaster House in Whalley Range and until 1982, and from then until 1992 the home of 'B' Squadron, shared with 202 Field Squadron Royal Engineers.

Members of A Squadron go into action at Holcombe Moor Training Camp during exercise "Inside Right" in October 1975.

Members of the DLOY Old Comarades Association with banner in reflective mood outside St. George's Church, Chorley, after a Regimental Church Parade in November 1981.

Regimental Guard at the opening of the Museum, Stanley Street, Preston in 1985.

A Chinook helicopter transporting DLOY Landrovers during annual camp in East Anglia in the summer of 1984.

The Colonel in Chief talking to members of C (HSF) Squadron on her visit to Altcar on 29th June 1985. The officers: (*left to right*) Lt. Col. D. A. Corbin, Col. S. P. E. C. W. Towneley, Hon. Col., Major H. C. D. Laing and Sgt. B. Bowes.

The Colonel-in Chief watching a display by members of B Squadron during her visit to Altcar in 1985; to the left of The Queen is Major Victor Seely, Royal Hussars (Training Major) and to her right Major A. J. Hammersley (OC B Squadron) and Lieutenant-Colonel D. A. Corbin (CO). This picture is reproduced by kind permission of the Editor of the *Lancashire Evening Post* who are the copyright holders.

The Colonel-in-Chief presenting the Duchy Shield to Major M. T. Steiger (OC D Squadron) on her visit to Altcar in 1985; the Honorary Colonel, Colonel S. P. E. C. W. Townley, is the Officer standing at the extreme left.

Members of D Squadron on the ranges at Altcar under the watchful eye of S/Sgt Best, 14/20 H, the Squadron Permanent Staff Instructor.

Cpl. Tierney (*left*) and Lt. Col. J. D. V. Woolley (*right*) at the Royal Tournament, July 1987, at which the Regiment staged a mounted historical pagent; Lt. Col. Woolley is dressed as a Bolton Light Horse volunteer c. 1820 and Cpl. Tierney as a 'skinhead'.

Lt. Col. J. D. V. Woolley handing over command to Lt. Col. M. T. Steiger TD., at Altcar Camp, 24th April 1988.

The Reverend Trevor Vaughan, Regimental Padre, cooking in the field at annual camp in 1988.

Colonel, Colonel Denis Bates, the wartime CO of the 78th (DLOY) Medium Regiment, the then RSM E. Sheen, Sergeant B. Richardson (late of the 78th) and a venerable Old Comrade, Mr R. Dean, who had served in the Boer War and the First World War.

In 1959 the Regiment suffered a grievous loss in the death of its most dedicated Honorary Colonel. On 13 September of that year Colonel Denis Houghton Bates, MC, TD died at his home, Chorlton Hall, Malpas, after a sudden illness. He was 73 years of age. The funeral, attended by members of the Regiment, was held at Childwall Parish Church (Liverpool), where his remains were interred in the family vault.

Denis Bates had served the Regiment since 1910 when he joined as 2nd Lieutenant. Commanding A Squadron in the Palestine Campaign of 1917–18, he gained his well-earned MC, while his Squadron's exertions as a mounted unit throughout earned the Regiment its unique distinction of shoulder chains in Service Dress. In 1930 he assumed command of the Regiment and ten years later became Honorary Colonel, an appointment he held until 1956. During this post-war period he also carried on a demanding civilian career: by 1953 he had become Chairman of the Cunard Steamship Company, Deputy Chairman of the Cunard White Star Ltd, Chairman and Manager of Thos Brocklebank Ltd, Director of the Oceanic Steam Navigation Company Ltd. Yet despite all these heavy responsibilities, he never ceased to apply time and energy to the interests of the Regiment and, as we have seen, to fight battles with authority on behalf of its honour and tradition. 'Devoted' seems a scarcely adequate adjective to describe Denis Bates. His portrait (depicting those shoulder chains) had an honoured place in the Officers Mess at Chorley.

Mundane duties, training and Annual Camp were followed in 1961 by Royal ceremonial not seen since 1909 when King Edward VII had presented a new Guidon to the Regiment at the then RHQ of Worsley Park. More than half a century on, this Guidon was now in need of replacement, and on 24 May 1961 King Edward's great grand-daughter honoured the Regiment by presenting a new one. The impressive ceremony was held at Belle Vue Stadium, Manchester, in perfect weather. With Colonel R. F. Hesketh, Honorary Colonel, in attendance on The Queen, the parade was commanded by Lieutenant-Colonel B. C. L. Tayleur (14/20 H) as CO. The No. 1 Guard of 69 all ranks was commanded by Major T. A. Marshall, the No. 2 Guard of 53 all ranks by Major J. A. Chartres. Bearing the Old Guidon was RQMS E. Durrant, while SSM D. Holdship bore the New. The RSM was WO1 E. Sheen.[7] For this event the Bandmaster, WO1 J. R. Cooney, had been able to muster 29 performers. All were in their blue Number One Dress except the two Queen's Orderlies and the Drum Party who were resplendent in their scarlet Full Dress and plumed helmets, with drawn swords. Also present were 47 Old Comrades under Lieutenant-Colonel W. R. Palmer, DSO, TD. While the parade was forming up the hordes of spectators from Manchester and elsewhere were entertained by music from the Band of the 4th/7th Royal Dragoon Guards who had travelled from their Regiment's location as RAC Training Regiment at Catterick.

Her Majesty, accompanied by The Duke of Edinburgh, was received on parade by a trumpet fanfare and the Royal Salute by the DLOY Band. After she had inspected her

---

7. Until 1822 cavalry Standards and Guidons were carried by subalterns (as with infantry Colours), but from that date they have been entrusted to Warrant Officers.

Regiment, the New Guidon was consecrated by the Chaplain-General and then formally handed over. The Old Guidon was ceremonially marched off parade and Her Majesty then addressed the Regiment. The following is an extract from her speech:

> Colonel Tayleur, Officers, Warrant Officers and men of The Duke of Lancaster's Own Yeomanry: it was in 1909 that King Edward VII came to Lancashire to present to your Regiment the Guidon which has just been marched off parade. Now, fifty-two years later I, his great grand-daughter have come as your Colonel-in-Chief to present its replacement to you on Lancastrian soil.
>
> The Regiment has been through many vicissitudes during these years, but whether as Cavalry or Gunners or part of the Royal Armoured Corps, it has always acquitted itself with honour and done credit to the name it so proudly bears. Now, as a Reconnaissance Regiment, you are fulfilling your traditional role once more, and I know that you do it with your traditional efficiency. I am confident that you of The Duke of Lancaster's Own Yeomanry will guard this new Guidon with the same care and pride as your predecessors have guarded the old one; and I hope that yet another half-century may pass away before this Guidon, in its turn, will be marched away to be laid up in honoured retirement.[8]

After the new Guidon had been ceremonially trooped through the ranks, the ceremony ended with a drive past and Advance in Review Order. Needless to say, this event had entailed weeks of rehearsal conducted by Colonel Tayleur and RSM Sheen, and the impeccable standard of turnout and drill was the subject of congratulatory messages from the GOC North West District and other senior staff officers present. It was generally agreed that the Regiment had excelled itself.

The Old Guidon was laid up in Manchester Cathedral, the New being displayed at RHQ, first in Clifton, Manchester, and then in the Chorley HQ.

Still in their Reconnaissance role, the DLOY spent the next six years with routine training and Annual Camps at Kirkcudbright, Bodney (Stanford Training Area, Norfolk), Nesscliffe, Shropshire, and in 1967 on the RAC ranges at Castlemartin, Pembrokeshire.

The latter Camp found the Regiment yet again reorganised with an addendum to its title. In December 1966 the Labour Government had announced radical changes in the Territorial Army to take effect from April the following year. What was now termed the Territorial and Army Volunteer Reserve was divided into three distinct bodies: a tiny band of 'Ever Readies' (T&AVR I); a 50,000 strong back-up force, mainly technical, medical and gunners (T&AVR II), and the remainder (T&AVR III), on greatly reduced establishments and committed only to Home Defence. In order to avoid disbandment many Yeomanry regiments in the T&AVR III were obliged to amalgamate with other units, and thus on 1 April 1967 the reduced DLOY merged with a Lancashire Territorial unit of the Royal Tank Regiment, the 40th/41st RTR. The title was now The Duke of Lancaster's Own Yeomanry (Royal Tank Regiment). Having been Gunners during the war,

---

8. Her Majesty's forecast was not entirely accurate. It must be recorded that in October 1990 the 29-year-old Guidon was replaced by a new one, presented by the Queen with similar ceremonial 'on Lancastrian soil' at Stonyhurst College.

the Regiment was now in theory 'Tankies' – in theory, because no tanks were seen and as before, all it had to train with were Land Rovers and 3-tonners. After some debate about badges, it was agreed that the DLOY cap badge would be retained, but the RTR badge would be worn as a collar badge, while a cloth tank badge was to be displayed beneath the right shoulder.

With RHQ at Clifton, Manchester, A Squadron was located at Oldham, B was split with SHQ and two Troops at Clifton and two at Preston, while C Squadron was at Bootle. The strength was now 20 officers and 196 other ranks, with Lieutenant-Colonel T. A. Marshall, TD in command. About 50 per cent of the strength was RTR and while at first there was a certain degree of friction between the two elements, this soon evaporated as each came to respect the other's point of view. Sadly, one result of the 1967 amalgamation was the demise of the Regimental Band which had performed since the reformation of 1947.

In September of that year Colonel Marshall retired, handing over command to another DLOY officer, Lieutenant-Colonel N. H. Phillips. And it was under him that the Regiment was to suffer the most traumatic period of its post-war existence. First on 16 January 1968, Prime Minister Harold Wilson announced in the House that drastic cuts were to be made in the Civil Defence services and the T&AVR III. The latter, including those Yeomanry regiments reserved for Home Defence, were to lose all financial support from the Government, which meant that unless they could fund themselves, there was no alternative but disbandment. Despite heated debate in the House, and the efforts of the Duke of Norfolk, Chairman of the T & AVR Association, the Government remained adamant.

As CO of DLOY (RTR), Colonel Norman Phillips was determined that his Regiment should not suffer extinction. He sent telegrams to the MPs for North West constituencies, urging support for his endeavours to save the Regiment. The outcome was that positive support was forthcoming from Lieutenant-Colonel Sir Walter Bromley-Davenport (MP for Knutsford Division) and Mr Stanley Orme, Member for Salford West (surprisingly, since he was Labour). At the same time, Colonel Phillips created a DLOY Regimental Trust to safeguard the Regimental silver and other property should disbandment ensue – which seemed probable. With the assistance of the above-mentioned, and with funds raised by the Regiment itself, it was possible to hold a four-day Annual Camp at Weeton, near Blackpool, where the 5th Royal Inniskilling Dragoon Guards generously provided facilities and lent vehicles. Land Rovers were also borrowed from the Cheshire Yeomanry. Some funds for the Camp were authorised by Brigadier H. M. H. Ley, CBE, Secretary of the East Lancashire branch of the T&AVR Association. At this Camp the strength was down to 20 officers and 75 other ranks.

As was feared, the Labour Government had not yet completed its destruction of the Territorial forces. In April 1969 Colonel Phillips learned that all the Yeomanry regiments of the T & AVR Home Defence force were to be reduced to pathetic cadres of eight all ranks. This was tantamount to disbandment, but, based in the old RHQ at Clifton, Colonel Phillips nobly preserved the Cadre intact and carried on training as best he could. The Cadre comprised the following:

    Lieutenant-Colonel N. H. Phillips   Sergeant D. V. Marshall
    Captain D. J. Claxton   "   J. D. Steven
    WO2 (RQMS) B. Richardson   Lance-Corporal C. Gillham
                                                  "   M. E. G. Trevor-Jones
                                                  "   M. Collinson

The only Yeomanry regiment remaining at full strength was a new conglomerate titled The Royal Yeomanry, and made up of single Squadrons from The Royal Wiltshire, Sherwood Rangers, Kent and County of London, North Irish Horse and Berkshire and Westminster Dragoons. In all, 17 regiments had been slashed to eight-strong cadres with little foreseeable future.

But hope springs eternal . . . Colonel Phillips and his DLOY cadre purchased a mini-bus and with some borrowed Land Rovers and radios, bravely carried out weekend training exercises. In June they even managed a two weeks' attachment to the 9th/12th Royal Lancers at Catterick for some training in tank driving and gunnery, although it seemed problematical whether such skills would ever be demanded of them. Part I Regimental Orders were dutifully compiled monthly and copies were sent to North West District Headquarters, principally as reminders that there was still a DLOY element in existence. In 1970 the Cadre was more adventurous for its Annual Camp. Colonel Phillips persuaded the 75th Royal Engineers (TA) to transport 'all ranks' (eight) to Germany where the first week was spent at Paderborn with the 14th/20th King's Hussars (still officially the affiliated Regiment), the second at Hameln with the 75th RE, whom they assisted with radio communications – 'part of the deal in return for free transport' as Colonel Phillips relates.

Just before the German expedition the Cadre learned the sad news of the death, at 69, of Colonel W. R. (Bobby) Palmer, DSO, TD who had commanded his Gunner element of the Regiment with such distinction during the war and reraised the DLOY in 1947. It was ironic that he had only recently achieved the ultimate peak of Honorary Colonel. The whole Cadre attended the Memorial Service in Liverpool Parish Church. The successor as Honorary Colonel was Colonel M. A. A. Birtwistle, TD who had commanded the Regiment from 1956 to 1959.

On 19 June 1970 Harold Wilson's Labour Government was defeated in the General Election and Edward Heath's Conservative party assumed power. Their pledge to repair some of the damage inflicted on the Reserve forces by their predecessors was quickly put into effect. In January 1971 a Ministry of Defence Instruction entitled 'Expansion of the Territorial and Army Volunteer Reserve 1971' was published.[9] The Cadres of ten Yeomanry regiments were to be expanded into full Squadrons, to be merged in three new 'conglomerate' regiments titled The Queen's Own Yeomanry, The Wessex Yeomanry and The Mercian Yeomanry, these being in addition to the already existing Royal Yeomanry. Some were to be armoured car regiments, others tanks. One of the former was The

---

9.   A/79/Gen/4067 (ASD I/5c) dated 29 January 1971.

Queen's Own which comprised squadrons from The Queen's Own Yorkshire Yeomanry, the Ayrshire, the Cheshire, and the Northumberland Hussars – all northern representatives.

In February 1971 Colonel Phillips, still in command of the DLOY Cadre, was given the option of raising a squadron to join this new Regiment, or to reform as a distinct DLOY Regiment, but in a Home Defence role as 'Dismounted Yeomanry'. After consultation with the Honorary Colonel, he chose the latter alternative, on the grounds (as he wrote) 'that the role *could* change, but once a Squadron, always a Squadron'.

And so, on 1 April 1971 The Duke of Lancaster's Own Yeomanry rose phoenix-like from the ashes of its Cadre to become the only Yeomanry regiment to exist as a corporate body under its original title. It is acknowledged that much of the credit for this emergence from limbo is due to the untiring efforts of Lieutenant-Colonel Norman Phillips.

Under Army Order 20/72 the title was officially changed back to The Duke of Lancaster's Own Yeomanry (dropping the suffix 'RTR'). Although remaining within the Royal Armoured Corps, the role was now that of an Infantry Home Defence unit, tasked with reconnaissance.

The reformed Regiment was quickly recruited up to strength with twelve officers and 232 other ranks. With RHQ still at Clifton, Manchester, there were three Squadrons: A at Wigan, B at Chorley and D at Preston. (C Squadron had been disbanded.)

The key posts at this historic date were as under:

RHQ

Lieutenant-Colonel N. H. Phillips	*Commanding*
Major J. A. Pharo-Tomlin (14/20 H)	*2 I/C*
Major B. F. B. Gaskin, TD	*Adjutant*
Major T. H. F. Jones, MBE	*Quartermaster*
Major D. W. J. O'Neill, TD	*RMO*
WO1 J. Morrow (9/12 L)	*RSM*
WO2 B. Richardson	*RQMS*

A Squadron

Major D. J. Claxton	*OC*
Captain G. D. Thompson	*2 I/C*
Lieutenant N. H. Fairclogh	*Troop Leader*
WO2 J. D. Steven	*SSM*
S/Sgt D. Harris (RTR)	*PSI*

B Squadron

Major J. A. Ferguson	*OC*
Captain R. A. Ferguson	*2 I/C*
WO2 R. Gorton	*SSM*
S/Sgt P. Midgley (14/20 H)	*PSI*

D Squadron

Major J. Stuart-Mills	OC
Captain R. B. Heaton	2 I/C
WO2 E. Thistlethwaite	SSM
S/Sgt R. Binkey	PSI

The first Annual Camp of the reformed Regiment was held at the Stanford Training Area, Thetford (Norfolk) in October 1971 when 155 all ranks attended. In the following May 199 all ranks went 'overseas' to Jurby, Isle of Man, when they were inspected by the GOC North Western District, Major-General C. W. B. Purdon, CBE, MC. On this occasion, and at the final Church Parade, music was provided by the Band of the 14th/20th Hussars.

May 1972 saw a detachment marching for the first time in the Cavalry Memorial Parade in Hyde Park, a ceremony which has been attended ever since. By now, Lieutenant-Colonel Norman Phillips had retired as CO. In April 1971 he handed over to a Regular, Lieutenant-Colonel J. D. Bastick, Royal Tank Regiment, who in 1973 was to publish his *Trumpet Call*, the first history of the DLOY. Norman Phillips had served the Regiment since 1960 as Subaltern, Squadron Leader and Commanding Officer, and as already seen, was instrumental in reforming the Regiment from its Cadre. At the time of writing he remains an active member of the Regimental and Museum Trusts.

Members of DLOY in camp at Tilshead 1956, training on a Dingo Scout Car.

CHAPTER X

Epilogue
1974–1990

By 1974 the Regiment's strength had risen to 17 officers and 301 other ranks, a creditable proportion of the authorised establishment of 392 all ranks. Some 200 attended the Annual Camp at Bellerby in Yorkshire. A Regimental team achieved the highest overall score in the District Skill-at-Arms competition. During this year there was a change of command: Lieutenant-Colonel Desmond Bastick (RTR) departed to HQ 1'(BR) Corps in Germany and Lieutenant-Colonel D. J. Claxton took over. A Yeoman, David Claxton had served the Regiment in every commissioned rank and had just been awarded his Territorial Decoration. One of the new subalterns joining A Squadron in the same year was 2nd Lieutenant M. T. Steiger, who was to emulate Claxton by rising to Commanding Officer (with a TD).

The following year saw the Regiment involved in the large-scale UKLF Mobilisation Exercise 'Inside Right', held between 19 and 22 October. For this the DLOY camped at the Altcar ranges, and besides acting as 'own Troops' on exercises, learned much of mobilisation procedures and the working of a Command Post. A novel and exciting feature of the exercise was the helicoptering of two Squadrons to reinforce a third 50 miles away on Holcombe Moor.

So far the DLOY had not seen their Royal Colonel-in-Chief since Her Majesty presented the new Guidon at Manchester in 1961. But in June 1977, as part of the Silver Jubilee tour, the Queen visited Lancashire, and on her arrival at Wigan on the 20th a Royal Guard of Honour was found by the Regiment.

In October 1978 the Regimental Newsletter reported the formation of the Regimental Association, made up of past and serving members, with the object of promoting and fostering the essential unity of the two elements. The President was to be Colonel R. F. Hesketh, TD, DL, the Chairman would be the Honorary Colonel while Members would include the Commanding Officer, Second-in-Command, the RSM and three Old Comrades. By the following year the Association was in business, and has flourished ever since. In January 1978 the Regiment bade farewell to Lieutenant-Colonel D. J. Claxton as CO, the post being assumed by a non-Yeoman, Lieutenant-Colonel P. D. W. Cable-Alexander, Royal Scots Dragoon Guards.

The next year brought another change in the Regimental hierarchy. In February 1979 Colonel M. A. A. Birtwistle, TD retired from his appointment as Honorary Colonel. With justifiable pride he recorded in the Newsletter, '1979 will mark for me the fortieth year of commissioned service with the Territorial Army [he was commissioned 2nd Lieutenant in the 4th Bn East Lancashire Regiment in 1939], and thirty two of these have been spent in The Duke of Lancaster's Own Yeomanry, as Squadron 2I/C, Squadron Leader,

Commanding Officer and Honorary Colonel'. Colonel Michael Birtwistle had long been a Deputy Lieutenant for the County of Lancaster, and only the previous year had been appointed High Sheriff. In the same month the Honorary Colonelcy was assumed by Colonel S. P. E. C. W. Towneley, JP, Lord Lieutenant of Lancashire. As a young subaltern, Simon Towneley had served during the Second World War with The King's Royal Rifle Corps and was in action with his Battalion in Italy. He was unique in the Regiment's roll of Honorary Colonels in being not only a gifted musician but an authority on musical history. He performed in chamber ensembles, contributed to the *New Oxford History of Music* and published his own esoteric work, *Venetian Opera in the Seventeenth Century* (1954).

By 1979 sundry bits and pieces of Regimental history in the shape of uniforms, arms, pictures, etc. were accumulating at Regimental Headquarters in Clifton, where neither space nor facilities were available to form a properly organised museum for classification and display. Something had to be done to preserve the Regimental memorabilia. Thus after negotiating with The National Trust, permission was obtained to house the collection in Rufford Old Hall, a splendid Elizabethan mansion near Ormskirk. Although now owned by The National Trust this had been the seat of the Hesketh family who had contributed many officers to the Regiment. No more than one room could be allotted, but it was foreseen that this could be only temporary accommodation, as indeed it was. To complete the Museum story, with chronological sequence ignored, we must leap forward to 1984. In that year agreement was reached with the Lancashire County Council and its Museums Service Director, John Blundell, to acquire premises in the Old Sessions House in Stanley Street, Preston. An imposing early 19th century building in the centre of town (next door to the old prison), this was, and is, the Headquarters of the Lancashire County Museum services, with its own exhibits. Three ground-floor rooms provided adequate space to display the Regiment's exhibits, while (to the satisfaction of historians) an upper floor library received documentary material. With due ceremony, the Regimental Museum was opened by Colonel Simon Towneley on 21 October 1984. Today it forms a truly representative visualisation of the DLOY's history, with uniforms, arms, equipment, pictures and remarkably realistic recreations of scenes, such as a First World War dugout with officer's kit, and even a contemporary newspaper on his camp desk. Old cavalrymen are greeted by a life-size model of a troop horse, saddled, bridled and accoutred with sword and SMLE rifle. A little later the Old Sessions House became hosts to the Regimental Museums of the 14th/20th King's Hussars and The Queen's Lancashire Regiment, so becoming a truly Lancashire Regimental Museum.

To revert to 1979, the Annual Camp was held at Fremington Training Camp near Barnstaple from 1–15 September, when 150 all ranks attended. Exercises involving navigation over Dartmoor were carried out, and during the second week the Regiment was visited by the Director Royal Armoured Corps, Major-General J. M. Palmer, son of the lately deceased Honorary Colonel, Bobby Palmer. Previously, in April, the Regiment had enjoyed the duty of providing radio communication in the Settle district of Yorkshire for the Pennine Long-Distance Ride which had been pioneered by Colonel Towneley's wife Mary, an accomplished horsewoman. Unusually, the weather was perfect, and in their various posts along the route, Lancashire 'townie' lads were able to admire the spectacular Yorkshire scenery of the Three Peaks.

In the 1970s the Regiment added female personnel to its strength as members of the WRAC, some being NCOs and Privates and some officers. Although mainly employed on radio, clerical and administrative duties, some became highly proficient with weapons. At the annual North West District Skill-at-Arms Meeting at Altcar in June 1979, the Championship WRAC Pistol competition was won by Lance-Corporal Priestley, with Private Meacock as runner-up. At this Meeting the DLOY team achieved second place overall, earning congratulations from the District GOC. Also in 1979 the Regiment was pleased to see WO2 (RQMS) J. D. Steven appointed MBE in the Queen's Birthday Honours. Later Captain (QM), Derek Steven had been a member of the 1969 Cadre, and was still serving when this history went to press. He was the first non-commissioned member of the Regiment to be honoured with the above award.

During 1979–80 some improvements were introduced to bring the General Reserve Battalions (including the dismounted Yeomanry) more into line with the NATO-roled TA units. A regular Training Major was authorised, even when the CO was a regular; a permanently established regular Adjutant was allowed. On the equipment side, new improved radio sets and field telephones were promised, while weapons would include the Carl Gustav anti-tank system, the 50mm. and 81mm. mortars As the contemporary Newsletter observed, 'all these proposals are destined to remove the poor brethren, second-class citizen image that Home Defence battalions have in comparison with NATO TA battalions'.

A stimulus to recruiting was the raising of the Annual Training Bounties to £100 after one year, £200 after the second and £300 after the third. Whether or not this was relevant, by April 1980 the Regiment's strength had reached an all-time peak of 24 officers and 443 other ranks. Among the former were one WRAC Captain and two Lieutenants.

Meanwhile, the Remembrance Sunday of November 1979 saw a memorable event in Chorley. The parade and church service were attended by all three squadrons, plus RHQ, this being the first time that the town had seen the entire Regiment on parade. The March Past outside the Drill Hall was led by Lieutenant-Colonel Cable-Alexander, the Salute being taken by Colonel Simon Towneley, Lord Lieutenant and Honorary Colonel. The Regimental March, 'John o' Gaunt', was performed by the Band of the Lancashire Constabulary, kindly provided for the ceremony in the absence of the Band of the affiliated 14th/20th Hussars in Germany.

Having witnessed this ceremonial, Chorley was now to become more permanently associated with the only Lancashire Yeomanry regiment. Since the reformation of 1947, the DLOY Regimental Headquarters had been located within the boundaries of Manchester, but with Squadrons and Troops dispersed as far afield as Preston, Wigan and Blackpool, it seemed to make sense to establish a more central location. Thus, in 1979 the old TA Drill Hall at Chorley was selected.[1] During the next two years extensive modifications to the interior of the building in Devonshire Road were carried out, to provide well-appointed premises. A new first floor was added to house Officers' and WOs' and Sergeants' Messes; on the ground floor were offices for CO, Adjutant, QM, RSM and

---

1. This had been erected in 1895 to house the Chorley Loyal Rifle Volunteers.

clerks, with a central parqueted 'parade area' surrounded by Regimental memorabilia and Rolls of Honour. Fittingly continuing the Manchester tradition, the new RHQ was named 'Lancaster House'.

In its issue for 12 November 1981 the *Chorley Guardian* splashed a banner headline, 'Bags of Swank as the Dukes Move In'. The ceremonial take-over on 7 November was performed with the Regiment, headed by the Band of a Light Infantry Battalion, marching past the Honorary Colonel, who later unveiled a plaque in the hall. Afterwards a Service of Remembrance was held in the Parish Church, followed by entertainment for the Mayor of Chorley and numerous guests, and in the evening the annual get-together of Old Comrades.

The Squadron locations were now as under:

Headquarters Squadron	Chorley
A Squadron	TA Centre, Powell Street, Wigan
B Squadron	TA Centre, Manchester Road, Clifton
D Squadron	The Keep, Fulwood Barracks, Preston
	(Troop detached at TA Centre, Talbot Road, Blackpool)

It will be seen that B Squadron had been obliged to move from their former SHQ at Chorley to the vacated RHQ at Clifton, which they now shared with 202 Field Squadron Royal Engineers (TA).

In June 1977 members of the Regiment had experienced their first spell of overseas training when 120 all ranks joined up with the 4th Battalion The King's Own Royal Border Regiment for what was now an annual Territorial exercise named 'Marble Tor' at Gibraltar. The DLOY's turn came round again in June 1980 when 128 all ranks spent a fortnight on the Rock.

Having been roled as infantry since 1971, in 1983 the Regiment underwent another change, that of a Home Defence Reconnaissance Regiment, and one which it has retained to the present day. To carry out reconnaissance duties covering the whole of North West England and Scotland, the Regiment was mounted with 70 Land Rovers equipped with Clansman radios and 12 four-tonne lorries as A Echelon. Arms comprised the SLR, the LMG, Carl Gustav anti-tank system and 50mm. mortar.

The total establishment allowed for 357 all ranks, including attached REME and other personnel, but such had been recruiting efforts that the actual figure stood at 396, or 31 officers and 365 other ranks. Among these were three WRAC officers and 22 WRAC NCOs and Privates. At this date the Commanding Officer was Lieutenant-Colonel D. A. J. Corbin (4th/7th Royal Dragoon Guards).

The re-roling evoked a two-page illustrated write-up in the Army's magazine *Soldier* for 30 July 1984. It was recorded that during the past twelve months the Regiment's vehicles had covered a total of 238,461 miles on training and weekend exercises. Recruiting had been very selective: out of 212 would-be members, only 131 were finally accepted, the rest being rejected on medical or other grounds (including 'civilian convictions'). Colonel David Corbin explained the Regiment's specific tasks:

> Our role is to provide the District Commander with a small reaction force capable of acquiring and reporting accurate information. This will allow my squadrons to be deployed throughout the North West of England and Scotland. In times of national emergency many troops are tied down defending vital installations ... If an incident occurs in some area, remote from other forces, it may be the military has to sort it out. A recce Troop is sent to the area and it may move in the last few kilometres on foot to identify an armed group. The Squadron Leader then moves up with elements of the Squadron to put in an attack to restore the situation ... We are developing expertise in the use of house searches, woods clearance, and we now have several search advisers in the Regiment, which increases our capability. We would also expect to assist the civilian authorities in the identification of explosive devices, though the EOD[2] boys would deal with them. We would expect to do escort duties, traffic control, and will develop our NBC recce capability.

Such were the tasks of the DLOY Reconnaissance Regiment, RAC (TA), and they have changed little as this history is completed. For the 1983 Annual Camp the Regiment motored up to Barry Buddon near Carnoustie on the Firth of Tay, when a creditable number of 277 all ranks attended. As A Squadron's Newsletter noted, 'with very little time to shake down ... time was taken up with firing the APWT (Annual Weapon Training Test), running, throwing grenades, running, driving, running, signalling, running, meeting the local Jocks and even more running'. Early morning runs, or PE, resulted in the DLOY becoming 'slimmer and fitter than ever in living memory'.

The year 1984 brought two more well-earned awards to members of the Regiment, when Captain Edmund Sheen was appointed MBE and Staff-Sergeant Brian Patrick Andrews received the British Empire Medal. Captain Sheen had served the DLOY for 25 years, as PSI, RSM and finally Quartermaster. His Citation recorded that 'without his extraordinary work, well beyond the call of duty, much of our operational training would have been nugatory ... Captain Sheen is an exceptional example of all that is excellent in a soldier totally dedicated to presenting the TA and the Regiment in a good light ...'[3] Staff-Sergeant Andrews' contribution as PSI had been 'outstanding'. His 'selfless and continued devotion to the discharge of his duties [were] far in excess of that normally expected of a Permanent Staff Instructor ...'

Since 1961 when the Queen presented the new Guidon, the Regiment as a whole body had not seen its Colonel-in-Chief on parade. But in June 1985 Her Majesty graciously agreed to visit Her Regiment at Altcar – 151 years after it had become the Sovereign's, or The Duke of Lancaster's Own. Travelling by train to Southport station on 29 June, she was met by Lancashire dignitaries, and then proceeded by Rolls Royce to Altcar Training Camp, to be greeted by a Guard of Honour at the Camp gates. She was there received by Colonel Towneley, Honorary Colonel, who presented the Director of the Royal Armoured Corps, Major-General S. C. Cooper and the Commanding Officer, Lieutenant-Colonel D. A. J.

2. Explosive Ordnance Disposal.
3. As this history was completed in 1990, Major E. Sheen, MBE was still serving as Quartermaster.

Corbin. The latter then presented the Adjutant, Captain H. A. O. Wicks (14th/20th Hussars) and the RSM, WO1 R. D. Stapley (Queen's Own Hussars).

Next, Her Majesty visited the Squadrons displaying their equipment and carrying out training activities, after which she entered the other ranks' cookhouse to see the Regimental Cooks preparing the soldiers' dinner. A visit to the WOs' and Sergeants' Mess followed, and the morning's programme ended with luncheon in the Officers' Mess, where the Colonel-in-Chief signed a specially inscribed page of the Visitors' Book. In the afternoon Her Majesty met Old Comrades and some of the Regimental families, and the day-long programme was concluded with a drive past by the Regiment in their Land Rovers.

The occasion was an unqualified success, and brought forth gracious appreciation from Her Majesty. Immediately after her departure she caused her Private Secretary to write thus to Colonel Corbin:

> PALACE OF HOLYROOD HOUSE
> 29th June 1955
>
> The Queen's enthusiasm for the way in which the Regiment conducted themselves during her visit today is, as anyone here at Holyroodhouse will testify, unbounded. Her Majesty has instructed me to write to offer her congratulations and warm thanks to all members of The Duke of Lancaster's Own Yeomanry on a day which was an outstanding success. Every facet of the programme worked, I should have thought, to your entire satisfaction and was greatly enjoyed by your Colonel-in-Chief. Her Majesty would like every man and woman under your command to know of this appreciation and of how much she admired the enthusiasm and professionalism with which the day's events were carried out...

This Royal Visit was a memorable occasion for all, but particularly so for officers and men of C (HSF) Squadron, which had only been raised six months previously. The volunteer Home Service Force had been created in 1982, as a sort of successor to the wartime Home Guard, with a Key Point Defence role. But there was nothing of the 'Dad's Army' image about the Force: not only were the squadrons and companies absorbed and administered by the Territorial regiments and battalions and required to train with them, but a large proportion were ex-servicemen of the Royal Navy, Army and RAF, bringing with them their former skills and expertise to form highly efficient units. Raised on 2 January 1985, C (HSF) Squadron of the DLOY enjoyed remarkably brisk recruiting, becoming 85 per cent up to establishment by the time of the Royal Visit in June. The three Troops were dispersed among the other Squadrons: 1st Troop (with SHQ) was attached to RHQ & HQ Squadron at Chorley; 2nd Troop was with A Squadron at Wigan, 3rd Troop with D at Preston.

The key posts in the Squadron were as under:

SHQ Chorley		
Major Hugh Laing		Squadron Leader
WO2 Gordon Hudson		SSM
WO2 Harry Fletcher		SQMS
Chorley Troop		
Lieutenant Ian Cowan		Troop Leader
Sergeant Brian Bowes		Troop Sergeant
Wigan Troop		
Lieutenant George Fulton		Troop Leader
Preston Troop		
Lieutenant Thomas Bowring		Troop Leader
Sergeant Gordon Heywood		Troop Sergeant

In November 1985 Lieutenant-Colonel D. A. J. Corbin handed over command to another regular cavalryman, Lieutenant-Colonel J. D. V. Woolley, 17th/21st Lancers. At this date the healthy strength return reported 33 officers and 416 other ranks.

Meanwhile, weekly drill nights, weekend exercises and Annual Camps proceeded as usual, and were well attended by officers and soldiers. The year 1987 saw a second spell of overseas service when, on 9 May, a composite squadron of 120 all ranks, named G Squadron, was flown to Gibraltar for Exercise Marble Tor. Commanded by Major John. Tustin, the Squadron had a busy and adventurous fortnight, practising fieldcraft, shooting, adventure training (abseiling, rock climbing, caving, canoeing, windsurfing) and taking part in Exercise 'Yeoman's Scramble' which involved being transhipped at sea into landing craft and landed (at night) to scale cliffs and rescue hostages held by 'insurgents'. Such diversions, as part of annual training, would surely have boggled the minds of part-time Territorial soldiers (and indeed, Regulars) of pre-war days.

The same year of 1987 was marked by another even more memorable event when in July a team of 70 members of the Regiment staged a display at the Royal Tournament at Earls Court, London. This was the first time for more than 70 years that the Territorial Army had been represented in this most popular Service charity event, and with C Squadron playing a leading role, it was also the first public exposure of members of the Home Service Force. The 'incident' devised by Major Laing of C Squadron, was the repulse and capture of enemy saboteurs from a Key Point, realistically enacted by members of A, B and D Squadrons in their Land Rovers. The performance ended with a parade representing the varied roles of the Regiment during its 189 years' service. First into the arena was the Commanding Officer, Lieutenant-Colonel Woolley, splendidly attired in 18th century kit as Commandant of the Bolton Light Horse Volunteers and mounted on a horse borrowed from The King's Troop RHA; then, similarly mounted, came the wife of Lieutenant Bowring (C Squadron) dressed as a soldier of the Imperial Yeomanry of Boer War vintage; she was followed by a mounted trooper in World War I service kit. Next was a towed field gun, representing the 77th and 78th (DLOY) Regiments of World War II, and finally came a 'Dingo' scout car.

There was tumultuous applause, led by the Minister of State for Defence, Lord Trefgarne, as the DLOY performers left the arena to their Regimental March, 'John o' Gaunt'. The first display by any Yeomanry for many decades, it was a resounding success, and did much to enhance the prestige of the only Yeomanry regiment still existing under its own title and still representing the County Palatine.

The year 1988 brought changes in the higher echelons of command. In March Colonel Simon Towneley, Honorary Colonel, retired, to be succeeded by Major-General Sir Michael Palmer, KCVO who held the appointment as this history went to press. As already mentioned, General Mike is the son of the late Lieutenant-Colonel Bobby Palmer, DSO, TD whose distinguished services in command of the DLOY's Gunner element in the Second World War were related in Chapter VIII. A regular cavalryman, the General was first commissioned 2nd Lieutenant in the DLOY's affiliated Regiment, the 14th/20th King's Hussars, in 1948, and as Captain served as Adjutant to the DLOY from 1955 to 1958. He commanded his own Regiment, 1969–72 and, having risen to Major-General, became successively Assistant Chief of Staff, Allied Forces Central Europe, Director of The Royal Armoured Corps, Defence Services Secretary and Colonel of the 14th/20th. Retiring from the Active List in 1985, he has since been heavily involved with business commitments in the City of London, and in 1989 was elected Master of The Worshipful Company of Salters.

The year of the new Honorary Colonel's appointment saw the Regiment involved in two large-scale exercises, 'Strong Link' in September, when RHQ and D Squadron practised their Home Defence operational role, closely followed by 'Bonnie Dundee' in which A and B Squadrons motored and 'yomped' among the hills and moors of the Inverness area. In the previous May the Territorial Army's campaign to 'sell' itself to industry and commerce was marked by Exercise 'Executive Stretch', when the Regiment hosted 34 young executives from Lancashire and elsewhere in the north west and gave them some idea of what Territorial soldiering was all about. Dubbed 'Yuppies' Yomp', this subjected the budding MDs to a weekend of such unwonted exertions as assault courses, command tasks, patrols and other diversions, all of which seemed to have imbued them with a healthy respect for part-time soldiers.

In November 1988 the Regiment said farewell to Lieutenant-Colonel John Woolley who relinquished command to take up a staff appointment at Western District Headquarters. His ceremonial send-off was fitting for one who had done much for the Regiment during his three year tenure: mounted in a horse-drawn carriage, accompanied by the new CO, Lieutenant-Colonel M. T. Steiger, TD, he was escorted by troopers in Full Dress.

It was Colonel Woolley who not only secured the funding and commissioning of this history, but also initiated the publication of the first Regimental Journal. Ably edited by Major Margaret Hammersley of the attached WRAC, *The Lancashire Yeoman* appeared in November 1987 and was a credit to the Regiment, brightly written, professionally printed and copiously illustrated.

As previously noted, Colonel Woolley's successor had joined the Regiment as 2nd Lieutenant M. T. Steiger in 1974 and quickly rose from Troop Leader to Sqn 2/IC then

Squadron Leader, and finally to his ultimate appointment. As Museum's Officer he had been largely instrumental in the creation of what is now one of the finest Yeomanry museums in the country. His TD was awarded in 1986. In addition to all his military responsibilities, he has carried on a busy civilian career in the Law, now practising as a barrister with Chambers in Manchester.

Martin Steiger is an example of that rare breed, musical Commanding Officer. An accomplished pianist, he is prone to entertain house guests with recitals of Beethoven sonatas – Yeomen have always been men of many talents.

In July 1986 A Squadron had been obliged to move from its old established Drill Hall, or TA Centre, in Powell Street, Wigan to temporary premises in the same town, this being due to an urban redevelopment scheme. Plans were put in hand for new and more spacious accommodation in the town's Canal Street (not far from the tourist-oriented development of 'Wigan Pier'). The premises were ready for occupation by October 1989 and with a happy historical hark-back, the new building was named Kearsley House, after Captain John Hodson Kearsley who had raised one of the DLOY's antecedents, the Wigan Volunteer Light Horse, in 1818.

The ceremonial opening was performed on 21 October 1989 by Lieutenant-General Sir David Ramsbotham, KCB, CBE, Inspector-General of the Territorial Army, who was received by a Guard of Honour found by A Squadron, under Major J. Tustin. The General Salute and subsequent music were performed by the Band of the 5th/8th (Volunteer) Battalion, The King's Regiment.

As in previous years, the 1989 role of the Regiment as a Home Defence Medium Reconnaissance unit involved training in a wide variety of tasks, such as:

> Investigation of 'incidents'
> Mounted and foot patrols
> Minor operations at Section level
> Vehicle check points
> Search operations
> NBC reconnaissance
> Escort duties
> Route reconnaissance
> Traffic control

In addition to all these, the normal pattern of training in shooting (rifle and LMG), radio and driving and maintenance had to be carried on. The Regiment had always distinguished itself in shooting, and the annual Skill-at-Arms Meeting held at Altcar in May was no exception. Competing against all units in the North West District, the 'A' Team won the Falling Plates TA Competition, C (HSF) Squadron won the HSF moving Target event, while the WRAC team triumphed in their competition. As observed in the previous chapter, the WRAC members had always demonstrated that the 'weaker sex' were by no means weaker than their male comrades when it came to handling weapons. At Bisley in July Officer-Cadet Jayne Ashworth carried off the coveted Gold Medal for the Women's Services Rifle Championship.

Every year Reservists of the Regular Army are required to report to certain military centres, to be recorded and 'processed' as part of their Reserve commitments. In February 1989 the Reporting Centre at Preston was manned by members of the Regiment, who in four days dealt with no fewer than 1,695 Reserve WOs, NCOs and men. For many years the DLOY has been honoured to provide a Guard on the Grand National trophies at Aintree, and on 8 April television viewers saw the Regiment's troopers in Full Dress of scarlet tunics and helmets, with drawn swords, guarding the cups as the winning jockey was acclaimed.

Not all activities were home-based. From 26 May to 26 June six NCOs and men were attached to the affiliated 14th/20th King's Hussars for the annual exercise 'Medicine Man' in the British Army's Training Unit area at Suffield in Canada, where schemes are carried out with live ammunition. Also in May, two NCOs from D Squadron flew to Hong Kong for attachment to the Royal Hong Kong Regiment, to take part in Chinese border patrols. In October, two subalterns enjoyed an attachment to the Garde Hussar Regiment of the Danish Army. The old slogan 'Join the Army and see the world' still had some relevance, even for Territorials.

In September 1989 the Regiment motored down to Devon for Annual Camp which, as usual, involved a variety of activities, mostly in anything but welcoming weather, with pouring rain. Officers and men of B Squadron endured arduous treks (on foot) across the wastes of Dartmoor, also indulging in such diversions as rock climbing and abseiling. Less physically demanding, but instructive, was the Medical Section's attachment to the Royal Naval Hospital at Plymouth, where they gained valuable experience in the treatment of battle casualties. Social events were marked by a Dinner Night in the Okehampton Officers' Mess where, in addition to the Guest of Honour, Major-General Nicholas Ansell, Director of The Royal Armoured Corps, the Commanding Officers of The Royal Wessex Yeomanry and Queen's Own Mercian Yeomanry were entertained. Music was kindly provided by the Royal Marines with their string band.

All this took place during the first week. The second week saw the Regiment navigating from Okehampton to the Sennybridge Training Area near Brecon, and thence to the Midlands. Finally, on 24 September the two-week Annual Training was concluded at the Holcombe Training Camp, near Bury 'with a highly enjoyable Regimental concert in which each Squadron provided a cabaret,' said the Regimental notes. The Yeomanry have always believed in the old adage 'All work and no play . . . '

The activities of 1989 came to an end on 9 December when a shooting weekend was held at the Altcar Ranges. Here, opportunity was taken to put on a Christmas lunch for the other ranks, who, following Army tradition, were served by the Commanding Officer, his officers and senior NCOs. 'This was a very popular event and the other ranks were well provided with paper hats, crackers and beer. Needless to say, there was no shooting in the afternoon.' Thus the busy year ended on a festive note.

With the year 1990 we come to the final paragraphs of this record of the Regiment's services over nearly two centuries. And the most memorable event of that year – indeed

Members of the Regiment's Ceremonial Guard on duty at Aintree for the Grand National 1988; the Regiment has guarded the trophies for the Grand National since 1985.

The A Squadron shooting team with a succesful clutch of trophies from the Regimental Skill-at-Arms meeting held at Altcar in April 1988; on the extreme left is the Squadron SSM, S/Sgt Taylor and at the extreme right the Squadron OC, Major John Tustin.

The Regimental Medical Officer, Major Cliff Godby and his staff preparing members of A Squadron to simulate casualties at Nesscliffe during annual Camp 1989.

Sir David Ramsbottom KCB, CBE, opening the new 'A' Squadron TA Centre at Canal Street, Wigan, 21st October 1989. The TA Centre was named after John Hodson Kearsley who raised the Wigan Light Horse Volunteers in 1819.

The TA Centre at Canal Street, Wigan opened in October 1989; the stonework in the foreground was brought from the previous TA Centre, Powell Street, Wigan, originally erected for the Lancashire Rifle Volunteers.

The Colonel-in-Chief sharing a joke with the Officers on her visit to Stonyhurst in October 1990. The Officers are as follows:

Front Row (*left to right*) Major Major G. Fulton (OC C HSF Squadron), Major A. R. F. MacKenzie (OC A Squadron), Lieutenant-Colonel A. J. Hammersley (CO NWD Specialist Training team), Major-General Sir Michael Palmer KCVO (Honorary Colonel), the Colonel-in-Chief, Lieutenant-Colonel M. T. Steiger (CO), Major J. Eastham (Second-in-Command), Major D. Lithgo-Smith (CO B Squadron).

Rear row (left to right) Major M. E. Hammersley WRAC, Captain E. N. Ryder, Captain M. A. C. Williams, 14/20H, Major I. S. Forbes-Cockell LG (Training Major), Captain S. R. C. Seawright, 14/20H (Adjutant), Captain T. G. Bowring, Captain M. E. Hayle.

This picture is reproduced by kind permission of the Editor of the *Lancashire Evening Post* who are the copyright holders.

Guidon Party and Scarlet Guard at the entrance to the Regimental Museum, Preston, on the occasion of the removal of the 1909 Guidon from Manchester Cathedral to the Museum on 10 April 1991.

Members of the Old Comrades Association in front of a 5.5" Howitzer gun as used by 77 and 78 Medium Regiments (DLOY) during the Second World War. The gun was ceremonially unveiled on 10 April 1991.

The DLOY Guidon being paraded before Her Majesty The Queen at Windsor Great Park on Sunday 17 April 1994 as part of the Royal Review to celebrate the 200th anniversary of the forming of the earliest yeomanry units in England. This parade was the first major parade since the amalgamation to form the RMLY. The Guidon is carried by WO2 N. Turner and escorted by S/Sgt P. Roden and S/Sgt L. Sutton

the most memorable since 1961 — was the presentation of a new Guidon by Her Majesty The Queen, Colonel-in-Chief, which took place in October.

As recounted in Chapter IX (pp. 143) Her Majesty had previously honoured the Regiment with the presentation of a new Guidon at Manchester in May 1961, which replaced that given by her great-grandfather, King Edward VII at Worsley Park, 52 years earlier. Normally, the period of service for Standards, Guidons or Colours of Territorial units is 30 years, and after only 29 years the 1961 Guidon (displayed at RHQ Chorley) was still in excellent condition. But Major-General Sir Michael Palmer, Honorary Colonel, felt that it would be fitting if it could be replaced during the tenure of a volunteer Yeoman Commanding Officer. Lieutenant-Colonel Martin Steiger, TD was due to hand over to a Regular at the beginning of November 1990, and so machinery was set in motion to bring forward the presentation.

As early as 1988 the Honorary Colonel had approached the Queen's Private Secretary suggesting that Her Majesty might be graciously pleased to make the presentation around the middle of October. To everyone's gratification, the date of 18 October was approved.

The venue for the ceremony had already been arranged — at Stonyhurst College, some 15 miles east of Preston. It so happened that Colonel John Cardwell, a former CO of the DLOY (1961–64), was a Stonyhurst Old Boy and it was at his suggestion that the college authorities were approached, proving enthusiastic and affording generous co-operation. This ancient Roman Catholic public school (originally founded in France in 1593) was not only an ideal setting with its spacious grounds and elegant 18th-century buildings, but it also boasted worthy military connections. Seven Old Boys had won VCs, including the first such awards in the First and Second World Wars.

The parade was planned to comprise four dismounted Guards of 30 men each, provided by the four Squadrons, all in No. 2 Dress with the distinctive shoulder chains; behind each Guard was a detachment of WRAC members in Land Rovers, while a feature which evoked much interest from Her Majesty was a Mounted Escort to the Guidon, one officer and three Yeomen in full scarlets with drawn swords. The officer was Lieutenant-Colonel Frank Hewitt, DLOY, who had arranged for black horses to be borrowed from the Guards Division Depot at Pirbright, and for a 'crash' course in equitation at the Knightsbridge barracks of the Household Cavalry. Perhaps 'crash' is not quite the appropriate term, for all successfully passed the course under the critical eye of the Riding Master with no involuntary dismounting. Also in full dress scarlet were the Queen's Yeomen orderlies and lance markers. Commanded by Lieutenant-Colonel M. T. Steiger, TD, the parade strength was 17 officers and 140 other ranks. The essential music was provided by the Band of the 1st Battalion, The Queen's Lancashire Regiment, kindly made available by the Commanding Officer, Lieutenant-Colonel A. F. Birtwistle.

Exactly at 1100 hours as planned, Her Majesty, preceded by the Mounted Escort, arrived in her Rolls Royce on the parade ground, to be received by a Royal Salute from the Band. Accompanied by the Colonel of the Regiment, Major-General Sir Michael Palmer, KCVO and Colonel Steiger, she then inspected the Regiment. After Her Majesty had returned to the dais, the Old Guidon was trooped through the ranks to a slow march and was then marched off parade to the emotive strains of 'Auld Lang Syne'. Next followed the Consecration of the New Guidon, resting on the silver kettle-drums. The service was conducted by the Deputy Chaplain General to the Forces, the Venerable G. H. Roblin, supported by four other clerics, including the Regimental Padre, the Rev. Trevor Vaughan who in his civilian ministry was Vicar of Settle.

When the consecrated Guidon had been handed over to RQMS Cavanagh by The Queen, Her Majesty addressed the Regiment. After recalling the previous Presentation in 1961, she continued:

> Much additional hard work is required of part-time soldiers to execute a Parade such as this. I am pleased, though not surprised, to see that all of you today have maintained that very high standard which I admired so much thirty years ago. You give me every confidence that the new Guidon will be cherished in the finest traditions of the Regiment. The excellence of the Parade is matched by the impressive surroundings Stonyhurst provides for this splendid occasion. On behalf of the Regiment I should like to express our gratitude to the School for allowing the use of their historic premises and for offering so much help and assistance ...
>
> It is pleasing to see so many Old Comrades here today, including the men of the 77th and 78th Medium Regiments who served with such distinction in the Second World War. Yeomen of Lancashire, it is to them, and to all of you past and present, that I give my thanks for your service to your country. I congratulate those on parade today on your commitment and military efficiency, achieved at the cost of many a leisure hour. The County Palatine has good reason to be proud of you.

Replying, Lieutenant-Colonel Steiger thanked Her Majesty for the signal honour in presenting the new Guidon, assuring her that 'we shall treasure our new Guidon, not only to keep faith with the traditions and glory of the past, but also to inspire in the next generation of Yeomen our unfaltering devotion to Your Majesty as Duke of Lancaster and our Colonel-in-Chief'. The ceremony ended with an Advance in Review Order and a March Past the Royal Dais.

After The Queen had been entertained to luncheon in the college refectory (when music was provided by the college orchestra), she was presented by the Honorary Colonel with a memento of the occasion in the form of an enamelled casket with the Regimental Badge, and was then shown some of the historic treasures of Stonyhurst College. Following group photographs, she took her leave of the College Rector, Headmaster, Honorary Colonel and CO and departed in her motorcade at 3.20 p.m. to a Royal Salute, Guidon dipped. It had originally been planned that the police should lead the royal car, but to the extreme gratification of the Regiment, Her Majesty specifically requested that the Mounted Escort should be accorded this honour, and so Lieutenant-Colonel Hewitt and his three scarlet-clad troopers, drawn swords at the 'carry' trotted ahead of Her Majesty down the length of the Stonyhurst drive.

The Guidon Parade was the climax, and finale, of Lieutenant-Colonel Steiger's two-year tenure of command. On 9 November he was dined out in the RHQ Mess at Chorley, to be succeeded by Lieutenant-Colonel S. M. P. Stewart of The Queen's Dragoon Guards.

Colonel Stewart was to be the last Commanding Officer of the Regiment.

The County Palatine had good reason to be proud of its only surviving Yeomanry Regiment, as Her Majesty had averred. But alas, the Government was soon to destroy that same Regiment that had served Her and Her predecessors for nearly 200 years. In 1991 the Secretary of State for Defence announced his "Options for Change" ("No Option but Change" as one Commanding Officer put it) in which both Regular and Territorial Army were slashed by amalgamations and disbandments.

Thus by 1 November 1992 the Duke of Lancaster's ceased to exist as a Regiment. It was ruthlessly cut to a single squadron, merged with the Queens Own Mercian Yeomanry to form the new conglomerate, the Royal Mercian and Lancastrian Yeomanry, deployed as under:

> RHQ and HQ Squadron (Shropshire Yeomanry) – Telford
> A Squadron (Queen's Own Warwickshire and Worcestershire Yeomanry) – Stourbridge
> B Squadron (The Staffordshire Yeomanry) – Dudley
> D Squadron (The Duke of Lancaster's Own Yeomanry) – Wigan

The old order changeth . . . and Regiments are abolished by politicians. But the name of the Duke of Lancaster's Own Yeomanry and its traditions live on in a single squadron, still proud to wear the unique No.2 dress shoulder chains that distinguished it from its partners in the new Regiment which has Her Majesty (Duke of Lancaster) as Colonel in Chief.

The Queen's Mounted Escort leading the Royal Cavalcade from Stonyhurst College after the Guidon Parade on 18 October 1990. The Escort were all serving DLOY volunteers mounted on horses kindly loaned by the Household Cavalry Regiment; Lieutenant Colonel F. E. Hewitt (*front*) commanded; from left to right behind him are Sergeant Valentine, Corporal Gaskell and Corporal Young.

This magnificent brass plaque records the service of 23 Company Imperial Yeomanry during the Boer War 1900–1902. The plaque has been displayed at all RHQ locations until 1992 and now hangs in the TA Centre, Canal Street, Wigan, Home of D (DLOY) Squadron, The Royal Mercian and Lancastrian Yeomanry.

APPENDIX I
ROLL OF HONOUR

THE DUKE OF LANCASTER'S OWN YEOMANRY

THE BOER WAR – 1899–1902

23rd (DUKE OF LANCASTER'S OWN) COMPANY, IMPERIAL YEOMANRY

Imp Yeo No. (if known)	Name	Rank	Date of Death	Details
2682	BARRY G.E.M.*	L/Cpl	30.5.1900	KIA Faber's Putt[1]
–	BINGHAM J.A.	Lieut	11.2.1902	DOW Middleport
2669	COULSTON W.*	Cpl	30.5.1900	KIA Faber's Putt[1]
2741	DERBYSHIRE J.W.*		30.5.1900	KIA Faber's Putt[1]
2718	DRANSFIELD J.W.*		27.11.1900	Died Kimerley (enteric fever)[2]
2677	HACKFORTH F.W.*		30.5.1900	KIA Faber's Putt[1]
25554	HALL W.S.		2.6.1902	KIA Craddock, Cape Colony
25573	HANLEY F.		2.6.1902	KIA Craddock, Cape Colony
2643	HOWCROFT W.		17.4.1902	Died Kroonstad (disease)
–	HUME		6.2.1902	KIA Middleport, Cape Colony
20511	ISHERWOOD R.*		6.2.1902	KIA Middleport, Cape Colony
20516	LANCASTER R.	Cpl	6.2.1902	DOW Middleport, Cape Colony
2680	LONGLAND C.F.		22.5.1901	Died Harpenden, Herts., from enteric fever contracted on homeward journey; served as cook to the 23rd Coy
2753	LOOKER W.*		20.1.1901	Died Johannesburg (disease)
2646	ORRELL P.*		30.5.1900	KIA Faber's Putt[1]
2788	REW D.*		30.5.1900	KIA Faber's Putt[1]
–	SPRATT H.D.	Lieut	2.6.1902	KIA Craddock, Cape Colony

FORMER MEMBERS OF THE REGIMENT WHO DIED SERVING WITH OTHER UNITS

Former DLOY number (if known)	Name	Date of Death	Details at time of Death
–	WHITAKER H.E.*	14.2.1901	Served with the 74th Coy Imp Yeo and later with the Imperial Light Horse; died 'from injuries'

* = known to have had previous service with the DLOY (numbers not known)
[1] = buried in the Garden of Remembrance, West End Cemetery, Kimberley
[2] = buried at Kimberley, in Gladstone, Kenilworth or West End Cemeteries

Key to Cemetery/Memorial Refs:

B 16	=	Dozinghem Military Cemetery, Westvleteren, Belgium
B 18	=	Mendinghem Military Cemetery, Proven, Belgium
DUBLIN 14	=	Grangegorman Military Cemetery, Co Dublin, Eire
E 1	=	Hadra War Memorial Cemetery, Alexandria, Egypt
E 6	=	Chatby War Memorial Cemetery, Egypt
E 9	=	Cairo War Memorial Cemetery, Egypt
E 15	=	Suez War Memorial Cemetery, Egypt
ESSEX 13	=	East London Cemetery, Plaistow, West Ham, Essex
EUR 1	=	Pieta Military Cemetery, Malta
FR 40	=	Etaples Military Cemetery, Etaples, France
FR 67	=	La Neuville Communal Cemetery, France
FR 300	=	St Pierre Cemetery, Amiens, France
FR 511	=	Peronne Communal Cemetery Extension, France
FR 628	=	Eclusier Communal Cemetery, Eclusier–Vaux, France
FR 1571	=	Mazargues War Cemetery, France
GALLIPOLI 1	=	Lancashire Landing Cemetery, Helles, Gallipoli
IRELAND 75	=	Drumcree Church of Ireland Churchyard, Co Armagh, N Ireland
ITALY 14	=	The Savona Memorial, Italy
LANCS 413	=	Kirk Maughold (St Machut) Churchyard, Isle of Man
MR 20	=	Arras Memorial at Faubourg–d'Amiens Cemetery, Arras, France
MR 21	=	Thiepval Memorial, France
MR 34	=	Jerusalem Memorial, Israel
MR 41	=	Chatby Memorial, Alexandria, Egypt
P 8	=	Gaza War Cemetery, Palestine
P 11	=	Haifa War Cemetery, Israel (formerly Palestine)
SYRIA 1	=	Beirut British War Cemetery, Lebanon, Syria
W/LAND 82	=	Kendal (Parkside) Cemetery, Cumbria (formerly Westmorland)

THE GREAT WAR – 1914–1918
DUKE OF LANCASTER'S OWN YEOMANRY

DLOY No.	Name	Rank	Date of Death	Cemetery/ Memorial	Details
4857	ADAMS W.H.		4.12.1917	ESSEX 13	Died UK (2/1st DLOY)
110735	ASHMAN L.A.		8.12.1917	MR 34	DOW Egypt
4180/110670	BERRY O.		5.11.1915	E 1	Died Egypt
–	BIBBY H.L.	Maj	4.5.1917	ITALY 14	Drowned Mediterranean (SS *Transylvania*)
3240/11026	BIRCH J.W.		4.2.1919	FR 1571	Died France & Flanders
3189	BURGESS S.	L/Cpl	6.10.1915	EUR 1	DOW received in Egypt?
–	CROOK P.J.	Lieut	7.11.1917	P *	KIA Palestine
11058	CRYER (J.)A.		3.4.1917	FR 511	DOW France & Flanders
1924	DEARDEN J.	Sgt	25.11.1915	GALLIPOLI 1	DOW Gallipoli (possibly divisional military police)
30404*	FLAVELLE T.H.		6.11.1918	IRELAND 75	Died UK
3327/110173	HARRIS A.	C/S/Sth	26.10.1918	SYRIA 1	Died Lebanon
3779	HARRISON J.		14.5.1916	E 15	Died Egypt
GS/13949**	HILLS H.		11.12.1918	E 1	Died Egypt; formerly 1872 Herts Yeo & D/14850 Corps of Dragoons
3357/110178	HUGHES H.E.		25.3.1917	FR 628	DOW France & Flanders
4026	JONES J.D.	Farrier	1.2.1916	W/LAND 82	Died UK (2/1st DLOY)
110604	McCLURE W.		30.3.1917	MR 21	KIA France & Flanders
3380	McKENNA B.		3.12.1914	E 9	Died Egypt
110660	MOORE G.W.		7.11.1917	P 8	KIA Palestine
13970	NICKELS W.C.		7.11.1917	P 8	KIA Palestine
1124	RIDYARD T.		4.1.1917	FR 67	Died France & Flanders
4030/110570	SIDDALL T.A.	L/Cpl	25.10.1918	P 11	Died Palestine
110631	SMALLEY T.		3.7.1918	?¹	Died UK
110868	SMITH A.		15.11.1918	SYRIA 1	Died Lebanon
3955/110553	STOTT H.		31.5.1919	FR 300	Died France & Flanders
3033	SUTCLIFFE R.		3.2.1916	LANCS 413	Died UK
3315	TURNER A.	S/Smith	30.9.1914	MR 41	Died in accident on SS *Atlantian* – Mediterranean
110501	WALKER G.		10.10.1918	DUBLIN 14	Drowned Irish Sea (RMS *Leinster*)
3831/110482	WHITAKER H.	L/Cpl	24.3.1917	MR 21	KIA France & Flanders
3287/110376	WILLIAMS J.H.		7.11.1917	MR 34	KIA Palestine
3395	WILLIAMS T.		17.10.1915	E 6	Died Egypt

SERVING ON DETACHMENT FROM THE REGIMENT

–	FAIR J.G.	2nd Lieut	19.3.1917	MR 20	KIA France & Flanders (attached to RFC)
–	FAWCETT F.	2nd Lieut	12.11.1918	FR 40	Died France & Flanders (attached to 64 Sqn RAF)
–	GREENALL J.E.D.	Capt	31.3.1918	FR 300	KIA France & Flanders (attached to RFC)
–	MORGAN H.R.	Lieut	8.11.1917	B 18	KIA France & Flanders (attached to 7th Sqn RFC)
–	SHEPHERD-CROSS C.H.S.	Maj	15.10.1917	B 16	KIA France & Flanders (attached to 197th Coy MGC)

FORMER MEMBERS OF THE REGIMENT
WHO DIED SERVING WITH OTHER UNITS

Former DLOY number (if known)	Name	Date of Death	Details at time of Death
5124	ADAMSON W.V.	17.8.1918	45476 Pte 2nd Btn South Lancashire Regt
110672	ALLEN T.	4.11.1918	245633 Pte 12th Btn Manchester Regt (MM)
110855	ANDERSON T.	26.10.1917	245642 Pte 12th Btn Manchester Regt
3407	ANNAHEIM G.H.	4.10.1918	Lieut (Temp) 1st Btn Royal Munster Fusiliers
5149	AUSTIN E.	8.11.1918	45497 Pte 2nd Btn South Lancashire Regt
4509	BAILEY C.T.	22.3.1918	32151 L/Cpl 2nd Btn South Lancashire Regt
3750	BARNES F.T.	27.10.1917	37244 A/Cpl 9th Lancashire Fusiliers
3849	BAUGH F.H.	10.3.1917	P/6120 Pte Mounted Military Police
4139	BAXENDALE R.	18.9.1918	260340 Pte 7th Btn Border Regt
3619	BIDDLE J.R.	29.9.1918	46463 Pte 11th Btn Manchester Regt
5050	BIRMINGHAM M.	4.11.1918	53415 Pte 16th Btn Lancashire Fusiliers
110713	BLACKBURN E.	9.9.1918	245498 Pte 12th Btn Manchester Regt
4308	BOWMAN L.J.	2.12.1916	37251 Pte 9th Btn Lancashire Fusiliers
4158	BOYES T.V.	30.7.1918	260493 Pte 7th Btn Border Regt
4893	BUCKLE F.E.	20.10.1918	32533 Pte 1/5th Btn East Lancashire Regt
5084	BULCOCK A.	26.4.1918	53417 Pte 2/5th Btn Lancashire Fusiliers
5054	CAIN J.A.	22.9.1918	53421 Pte 2/5th Lancashire Fusiliers
111196	CHADWICK H.	5.5.1918	53361 Pte 1st Btn Lancashire Fusiliers
110609	CHESTER H.	20.10.1918	245505 Pte 1/10th Btn Manchester Regt
5052	CLARKE A.	11.8.1918	53420 Pte 2/5th Btn Lancashire Fusiliers
3996	COLEMAN J.A.	24.10.1917	46499 Cpl 21st Btn Manchester Regt
5053	COOPER E.	10.5.1918	53422 Pte 2/5th Btn Lancashire Fusiliers
4345	CRISPIN F.V.	22.10.1917	46517 L/Cpl 23rd Btn Manchester Regt
110068	CROSTON G.	16.10.1917	245635 Pte 12th Btn Manchester Regt
4237	CROWTHER R.	25.8.1918	46510 Pte 12th Btn Manchester Regt
4748	DARCY W.C.	2.6.1918	46505 Pte 2nd Btn South Lanchashire Regt
4500	DEVANEY N.	1.8.1917	242885 Pte 1/5th Btn South Lancashire Regt
5008	DICKINSON W.	21.3.1918	53366 Pte 2/8th Btn Lancashire Fusiliers
4942	DOBBIE F.L.	26.5.1918	45483 Pte 2nd Btn South Lancashire Regt
2996	DODD S.	7.12.1919	439960 Cpl Royal Engineers
5153	DODGSON W.G.	5.10.1918	63275 Pte 16th Btn Lancashire Fusiliers
1736	DRINKWATER L.W.	3.10.1917	2nd Lieut Royal Field Artillery (TF)
110107	EDGE T.	5.8.1918	245512 Pte 12th Btn Manchester Regt
5154	EDMUNDSON W.G.	25.3.1918	53457 Pte 1/8th Btn Lancashire Fusiliers
–	FAWCETT L.G.F.E.	6.11.1917	Capt Royal Scots Fusiliers
110114	FINK S.	26.10.1917	245679 Pte 12th Btn Manchester Regt
110693	FISHER W.	21.11.1917	245638 Pte 12th Btn Manchester Regt
4570	FLETCHER G.	14.6.1917	32153 Pte 2nd Btn South Lancashire Regt
4409	FLETCHER L.	23.8.1918	37263 L/Sgt 16th Btn Lancashire Fusiliers
4934	FLINT J.W.	13.4.1918	53343 Pte 1st Btn Lancashire Fusiliers
4313	FODEN R.E.	24.11.1918	58081 Pte 18th Btn Liverpool Regt
110643	FORESTER A.L.	10.11.1917	245514 Pte 12th Btn Manchester Regt
3058	FOX S.H.	12.9.1917	GS/13935 Pte Corps of Dragoons
3646	GARDE F.O.	9.9.1918	245566 Pte 12th Btn Manchester Regt
4897	GIBSON J.T.	20.11.1917	40770 Pte 2/5th Btn Lancashire Fusiliers

FORMER MEMBERS OF THE REGIMENT
WHO DIED SERVING WITH OTHER UNITS (cont.)

Former DLOY number (if known)	Name	Date of Death	Details at time of Death
4514	GIBSON T.	21.3.1918	260355 Pte 1/5th Btn Border Regt
4685	GLEDHILL W.	20.11.1917	28583 Pte 12th Btn Manchester Regt
3809	GLENNER H.	31.3.1918	25693 Pte 1st Btn Border Regt
2982	GOLDING J.A.	3.10.1917	P/10739 Pte Mounted Military Police
4245	GREATOREX J.	4.6.1917	242895 Pte 1/5th Btn South Lancashire Regt
4365	GREENACRE C.A.	22.10.1917	46523 Pte 23rd Btn Manchester Regt
4684	GREGSON G.	13.8.1917	28585 Pte 1st Btn Border Regt
–	GWYER C.	27.8.1918	2–Lieut 2nd Btn Grenadier Guards
110467	HAMER H.	22.3.1918	245637 Pte 12th Btn Manchester Regt
110546	HAMER W.W.	5.2.1918	245561 Pte 12th Btn Manchester Regt
4900	HARDING J.	4.10.1917	28567 Pte 1st Btn Border Regt
3264	HARROP J.	18.8.1917	37223 Pte 9th Btn Lancashire Fusiliers
4901	HITCHCOCK W.G.	20.11.1917	40354 Pte 2/5th Btn Lancashire Fusiliers
4576	HOYLE W.	11.1.1918	245765 Pte 12th Btn Manchester Regt
4464	HUNT R.	13.9.1918	54252 Pte 12th Btn Manchester Regt
5147	HUTCHINSON A.E.	2.6.1918	46508 Pte 2nd Btn South Lancashire Regt
110581	JACKSON F.C.	10.11.1917	245522 Pte 12th Btn Manchester Regt
110582	JOHNSON H.	9.11.1917	245643 Pte 12th Btn Manchester Regt
3618	JONES B.	24.5.1917	38585 Pte 13th Btn Manchester Regt
110474	KANE R.	2.9.1918	245770 Pte 12th Btn Manchester Regt
110199	KEMBER S.	25.10.1917	245616 Pte 12th Btn Manchester Regt
110678	KIRKWOOD W.	1.12.1917	245665 Pte 12th Btn Manchester Regt
5071	KNOTT W.	22.5.1918	53429 Pte 2/5th Btn Lancashire Fusiliers
110708	LANCASHIRE H.	4.1.1918	245526 Pte 12th Btn Manchester Regt
4692	LEE J.W.	16.8.1917	28592 Pte 1st Btn Border Regt
5072	LEIGH C.	5.4.1918	53407 Pte 1/8th Btn Lancashire Fusiliers
3797	LORD J.W.	21.3.1918	37236 Pte 1/6th Btn Lancashire Fusiliers
–	MACK A.S.	9.4.1917	Lieut 1st Btn King's Own Royal Lancashire Regt*
110413	MAYO F.	10.10.1917	245531 Pte 12th Btn Manchester Regt
111365	MORPHET T.H.	25.3.1918	53458 Pte 1/8th Btn Lancashire Fusiliers
3818	MOTTERSHEAD L.	16.4.1917	46477 Pte 23rd Btn Manchester Regt
4699	NUTTALL E.	26.4.1918	46511 Pte 2nd Btn South Lancashire Regt
5076	O'FALLON R.R.	9.4.1918	53432 Pte 2/5th Btn Lancashire Fusiliers
4315	OWEN E.	24.4.1918	205385 Pte 1st Btn Sherwood Foresters
5202	PALIN T.H.	21.8.1918	45489 Pte 2nd Btn South Lancashire Regt
110838	PARTINGTON A.	5.11.1918	245581 Pte 12th Btn Manchester Regt
4395	PEARSON H.	5.12.1916	37261 Pte 9th Btn Lancashire Fusiliers
3926	PEARSON T.J.	28.9.1918	37242 Pte 1st Btn Lancashire Fusiliers
4011	PENTLAND T.E.	10.1.1917	37246 A/Sgt 9th Btn Lancashire Fusiliers
4770	PRESTWICH H.	30.9.1918	28598 Pte 1st Btn Border Regt
4734	QUINLAN J.	2.10.1917	28599 Pte 1st Btn Border Regt
3548	ROBERTS F.	5.9.1917	37227 Pte 2/8th Btn Lancashire Fusiliers
4760	ROBINSON F.	9.10.1918	28600 Pte 7th Btn Border Regt
2999	ROBINSON J.J.H.	29.10.1917	260320 Pte 7th Btn Border Regt
4176	SCHOFIELD J.	9.10.1918	260537 Pte 7th Btn Border Regt

FORMER MEMBERS OF THE REGIMENT
WHO DIED SERVING WITH OTHER UNITS (cont.)

Former DLOY number (if known)	Name	Date of Death	Details at time of Death
5023	SHACKLETON M.	12.4.1918	53353 Pte 1st Btn Lancashire Fusiliers
4764	SHARPLES J.	1.4.1918	28750 Pte 1st Btn Border Regt
3689	SHAW W.	22.10.1917	46466 Pte 23rd Btn Manchester Regt
4931	SMETHURST J.	12.4.1917	53354 Pte 1st Btn Lancashire Fusiliers
110323	SMITH A.	4.12.1917	245670 Pte 12th Btn Manchester Regt
110507	SMITH A.J.	9.6.1918	245677 L/Cpl 12th Btn Manchester Regt
–	SNELL C.H.	9.11.1917	Lieut 12th Btn Manchester Regt
–	STRATTON F.A.	27.1.1917	Lieut IARO, att'd to 87th Punjabis[1]
110781	TAYLOR S.H.	22.3.1918	245659 Pte 12th Btn Manchester Regt
4714	THOMAS P.	25.10.1918	53451 L/Cpl 2/5th Btn Lancashire Fusiliers (MM)
5144	THORNTON T.	1.6.1918	53452 Pte 2/5th Btn Lancashire Fusiliers
–	TILNEY L.A.	9.3.1918	2nd Lieut Royal Horse Guards, att'd 40th Sqn RFC (MC)
4347	TOMLINSON J.	10.7.1918	46518 Pte 1/10th Btn Manchester Regt
110802	TONGUE A.	19.5.1918	245544 Pte 12th Btn Manchester Regt
110484	TURNER A.W.	22.9.1918	245543 L/Cpl 12th Btn Manchester Regt
4419	WADDINGTON E.	5.12.1916	37265 Pte 9th Btn Lancashire Fusiliers
4880	WAITE A.E.	14.9.1918	53404 Cpl 2/5th Btn Manchester Regt
4032	WALL W.E.	22.10.1917	46503 Pte 23rd Btn Manchester Regt
4603	WALSH J.	16.8.1917	28607 Pte 1st Btn Border Regt
4037	WARBURTON R.	10.4.1918	235487 Pte 9th Btn Loyal North Lancashire Regt
3776	WARE H.	26.8.1917	46472 Cpl 23rd Btn Manchester Regt (DCM)
4738	WEBSTER A.	24.7.1917	28585 Pte 1st Btn Border Regt
4401	WHITELEGG A.	24.2.1917	46531 L/Cpl 23rd Btn Manchester Regt
110369	WHITFIELD G.	26.10.1917	245674 L/Cpl 12th Btn Manchester Regt
3430	WILSON A.H.	[2]7.10.1918	D/18117 Sgt 6th Reserve Regt of Cavalry
4045	WILSON G.E.	27.9.1918	46506 Pte 11th Btn Manchester Regt
4884	WILSON J.P.	14.8.1917	28569 Pte 1st Btn Border Regt
5167	WINDER A.	3.6.1918	46517 Pte 2nd Btn South Lancashire Regt
3379	WINDRIDGE T.	5.7.1918	361442 Pte Labour Corps
3755	WINSTANLEY T.A.	4.9.1917	37234 Cpl 9th Btn Lancashire Fusiliers

* = Name appears on Southport War Memorial under 'DLOY' – this may be an error, and Mack may have had no regimental connection

[1] = One source states 82nd Punjabis

[2] = 1914–15 Star Medal Roll gives date of death as 8.10.1918

[168]

THE SECOND WORLD WAR – 1939–1945

77th (DLOY) MEDIUM REGIMENT, ROYAL ARTILLERY

Former DLOY number (if known)	Name	Rank	Date of Death	Details at time of Death
110845	BLAYNEY F.S.	Gnr	8.11.1943	–
172944	DIMBLEBY H.W.	Capt	18.7.1944	KIA Bourgebus, France
878125	DONNELLY A.	Gnr	29.3.1945	DOW Oploo, Netherlands
32521539	ETCHELLS E.	Gnr	1.7.1944	KIA St Mauvieux, France
114223119	GOLDSMITH W.	Gnr	12.10.1944	DOW Oploo, Netherlands
118427	HOLLINS P.T.	Maj	26.4.1944	KIA Cheux, France
409966	IRVING A.	Gnr	30.7.1944	KIA Caumont, France
1101797	JONES R.	Gnr	15.8.1944	DOW
972999	JONES T.A.	L/Bdr	21.3.1942	
325618	MURPHY J.F.	Gnr	2.7.1940	
1089130	O'BRIEN T.J.	Gnr	12.9.1944?	DOW Oploo, Netherlands
1104667	POWELL E.N.	Gnr	30.7.1944	KIA Caumont, France
325641	SHEPHERD H.	Bdr	25.5.1940	
1089130	SYASS R.H.	Gnr	12.10.1944	
999470	WEST S.G.	L/Bdr	12.10.1944	

78th (DLOY) MEDIUM REGIMENT, ROYAL ARTILLERY (cont.)

Former DLOY number (if known)	Name	Rank	Date of Death	Details at time of Death
962278	BOWES F.	Gnr	2.7.1944	KIA Italy
962261	BURKE M.	Gnr	8.10.1946	Died UK (Middlesborough)
948320	BURNS M.J.	Gnr	12.5.1944	KIA Cassino, Italy
972281	CRAWFORD C.E.	Sgt	23.11.1945	Died
323335	DAGNALL F.	Gnr	8.5.1944	KIA Italy
114008	EDWARDS A.	Gnr	8.5.1944	KIA Italy
154618	ELLIS J.R.	Gnr	10.5.1955	KIA Cassino, Italy
962823	FERN J.	L/Bdr	7.7.1944	KIA Italy
1141572	FOX W.S.	Gnr	17.8.1942	Died UK
613800	GILES D.A.N.	Gnr	30.4.1944	Italy (KIA?)
14272801	GRAINGER J.	Gnr	16.2.1945	DOW Italy
1115220	GRAY C.A.	Gnr	11.4.1945	Battle accident, Italy
1091276	GREEN C.C.	Gnr	17.1.1944	KIA Italy
947720	HAWITT A.	Gnr	12.5.1944	KIA Cassino, Italy
940954	HOLM A.E.	Gnr	12.5.1944	KIA Cassino, Italy
1101799	LERWILL F.	Gnr	1.11.1943	Died Middle East
980370	McKAY J.	Gnr	17.2.1945	Died Italy
14272856	MORAN F.	Gnr	12.5.1944	KIA Cassino, Italy
13047904	MURPHY T.	Gnr	12.5.1944	KIA Cassino, Italy
1141805	PATRICK H.W.	Gnr	12.5.1944	KIA Cassino, Italy
323958	PEARSON F.	Gnr	11.4.1942	Died UK (Cornwall)
1140741	PEARSON J.A.	Gnr	6.7.1944	KIA North West Europe*
–	SEDDON-BROWN D.	Maj	12.5.1944	KIA Cassino, Italy
974902	SHAW J.H.M.	Gnr	?	**
1123801	SMITH S.S.	Gnr	17.1.1944	KIA Italy
962285	STEWART J.W.	Gnr	25.7.1940	Died UK (Haverfordwest)
–	STRAKER L.H.	Lieut	12.5.1944	KIA Cassino, Italy (att'd to Regt)
410417	THORNTON J.D.	L/Bdr	11.4.1942	Died UK (Cornwall)
1140854	THORPE B.	Gnr	4.10.1944	DOW Italy
402905	TURNER J.C.	WO2	12.5.1944	KIA Italy
935612	WHITE W.M.	Gnr	30.4.1944	KIA Italy
404369	WILSON A.E.	L/Bdr	17.1.1944	Died Italy
322101	WILSON R.O.	L/Bdr	5.5.1940	Died UK (Pembroke)

Notes:
* Appears in a Regimental list of the 78th; perhaps dies while on attachment (to 77th?)
** The Commonwealth War Graves Commission find no trace of this man, although he appears in a Regimental list

APPENDIX II

HONOURS, AWARDS and DECORATIONS

THE DUKE OF LANCASTER'S OWN YEOMANRY

A. Honours & Awards

THE BOER WAR – 1899–1992

23rd (DUKE OF LANCASTER'S OWN) COMPANY, IMPERIAL YEOMANRY

Imp Yeo No. (if known)	Name	Rank	London Gazette entry	Details of Award
–	BROCKLEBANK J.J.	Lieut	8.2.1901	Mentioned in Despatches (Commander Colt Gun Section)
			–	Distinguished Service Order
2672	ELCE D.		–	Distinguished Conduct Medal
2673	FAIRCLOUGH R.	Sgt	–	Distinguished Conduct Medal
2159	GRIFFITHS W.H.	Sgt Maj	–	Distinguished Conduct Medal
–	HUNTINGTON A.W.	Lieut	8.2.1901	MID
			–	Distinguished Service Order
–	KEMP	Capt	8.2.1901	MID
2753	LOOKER W.		–	Distinguished Conduct Medal

All the above awards were made in respect of the action at Faber's Putt

[171]

THE GREAT WAR – 1914–1918
DUKE OF LANCASTER'S OWN YEOMANRY

DLOY No. (if known)	Name/Initials	Rank	London Gazette entry	Details of Award
–	BATES D.H.	Lieut(T/Cpt)	6.7.1917	MID
		Capt	3.6.1918	Military Cross (for Egypt)
3557/110045	BATES G.H.	Sgt	6.7.1917	MID
3088/110017	BLYTHE A.	Sgt	26.5.1917	Military Medal
23474	BOWE W.	Pte	1918	MM (s/w 12th Btn Manchester Regt.)
3226	BROWN W.	Cpl	–	MID
75021	BUCKLEY J.	Pte	14.5.1919	MM (s/w 12th Btn Manchester Regt.)
3349	CATTERALL E.	S/Smith	23.3.1917	Military Medal
–	CLARK C.F.	Lieut	–	Croix de Guerre
	FITZHERBERT– BROCKHOLES J.W.	Lieut	4.6.1917	Military Cross
3902/110512	FRANCIS W.	Pte	16.1.1918	MID (for Egypt)
2961/111022	GARDNER S.	Pte(A/L/Cpl)	4.6.1918	MID
110125	GEE J.	Sgt	15.5.1917	MID
23474	HADFIELD S.	Pte	1918	MM (s/w 12th Btn Manchester Regt.)
–	HARTLEY C.R.	2nd Lieut(T/Lt)	6.7.1917	MID
3004	HAY C.H.	Cpl	9.12.1916	Military Medal
–	HEATON B.W.	2nd Lieut	15.5.1917	MID
		Lieut	1.1.1919	MC (s/w 12th Btn Manchester Regt)
3378/110408	HINDLE T.B.	Sgt(A/SQMS)	26.4.1917	Distinguished Conduct Medal*1
			6.7.1917	MID
			31.8.1917	Italian Medal for Military Valour (Bronze)
110190	JACKSON A.	Pte(A/Sgt)	6.7.1917	MID
110534	JACKSON E.	L/Sgt	10.4.1918	Military Medal
3014/110183	JARVIS A.L.	Cpl(A/Sgt)	10.4.1918	Military Medal
3232	MASON G.H.	SQMS	–	MID
110554	MATLEY W.	Pte(A/QMS)	1.1.1919	MSM (for Egypt); later 621901 Labour Corps. From Longsight
2894/110221	MEREDITH J.S.	Sgt	11.3.1920	DCM (for Palestine)*2
110611	NICHOLLS E.	Pte(L/Cpl)	3.6.1919	MSM (for Italy)
–	PERCIVAL F.N.	2nd Lieut(T/L)	15.5.1917	MID
3173	REED G.	Sgt	9.12.1916	Military Medal
3725	ROBERTS E.H.	Pte	9.12.1916	Military Medal
–	ROYDS W.E.	Maj	–	MID

[172]

THE GREAT WAR – 1914–1918

DUKE OF LANCASTER'S OWN YEOMANRY (cont.)

DLOY No. (if known)	Name/Initials	Rank	London Gazette entry	Details of Award
–	SANDERSON B.	2–Lieut	14.11.1916	Military Cross*3
		2nd Lieut(T/Cpt)	15.5.1917	MID
		Lieut(A/Capt)	16.9.1918	Military Cross (second award)*4
			5.7.1919	MID (second award)
2886/110287	SPRITTLES F.F.	Cpl S/S	6.7.1917	MID
110460	SUDELL W.	SSM	3.6.1919	Meritorious Service Medal; 2/1st DLOY (possibly for service in Ireland)
3050	SUTHERLAND A.	Cpl	9.12.1916	Military Medal
3133/110295	SULLIVAN W.	Sgt	31.8.1917	Italian Medal for Military Valour (Bronze)
–	TILNEY R.H.	Lieut–Col	15.5.1917	MID
			4.6.1917	Distinguished Service Order
			30.12.1918	MID (second award)
3263	WHITHAM R.	Pte	9.12.1916	Military Medal

SERVING ON DETACHMENT FROM THE REGIMENT

–	HILL N.G.		15.10.1918	Military Cross (att'd 1/5th Btn King's Own Regt)
	,,	Lieut	10.12.1919	Bar to MC*5 (att'd 1/5th Btn King's Own)

*1 'For conspicuous gallantry and devotion to duty. He rendered invaluable service throughout the operation in getting supplies forwardto the front line.'

*2 'For conspicuous gallantry, devotion to duty, and consistent good service. He has several times acted as troop leader, no officerbeing available, and when in command of his troop the way he has handled his men and the example he has set under all conditions hasbeen of very exceptional value.'

*3 'For conspicuous gallantry during operations. He constantly carried out dangerous reconnaissances, regardless of the enemy's fire,and rendered valuable reports.'

*4 'For conspicuous gallantry and devotion to duty. During a heavy engagement this officer went forward with complete disregard forhis own safety under heavy shell fire to clear up the situation, which at the time was obscure. He returned with very valuableinformation. He performed his staff duties under most trying circumstances cheerfully and with cool and skilful precision on alloccasions.'

*5 'For conspicuous gallantry and devotion to duty near Ere, on 5 November 1918, when he led an attack on an enemy position inbroad daylight across open fields with great skill and daring, entering the hostile trench and shooting one of the garrison himself. Hisparty came under heavy machine–gun and rifle fire on their return, but he managed to get all his men under cover before retiring himself.'

FORMER MEMBERS OF THE REGIMENT
WHO WERE HONOURED WHILE SERVING WITH OTHER UNITS

Former DLOY No. (if known)	Name	Award	Details at time of award
110672	ALLEN T.	Military Medal	245633 Pte 12th Btn Manchester Regt
–	APPLETON J.H.	Military Cross	4th Reserve Regiment of Cavalry
3403	BUCKMAN J.N.	Military Medal	325837 Pte (Reserve Regt of Dragoons?)
Att'd DLOY	GREEN F.J.	Military Cross	Major RAMC (TF)
3209	HARRISON B.H.	Military Cross	Lieut 1st Btn Royal Munster Fusiliers
–	JACKSON A.	DCM	P–10738 L/Cpl(A/Sgt) Military Mounted Police Award for Italy
3041	LYNCH J.P.	Military Cross	Lieut Royal Field Artillery
3210	MARSDEN C.W.	Military Cross	Capt 1st Btn Royal Munster Fusiliers
–	MOLLOY L.G.S.	DSO	Major (Reserve)(TF)
3556	SMALLEY R.	Military Cross	Lieut Royal Field Artillery (Special Reserve)
4714	THOMAS P.	Military Medal	53451 L/Cpl 2/5th Btn Lancashire Fusiliers
–	TILNEY L.A.	Military Cross	Lieut Royal Horse Guards, att'd 40th Sqn RFC?
		Order of Crown (Belgium)	Lieut MC Royal Horse Guards
		MID	
3236	WALKER F.S.	MC	Lieut Cheshire Regt
3776	WARE H.	DCM	46472 Cpl 23rd Btn Manchester Regt

THE SECOND WORLD WAR – 1939–1945

The following citations have been traced:

77th (DLOY) MEDIUM REGIMENT, ROYAL ARTILLERY

DISTINGUISHED SERVICE ORDER

27014 T/Lieut Col Frederick George WINTLE, MBE

This officer has commanded the 77 Medium Regt throughout the operations in North–West Europe. The Regiment has been outstanding in producing quick and accurate fire for the engagement of hostile batteries on the MEUSE; the support of our Airborne Forces at the crossing of the RHINE; and the support of the 6th (Guards) Armoured Brigade in the operations before MUNSTER.

The credit for this conspicuous success belongs to this officer who by his personality, cheerfulness in the face of difficulties and danger, has inspired all ranks of the Regiment with a very high sense of duty. (8 May 1945)

MILITARY CROSS

174599 W/Capt (T/Major) Laurence James THOMAS

This officer has commanded 103 Medium Battery during all the engagements in which the Regiment has taken part. During this period he has set an outstanding example to all ranks by endeavouring to reach the best possible observation posts, often under heavy fire from guns, machine–guns and mortars, in particular at CHEUX, ESQUAY and CAEN in June and July 1944. By his action the Regiment was frequently able to engage targets which otherwise would have been missed. By his example of devotion to duty and courage he has shown the way to his battery to fulfil its tasks under the most difficult circumstances. (20 August 1944)

78th (DLOY) MEDIUM REGIMENT, ROYAL ARTILLERY

DISTINGUISHED SERVICE ORDER

26565 T/Lieut Col William Robert PALMER

This officer has shown consistent gallantry and devotion to duty since his Regiment first came into action in November 1943 on the River SANGRO. He has repeatedly reconnoitred advance observation points in the face of heavy fire to aid the infantry, in particular at CASSINO and during the subsequent advance to FLORENCE. On at least two occasions he has by his presence and quiet courage steadied the batteries of his Regiment when engaged on a fire plan in support of infantry attacks whilst under heavy and accurate enemy shell fire, from a variety of calibres from 105 mm to 17 cm. On one such occasion at CASSINO a 17 cm shell burst under the trail of a gun, killing the whole detachment and his Second–in–Command who was in the pit, setting charges alight and exploding shells in the pit; he calmly directed salvage operations so successfully that the gun was again in action the next day. His coolness and bearing under fire are an example to the officers and men of his Regiment.

Citations (cont.):

MILITARY CROSS

224901 W/Lieut (T/Captain) John ARROWSMITH

Until recently becoming adjutant, this officer in his capacity at Tp Comd has been constantly engaged in observation post duties for the previous twelve months. He has frequently shown outstanding qualities of courage, resource and initiative, and on many occasions has of his own volition moved forward his observation post at considerable personal risk in order to obtain better observation.

In January 1945, Capt Arrowsmith was occupying an observation post in the FRASINETTO area when a company of the Royal Irish Fusiliers was subjected to heavy mortar fire from an area which, owing to the forward slope being convex, he was unable to see. To get to the only position from which fire could be observed necessitated a crawl of some 600 yards over exposed ground and while on the way he was himself fired on by mortars, but he reached his objective, and by means of a 38 set carried out a shoot which successfully neutralized the mortars.

This officer is always very reticent about his exploits and there has only come to light recently the story of a very brave attempt he made to rescue the crew of a burning tank. Last July during the advance into GRASSINA, South of FLORENCE, Capt Arrowsmith was using as an observation post a turretless Honey tank, in which he was accompanying a task force of the 25th Army Tank Brigade, whose mission was to prevent the demolition of the bridges at GRASSINA. When coming into view of the high ground north of the village, the force came under heavy direct fire from German 88 mm guns, resulting in the 'brewing up' of a Churchill and a Sherman, the latter tank being immediately in front of Capt Arrowsmith's Honey. He immediately dismounted from his own tank and calling to his signaller to assist him, climbed on to the turret of the now blazing tank and succeeded in opening half of the roof, out of which shot a pillar of fire and black smoke and almost immediately the small arm ammunition within the tank started to explode. Despite this Capt Arrowsmith succeeded in getting a grip under the tank commander's shoulders, but owing to the intense heat his hold relaxed, and all he could extract were the binoculars which had been round his neck. Seeing that further efforts at rescue were impossible, and in view of his own crew being exposed to the continued heavy fire, Capt Arrowsmith and his signaller returned to their tank. Shortly afterwards he succeeded in occupying a static observation post from where he successfully neutralized the area from which the 88s had been firing. As an inspiring leader of men Capt Arrowsmith's services have been invaluable to the Regiment.

224904 W/Lieut (T/Capt) Stanley Ernest CATTERALL

This officer has been constantly employed on observation post duties for the last twelve months, except for a period of two months while recovering from wounds sustained when accompanying the leading infantry in the crossing of the RAPIDO river. During this period he has successfully carried out many highly important shoots in close support of the infantry, to accomplish which he has shown great courage on frequent occasions on occupying exposed positions in order to obtain better observation.

Citations (cont.):

MILITARY CROSS (cont.)

Capt Catterall showed particular fortitude and stamina during the attack on the GOTHIC line when he went with the left coy of the 1/5 Royal Gurkha Rifles in their assault on MONTE VITIGLIANO. To reach the objective entailed a four hour walk from jeep head during which one of the OP mules was killed necessitating half their load being man-hauled up the steep mountain side. This officer remained with the infantry coy for three days in a very exposed position and under constant harassing fire, and although observation was impaired by low cloud and almost continuous rain he carried out many invaluable shoots on enemy FDLs, mortar areas and communications along the CRESPINO road, not only with his own guns, but with those of the 75th Heavy Regt RA as well.

Capt Catterall is an inspiring leader who at all times sets his men a splendid example of courage and devotion to duty.

68043 Capt (T/Major) Richard HEATON

During the period under review the officer has shown consistent devotion to duty, complete disregard of danger and has set a very high example to those under him. In particular during the period Nov–Dec 1943 – Jan 1944 he kept and maintained a series of observation posts in the FDLs at ARIELLI. Frequent changes of locality being necessary owing to the intense bombardment of the houses occupied by him as OPs from all natures of enemy artillery from HVSP guns to 77 cm. On at least two occasions when his OP was under bombardment and received several direct hits from 17 cm shells he remained in the top storey of the houses and gave valuable supportto the infantry with well directed fire on Mortars and Nebelwerfers which were causing casualties amongst the infantry.

160269 Lieut (T/Capt) Leonard Arthur RIDDETT

This officer has been constantly employed on observation post duties since Jan 1943, except for an absence from the Regt of one month while recovering from wounds. During the advance from CASSINO onwards he showed at all times complete disregard of his personal safety in order to obtain satisfactory observation, and he has occupied many positions where movement and replenishment were only possible at night. During the storming of the GOTHIC line in particular, Capt Riddett gave a magnificent example of fortitude and stamina when accompanying the right coy of the 1/5 Royal Gurkha Rifles on to MONTE FEMINA MORTE, which necessitated a six hour walk from jeep head. He remained for three days in almost continuous rain in a very exposed position with the leading platoon of this coy during which time he carried out many successful neutralization shoots particularly on the enemy's mortar positions, without the aid of which the coy comd stated the position could not have been held.

Capt Riddett is an inspiring leader of his OP party, a team fully confident to successfully carry out any task allotted to it.

QUEENS SOUTH AFRICA MEDAL ROLL
(Set out in Troops as per L. H. Johnson's book)

23rd Company 8th Battalion Imperial Yeomanry Boer War

* = Medals known

	Cape Colony	Transvaal	Orange Free State	SA 1901	Remarks
A Troop					
Captain G. Kemp	•	•	•	•	Also SA 1902
Lieut J. A. B. Heap	•		•		As Lieut 23rd Coy
* Sgt W. N. Griffiths	•		•		
2746 Sgt A. G. Herrington	•	•	•		
2710 Sgt Farr R. Miller	•	•	•		
2700 Cpl J Wilson	•		•	•	
2713 Tpr W. Ashworth	•		•	•	
2690 Tpr W. Brooks	•	•	•		
2685 Tpr G. Brooks	•		•		sev. wounded 22.4.? Middlewater
2717 Tpr A. Brooksbank	•		•		
* 2709 Tpr F. Brierley	•		•		
2763 Tpr E. S. Brierley	•		•		
2701 Tpr S. Casson	•		•		
2718 Tpr D. W. Dransfield	•		•		Died Kimberley 27.11.1900
2687 Tpr W. Halliwell	•		•		
2698 Tpr T. Coulthard	•		•		
2691 Tpr W. W. Handley	•		•		
2696 Tpr J. Hargreaves	•		•		
2684 Tpr F. Hollingworth	•		•		
* 2719 Tpr E. Jones	•	•	•	•	Wounded 23.10.1900 Hoopstad
2737 Tpr E. W. Kay	•		•	•	
2712 Tpr J. H. Kershaw	•		•	•	
2686 Tpr F. Lewin	•		•	•	
2711 Tpr F. A. Makin	•				
2708 Tpr T. W. Ormrod	•				
2688 Tpr E. Pearson	•				
2715 Tpr W. H. Priestley	•	•	•		
2703 Tpr H. Rigg	•	•	•		
2720 Tpr G. Rodgers	•		•	•	
2697 Tpr M. Smith	•		•	•	
2714 Tpr C. L. Travis	•			•	
2706 Tpr J. B. Wild	•		•	•	promoted Cpl
B Troop					
* Lieut H. M. Hardcastle	•	•	•	•	Medals in museum
2673 Sgt R. Fairclough	•		•	•	Slightly wounded 30.1.1901 Largekloof
2641 E. H. Ashworth	•	•	•		
2650 Cpl T. Scowcroft	•	•	•		
2730 Bugler J. H. Barlow	•			•	
2659 Tpr C. Crowther	•		•	•	
2654 Tpr W. Crowther	•	•	•	•	Wounded 23.10.1900 Hoopstad

QUEENS SOUTH AFRICA MEDAL ROLL (cont.)
(Set out in Troops as per L. H. Johnson's book)

23rd Company 8th Battalion Imperial Yeomanry Boer War

* = Medals known

	Cape Colony	Transvaal	Orange Free State	SA 1901	Remarks
2651 Tpr J. A. Gee	•				
2755 Tpr E. Gornall	•	•	•		
2652 Tpr G. Haslam	•	•	•		Trans to 24th Coy
2643 Tpr S. Howcroft	•	•	•	•	
2644 G. K. Hutchinson	•	•	•	•	
2647 Tpr W. A. Hutchinson	•		•	•	
2600 Tpr L. H. Johnson	•		•	•	
2738 Tpr S. Jones	•		•	•	
2688 Tpr C. H. Kelsall	•		•		
2659 Tpr F. H. Leyland	•		•	•	
* 2680 Tpr C. F. Longland	•	•	•	•	Died 22.5.1901 after return to UK. Enteric
2642 Tpr C. D. Mucklow	•	•	•		
2646 Tpr P. Orrell	•				Killed 30.5.1900 Faber's Putt
2739 Tpr R. G. Peel	•		•	•	Promoted Cpl in SA
2658 Tpr G. H. Pickstone	•		•	•	
2653 Tpr E. Poole	•		•	•	Wounded 30.5.1900 Faber's Putt
2645 Tpr E. Rixen	•	•	•		
2655 Tpr H. B. Seed	•	•	•	•	
2661 Tpr J. Sherrington	•	•	•	•	
2656 Tpr F. G. Torry	•	•	•	•	
2649 Tpr S. Wolfenden	•				
2740 Tpr H. H. Yates			•	•	
2681 Tpr A. Yates			•	•	
C Troop					
Lieut C. H. Bibby-Hesketh	•				
2699 Sgt S. Sales	•		•	•	
* 2728 Cpl W. S. Earnshaw	•	•	•	•	Also awarded Kings Medal
2749 Sh Smith W. H. Niccolls	•		•	•	
2766 Sdlr J. T. Fearns	•	•	•	•	
2748 Tpr P. R. Agnew	•				Wounded 30.5.1900 Faber's Putt
2731 Tpr G. H. Barnes	•				
2747 Tpr R. Bradshaw	•	•	•	•	
* 2724 Tpr C. H. Brunner	•		•	•	Wounded 30.5.1900 Faber's Putt
2754 Tpr J. Byrne	•	•	•	•	
2728 Tpr S. P. Chambers	•	•	•	•	
2761 Tpr F. Clark	•		•	•	
2741 Tpr J. W. Derbyshire	•				Killed 30.5.1900 Faber's Putt

QUEENS SOUTH AFRICA MEDAL ROLL (cont.)
(Set out in Troops as per L. H. Johnson's book)

23rd Company 8th Battalion Imperial Yeomanry Boer War

* = Medals known

	Cape Colony	Transvaal	Orange Free State	SA 1901	Remarks
2742 Tpr D. Featherstone	•		•	•	
2752 Tpr W. Graham	•	•	•	•	
2762 Tpr J. W. Hulton	•		•	•	
2729 Tpr L. B. Haddock	•		•		
2760 Tpr A. Hilton	•		•		
2750 W. C. Jackson	•		•		
2923 Tpr T. Jackson	•		•	•	
Tpr T. B. Job					Commissioned Lt. S.A
2759 Tpr R. E. Launn	•		•		
2743 Tpr A. Marsh	•	•	•	•	
2722 Tpr J. E. Maxwell	•				
2745 Tpr W. A. Royle	•	•	•	•	
2725 Tpr J. F. Scott	•	•	•	•	
2751 Tpr J. H. Stopford	•		•		
2736 Tpr J. Ward	•		•		
2727 Tpr S. Williams	•	•	•	•	
2756 Tpr A. W. Wright	•		•	•	Wounded 30.5.1900 Faber's Putt

D Troop

	Cape Colony	Transvaal	Orange Free State	SA 1901	Remarks
Lieut A. W. Huntington	•		•	•	Awarded DSO
2758 Sgt W. Mason	•	•	•	•	Wounded 30.5.1900 Faber's Putt
2669 Cpl W. Coulston	•				Killed 30.5.1900 Faber's Putt
2744 Sh Smith G. Gibbs	•				Wounded 30.5.1900 Faber's Putt
2683 Bglr G. Bullough	•		•	•	
* 2682 Tpr G. E. Barry	•				Killed 30.5.1900 Faber's Putt
2662 Tpr H. A. Brown			•	•	
2670 Tpr R. B. Carter	•				Wounded 30.5.1900 Faber's Putt
* 2695 Tpr J. Clegg	•				
2758 Tpr A. F. Mason	•		•		
2678 Tpr J. E. Culeen	•				
* 2664 Tpr A. Edmonson	•		•		Awarded Kings SA Medal
2672 Tpr D. Elce	•		•	•	
2679 Tpr F. Fletcher	•		•	•	
2677 Tpr F. W. Hackforth	•				Killed 30.5.1900 Faber's Putt
2671 Tpr G. R. Jacques	•	•	•	•	Trans to 24th Coy Also SA 1902
2667 Tpr W. E. Kay	•		•	•	Wounded 30.5.1900 Faber's Putt

QUEENS SOUTH AFRICA MEDAL ROLL (cont.)
(Set out in Troops as per L. H. Johnson's book)

23rd Company 8th Battalion First Yeomanry Boer War

* = Medals known

		Cape Colony	Transvaal	Orange Free State	SA 1901	Remarks
	2753 Tpr W. Looker	•			•	Trans to Pretoria Police Died 20.1.1901
	2694 Tpr J. M. Partington	•	•	•	•	
	2693 Tpr T. Royce	•	•	•	•	Also S.A 1902
	2734 Tpr S. Starkie	•	•	•	•	
	2674 Tpr J. N. Thornton	•	•	•	•	
*	2675 Tpr J. Turner	•			•	Wounded 30.5.1900 Faber's Putt Lt Huntington's servant
	2716 Tpr H. Waterfield	•		•		
	2704 Tpr C. P. Webster	•		•	•	
	2663 Tpr F. Whalley	•		•	•	
*	2689 Tpr R. J. Whittaker	•		•	•	
	2660 Tpr L. Whitehead	•		•	•	
Gun Section						
	Lieut J. J. Brocklebank	•				Joined 1st KDG. DSO
	2692 Sgt C. Storey	•		•		Wounded 30.5.1900 Faber's Putt
	2778 Cpl G. L. Reynolds	•		•		
	2765 Cpl W. Lupton	•			•	Wounded 30.5.1900 Faber's Putt
	2777 Tpr F. Brownrigg	•		•		
	2772 Tpr E. Dean	•		•	•	Trans to 24th Coy 8th IY
	2769 Tpr W. Ellis	•				
	2768 Tpr M. Elphinstone	•	•	•	•	Trans to 24th Coy 8th IY
	2790 Tpr E. A. Heap	•		•		
*	2770 Tpr C. S. Matthews	•		•	•	
	2780 Tpr J. B. Mould	•		•	•	Accidentally wounded 10.6.1900 Campbell
	2767 Tpr W. M. M. Radford	•		•	•	
	2773 Tpr G. H. Richards	•		•	•	
	2779 Tpr V. H. Stott	•		•	•	
	2775 Tpr F. Thompson	•		•	•	
	2774 Tpr S. M. Tyson	•		•	•	
	2764 Tpr J. Warren	•	•	•	•	Trans to 24th Coy 8th IY
*	2776 Tpr C. W. Whittaker	•		•	•	
Battalion Staff						
	Surg Capt Charnley Smith					Medal entitlement unknown
*	Vet Lieut H. G. Westgate	•	•	•		Also served 32nd Bn IY
	2786 Tpr W. E. Cowie	•	•	•	•	
	2787 Tpr R. B. Chadwick	•		•	•	
	2788 Tpr D. Rew	•				Killed 30.5.1900 Faber's Putt
	2791 Tpr H. Wardell	•		•		

B. Decorations
IMPERIAL YEOMANRY LONG SERVICE AND GOOD CONDUCT MEDAL

* = Medals known

	No.	Rank	Name	Date	Remarks
*	449	Sgt	W. Booth	Feb 1905	
	358	Sgt	A. Brooksbank	Nov 1906	QSA
	331	Trumpeter	G. Bullough	Nov 1906	QSA awarded for Boer War
	909	Far Sgt	S. Collison	Feb 1905	
	460	SQMS	C. Cormack	Feb 1905	
	1051	SQMS	T. Dean	Feb 1905	
	945	Sgt	R. Dewhurst	May 1907	
	618	SSM	J. Farrington	Feb 1905	
*	906	RSM	Ffrance	Feb 1905	
	425	SSM	J. Green	Feb 1905	
	523	Sgt	A. Hilton	Aug 1905	Awarded QSA and 1911 Coronation Medal
	426	Sgt	R. Ingham	Feb 1905	
	944	SSM	G. Kennerdine	Nov 1907	Photo in Regt Collection
	1155	Sgt	P. McDonald	Feb 1905	
	950	SQMS	F. Ormrod	Nov 1907	Joined RAF WWI Medal & BWM known
	508	Far Sgt	W. Pugh	Feb 1905	
	1124	Pte	T. Ridyard	Feb 1905	
	282	LSgt	J. Sykes	Feb 1905	
	248	SSM	J. B. Wild	Feb 1905	QSA
	551	Sgt	T. R. Wood	Nov 1905	

TERRITORIAL DECORATIONS
FOR THE DUKE OF LANCASTER'S OWN YEOMANRY

There are four separate decorations:

(a) Territorial Decoration 1908–1930
(b) Efficiency Decoration (Territorial) 1930–1969
(c) Efficiency Decoration (Territorial and Army Volunteer Reserve) 1969–1982
(d) Efficiency Decoration (Territorial) 1982– to date

The following decorations are known to have been awarded:

(a) Territorial Decoration 1908–1930

London Gazette Date	Page	Name
2 April 1909	2597	Lieutenant Colonel and Honarary Colonel J Rutherford
2 April 1909	2597	Major R H Tilney
17 December 1912	4576	Major H M Hardcastle
7 July 1916	6743	Major T A S Shepherd-Cross

From 12 December 1916 until 2 January 1919 all Yeomanary officers are shown together without any specific unit title.

4 November 1919	13518	Captain F Shaw
31 December 1920	12817	Major W E Reyods
31 December 1920	12817	Captain T B Forwood
31 October 1924	7861	Major D H Bates MC
30 January 1925	688	Major W Hesketh

(b) Efficiency Decoration (Territorial) 1930–1969

20 December	1938	Lieutenant Colonel J Heaton

From 6 February until 1941 all awards are grouped together as Yeomanry without any specific unit title

13 February 1948	1027	Major D B Stewart
21 April 1950	1924	Major B Greenwood
21 April 1950	1924	Captain (acting Major) J D M Wilson
16 March 1951	1417	1st Clasp to Major D B Stewart TD
25 May 1951	2866	Captain D R Poynton and 1st Clasp
19 February 1952	980	Captain (acting Major) M A A Birtwistle and 1st Clasp
20 May 1958	3166	Major (acting Lieutenant Colonel) M A A Birtwistle TD 2nd Clasp

[183]

(b) Efficiency Decoration (Territorial) 1930–1969 cont.

London Gazette Date	Page	Name
16 September 1960	6329	Major J N B Cardwell
17 March 1964	2380	Captain J R S Hart
18 September 1964	7922	Captain (Honorary Major) H B Dunstan
14 January 1966	433	Lieutenant Colonel T A Marshall
14 January 1966	433	Captain (acting Major) E S Swindells
13 May 1966	5693	Major J A Chartres
13 November 1966	12303	Captain JJ Condon
14 May 1968	5448	Major L G Dodgson

(c) Efficiency Decoration (Territorial and Army Volunteer Reserve) 1969–1982

3 June 1969	5730	Major J Clemence
3 June 1969	5730	Major C R Greaves
18 May 1971	5153	Major F E Hewitt (as Major 5RRF)
17 July 1973	8288	Major D J Claxton
15 January 1974	584	Major J Stuart-Mills
15 January 1974	584	Captain R A Ferguson
15 July 1975	8999	Captain (acting Major) R B Heaton
13 April 1976	5471	Major J Swift
1 June 1982	7225	Major J Stuart-Mills, Clasp to ED (T & AVR)

(d) Efficiency Decoration (Territorial) 1982–1992

7 December 1982	15997	Captain (now Major) G D Thompson
17 December 1982	15998	Major B L Greenwood
6 December 1983	16124	Lieutenant Colonel R A Ferguson, Clasp to TD
4 Sept 1984	12030	Major J Eastham
5 March 1985	3109	Captain A J Hammersley
24 February 1987	2470	Major M T Steiger
14 June 1988	6893	Major J S Collis
29 November 1988	13394	Major J Tustin
29 November 1988	13394	Captain A P Berry
30 May 1989	6387	Major J Eastham, Clasp to TD
25 August 1992	14363	Lieutenant Colonel F E Hewitt TD, 1st, 2nd and 3rd Clasps to E D (T & AVR)
25 August 1992	14365	Lieutenant Colonel A J Hammersley, 1st Clasp

TERRITORIAL EFFICIENCY MEDAL
and
EFFICIENCY MEDAL (TERRITORIAL) 1909-1991

* = Medals known

	No.	Rank	Name	Date	Remarks
	1924	Trumpeter	Dearden J.	Jan 1909	
	1736	Sgt	Drinkwater L. W.		
	544	Sgt	Williams S.		
	2194	Cpl	Stringer F.	Apr 1909	
	1645	Sgt	Glover A. E.	Jul 1909	
	1254	SSM	Wilding F. M.		
*	1315	Sgt	Dunbar E.	Jan 1910	
	1907	Pte	Rhind P.		
	2237	Pte	Roberts W.		
	1341	Sgt	Denley J. S.	Apr 1910	
	1365	SSM	Howarth W. E.		
*	2029	L/Cpl	Appleton J. H.	Jul 1910	Awarded MC WWI Medals in Museum
	1444	Farr Sgt	Greenlees C.		
	1443	SQMS	Heap E.W.		
	1466	SQMS	Stott J.		
	1427	Sgt	Waterhouse F. J.		
	2173	L/Sgt	McIntyre A. W.	Oct 1910	
	1532	Sgt	Mottram W. G.		
	1558	Sgt	Page A. T.		
	1398	Sgt	Roche A.		
	2492	Cpl	Bowerbank W.	Jan 1911	
	2165	Pte	Cox W. H.		
	1321	SQMS	Parker R. G.		
	1602	Cpl	Pullen J. G.		
	2337	Pte	Carruthers G.	Apr 1911	
	1587	L/Sgt	Frankland H.		
	2017	L/Sgt	Jackson A.		
*	1802	Sgt	Crossley C. H.	Oct 1911	
	1739	Sgt	Fudge H.		
	1638	Pte	Hill T.		
	1719	Cpl	Rigby R. H.		
	1734	Sgt	Self N.		
	1865	Cpl	Ferguson F. S.	Jan 1912	
	1801	Cpl	Jump W. J.		
	1820	Sgt	Larkin W.		
	1818	Sgt	Turner E.		
	1946	Sgt	Hibbert G. H.	Jul 1912	
*	1979	Sgt	Holden J.		
	2536	Pte	Pile W.		
	2515	Pte	Thompson A.		
	1826	Sgt	Gosling G.	Jan 1913	
	2702	Pte	Critchley H.M.	Apr 1913	
	2049	Sgt	Dixon T. P.		
	1922	Sgt	Friedental F.		
	1992	Pte	Howard C.		

TERRITORIAL EFFICIENCY MEDAL and EFFICIENCY MEDAL (TERRITORIAL) 1909-1991   (cont.)

* = Medals known

No.	Rank	Name	Date	Remarks
2621	Pte	Hume A.		
2031	L/Cpl	Walker W.		
2051	Sgt	Carman H. J.	Oct 1913	
2341	L/Sgt	Lewis J. C.		
2050	Sgt	Norris D.		
2792	Cpl	Roberts H. E.		
2217	Sgt	Capper J. D.	Apr 1914	
2169	Pte	Finlayson D. C.		
2214	Cpl	Greenfield U. F.		
2002	Pte	Halstead J.		
2246	L/Sgt	Lane W.		
2135	Sgt	Patchett J. J.		
2104	L/Cpl	Speakman A.		
2155	Farr-Sgt	Swift J. R		
2184	L/Cpl	Williams A. S.		
2242	Sgt	Cragg F.	Nov 1915	
3167	L/Cpl	Griffiths E.		
2297	Sgt	Dean F.	Apr 1916	
2330	S.S.M.	Sudell W.		
2598	SGT	Courcy C. de	Oct 1916	
2318	Pte	Dean R. H.		
3893	Sgt	Drinkwater W. F.		
1966	Sgt	Farran J.		
2437	L/Sgt	Guy R. W.		
2244	Sgt	Holmes J. J.		
2567	Pte	King W. B.		
2999	L/Sgt	Robinson J		
1951	L/Cpl	Thurnham J. J.		
* 110110	Sgt	Farron J. R.	Nov 1917	
110152	Sgt	Holmes J. J.		
110872	Sgt	Smith W.		
110156	Cpl	Hay C.		
110219	Pte	Marland T.		
110331	Pte	Smith W.		
110014	Sgt	Brooksbank P. L.	May 1918	
110077	SQMS	Dalzell R. G.	Aug 1918	
111462	Sgt	Lees F.		
110076	Cpl(Act-Sgt)	Daniel B.	Feb 1919	
110154	Pte	Holding W.		
1355	Sgt	Biggs F. H. (Later Commissioned)	May 1919	
3068	Sgt	Lynch D. D. (Later 38078 Norfolk Regt)		
2967	Pte(A-L/Cpl)	Grundy R.	Aug 1919	
110363	Trumpeter	Wood D.		
110267	Far-S/Sgt	Robertson R.	Oct 1919	
110221	Sgt	Meredith J. S.		
110111	Pte(Act-Cpl)	Farnworth J. H.		

TERRITORIAL EFFICIENCY MEDAL
and
EFFICIENCY MEDAL (TERRITORIAL) 1909-1991 (cont.)

* = Medals known

No.	Rank	Name	Date	Remarks
110287	Sh.Smith-Cpl	Sprittles F.		
110334	Pte(A/Cpl)	Turner J.		
110187	Pte	Jackson E. H. (Later Commissioned)	Feb 1920	
2683	Sgt	Drinkwater M. F. (Later Commissioned)	Apr 1920	
2754	Sgt	Hilton G. H. (Previously 51969 MGC Cav)		
110016	Cpl	Brierley J. J.	Nov 1920	
3044	Pte(L/Cpl)	Gilchrist J. (Previously 415570 Labour Corps)		
110017	Sgt	Blythe A.	Feb 1921	
110242	Sgt	Overens H. W.		
*110183	Cpl	Jarvis A. L.		
110002	**Pte**	Atkinson J.		
3054	**Cpl**	Bishop H. O. (Later Commissioned)	May 1921	
396915	**Pte**	Sanderson D.	May 1922	
2788	Pte(A/Sgt)	Anderson F.	Aug 1922	
396959	Pte	Hall J.		
397015	Pte	Hunt J. A.		
2980	Pte	Higgins J. (Previously 30648 Lanc Fus)		
2317	WO2	Parry R. (Later 397401)	Nov 1922	
396960	Pte	Foden A.	Aug 1923	
397028	Sgt	Spencer S. D.	May 1924	
*396909	WO2	Knowles F. H.	Nov 1924	
396911	SQMS	Morris F.		
397067	Sgt	Hartley C. MM		
2597	Tpr	McConkey S. J.		
3803	Sgt	Howson F. (Later Commissioned)	May 1925	
397068	Sgt	Simpson A.	Jun 1926	
3052	Tpr	Wild G. (Later P/10750 CMP)	Aug 1926	
27094	Tpr	Kenkinson J.	Feb 1927	
30405	Sgt	Brand H. G. S.	Aug 1927	
396806	WO2	Williams R. E.	May 1928	
396958	Sgt	Jones J. R.	May 1929	
396817	Tpr	Wall L.	Aug 1929	
396805	Tpr	Wilson W.		
36908	Sgt	Blackburn F. S.	Nov 1929	
396804	WO2	Knott S.	Feb 1930	
396910	Sgt	Bishop C. M.	May 1930	
396815	Tpr	Jones W.		
531651	Sgt	Langan R. J.	Nov 1930	

TERRITORIAL EFFICIENCY MEDAL and EFFICIENCY MEDAL (TERRITORIAL) 1909-1991 (cont.)

* = Medals known

No.	Rank	Name	Date	Remarks

All below are Efficiency Medal Bar Territorial unless specified otherwise.

No.	Rank	Name	Date
27092	Tpr	Farr R.	Aug 1932
396911	SQMS	Morris F.	Nov 1932
3511780	Tpr	Ryall R.	Feb 1933
397130	SQMS	Jackson E. H.	May 1934
397114	Sgt	Gilchrist J.	
396904	Sgt	Griffiths H.	
396831	Sgt	Hewitt W. A.	
397096	Sgt	Moss J. E.	
397131	Sgt	Williamson W. J.	
397263	Sgt	Denny T.	Aug 1934
397297	Sgt	Riley W.	
397523	Bndsmn	Mortimer H.	
539385	WO2	Anderson F.	Nov 1934
397210	WO2	Lewis W.	
397239	S/Sgt	Bebbington H.	
397519	Sgt	Hatch R.	
392128	Sgt	Openshaw A.	
397526	Bndsmn	Boyd A. H. C.	
741791	Bndsmn	Earnshaw J.F.	
397525	Bndsmn	Garner W.F.	
397517	Bndsmn	Prosser A. H.	
529704	Cpl	Astington J. F.	Feb 1935
397802	Cpl	Settle F. W.	May 1935
32761	S/Sgt	Horton G.	Aug 1935
3517386	Sgt	Gadd G. L.	
397899	Sgt	O'Neill V.	
398011	Cpl	Bratby J.	
397973	Tpr	Norman A. V.	
397748	Sgt	Bellis L. O.	Nov 1935
396958	SQMS	Jones J. R.	Feb 1936
398558	Cpl	Jones D.	Aug 1936
398732	Cpl	Hannan	Nov 1936
396909	WO2	Knowles F. H.	Feb 1937
397067	Sgt	Hartley C. MM	

[188]

TERRITORIAL EFFICIENCY MEDAL and EFFICIENCY MEDAL (TERRITORIAL) 1909-1991 (cont.)

* = Medals known

No.	Rank	Name	Date	Remarks
398715	Sgt	Hind S.		
399102	Sgt	Pierce A.		
399454	Cpl	Williamson D. E.	Aug 1937	
399440	Tpr	Balshaw J. W.		
3439471	Tpr	Galvin H.		
534769	SQMS	Hyland G. R.	Nov 1937	
399715	Bndsmn	Bedwell G.		
399979	Cpl	Chevin J. H.	Feb 1938	
396814	Tpt-Maj	Purvis F.	Aug 1938	
400446	Sgt	Blackburn G. E.		
400174	Sgt	Wilson S.		
400194	Tpr	Clarkson J.		
400469	Cpl	Henderson J.	Nov 1938	
400196	Tpr	Peddie O. C.		
146150	Pte	Bland J. W.	Feb 1939	
400883	Tpr	Fletcher J. R.	May 1939	
401460	Sgt	Kitchen C. E.	Aug 1939	
401232	Sgt	Long P.		
400459	Sgt	Walmsley J.		
2021910	Tpr	Callagman A.		
401210	Bndsmn	Welch W. H.		
3511574	Sgt	McDonough A.	Nov 1943	
326706	Cpl	Jolly A.	Mar 1946	
322475	Cpl	Southam J.		
318279	Tpr	Lea H.		
322990	Tpr	Taylor J. H.		
322465	Cpl	Bellis F. R.	List 4 1946	
3852946	Tpr	Fishwick F.		
322733	Tpr	Pennington J.	List 9 1948	
1927617	SQMS	Compton A.	List 23 1954	
7963606	WO2	Holdship D.	List 39 1958	
2364346	Sgt	Holdship H.		
7917873	Sgt	Prunty J. M.	List 44 1959	
22206645	Sgt	Gadman W.	List 49 1961	
22297398	WO2	Durrant W. E.	List 54 1962	
22297283	Sgt	Betteridge T.		
22297945	Sgt	Cain R.	List 56 1962	
22297880	Sgt	Eyre R.		
22297976	Sgt	Northwood W. H.		
22516725	Sgt	Crossley D.	List 58 1963	
22104946	Sgt	Taylor B. R.		
22206737	Sgt	Jackson M. W.	List 59 1963	
22094942	Sgt	Whitehead R.		
22544470	Sgt	Campbell C.	List 60 1963	
22544451	Sgt	Richardson B.		

TERRITORIAL EFFICIENCY MEDAL
and
EFFICIENCY MEDAL (TERRITORIAL) 1909-1991   (cont.)

* = Medals known

No.	Rank	Name	Date	Remarks
22516206	Cpl	Jones W.		
22516959	Cpl	Bunner R. F.	List 61 1964	
22115572	WO2	Torkington D. A.	List 65 1965	
22185006	S/Sgt	Denny E.		
22115516	L/Cpl	Goodwin T. J.		
22409632	Sgt	Gowen A.	List 67 1965	
21001551	Sgt	Johnson J. W.	List 68 1965	
22841325	Sgt	Armstrong F. J.	List 72 1966	
22409638	Sgt	Kitchen R. H.		
22841146	Sgt	Mulvaney W. H.		
22592233	Sgt	Thistlethwaite E.	List 73 1966	
22841922	Cpl	Brereton B.	List 83 1969	
23221177	L/Cpl	Jones J. A.		
22680925	Cpl	Fairbrother J.	List 84 1969	
23955398	Cpl	Trevor-Jones M. E. G.	List 109 1976	
23974138	Sgt	Gillham C.	List 110 1976	
23979915	Sgt	Steward F. M.	List 111 1976	
24004763	S/Sgt	Sudworth B.	List 117 1978	
22130882	WO2	Steven J. D.	List 123 1979	
24236880	WO2	Myers J.	List 143 1985	
24236591	S/Sgt	Kershaw G. L.		
24256039	Sgt	Gair B. J.		
24236913	Sgt	Lake J. W.		
24236200	Cpl	Potter C.		
24256352	S/Sgt	Norburn J.	List 144 1985	
23845132	Cpl	Bligh J. A.		
24292137	Cpl	Browne K. J.	List 147 1986	
23891453	Sgt	West D.	List 148 1986	
24292149	WO2	Stride D. G.	List 149 1986	
24292899	S/Sgt	Burgess P. K.	List 152 1987	
24358110	Sgt	Jackson R. M.	List 156 1988	
24358071	Cpl	Fortin I. P.	List 157 1988	
24323586	WO2	Cavanagh J.	List 158 1988	
24381108	Sgt	Jackson B. P.	List 159 1989	
24381165	L/Cpl	Cannell J.		
23703154	Sgt	Sutton J.	List 160 1989	
24381471	Sgt	Bennett G.	List 161 1989	
24256293	Cpl	Bradshaw A.		
24381521	Sgt	Sutton L.	List 162 1990	
24193231	L/Cpl	Blowe P.		
23928335	Cpl	Williams C. D.	List 163 1990	
23703204	S/Sgt	Roache J.B.	List 164 1990	
24381573	S/Sgt	Bowker B. R.	List 165 1990	
24416040	Sgt	Rose E. J.	List 166 1990	
24416055	Sgt	Samson P. M.		

TERRITORIAL EFFICIENCY MEDAL and EFFICIENCY MEDAL (TERRITORIAL) 1909-1991 (cont.)

* = Medals known

No.	Rank	Name	Date	Remarks

BARS AWARDED

No.	Rank	Name	Date
27092	Tpr	Farr R.	Aug 1938
		Medal awarded Aug 1932	
397899	WO2	O'Neill V.	List 6 1947
397899	WO2	O'Neill V. (second clasp)	
3511574	Sgt	McDonough A.	
1927617	WO2	Crompton A.	List 43 1959
21001053	Cpl	Trigg H. C. R. (first clasp)	
21001053	Cpl	Trigg H. C. R. (second clasp)	List 59 1963
1927617	WO2	Crompton A. MBE (second clasp)	List 67 1965
22206645	Sgt	Godman W.	List 73 1966
22516725	S/Sgt	Crossley D.	List 82 1969
22544451	WO2	Richardson B.	List 84 1969
22664038	WO2	Kerans F.	List 109 1976
22134489	Sgt	Wilbraham A.	
22130882	WO2	Steven J. D.	List 116 1977
23974138	WO2	Gillham C.	List 135 1982
23979915	WO2	Steward F. M.	
22664038	WO2	Kerans F. (second clasp)	List 149 1986
22664038	WO2	Kerans F. (third clasp)	
24236131	S/Sgt	Jones A.	List 165 1990
24256039	S/Sgt	Gair B. J.	List 167 1990
24236591	S/Sgt	Kershaw G. C.	
24236200	Cpl	Potter C.	
24236913	S/Sgt	Lake J. W.	List 169 1991
23845132	Cpl	Bligh J. A.	

George Batley, the Regimental Band Master between 1884 and 1902 is here seen mounted and carrying a trumpet. Around him are the band in a variety of relaxed poses and the Regiment's silver kettledrums can be seen mounted to Band Master Batley's left. This picture was taken some time between 1898 and 1902 when Mr. Batley retired.

APPENDIX III

Regimental Music

(1) THE BAND

On the conclusion of the Crimean War in 1856 a splendid review of some 16,000 British and French troops was held at Scutari before the Allied Commander-in-Chief and a vast concourse of senior military officers and civilian dignitaries. The ceremony commenced with the performance of the two National Anthems, and the result was distressing cacophony. Not only were the massed regimental bands playing different arrangements, in different keys, but their instruments were not all of the same pitch. This dreadful dissonance so horrified the Duke of Cambridge (one of the military dignitaries) that he determined to do something to create harmony among British Army bands.

On returning home and assuming the post of Commander-in-Chief, he inaugurated a 'Military Music Class' at Twickenham with the object of producing qualified Bandmasters and introducing uniformity among their bands. This was the origin of today's Royal Military School of Music, housed in the Twickenham mansion built for Queen Anne's court painter and known as Kneller Hall.

As was only too audibly evident at Scutari, prior to this development, regimental bands had been entirely subject to the whims of the regiments themselves, or rather their officers, who funded all expenses for instruments and music, and paid the salaries of the hired 'Music Masters' who were usually German or Italian civilian musicians. Horse Guards (War Office) took no interest other than periodically restricting the maximum number of soldiers allowed to be 'milked' from the ranks as bandsmen. Seldom musically-minded, the officers were content to leave such recondite matters as choice of music and performance entirely in the hands of the Music Masters. Although, as always, the Yeomanry were a law unto themselves and unaffected by Horse Guards' mandates, such was the lack of interest and the utterly disorganised state of musical matters generally in the Army, it is not to be wondered at that records of the early bands of the DLOY's progenitors are fragmentary in the extreme.

And here, for the benefit of non-musical readers, we should distinguish between what evolved as 'military bands' and 'brass bands'. The former deploy not only such brass instruments as trumpets, cornets, horns and trombones, but also the woodwind section: flutes (and piccolo), oboes, clarinets, bassoons. As its name implies, the brass band dispenses with the woodwind, having only the brass section, including some instruments not found elsewhere, such as the flugel horn. Lancashire and Yorkshire have long been noted for their civilian brass bands – Bessies o'th' Barn and Black Dyke Mills, for example – and many members of these originated as Army bandsmen.

In the days of the horse all cavalry bands, Regular and Yeomanry, performed mounted when on parade or on the march, but as they were seldom asked to exceed a sedate walk, horsemanship was less important than musicianship.

The earliest reference to a DLOY band (or one of its antecedents seems to be that recorded in *The Military Musician* (Kneller Hall journal) of October 1937. According to this, around 1818 a band was formed by Colonel Ralph Fletcher, Commandant of the Bolton Militia, and this was later attached, or loaned, to the Bolton Light Horse Volunteers. The civilian Master was a Mr George Slater, a noted bassoon player and close friend of Mr Charles Godfrey, Bandmaster of the Coldstream Guards and father of two distinguished Guards Directors of Music, one of whom became the first to be commissioned, in 1887.

By 1828 the band of what had now become the Lancashire Yeomanry Cavalry under Mr Slater could muster flute, piccolo, nine clarinets, three bassoons, four horns, two trumpets, one trombone and two of that convoluted wooden bass instrument aptly termed Serpent, which grunted the 'oomp' of the 'oompah' in a march rhythm.

By 1831 the band seems to have been depleted of its woodwind, for on 16 October of that year *The Bolton Chronicle* reported a parade of the Regiment in the Market Place 'attended by their new Brass Band'. However, in 1838 the instrumentation was increased by the addition of woodwind from the private band of Lord Francis Egerton (later 2nd Earl of Ellesmere) of Worsley Park, who was later to command the Regiment. His Lordship also provided the successor to George Slater in the person of Thomas Lee, an accomplished clarinetist. For some years Mr Lee had played in the celebrated Bessies o' th' Barn band, which at that time included woodwind as well as brass.

When Queen Victoria visited the Earl of Ellesmere at Worsley in October 1851, 'Her Majesty was received by a Royal Salute by the band of the Earl of Ellesmere, which afterwards discoursed an entertaining programme of music'.(*Bolton Chronicle* 11 October)

In the following year another professional musician took over the band. George Ellwood, of Lancaster, was a noted trumpet player and for many years had played in Manchester under Charles Hallé (later Sir Charles), founder of the Hallé Orchestra. He remained in charge for the remarkable span of 32 years, during which he brought the ensemble to a very high standard of performance. In June 1864 the Regiment made one of its several visits to Lancaster for 'Permanent Duty' (Annual Camp), and the band evoked favourable comment in the columns of *The Lancaster Gazette* of 25 June: 'It is one of which Lancaster may be proud, because the perfection it has attained is owing to the instruction and supervision of a townsman – Mr Ellwood, the talented bandmaster of the regiment. Nightly this fine band has delighted crowds of our townsfolk, either assembled in the street or at the neighbouring windows.' The *Lancaster Gazette* also published the programme performed at a closing dinner in The King's Arms Hotel, and it is instructive to compare this selection with the repertoire preferred by regimental bands (and public) today:

March	–	*Le Reveil de Jeanne d'Arc*	–	Matizieux
Overture	–	*Die Zauberflöte*	–	Mozart
Quadrille	–	*Le Fete des Lilas*	–	Lamotte
Selection	–	*Robert le Diable*	–	Meyerbeer
Valse	–	*Faust*	–	Gounod

Selection	–	*Les Huguenots*	–	**Meyerbeer**
Mazurka	–	*Wanda*	–	Telexey
Euphonium Solo	–	*Maria Stuarda*	–	Donizetti
Selection	–	*La Favorita*	–	Donizetti

Eight years later the band, still under Mr Ellwood, gave a public concert in Avenham Park, Preston, when the *Preston Guardian* of 22 June 1872 reported that 'a large gathering of pleasure seekers was entertained by the exquisite strains of this band'. As usual, the programme was exclusively classical, featuring Mozart, Boieldieu, Suppé, Weber and other lesser-known names.

The general public might be enthralled by the 'exquisite strains' of military bands, but evidently the musical cognoscenti had other tastes. Reporting a piano recital in the Philharmonia Rooms, London, *The Musical Times* of March 1862 added: 'afterwards a wind band of some regiment was unfortunately let into the room and contrived to make a most distressing noise'. *Chacun à son goût!*

By 1878 the DLOY Band could parade a creditable brass-and-woodwind ensemble of 27 musicians.

In 1884 the veteran George Ellwood retired, handing over to yet another talented musician. Mr George A. Batley was the son of Trumpet-Major W. H. Batley who served for 32 years in the Life Guards. George had joined the DLOY Band as cornet player in 1846 at the age of fourteen, when he was so small that he had to be lifted onto his horse. Like Ellwood, he also played under the baton of Charles Hallé in Manchester. His brother, also Thomas, became Bandmaster of The Lancashire Hussars in 1871, thus giving rise to confusion between the two.

Perhaps it should be mentioned that while the musical education and performance of a band was solely in the hands of the Bandmaster, all matters of discipline, drill and turnout were the responsibility of the Trumpet-Major. He also taught the trumpeters the numerous regulation 'sounds' or calls, such as 'Reveille', 'Boot and Saddle', 'Stables' and the rest. These routine calls were sounded on the brass E-flat duty trumpet which as a 'natural' instrument (no valves) had a practical compass of eight notes.[1] In the field, the B-flat bugle, with only five notes, was used for executive calls – 'Mount', 'Walk March', 'Trot', 'Troops right Wheel' and so forth. In all, the trumpeters were required to master a total of 38 such field calls, and Squadron and Troop Leaders (however unmusical) were expected to recognise them and act upon them.

George Batley was remarkable in being not only an accomplished musician but equally accomplished as a horseman, swordsman and marksman with the rifle, for which latter skills he won many silver cups presented by the Earl of Ellesmere.

1. As a matter of interest, the venerable routine calls, unchanged to the present day, were first officially published by Horse Guards in 1798 – the year that saw the creation of the DLOY's progenitor, the Bolton Light Horse. They had been collated (if not composed) by a Yeoman, one Trumpet-Major Hyde of the Westminster Light Horse Volunteers.

Although, as we have seen, after the formation of the Royal Military School of Music at Kneller Hall in 1857, all regular Bandmasters had to qualify as such at this establishment, there was no requirement for their Yeomanry counterparts to do so, and thus the present Kneller Hall archives have no records of any DLOY musicians so qualified. As with other members of the Regiment, Bandmasters (and Bandsmen) were co-opted from civilian life.

Until after the First World War the band remained mounted, and on parade was led by the noble heavy Drum Horse (traditionally piebald or skewbald) bearing the pair of silver kettle drums decked with embroidered banners. In 1899 new Drum Banners were presented by Major P. Hargreaves and Major W. C. Jones, for use with a fine pair of silver kettle drums donated by Major Jones on his retirement from second-in-command in 1898.

A photograph of the band on a mounted parade at Southport in 1898 shows it clad in Full Dress finery of scarlet tunics, white metal, plumed helmets, and led by what appears to be a piebald Drum Horse. Another (dismounted) group photograph of c. 1905 depicts 22 performers in scarlet patrol jackets with the gold aiguilettes introduced in 1899 and pill-box hats. It is not possible to make out the complete instrumentation, but clearly visible are four clarinets, a flute, an oboe, two cornets, two trombones, a euphonium, a B-flat bass (or tuba) and a string double-bass, plus side drum and bass drum.

The Bandmaster was then Mr William Smart who reformed the band after the 1914–18 war and continued with the baton until 1922. Little is known of him, but in that year he was succeeded by Mr Henry Mortimer, and here some confusion has arisen with his better-known namesake. The latter was long a leading light in the brass band world, conductor of several championship bands and in recent years occasionally appearing as guest conductor of the Kneller Hall Band. Both Harry Mortimers (unrelated) studied together at the Royal Manchester College of Music – now the Royal Northern College of Music – the one on the clarinet, the other on trumpet and cornet. And both played in the Hallé Orchestra under Sir Hamilton Harty, and in the Royal Liverpool Philharmonic. Small wonder that the two have been confused.

However, although the DLOY's 'Harry' never achieved the celebrity of his brass band namesake, he left a legacy to the Regiment, in his composition of the Regimental march, 'John o' Gaunt'. He resigned in 1934 when Mr H. F. Morton took over.

It was during Morton's tenure that the pitch of military band instruments was altered to the present international standard, with the note A above middle C equalling 440 cps. The DLOY Band conformed, which meant the replacement of all the old 'high pitch' brass and woodwind – at the Regiment's expense. What this cost is not revealed, but the band had fallen into line by the 1930s, at the urging of Mr Morton. A photograph of the band reproduced in *The Military Musician* of October 1937 shows 25 performers, plus Mr Morton, but all the instruments are not clearly identifiable.

As in the First World War, the band ceased to function during the Second, but many of the Bandsmen joined the ranks as medical orderlies or gunners. With the reconstitution of the DLOY in 1947, the band too was reformed, again under Mr Morton. After more than 30 years' civilian and military music making, he handed over in 1950 to WO1 J. R. Cooney, who had served for 24 years in the band of the 3rd The King's Own Hussars, in which he became Band Sergeant. His own instruments were the tuba and the bass trombone and he was well known in Manchester and Liverpool orchestral circles as a deputy performer with the Hallé and Royal Liverpool Philharmonic Orchestras, also the BBC Northern Orchestra. It was under his baton that the band excelled itself, both in music and drill, at the ceremony in Belle Vue Stadium Manchester in 1961 when Her Majesty the Colonel-in-Chief presented the new Guidon. Formerly, the Bandsmen who were rarely seen on parade, and then only on very special occasions, had not been remarkable for their precision of marching and drill, and somewhat unkindly they were known to the rest of the Regiment as 'Cooney's Loonies'. But this was no reflection on their musical abilities, and the Guidon Parade proved that they could hold their own with the best-drilled band when called upon.

Mr Cooney retired in 1963 and was succeeded by Mr A. Hurst, destined to become the last Bandmaster of the DLOY. When, in April 1967 the Regiment was amalgamated with 40th/41st Royal Tank Regiment, the band was disbanded (apt term) and sadly, has never since been resuscitated, which has meant calling on the co-operation of the affiliated 14th/20th King's Hussars and certain Territorial units for music on ceremonial occasions.

The final *nunc dimittis*, however, came in 1987, when the Regimental journal, *The Lancashire Yeoman*, reported the sale of all the old band music. The £1,400 raised may have been a welcome addition to Regimental funds, but might perhaps be regretted should the band ever be reborn.

For the record, it may be mentioned that the Territorial Army still deploys 24 bands, four being Yeomanry, the rest Artillery, Signals or Infantry.

(2) REGIMENTAL MARCH

Since the earliest days of the British Army all regular regiments have adopted some melody as their own exclusive march, accorded almost the same honours as the National Anthem, to be played when marching on or off a ceremonial parade, ranking past a saluting base, or concluding a concert performance. In the days of the horse all cavalry regiments rode past to their Slow March, the tempo being more suited to the walk pace of a horse (and more *maestoso*) than the sprightly quicksteps of infantry marches. All these regimental marches were officially authorised in the 1880s, and are duly recorded at Kneller Hall. But, as we have seen, that Alma Mater of military musicians has never concerned itself with Territorial regiments, and thus (with scant regimental records), we have no knowledge of what exclusive airs were adopted by the DLOY until the 1930s. Newspaper reports of the 1870s–1900s describe the Regiment trotting past to 'the regimental march' of 'Monymusk' or cantering past to 'Bonnie Dundee'. The former, with its bouncing two-four rhythm, was ideal for the sitting trot (always ridden on ceremonial and drill parades), while the swinging six-eight of 'Bonnie Dundee' was equally appropriate to the three-time canter pace. But neither of these could really be claimed as

'Regimental Marches', for they were common to all mounted units (and can still be heard today in the displays by The King's Troop RHA and The Household Cavalry).

It was not until the advent of Mr H. Mortimer as Bandmaster of the DLOY that the Regiment acquired its own distinctive march, aptly entitled 'John o' Gaunt'. Mr Mortimer is claimed to have composed the original score in the 1920s, while the introductory fanfare and concluding section in change of key were added by Bandmaster A. Hurst in the 1960s.

Although at the date of composition the Regiment was mounted, the march did not conform to the customary cavalry marches with their slow common or four-four time, but is in a jaunty six-eight style, more appropriate to an infantry quickstep, while the melody is somewhat reminiscent of a traditional folk song or dance. With the demise of Mr Mortimer, and no information forthcoming from Kneller Hall, it is not possible to say whether it was an original composition or based on something like the above.

This Appendix would not be complete without mention of a 'Pavane or Fanfare' composed by the talented Colonel Roger Hesketh in 1975, when there were hopes (unfulfilled) that the band might be reformed. Arranged for full military band, this was performed at the Guidon Parade in October 1990.

(3) THE REGIMENTAL TRUMPET CALL

Until the advent of technology in the form of radio (and telephone) the chief means of relaying orders in the field and in quarters were the age-old ones of trumpet and bugle calls. As we have seen, these were first authorised and published in 1798, when all regiments were required to employ the identical calls (or 'sounds'). It can readily be imagined that when two or more units were encamped or quartered together, each within earshot of the other's trumpeters, there could be no doubts as to which call was intended for whom. Thus around 1838 each regiment was given its own distinctive Regimental Call – a kind of 'signature tune' of three or four bars, to be sounded before any other call, and so removing doubts. In the Regular Army all these Regimental Calls were published in successive editions of the official *Manual of Trumpet and Bugle Sounds for the Army*, but

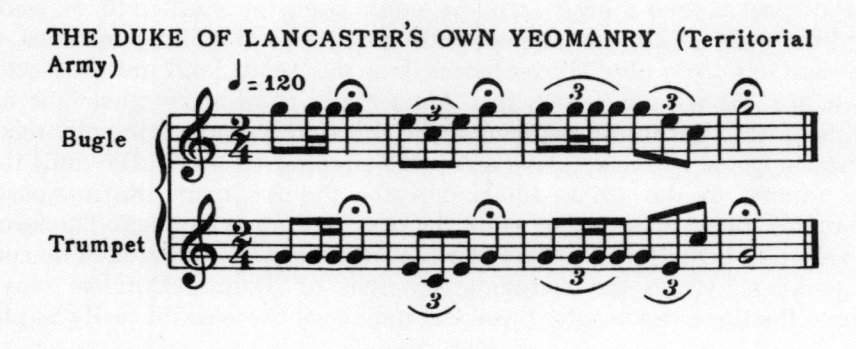

THE DUKE OF LANCASTER'S OWN YEOMANRY (Territorial Army)

it was not until after the Second World War that the Yeomanry's Calls were included, and it is not possible to say when they were first adopted. That for The Duke of Lancaster's Own Yeomanry appeared in *Trumpet and Bugle Calls for the Army, 1966*, and is given below. It will be seen that it could be sounded on either trumpet or bugle, but the former instrument was always used in quarters.

Bandmasters of The Duke of Lancaster's Own Yeomanry and its Predecessors

1818	George Slater	1902	W. Smart
1838	Thomas Lee	1922	Henry Mortimer
1852	George Ellwood	1934	Harold F. Morton
1884	George A Batley	1950	WO1 Joseph R. Cooney
		1963	WO1 A. Hurst

The Kettle Drums, 1899

At the Annual Training at Southport in 1899 a pair of handsome drum banners was presented to the regiment through the generosity of Major P. Hargreaves and Major W. C. Jones. In this photograph, Drummer Johnson proudly parades the newly presented banners on Southport sands. The bandsmen were distinguished by having scarlet rather than white plumes on their helmets and by the wearing of heavy yellow aiguillettes on the left shoulder; the drum horses had the added distinction of a scarlet throat plume.

This shows a detachment of the Regiment together with the band on the steps of Worsley New Hall, the seat of Lord Ellesmere. The band wore scarlet plumes in their helmets together with aiguillettes. Photograph c. 1900.

The Regimental March

of

The Duke of Lancaster's Own Yeomanry

(John O' Gaunt)

[202]

[203]

[204]

4
19
20
21
22
23
24
Flute/ Piccolo
E♭ Clarinet
Oboe
Solo
1 Rep
Clarinets
2
3
Alto Saxophone
Tenor Saxophone
Bassoon
Horns
1
Cornets
2
1
2 Trombones
Bass
Euphonium
Basses
Percussion

25
26
27
28
29
30
5
Flute/
Piccolo
E♭ Clarinet
Oboe
Solo
1
Rep
Clarinets
2
3
Alto
Saxophone
Tenor
Saxophone
Bassoon
Horns
1
Cornets
2
1
2
Trombones
Bass
Euphonium
Basses
Percussion

[207]

[208]

[209]

[210]

[211]

[212]

D.S al Fine

This illustration is taken from *Earle's Lancashire Hussars* and shows the Regiment's distinctive Field Dress in 1848, the year of formation.
Note the Belgian style shako and pelisse; the shako and overalls were cerise and the lace originally gold although later changed to silver. Full Dress was even more elaborate and a splendid example is on view in the foyer of the Regimental Museum, Preston.

[214]

APPENDIX IV

The Lancashire Hussars

In August 1848 the following letter was sent by the Adjutant-General's secretary to Lord Fitzroy Somerset, Military Secretary at Horse Guards:[1]

                                              Whitehall
                                         31 Aug. 1848

    My Lord
    I am directed by Secretary Sir George Grey to acquaint your Lordship, for the information of the General Commanding in Chief, that the Queen has been pleased to accept the services of a Corps of Yeomanry to be raised in the County of Lancaster, consisting of Two Troops and 140 private men. Her Majesty has also approved of this Corps being styled the 'Lancashire Hussars' and of the appointment of Sir John Gerard as Major Commandant.
                                                  I have etc.
                                    (Sd.) *G. Cornewall Lewis*

As mentioned in Chapter II, tradition had it that Sir John Gerard, member of the wealthy Catholic family from Garswood, near Ashton-in-Makerfield, was serving in the DLOY when he departed to raise his own Regiment, taking with him Catholic officers and men from the preponderantly Anglican make-up of the DLOY. But in 1889 a well-researched history of The Lancashire Hussars was privately published by Lieutenant T. Algernon Earle (later Lieutenant-Colonel in command) of that regiment, and this effectively disposes of the tradition.[2]

Major Sir John Gerard was never a member of the DLOY, but since 1842 had commanded the 3rd Royal Lancashire Militia (Duke of Lancaster's Own). With that subtitle, it is not difficult to imagine how this regiment became confused with the DLOY. And incidentally it shows that the latter's title was not unique – that is until 1881 when the six Battalions of Royal Lancashire Militia (DLO) were absorbed by other Lancashire infantry regiments.

The first Troop of the Hussars was raised in September 1848 from tenants and others on Sir John's Garswood estate, and shortly afterwards a second Troop was formed at St Helens, 'to which also some Ormskirk and Liverpool men were admitted'.(Earle) Sir John spared no personal expense in kitting out and arming his command, 'providing them with swords, belts &c. of a much superior kind'. A dress distinction that must have evoked comment elsewhere were the crimson Full Dress overalls of the officers – formerly the exclusive prerogative of the 11th (Prince Albert's Own) Hussars, being granted to them by the Queen in 1840. How and why Sir John managed to usurp this unique

---

1. Public Record Office. Ref. HO51/166.
2. *List of Officers who have served in The Lancashire Hussars Yeomanry Cavalry with some Notes and Annals of the Regiment . . . 1848 to the Present Time* (1889) (Copy in DLOY Museum)

privilege is not revealed, but by 1850 the crimson had been replaced by the normal Hussars' blue – perhaps after protest from the 11th?

The first Annual Camp (or 'Permanent Duty') was held at Garswood in 1849, but the following year saw the Regiment at Southport, a venue which was visited during the next 40 years. In 1854 the founder, Sir John Gerard, died, and his brother Robert succeeded to the title and the command. In the following year the Hussars joined with their Lancastrian comrades, the DLOY, for annual training at Liverpool, and there was another similar meeting in 1856 when both regiments were together at Lancaster. By 1859 the Hussars could deploy four Troops, with a strength of 14 officers and 220 other ranks.

The succeeding years saw the Regiment carrying out the normal Yeomanry routine of weekly drills, annual training (always at Southport), while Regimental Headquarters was permanently located at Ashton-in-Makerfield.

The training camp at Southport in May 1896 gave the good citizens of that town their first opportunity of witnessing a polo match. Playing on the sands, the Hussars' team decisively beat the Liverpool Polo Club by three goals to nil, 'and the game, watched by an enormous crowd, proved a great success in spite of the occasional disappearance of the ball into the sand'.(Earle) Next year there was another match against a 3rd Hussars' team when the Yeomanry suffered an equally decisive defeat.

By the outbreak of the Boer War in 1899 the Regiment mustered 17 officers and 437 other ranks. In common with the rest of the Yeomanry, all those fit enough volunteered for active service in the newly-created Imperial Yeomanry. And like the others, they served as mounted infantry, forming the 32nd Company, 2nd Battalion IY, and 77th Company, 8th Battalion. On the conclusion of hostilities, The Lancashire Hussars reverted to their original role as horsed cavalry, being attached to the Welsh Border Mounted Brigade in Western Command.

By August 1914 the Regiment was deployed thus: RHQ was now at Prince Albert Road, Liverpool; A Squadron was at Ashton-in-Makerfield, with drill halls at Wigan and Liverpool; B Squadron was at St Helens; C at Newton-le-Willows, and D at Rainhill. In command was Lieutenant-Colonel T. A. Earle, author of the history. War services were very similar to those of the DLOY, the Regiment being split into divorced Squadrons, some serving in Egypt, others in France to form a Corps Cavalry Regiment, where they were later joined by the others. In July 1917 this Regiment was dismounted and in September 16 officers and 290 other ranks were absorbed by the 18th (Lancashire Hussars) Battalion, The King's Regiment (Liverpool), and as such served until the Armistice.

The post-war years brought radical changes. In 1921 the Regiment was ordered to merge with The Duke of Lancaster's Own to form the 2nd (Lancashire Yeomanry) Army Brigade Royal Field Artillery. As recounted in Chapter VII (p 100), the DLOY managed to evade this unwelcome transformation, leaving their partners to emerge as the 106th (Lancashire Yeomanry) Brigade, with two Batteries.

This was virtually the end of The Lancashire Hussars as a distinct Yeomanry Regiment. It no longer appeared in the Army Lists under its title, but like other Territorial units of the Royal Artillery remained anonymous. In the Second World War, as 149 Anti-Tank Regiment RA, it served in Egypt and the Western Desert, Italy and Greece.

On the reformation of the Territorial Army in 1947 the Regiment lost all vestiges of its origins when it became 349 Light Anti-Aircraft and 306 Heavy Anti-Aircraft Regiments. Finally, these were absorbed by the Lancashire Territorial Artillery.

However, The Lancashire Hussars are not forgotten. They never managed to form a regimental museum of their own, but that of the DLOY at Preston preserves several memorabilia of its Lancastrian brethren, including a splendid Ferneley painting depicting a Full Dress mounted parade of the Regiment in 1851, with Colonel Sir Robert Gerard (brother of the founder) in command.[3]

3. John Ferneley (1782–1860) was the most admired sporting and military artist of his day. The picture was auctioned at Christies in July 1987 and, thanks to the generosity of members and friends of the DLOY, funds were available to make the successful bid of £6,000.

1882
Colonel the Hon A. F. Egerton

1896
Colonel F. C. G. Egerton, Earl of Ellesmere

1915
Colonel P. Hargreaves

1922
Colonel Sir John Rutherford, Bt, TD

1932
Colonel H. M. Hardcastle, TD

1940
Colonel D. H. Bates, MC, TD

1956
Colonel R. F. Fleetwood-Hesketh, TD, DL, JP

1970
Colonel W. R. Palmer, DSO, TD

1979
Colonel M. A. A. Birtwhistle, **TD**

1979
Colonel S. P. E. C. W. Towneley, Ld Lieut, JP

1988
Major-General Sir Michael Palmer, KCVO

Note
The pictures reproduced here do not necessarily show the individuals when holding office as Honorary Colonel.

APPENDIX V

(1) HONORARY COLONELS

Note   It was not until 1850 that Honorary Colonels began to be appointed to Yeomanry regiments, though there had previously been a somewhat similar appointment of Lieutenant-Colonel Commandant. As seen below, the first DLOY Honorary Colonel as such appeared only in 1882.

1882	Colonel the Hon. A. F. Egerton
1896	Colonel F. C. G. Egerton, Earl of Ellesmere
1915	Colonel P. Hargreaves
1922	Colonel Sir John Rutherford, Bt,TD
1932	Colonel H. M. Hardcastle, TD
1940	Colonel D. H. Bates, MC, TD
1956	Colonel R. F. Fleetwood-Hesketh, TD, DL, JP
1970	Colonel W. R. Palmer, DSO, TD
1970	Colonel M. A. A. Birtwistle, TD
1979	Colonel S. P. E. C. W. Towneley, Ld Lieut, JP
1988	Major-General Sir Michael Palmer, KCVO

(2) COMMANDING OFFICERS

1798–1816	Major John Pilkington (Bolton Light Horse Volunteers)
1819–1828	Major Thomas Richmond Gale Braddyll (Furness Troop of Yeomanry Cavalry)
1819–1828	Captain James Hodson Kearsley (Wigan Troop)
1819–1828	Captain James Kearsley, JP (Bolton Troop)
1828–1834	Major T. R. G. Braddyll (Lancashire Yeomanry Cavalry)
1834–1841	Colonel T. R. G. Braddyll (The Duke of Lancaster's Own Yeomanry)
1841–1857	Lieutenant-Colonel Lord Francis Egerton, Earl of Ellesmere
1857–1862	Lieutenant-Colonel G. G. F. Egerton
1862–1882	Lieutenant-Colonel The Hon. A. F. Egerton
1882–1884	Lieutenant-Colonel V. Grey de Wilton
1884–1891	Lieutenant-Colonel R. H. Ainsworth
1891–1896	Lieutenant-Colonel F. C. G. Egerton
1896–1902	Lieutenant-Colonel C. M. Royds, MP
1902–1906	Lieutenant-Colonel P. Hargreaves
1906–1912	Lieutenant-Colonel J. Rutherford, TD, MP
1912–1919	Lieutenant-Colonel R. H. Tilney, DSO, TD (CO DLOY 1912–1916) (CO 3rd Corps Cavalry Regt. 1916–1919) (CO DLOY Reinforcement Regt. 1917–1919)

1916–1923	Lieutenant-Colonel H. M. Hardcastle, TD
	(CO DLOY Reinforcement Regt. 1916–1919)
	(CO 12 (DLOY) (Manchester Bn. 1919–1921)
	(CO DLOY 1919–1923)
1917–1918	Lieutenant-Colonel T. W. Bullock
	(CO 12 (DLOY) Manchester Bn.)
1918	Lieutenant-Colonel E. G. S. Truell
	(CO 12 (DLOY) Manchester Bn.)
1918–1919	Lieutenant-Colonel S. Danby, DSO, MC
	(CO 12 (DLOY) Manchester Bn.)
1923–1924	Lieutenant-Colonel T. B. Forwood, TD
1924–1930	Lieutenant-Colonel H. A. Bromilow, TD
1930–1934	Lieutenant-Colonel D. H. Bates, MC, TD
1934–1938	Lieutenant-Colonel J. Heaton, TD
1938–1940	Lieutenant-Colonel W. N. Musgrave-Hoyle, MC
	(CO DLOY 1938–1940)
	(CO 77 (DLOY) Med. Regt. RA 1940)
1940–1942	Lieutenant-Colonel F. H. C. Rogers, MC
	(CO 77 (DLOY) Med. Regt. RA)
1942–1945	Lieutenant-Colonel F. G. Wintle, DSO, MBE
	(CO 77 (DLOY) Med. Regt. RA)
1945	Lieutenant-Colonel L. J. Thomas, MC
	(CO 77 (DLOY) Med. Regt. RA)
1940	Lieutenant-Colonel R. Fleetwood-Hesketh, TD
	(CO 78 (DLOY) Med. Regt. RA)
1940–1941	Lieutenant-Colonel V. A. Young, MC
	(CO 78 (DLOY) Med. Regt. RA)
1941–1943	Lieutenant-Colonel E. M. Tyler, MC
	(CO 78 (DLOY) Med. Regt. RA)
1943–1949	Lieutenant-Colonel W. R. Palmer, DSO, TD
	(CO 78 (DLOY) Med. Regt. RA)
	(CO DLOY 1947–1949)
1949–1952	Lieutenant-Colonel E. B. Studd, 14/20H
1952–1956	Lieutenant-Colonel D. B. Stewart, TD
1956–1959	Lieutenant-Colonel M. A. A. Birtwistle, TD
1959–1961	Lieutenant-Colonel B. C. L. Tayleur, OBE 14/20H
1961–1964	Lieutenant-Colonel J. N. B. Cardwell, TD
1964–1967	Lieutenant-Colonel T. A. Marshall, TD
1967–1972	Lieutenant-Colonel N. H. Phillips
	(CO DLOY (RTR) 1967–1969)
	(CO Cadre 1969–1971)
	(CO DLOY 1971–1972)

1972–1974	Lieutenant-Colonel J. D. Bastick, MBE, RTR
1974–1978	Lieutenant-Colonel D. J. Claxton, TD
1978–1980	Lieutenant-Colonel P. D. W. Cable-Alexander, Royal Scots DG
1980–1983	Lieutenant-Colonel R. A. Ferguson, TD
1983–1985	Lieutenant-Colonel D. A. J. Corbin, 4/7 RDG
1985–1988	Lieutenant-Colonel J. D. V. Woolley, 17/21L
1988–1990	Lieutenant-Colonel M. T. Steiger, TD
1990–1992	Lieutenant-Colonel S. M. P. Stewart, MBE, QDG

INDEX

Battles, actions etc., are indexed under Campaigns.
Ranks shown are those ultimately attained and not necessarily current at dates of reference.

Abbot, Pte P. H. 82
Abridgement of the Regulations for the Formation and Movements of the Cavalry. 20
Adams, Sgt Major W. 27
Affiliated regular regiment (14th/20th King's Hussars). 124; 138
Agnew, Maj K. M. 100
Agnew, Pte P. R. 52
Ainsworth, Lt Col R. H. 198
Aircraft, first military use of 62
Aldershot 32, 59, 62, 83, 85, 127
Allen, Pte T. 95
Allenby, Gen Sir Edmund xv, 77 78, 79, 91
Altcar 59, 61, 111, 149, 151 153–54, 157–58
Andrews, S/Sgt B. P. 153
Anglesey, Marquess of vii, 33
Ansel, Maj Gen N. 158
Anzacs xvi, 77, 78, 91
Army Remount Service 110
Artillery, conversions to 99, 111 *et seq*

Babbington, Maj Gen J. M. 83
Badges, regimental 68, 113, 138–39
Bailey, Lt E. W. 130 136
Baker, Bdr A. 136
Baldwin, Capt H. 111
Bands 19, 37, 38, 94, 145, 193–97
Barry, L/cpl G. E. M. 44, 51
Bastick, Lt Col J. D. 71fn, 148, 149, 221
Bates, Col D. H. 76, 78, 81, 95, 100, 102, 104, 105, 115, 137, 139, 143, 219, 220
Bates, Major Philip vii
Battle Honours v, 82, 86, 90, **102**, 141–42
Bibby, Maj H. L. 74, 76
Bibby-Hesketh, Lt Col C. H. 42
Birtwistle, Col M. A. A. 137, 140, 141–42, 146, 149–50, 219, 220
Blackburn Troop (DLOY) 38
Blackpool 43, 44
Blackpool Troop (DLOY) 29, 60
Bloemfontein 55
Blundell, John D. vii, 150
Blythe, Sgt A 95
Boardman, Ralph 5, 10

Boddington, 2/Lt P. 84, 91, 92
Bolling, Edward 5, 10
Bolton 4, 20, 22, 23, 27
Bolton Light Horse Volunteers 5 *et seq* 19, 23
Bolton Troop (DLOY) 29, 30 38
Bourke, Capt W. L. 38, 39
Bourne, Lt B. S. 138
Bowring, 2/Lt R. H. 109
Bowring, Lt T. 155
Braddyll, Col T. R. G. 13–15, 17, 18, 23, 219
Braddyll, Capt E. R. G. 15
Braddyll, Capt T. G. 13, 18
Bridgewater, 3rd Duke of 71fn
Brigades, Yeomanry 35–36, 63
British Army Training Unit Suffield (Canada) 158
Brocklebank Lt J. J. 42, 48, 51, 52, 54
Bromilow, Lt Col H. A. 100, 101, **104**, 220
Brooke, Mrs Geoffrey 81
Brooke Hospital for Animals 81
Broughton Troop (DLOY) 29, 38
Brownrigg, Tpr F. 49–51, 52
Bullock, Lt Col T. W. 91, 220

Cable-Alexander, Lt Col P. D. W. 149, 221
Caerwys (Wales) 65
Cambridge, FM The Duke of 193
CAMPAIGNS, BATTLES, ACTIONS
    Boer War
        Achterkop 55
        Faber's Putt 46–53
        Hoopstad 54
        Luckoff 55–56
    Egypt and Palestine
        Agagiya 76
        Canal Defence Force 75, 76
        Gaza 77, 78
        Rumani 76
        Wadi Hesi 78
    France and Flanders (WWI)
        La Boiselle 88
        Bois Grenier 86
        Flers 89
        Havrincourt 93
        Mormal Wood 94

    Selle River 93–94
    Somme (1916) 87–89
    Ypres 90–91
  France and NW Europe (WWII)
    Asten 130
    Blerwick 131
    Falaise Pocket 129
    Lantheuil 128
    Munster 133–34
    Norrey-en-Bessin 128
    Overloon 130
    "Overlord" 127
    Rhine Crossing 132–33
    Venraij 130
  Italy (WW II)
    Appenines 122, 123
    Cassino 118–121
    Gothic Line 122
    Medicina 124
    San Eusanio 118
Cape Town 45
Cardwell, Visct Edward 30
Cardwell, Lt Col J. N. B. 159, 220
Carlisle 37, 38
Catterall, Maj S. E. 117, 120, 123, 124, 136
Cavalry Journal 62
Cavalry Memorial Parade (Hyde Park) 148
Cavalry Training (Manual) 31, 62, 107
Chamberlain, Neville (Prime Minister) 109
Chartist riots 22–23
Chartres, Maj J. A. 143
Cheshire Yeomanry 73, 100, 101, 112, 126, 145
Childers, Erskine 61–62
Chorley (Lancashire) 11, 151–52
Clark, Gen Mark 121
Claxton, Lt Col D. J. 146–47, 149, 221
Clegg, Capt C. B. 109
Clemence, Lt P. G. 138
Clifton (Manchester) 145, 150, 152
Cooney, WO1 J. R. 143, 196, 197, 198
Corbin Lt Col D. A. J. 152–53, 154, 155, 221
Corps Cavalry regiments 74, 78, 87
County Associations 63, 64, 69
Cyclist units 84, 96, 97

Danby, Lt Col S. 220
Dartmoor 115, 150, 158
De Lisle, Gen Sir Beavoir 55
Derby, Earls of 4, 11, 12, 15, 64
Desert Mounted Corps xv, 77
Dickson, Capt B. 62fn
Dimbleby, Capt H. W. 128–29
Discpline 7–8, 16, 20, 35, 70
Divisional Cavalry 74, 77, 78, 83, 84, 85, 87, 100
Douglas, Maj Gen Sir William 75

Dowse, Maj Gen M. B. 139
Duke of Edinburgh's Own Volunteer Rifles 45, 47, 48, 50, 54
Durrant, RQMS 143

Earle, Lt Col T. A. 215, 216
Edward VII, King 60, 65, 68
Edward VIII, King 106
Egerton, Col the Hon. A. F. 29, 36, 219
Egerton, Col F. C. G. 36, 70–71, 219
Egerton, Lt Col G. G. F. 29, 219
Elizabeth II, Queen 139, 140, 142, 143–44, 149, 153–54, 159–60
Ellesmere, Earls of 26 *et seq*
Ellwood, George (Bandmaster) 194–95, 199
"Ernie", Tpr 45

Faber's Putt *see* "Campaigns, ..."
Fair Clough, Lt N. H. 147
Fencibles 3
Ferguson, Maj J. A. 147
Ferguson, Lt Col R. A. 147, 221
Firth, Maj Gen C. E. A. 141–42
Fisher, Major E. H. L. 123
Fishguard 113
Fitzherbert-Brockholes, Capt J. W. 84, 95
Fleetwood-Hesketh, Col R. F. 109, 113, 114, 143, 194, 219, 220
Fleetwood-Hesketh, Capt C. P. F. 109
Fleetwood-Hesketh, Lt F. C. B. 109
Fletcher, WO2 H. 155
Fletcher, Lt J. 15, 18, 23
Fletcher, Capt M. 5, 10
Fletcher, Col Palph 5, 10, 11, 194
Fortescue, Sir John xiv, 7fn, 27fn
Forwood, Lt Col T. B. 91, 220
Fulton, Lt G. 155
Furness Troop (DLOY) 13–15, 16, 18, 30

Gailbraith, L/Bdr E. 136
Gallipoli 75,76
Garswood (Lancashire) 215, 216
Gaskin, Maj B. F. B. 147
"Gentlemen and Yeomanry" 2 *et seq*
George IV, King 15
George V, King 68, 106
George VI, King 106
Gerard, Maj Sir John 24, 215, 216
Gerard, Col Sir Robert 217
Gibbs, Pte T. 52
Gibraltar 152,155
Gilpin Dr B. 14
Gieves & Hawkes 30

[224]

Gillham, L/Cpl C 146
Gladstone, E. W. 117fn
Godman, Lt Col R. T. 36
Gorst, Lt S. 138
Gorton, WO2 R. 147
Grand National 158
Green, Maj F. 95
Greenall, Capt J. E. 91
Greenhalgh, Sgt N. 10
Greenwood, Capt B. 109, 137
Grierson, Lt J. A. 84
Guidons 7, 29, 143, 159–61

GUNS
    4.5in (howitzer) 115, 117
    5.5in (gun-howitzer) 116, 118, 119, 126, 136
    5.9in (German) 88, 92, 93
    6in (howitzer) 113, 115, 126
    88mm (German SP) 133fn
    12in (railway mounted) 88–89
    15pdrs 55
    25pdrs 116, 117
    60pdrs 113
Gwyer, Lt C. 84, 91

Hackforth, Pte F. W. 51
Haddock, Maj N. vii
Haig FM Earl 86,89
Haldane, Visct R. xv
Hallé, Sir Charles 194
Hallé Orchestra 194, 196, 197
Hamburg 135
Hardcastle, Col H. M. 38, 99, 100, 219, 220
Hargreaves, Gnr L. vii
Hargreaves, Col P. 38, 60, 61, 71, 101, 219
Harrington, Lt Gen Sir Charles 99
Harris, Sgt A. vii
Harrison, Capt C. 130, 136
Harrop, Maj J. R. G. vii
Hartill, Gnr A. vii
Hartington, the Marquess of 36
Hawkshaw (Lancashire) 110
Hay, Cpl C. H. 95
Heath, Edward (Prime Minister) 146
Heaton, Lt B. W. 95
Heaton, Lt Col J. 106, 220
Heaton, Capt R. B. 148
Heaton, Maj R. E. 109, 123, 136
Heaton, Maj T. M. 109, 123
Hesketh, Lt T. M. 109
Hightown (Lancashire) 59
Hill 2/Lt N. G. 91
Hitler, Adolf 107, 135
Hollins, Maj P. T. 128

Home Service Force 154–55
Hong Kong 158
Hornby (Lancashire) 104
Horses 8, 35, 43, 45, 48, 51, 57, 61, 65, 74, 77, 80, 81,
    83, 86, 104, 105, 110, 111, 112, 125
Huntington, Capt A. W. 38, 42, 52, 57
Hurst WO1 A. (Bandmaster) 197, 198
Hurt, Maj F. C. A. 84

Imperial Yeomanry 41 *et seq*
Infantry, Services as 86 *et seq*
Ireland 1, 61, 97, 126
IRA 61fn 97
Irish Republican Brotherhood 97
Isle of Man 148
Ismay, Joseph Bruce 44

"Jack" (dog) 37
Jackson, L/Sgt E. 95
Jackson, Sgt E. W. 82
Jameson 2/Ltd H. 91
Jenkinson, Gnr P. 114
"John o' Gaunt" *see* Regimental March
Johnson, Tpr C. H. 42, 53–54, 55, 56
Johnson, Maj E. 38, 60
Johnson-Ferguson, Lt A. J. 38
Jones, Maj T. H. F. 147

Kearsely, Capt J. 15, 18, 19, 20, 219
Kearsely, Capt J. H. 16, 18, 157, 219
Kemp, Lt Col G. 38, 42, 44, 52, 56, 59
Kershaw, Capt R. 29
Kesselring, FM K. 117, 118, 121, 122
Kimberley 54
King's Troop RHA 39, 66
Kinmel Park 104
Kirkudbright 144
Kneller Hall (Royal Military School of Music) 193,
    194, 195, 197
Kressenstein, Gen K. von 76, 77
Kruger, President Paul 41

Laing, Maj H. 155
Lancashire County Museums Service vii
Lancashire Hussars 5, 24, 25, 99, 100, 195, 215, *et seq*
Lancashire Regiment of Yeomanry Cavalry 15
Lancashire Yeoman (Regimental Magazine) 156
Lancaster 19, 25, 37, 194
Langshaw, Maj J. 15, 18, 26

[225]

Larkhill (School of Artillery) 113
Lawson, Maj G. 136
Lee, Thomas (Bandmaster) 194, 198
Lees, Maj A. E. 38, 59
Ley, Lt G. G. 109
Light Armoured Car Battery 79, 80
Lindner, Brig J. F. vii, 136
Liverpool 15, 25, 29, 44, 60, 70, 73, 101, 216
Liverpool Philharmonic Orchestra 197
Llandrindod Wells 113
Lonsdale, Earl of 36, 38
Looker, Pte W. 52
Lord, Lt J. 18
Lords Lieutenant 2, 3, 7, 13, 63, 69
Love, Capt E. W. 85
Lowe, Gnr Arthur 127
Lowther Park 65, 104
Luddites 10
Lupton, Cpl W. 52

"Mainwaring, Capt" see Lowe, Arthur
Maitland (South Africa) 45
Malcolm, Lt J. C. S. 81
Manchester 25, 42, 60, 64, 73, 99, 101, 102, 139, 144, 147
Manchester Regiment, 12th (DLOY) Bn 91 et seq, 99
Mangall, Cpl J. 10
Marshall, Lt Col T. A. 143, 145, 220
Mason, Sgt W. 52
Mechanisation 106, 111
Meredith, Sgt J. S. 82, 95
Michaelson, Capt T. 24
Militia 1, 3
Molloy, Maj L. G. S. 68, 85, 95
Molyneux, Capt C. B. 36
Montgomery, FM Visct 132
Mortimer, Harry (Bandmaster) 196, 197, 198
Morton, H. F. (Bandmaster) 196, 198
Mounted Police unit (DLOY) 125–126
Museum, Regimental 106, 150, 217
Musgrave-Hoyle, Lt Col 107, 109, 113, 114, 220

NATO 140, 151
National Service 140
Northern Ireland 126

Okehampton 158
Oldham 29, 42, 64, 73
Oldham Troop (DLOY) 29, 30, 38
O'Neil, Maj D. W. J. 147
Options for Change xvii, 161
Orme, Stanley, MP 145
Otterburn 127
Oulton Park (Tarporley) 101

Paget, Gen Sir Henry 24fn
Paget's Horse 45, 49, 50
Palestine xv–xvi, 77 et seq
Palmer, Maj J. E. 109, 126–127
Palmer, Maj Gen Sir Michael 115fn, 150, 198
Palmer, Lt Col W. R. 109, 115–16, 118, 121, 122–23, 124, 125, 126, 136, 137, 138, 146, 156, 159, 219, 220
Paramor, Lt 81, 82
Pay Rates 7, 20, 21, 34, 63, 100
Peake, Capt J. A. 140
Pembroke 112, 114
Penrith, 36, 70
Percival, Capt N. F. 79, 80 81, 86
'Peterloo Massacre' 22
Phillips, Lt Col N. H. 145, 146, 147, 148, 220
Pilkington, Maj John 4–5, 7, 9, 10, 11–12, 17
Pitt, William (Prime Minister) 1
Plug riots 22
Polo 216
Poole, L/Cpl E. 52
Poynton, Capt D. R. 137
Precedence (of Yeomanry) 32, 100
Preston (Lancashire) 36, 64, 70, 73, 101, 138, 145, 150, 152, 155, 195, 217
Provisional Cavalry 4
Purchase System (commissions) 2, 30

Quad (gun tractor) 115, 115fn

Rainforth, Cpl J. 10
Ramsbottom (Lancashire) 110
Ramsbottom, Lt Gen Sir David 157
Regimental Association 149
Regimental March 197–98, 201
Regimental Trumpet Call 198
Regulations for the Territorial Force and County Association 69
Regulations for the Yeomanry Cavalry 32
Reserves (DLOY) 96–97
Rhyl (North Wales) 65, 100, 104
Richardson, RQMS B. vii, 120
Riddett, Maj L. A. H. 136, 146, 147
Roberts, FM Earl 60, 61, 62
Rochdale Troop (DLOY) 29, 30, 36, 38, 64, 73, 106
Rogers, Lt Col F. H. C. 114, 126, 136, 220
Royal Armoured Corps 137, 141, 147
Royal Mercian and Lancastrian Yeomanry xvii, 161
Royal Military School of Music see Kneller Hall
Royal Tank Regiment 144
Royal Tournament (1987) 155–56
Royal Wiltshire Yeomanry 26, 100
Rutherford, Lt Col Sir John 38, 64, 101, 217

Saddlery 19, 66
Salisbury Plain 64, 68
Sanderson, Capt B. (Baron Sanderson) 82, 85, 87, 88–89, 90, 95,
Sanderson, Capt R. T. 109
Seddon-Brown, Major D. W. 116, 120
Sennybridge Training Area (Brecon) 114, 158
Sharp, Sgt N. J. vii, 129
Sheen, Maj E. vii, 144, 153
Shepherd-Cros, Capt H. 29
Shepherd-Cross, Maj T. A. S. 29, 38, 60
Shoulder chains 101–103
Shropshire Yeomanry 110fn, 117
Slater, G. (Bandmaster) 194, 198
Smart, W. (Bandmaster) 196, 198
Soldier (British Army Magazine) 152
Southport 15, 25, 38, 196, 216
Steiger, Lt Col M. T. vii, 156–57, 159, 160, 161, 221
Steven, Capt J. D. 146, 147, 151
Stewart, Lt Col D. B. 220
Stewart, Lt Col S. M. P. 161, 221
Stocker, Capt B. G. vii
Stonyhurst College 159, 160
Storey, Sgt C. B. E. 43, 52
Stuart-Mills Maj J. 148
Surrey Yeomanry 74, 84, 87, 91
Sutherland, Cpl A. 95

Tanks xvi, 89, 90, 106, 138
Taranto 117
Tayleur, Lt Col B. C. L. 143, 220
Territorial Reserve Forces Act (1907) 63
Thomas, Lt Col L. J. 127fn, 128, 131, 133, **136, 220**
Thwaites, Capt J. J. 137
Tidworth 106
Tilney, Lt Col R. H. 38, 70, 73, 83, 85, 87, 91, 95, 99, 219
Tito, Marshal 125
Towneley, Col S. P. E. C. W. 150, 153, **156**, 219
Trieste 125
Trooper (rank) 101
Truell, Lt Col E. G. S. 220
Tustin, Maj J. 155, 157
Tyler, Lt Col E. M. 115, 220
Tyrell, Lt Col G. G. M. 78

Ulverston 13
UNIFORM (General) 6, 17, 18, 25, 30, 34–35, 67
    Battle dress 117
    Cap badge *see* "Badges, regimental"
    Cuirasses 14
    Facings 25

Helmets 6, 14, 17, 25, 39, 67
Khaki service Dress 43, 65, 107
Number Two Dress 65
Putees 43
Shoulder chains 101–103
Tropical 75

VE Day 135
VEHICLES (*see also* Tanks)
    Daimler Scout Cars (Dingos) 141
    Gun tractors 115, 123, 131
    Land Rovers 141, 145, 146
    Motor cars 62
Victoria, Queen 24–25, 194
Volunteer Force (1859) 24

Waddington, Rt Hon David 140
Walker, Capt R. C. D. 137
Ward, Maj Gen A. D. 122
Warren, Lt Gen Sir Charles 45 *et seq*
Wellington, Duke of 22
WEAPONS (*see also* "GUNS")
    Carbines 20, 23–24, 31, 33, 37
    Carl Gustav Anti-tank 151
    Machine guns 33–34, 42–43, 54, 75, 101 110
    Mortars 151
    Pistols 6, 32, 33
    Rifles 43, 67, 75, 107
    Swords 6, 31, 33, 39, 67 75, 107
Westmorland and Cumberland Yeomanry 36, 37, **42**, 44, 49, 52, 56, 96
Whitham, Pte R. 95
Wigan 140, 149, 152, 157, 216
Wigan Troop (DLOY) 15, 18, 29
William IV, King xvii, 17, 18, 138
Williams, Sgt Maj R. H. 26, 27
Wilson, Harold (Prime Minister) xvii, 145, 146
Wilson, BSM J. vii, 134
Wintle, Lt Col F. G. 126, 136, 220
Women's Royal Army Corps 151, **152**, 157
Woolley, Lt Col J. D. V. vii, 155, **156**, 221
Worsley 26, 36, 42, 64, 70

Yeomanry, raising of 2, 4
Yeomanry Regulations (1893) 35
Young, Lt Col V. A. 114, 115, 220
Yugoslavia 125